OXFORD HISTORICAL MONOGRAPHS

Editors

A BYZANTINE GOVERNMENT IN EXILE

Government and Society Under the Laskarids of Nicaea (1204–1261)

BY

MICHAEL ANGOLD

OXFORD UNIVERSITY PRESS
1975

Oxford University Press, Ely House, London W.1

GLASGOW NEW YORK TORONTO MELBOURNE WELLINGTON
CAPE TOWN IBADAN NAIROBI DAR ES SALAAM LUSAKA ADDIS ABABA
DELHI BOMBAY CALCUTTA MADRAS KARACHI LAHORE DACCA
KUALA LUMPUR SINGAPORE HONG KONG TOKYO

ISBN 0 19 821854 0

PRINTED IN GREAT BRITAIN BY
BUTLER & TANNER LTD
FROME AND LONDON

TO
MONICA

PREFACE

It can hardly be claimed that the history of the Nicaean Empire has been neglected by Byzantine scholars. Yet the fact remains that the last full-scale history of the period dates from 1912.[1] This is an admirable narrative history; and it is not my intention to embark upon another narrative history of the Nicaean Empire. The aim of this book is rather to examine its social and administrative structure. This has seemed to me to be a worthwhile undertaking largely because of the happy conjuncture of the place that the Nicaean Empire holds in the later history of Byzantium and the nature of the sources.

I think that it is true to say that the study of the social and administrative history of the Byzantine Empire during the period of its greatness is hampered by the nature of the sources. Scholars are forced to rely very heavily upon imperial legislation and government handbooks. These sources provide a rather artificial picture of Byzantine society and administration, since they present the government's idealized view of how they ought to function. It is a bias that is not offset by the other available sources, such as histories, chronicles, and saints' lives. Documentary sources, which allow us a glimpse of how the machinery of government worked in practice, only begin to survive in any numbers from the mid-eleventh century, and only in substantial quantities after the fall of Constantinople to the Latins in 1204. Thanks largely to the riches of the cartulary of the monastery of Lemviotissa near Smyrna,[2] it is possible to examine in some detail the workings of government and society during the period of exile at Nicaea. This is perhaps the first time in Byzantine history that such an undertaking is feasible. There are of course difficulties. The Lemviotissa cartulary only casts its beam of light on conditions in the region of Smyrna, but to a degree it is possible to use other sources to test how far the picture it gives of

[1] A. Gardner, *The Lascarids of Nicaea. The Story of an Empire in Exile*, London, 1912.

[2] The new edition which Mme H. Ahrweiler has promised for some time now had not appeared at the time of writing.

government and society in that district has any general application.

The strengths and weaknesses of the Byzantine Empire are illuminated however weakly at a crucial period in its history. One glimpses the perennial conflict between the forces of order represented by the government and an underlying instability that derived from the opposing interests of different social groups. The Empire was restored in exile; imperial government appeared to have triumphed, but at the same time the final dissolution of the Byzantine Empire was being prepared; for, if the seat of Empire was restored by the Nicaeans to Constantinople in 1261, the rich provinces of western Asia Minor which had formed the core of the Nicaean Empire were to fall to the Turks in the course of the next fifty years. This book is therefore concerned not only with the problem of the astonishing recovery of the Byzantine Empire after the fall of Constantinople to the Latins in 1204, but also with the problem of its collapse before the Turks. In a sense, the Empire of Nicaea appears to mediate between the fall of the City to the Latins and its final fall to the Ottomans in 1453.

This book took shape as a doctoral thesis which was submitted in May 1967 to the History Faculty Board of the University of Oxford. Since then, it has been largely rewritten and reshaped, mostly during the year 1971/1972. I have naturally incurred many debts of gratitude over the long period during which this book has been in gestation. I am particularly indebted to my supervisor, Professor Dimitri Obolensky, who has guided this work with great care and patience through its many stages and guises. I also benefited from Professor Donald Nicol's generous help and advice at a very delicate period of revision. Professor Nikos Oikonomides was kind enough to let me examine photocopies and transcripts he had made of a number of documents from the archives of the monastery of St. John of Patmos. It was due to the generosity of Professors Gerald Aylmer and Gwyn Williams of the University of York, where I taught for a while, that I had the time and money to make a tour of the Empire of Nicaea in the spring of 1969. Finally, I should like to acknowledge my debt to Alec Gaydon, whose assistant I was on the Victoria History of Shropshire and who did a great deal to shape my historical interests.

I have dedicated this book to my wife not so much because of her devotion to Byzantium, more because of her sustaining and entertaining attitude to the 'Grove of Academe'.

Edinburgh
September 1973

Michael Angold

CONTENTS

A NOTE ON TRANSLITERATION xiii

LIST OF MAPS xiv

ABBREVIATIONS AND SHORT TITLES xv

INTRODUCTION 1

PART I.
THE EMPIRE OF NICAEA AND BYZANTIUM

I. The Problem of the Unity of the Byzantine World after 1204 9

PART II.
POLITICS AND THE CONSTITUTION

II. The Byzantine Constitution: Theory and Practice 37

III. The Emperor and the Church 46

IV. The Emperor and the Aristocracy 60

V. The Usurpation of Michael Palaiologos 80

PART III.
THE ECONOMY AND SOCIETY OF THE NICAEAN EMPIRE

VI. The Nicaean Economy 97

VII. The Structure of Rural Society in the Nicaean Empire 121

PART IV.
THE CENTRAL ADMINISTRATION

Introduction. The Restoration of Central Government 147

VIII. The Emperor and Household Government 151

IX. The Military Organization of the Nicaean Empire 182

X. The Fiscal Organization of the Nicaean Empire 202

PART V.
THE PROVINCIAL ADMINISTRATION OF THE NICAEAN EMPIRE

Introduction. The Restoration of Provincial Administration 239

XI. The Administrative Divisions of the Asiatic Provinces of the Nicaean Empire 243

XII. The Administration of the Asiatic Provinces of the Nicaean Empire 250
XIII. The European Provinces of the Nicaean Empire 279
BIBLIOGRAPHY 297
I. GENERAL INDEX 315
II. INDEX OF TECHNICAL TERMS 328
III. INDEX OF OFFICES AND OFFICE HOLDERS OF THE NICAEAN COURT 330

A NOTE ON TRANSLITERATION

I have tried to avoid the Latin transliteration of Greek proper names. Normally I have used a Greek form, e.g. Angelos instead of Angelus, Kantakouzenos instead of Cantacuzenus, but in certain cases such a transliteration appears to offend common English usage; and I have preferred Nicaea to Nikaia, and Constantinople to Konstantinoupolis.

For the titles of offices I have used, where possible, an appropriate English equivalent: Steward for *epi tes trapezes*, Butler for *pinkernes*, Chamberlain for *parakoimomenos*, Grand Constable for *megas konstavlos*. Where there is no appropriate equivalent I have simply transliterated, e.g. *protovestiarios, kastrophylax*. I have similarly transliterated all technical terms, but with one exception: I have sometimes translated *vestiarion* as Wardrobe, but occasionally, particularly in rather technical passages, it seemed better to transliterate rather than translate.

I have not been entirely consistent in my use of place-names. I have normally given Anatolian place-names in their Greek form, rather than in their modern form, e.g. Smyrna, not Izmir; Philadelphia, not Alaşehir, but I have normally included in brackets the Turkish name, if the town or city in question was occupied by the Turks during the period 1204–61, e.g. Dorylaion (Eskisehir). I have followed a rather different practice in the case of European place-names. Where the modern place-name remains close to the medieval Greek name, I have for convenience sake used the modern, e.g. Skoplje for Skopia, Veles for Velesos, but where the modern name is further removed from the medieval, I have used the latter, e.g. Philippopolis and not Plovdiv, Stenimachos and not Asenovgrad, Tzouroulon and not Çorlu, Adrianople and not Edirne.

LIST OF MAPS

1. The Nicaean Territories in Asia Minor facing p. 243
2. The Nicaean Territories in Europe 281

ABBREVIATIONS AND SHORT TITLES

1. PERIODICALS

B	*Byzantion*, Brussels, 1924–.
BCH	*Bulletin de Correspondance hellénique*, Athens/Paris, 1877–.
BNJ	*Byzantinisch-Neugriechische Jahrbucher,* Berlin, 1920–5, Athens, 1926–.
BS	*Byzantinoslavica*, Prague, 1929–.
BZ	*Byzantinische Zeitschrift,* Leipzig/Munich, 1892–.
DOP	*Dumbarton Oaks Papers*, Cambridge, Mass., 1941–.
EB	*Études Byzantines*, 1–3, Bucharest, 1943–5 (continued as *Revue des Études Byzantines* [*REB*], q.v.).
EEBS	*'Επετηρὶς 'Εταιρείας Βυζαντινῶν Σπουδῶν*, Athens, 1924–.
EO	*Échos d'Orient*, Istanbul/Paris, 1897–1942 (continued as *Études Byzantines* [*EB*], q.v.).
JOB	*Jahrbuch der österreichischen Byzantinistik*, Vienna, 1969–.
JOBG	*Jahrbuch der österreichischen byzantinischen Gesellschaft,* Vienna, 1951–68 (continued as *Jahrbuch der österreichischen Byzantinistik* [*JOB*], q.v.).
NH	*Νέος 'Ελληνομνήμων*, Athens, 1904–27.
OCP	*Orientalia Christiana Periodica*, Rome, 1935–.
REB	*Revue des Études Byzantines*, Bucharest/Paris, 1946–.
REG	*Revue des Études Grecques*, Paris, 1888–.
RSI	*Rivista Storica Italiana*, Naples, 1888–.
VV	*Vizantijskij Vremennik*, old series, St. Petersburg, 1894–1927; new series, Leningrad, 1947–.

2. SOURCES

Acropolites	*Georgii Acropolitae Opera*, ed. A. Heisenberg, I: *Historia, Breviarium historiae, Theodori Scutariotae additamenta*; II: *Scripta minora*, Leipzig, 1903.

Actes de Dionysiou	Nicolas Oikonomidès, *Actes de Dionysiou* (Archives de l'Athos IV), Paris, 1968, 2 vols.
Actes de Xéropotamou	J. Bompaire, *Actes de Xéropotamou* (Archives de l'Athos III), Paris, 1964, 2 vols.
Actes de Zographou	W. Regel, E. Kurtz, and B. Korablev, *Actes de Zographou, VV*, 13, Supplement (1907).
Anna Comnena	*Annae Comnenae porphyrogenitae Alexias*, ed. B. Leib, Paris, 1937–45, 3 vols.
Blemmydes	*Nicephori Blemmydae Curriculum Vitae et Carmina*, ed. A. Heisenberg, Leipzig, 1896.
Cantacuzenus	*Ioannis Cantacuzeni eximperatoris Historiarum Libri IV*, ed. L. Schopen, Bonn, 1828–32, 3 vols.
C.I.G.	*Corpus Inscriptionum Graecarum*, IV, ed. A. Boeck, Berlin, 1877.
Cinnamus	*Ioannis Cinnami Epitome rerum ab Ioanne et Alexio Comnenis gestarum*, ed. A. Meineke, Bonn, 1836.
Delehaye, *Typica*	H. Delehaye, *Deux typica byzantins de l'époque des Paléologues*, Brussels, 1921.
Dölger, *Reg.*	F. Dölger, *Regesten der Kaiserurkunden des oströmischen Reiches* (*Corpus der griechischen Urkunden des Mittelalters und der neueren Zeit*, Reihe A, Abt. I), Munich/Berlin, 1924–65, 5 vols.
Dölger, *Schatzkammern*	F. Dölger, *Aus den Schatzkammern des Heiligen Berges. 115 Urkunden und 50 Urkundensiegel aus 10 Jahrhunderten*, Munich, 1948, 2 vols.
Gregoras	*Nicephori Gregorae Byzantina Historia*, ed. L. Schopen, Bonn, 1829–55, 3 vols.
Gregory of Cyprus	*Γρηγορίου τοῦ ἁγιωτάτου καὶ μακαριωτάτου οἰκουμενικοῦ Πατριάρχου περὶ τοῦ καθ' ἑαυτὸν βίου ὡς ἀπ' ἄλλου προσώπου*, in W. Lameere, *La Tradition manuscrite de la correspondance de Grégoire de Chypre, patriarche de Constantinople (1283–1289)* (Études de philologie et d'histoire anciennes publiées par l'Institut historique belge de Rome II), Brussels/Rome, 1937, pp. 176–91.
Heisenberg, 'Neue Quellen'	A. Heisenberg, 'Neue Quellen zur Geschichte des lateinischen Kaisertums und der Kirchenunion. I. Der Epitaphios des Nikolaos Mesarites auf seinen Bruder Johannes; II. Die Unionsverhandlungen vom 30. August 1206; III. Der Bericht des Nickolaos Mesarites über die

	politischen und kirchlichen Ereignisse des Jahres .1214', *Sitzungsberichte der bayerischen Akademie der Wissenschaften,* philos.-philol. und hist. Klasse, 1922, Abh. 5; 1923, Abh. 2–3, Munich, 1923.
Heisenberg, 'Palaiologenzeit'	A. Heisenberg, 'Aus der Geschichte und Literatur der Palaiologenzeit', ibid. 1920, Abh. 10, Munich, 1920.
Laurent, *Bulles métriques*	V. Laurent, *Les Bulles métriques dans la sigillographie byzantine*, Athens, 1932.
Laurent, *Regestes*	V. Laurent, *Les Regestes des actes du Patriarcat de Constantinople*, I, fasc. 4: *Les Regestes de 1208 à 1309* (Le Patriarcat Byzantin. Recherches de diplomatique, d'histoire et de géographie ecclésiastiques publiées par l'Institut d'Études Byzantines, Paris, Série 1), Paris, 1971.
Michael Choniates	*Μιχαὴλ Ἀκομινάτου τοῦ Χωνιάτου τὰ σωζωμένα*, ed. Sp. Lampros, Athens, 1879–80, 2 vols.
Migne, *P.G.*	J. P. Migne, *Patrologiae cursus completus, Series graeco-latina*, Paris, 1857–66.
Migne, *P.L.*	J. P. Migne, *Patrologiae cursus completus, Series latina*, Paris, 1844–55.
Miklosich and Müller	F. Miklosich et J. Müller, *Acta et diplomata graeca medii aevi sacra et profana*, Vienna, 1860–90, 6 vols.
Nicetas Choniates	*Nicetae Choniatae Historia*, ed. I. Bekker, Bonn, 1835.
Pachymeres	*Georgii Pachymeris de Michaele et Andronico Palaeologis libri tredecim*, ed. I. Bekker, Bonn, 1835, 2 vols.
Pseudo-Kodinos	Pseudo-Kodinos, *Traité des offices*, ed. J. Verpeaux (Le Monde Byzantin 1), Paris, 1966.
Rhalles and Potles	G. A. Rhalles and M. Potles, *Σύνταγμα τῶν θείων καὶ ἱερῶν κανόνων*, Athens, 1852–9, 6 vols.
Sathas	K. N. Sathas, *Μεσαιωνικὴ βιβλιοθήκη* (*Bibliotheca graeca medii aevi*), Venice/Paris, 1872–94, 7 vols.
Scutariotes	*Theodori Scutariotae Additamenta ad Georgii Acropolitae Historiam*, in Acropolites (q.v.) I, pp. 275–302.
Tafel and Thomas	G. L. F. Tafel and G. M. Thomas, *Urkunden zur älteren Handels- und Staatsgeschichte der Republik*

	Venedig (Fontes Rerum Austriacarum, Abt. 2, XII–XIV), Vienna, 1856–7, 3 vols.
Theodore Lascaris	*Theodori Ducae Lascaris Epistolae CCXVII*, ed. N. Festa, Florence, 1898.
Villehardouin	Villehardouin, *La Conquête de Constantinople*, ed. E. Faral, Paris, 1961, 2 vols.
Zepos, *Ius*	J. and P. Zepos, *Ius graecoromanum*, Athens, 1931, 8 vols.

3. MODERN WORKS

Ahrweiler, *Byzance et la mer*	H. Ahrweiler. *Byzance et la mer. La marine de guerre, la politique et les institutions maritimes de Byzance aux VIIe–XVe siècles* (Bibliothèque Byzantine, Études 5), Paris, 1966.
Ahrweiler, 'Smyrne'	H. Ahrweiler, 'L'Histoire et la géographie de la région de Smyrne entre les deux occupations turques (1081–1317), particulièrement au XIIIe siècle', *Travaux et Mémoires*, 1(1965), 1–204.
Andreeva, *Očerki*	M. A. Andreeva, *Očerki po kul'ture vizantijskago dvora v XIII veke* (*Studies in the culture of the Byzantine Court in the thirteenth century*) (Travaux de la société royale des sciences de Bohême, Classe des Lettres, N.S. VIII, No. 3), Prague, 1927.
Beck, *Kirche und theologische Literatur*	H.-G. Beck, *Kirche und theologische Literatur im byzantinischen Reich* (I. Müller-W. Otto, *Handbuch der Altertumswissenschaft*, XII, 2, 1), Munich, 1959.
Bon, *Le Péloponnèse byzantin*	A. Bon, *Le Péloponnèse byzantin jusqu'en 1204* (Bibliothèque Byzantine, Études 1), Paris, 1951.
Bratianu, *Le Commerce génois*	G. I. Bratianu, *Recherches sur le commerce génois dans la Mer Noire au XIIIe siècle*, Paris, 1929.
Bréhier, *Institutions*	L. Brehier, *Les Institutions de l'Empire byzantin, Le Monde byzantin II* (L'évolution de l'humanité, 32bis), Paris, 1949.
Cahen, *Pre-Ottoman Turkey*	C. Cahen, *Pre-Ottoman Turkey. A general survey of the material and spiritual culture and history c. 1071–1330*, London, 1968.
Dölger, *Finanzverwaltung*	F. Dölger, *Beiträge zur Geschichte der byzantinischen Finanzverwaltung, besonders des 10. und 11. Jahrhunderts* (Byzantinisches Archiv 9), Leipzig/Berlin, 1927.

Dölger, *Byz. Diplomatik*	F. Dölger, *Byzantinische Diplomatik. 20 Aufsätze zur Urkundenwesen der Byzantiner*, Ettal, 1956.
Dölger, *PARASPORA*	F. Dölger, *ΠΑΡΑΣΠΟΡΑ. 30 Aufsätze zur Geschichte, Kultur und Sprache des byzantinischen Reiches*, Ettal, 1961.
Geanakoplos, *Michael Palaeologus*	D. J. Geanakoplos, *Emperor Michael Palaeologus and the West 1258–1282. A Study in Byzantine–Latin Relations,* Cambridge, Mass., 1959.
Hendy, *Coinage and Money*	M. F. Hendy, *Coinage and Money in the Byzantine Empire 1081–1261* (Dumbarton Oaks Studies XII), Washington, D.C., 1969.
Každan, *Agrarnye Otnošenija*	A. P. Každan, *Agrarnye Otnošenija v Vizantii XIII–XIV vv.* (*Agrarian Relations in Byzantium in the 13th and 14th centuries*), Moscow, 1952.
Longnon, *L'Empire latin*	J. Longnon, *L'Empire latin de Constantinople et la principauté de Morée*, Paris, 1949.
Nicol, *Kantakouzenos*	D. M. Nicol, *The Byzantine Family of Kantakouzenos (Cantacuzenus) c.1100–1460. A genealogical and prosopographical study* (Dumbarton Oaks Studies XI), Washington, D.C., 1968.
Norden, *Das Papsttum und Byzanz*	W. Norden, *Das Papsttum und Byzanz. Die Trennung der beiden Mächte und das Problem ihrer Wiedervereinigung bis zum Untergange des byzantinischen Reiches*, Berlin, 1903.
Ostrogorskij, *Féodalité*	G. Ostrogorskij, *Pour l'histoire de la féodalité byzantine* (Corpus Bruxellense Historiae Byzantinae, Subsidia I), translated by H. Grégoire and P. Lemerle, Brussels, 1954.
Ostrogorskij, *Paysannerie*	G. Ostrogorskij, *Quelques problèmes d'histoire de la paysannerie byzantine* (Corpus Bruxellense Historiae Byzantinae, Subsidia II), Brussels, 1956.
Ostrokorsky, *Byzantine State*	G. Ostrogorsky, *History of the Byzantine State* (translated by J. Hussey), 2nd edn., Oxford, 1968.
Pauly–Wissowa	A. Pauly, G. Wissowa, and W. Kroll, *Real-Encyclopädie der classischen Altertumswissenschaft*, Stuttgart, 1894–.
Polemis, *Doukai*	D. I. Polemis, *The Doukai. A Contribution to Byzantine Prosopography*, London, 1968.
Ramsay, *Hist. Geography*	Sir W. H. Ramsay, *The Historical Geography of Asia Minor* (Royal Geographical Society's Supplemental Papers IV), London, 1890.

Stadtmüller, *Michael Choniates*	G. Stadtmüller, *Michael Choniates, Metropolit von Athen* (Orientalia Christiana Analecta, 33, 2), Rome, 1934.
Svoronos, *Le Cadastre de Thèbes*	N. G. Svoronos, *Recherches sur le cadastre byzantin et la fiscalité aux XIe et XIIe siècles: le cadastre de Thèbes*, Athens/Paris, 1959 (extract from *BCH* 83 (1959), 1–145, 805–25).
Thiriet, *La Romanie vénitienne*	F. Thiriet, *La Romanie vénitienne au moyen âge. Le développement et l'exploitation du domaine colonial vénitien (XIIe–XVe siècles)* (Bibliothèque des Écoles françaises d'Athènes et de Rome, 193), Paris, 1959.
Tomaschek, 'Topographie'	W. Tomaschek, 'Zur historischen Topographie von Kleinasien im Mittelalter', *Sitzungsberichte der kaiserlichen Akademie der Wissenschaften*, philos.-hist. Classe, 124, Abh. 8, Vienna, 1891.
Zakythinos, *Despotat*	D. A. Zakythinos, *Le Despotat grec de Morée*, Paris, 1932–53, 2 vols.

INTRODUCTION

The fall of Constantinople to the Latins on 13 April 1204 and the establishment of a Latin Empire of Constantinople has always been taken as a turning-point in Byzantine history. The very existence of Byzantium hung in the balance. The continuity of its history stretching back to the 'World of Late Antiquity' appeared to have been broken; but only momentarily. Byzantine traditions of culture and government were to be preserved in a series of successor states that grew up on the ruins of the Byzantine Empire. The most important of these was one centred in western Asia Minor, which we have come to know as the Empire of Nicaea. It was founded by Theodore Laskaris, a son-in-law of a previous Byzantine emperor, Alexios III Angelos. He had himself proclaimed emperor at Nicaea, probably in 1206, and two years later had a patriarch installed. The new patriarch's first official act was to crown Theodore emperor. Thus was the Byzantine Empire reconstituted in exile.

Theodore's son-in-law and successor, John Vatatzes, in the course of a long and successful reign (1222–54) made his state the most powerful one in the Aegean region. He secured control of the whole of western Anatolia and the islands along its coast, as well as conquering Thrace and Macedonia. Constantinople was ringed around by Nicaean territory, and it was to fall on 25 July 1261 to a small Nicaean force. The seat of Empire was restored to Constantinople. The task of the Nicaean Empire was completed.

The Empire of Nicaea forms by far and away the most important bridge between the Empire destroyed in 1204 and the Empire restored in 1261. The history of the last phase of Byzantium from 1261 down to the final fall of Constantinople in 1453 is virtually incomprehensible without reference to the history of the Nicaean Empire; for the experience of exile shaped the restored Empire.

The essentials of Byzantium were preserved in exile. The theory of empire inherited from Eusebius of Caesarea and

Justinian was maintained unimpaired. The prerogatives of the Byzantine emperor and patriarch were upheld. Nicaea was recognized as the new centre of the 'Orthodox World'. What is more, the traditions of Byzantine scholarship and education were kept alive by Nicaean emperors and scholars. The flowering of Byzantine scholarship that took place after the recovery of Constantinople has its roots in their work.

These traditional facets of Byzantine government and culture were of great importance for Byzantine self-respect and a sense of identity. They ensured a considerable measure of continuity, but beneath this façade there were changes. If the claims of the emperors of Nicaea to be the heirs of the emperors of Byzantium were to have any validity, they would have to be adapted to the circumstances prevailing during the period of exile. Currents of change that had been building up in the course of the twelfth century could no longer be ignored. The autonomy of the churches in Bulgaria and Serbia was officially recognized by the emperors of Nicaea; and they showed themselves to be realists in another way. In the course of the period of exile treaties with foreign powers ceased to be drawn up in the form of an imperial bull. A claim to oecumenical authority was quietly abandoned.

The problem of how the Byzantine legacy was preserved during the period of exile and of how the emperors and patriarchs of Nicaea attempted to give a degree of unity to the fragments of the fallen Byzantine Empire, in short, of how the Empire of Nicaea fared as the successor of Byzantium, provides the general context of this study, but its main purpose is more specific. It is to examine the fate of the Byzantine legacy in government during the period of exile. In what form was it preserved and handed on to the restored Empire? There is an intermingling of decisive change and marked conservatism. If the theory of imperial autocracy survives unchanged, the structure of government is altered in response to the conditions that exile brought and is adapted to the changing structure of society.

This is not a theme that lends itself to a straightforward narrative treatment. In any case, there have been a number of good narrative histories of the period of exile.[1] Nor is it intended simply to describe the structure of the administration. It is rather an attempt to see government in the round, by examining the administrative structure (Parts IV–V) against the background of constitutional problems (Part II) and the changing character of the economy and society (Part III). The history of the Nicaean Empire lends itself rather well to this approach. It was reasonably self-contained and its society was reasonably homogeneous. The sources too are perfectly adequate. The combination of a history written by one of the chief ministers of the Empire, George Akropolites, and the documentary material contained in the cartularies of various monasteries of western Asia Minor, not to mention the archives of the monastery of St. John of Patmos, provides a solid foundation. Nevertheless, the problems of government and society in the Nicaean Empire have not yet been tackled comprehensively, although the work of Mme Ahrweiler provides a valuable starting-point.[2]

The character of government at Byzantium depended upon the way in which imperial autocracy was exercised. Before 1204 this had been through the instrument of a bureaucracy. It succeeded in holding the Empire together through many centuries, but its defects were many; and they became increasingly apparent in the last decades of the twelfth century. This bureaucratic system of government was not able to survive the fall of Constantinople in 1204 with the attendant destruction of the departments of state and their archives.

The form of government that came into being during the period of exile and was bequeathed to the restored Empire is perhaps best described as a 'household government'. It was not clearly divided into departments with special functions and personnel. The vestiges of a bureaucracy survived only in the Imperial Wardrobe where the fiscal administration was concentrated. Virtually all other business coming before the

[1] e.g. A. Meliarakes, *Ἱστορία τοῦ Βασιλείου τῆς Νικαίας καί τοῦ Δεσποτάτου τῆς Ἠπείρου (1204–1261)*, Athens, 1898; A. Gardner, *The Lascarids of Nicaea. The Story of an Empire in Exile*, London, 1912; D. M. Nicol, *The Despotate of Epiros*, Oxford, 1957; D. M. Nicol, 'The Fourth Crusade and the Greek and Latin Empires, 1204–1261', in *Cambridge Medieval History* IV, part 1.

[2] Now collected in H. Ahrweiler, *Études sur les structures administratives et sociales de Byzance* (Variorum Reprints), London, 1971.

central administration was conducted in the imperial court. Members of the imperial household and imperial clerks carried out most of the routine administrative work, while the chief officers of the imperial household, such as the Steward, the Butler, and the Chamberlain, were entrusted with important administrative and military posts and missions. Provincial governors, as well as imperial commissioners sent out to the provinces, were drawn from the officers and members of the imperial household.

Although the creation of a household system of government marks a new stage in the history of Byzantine government, there was no complete break with the past, for the emperors of Nicaea were building on earlier administrative practice. The new form of government can be traced back in embryo long before 1204. In the course of the twelfth century the members of the private imperial chancery and other officers attached to the imperial household came to have a greater say in the direction of government and the formulation of policy. This 'imperial cabinet' was an ideal basis on which to restore the central administration after 1204.

The changes that occurred in the organization of the state during the period of exile were prepared by developments already apparent in the twelfth century. Their main characteristics were the simplification of the machinery of government and the association of members of the aristocracy in many aspects of government through the offices they held and the franchises they were granted. The old bureaucratic superstructure was swept away in 1204 and there emerged a household system of government.

This system of government reflected more clearly the shape of society. It appeared to provide a means of reconciling imperial prerogative and aristocratic privilege. This perhaps explains the comparative effectiveness of imperial administration during the period of exile and the apparent vitality and strength of the Nicaean Empire. Any weaknesses tended to be masked by the burning desire to recover Constantinople from the Latins, which united all sections of Nicaean society behind the emperor. They were only fully revealed after the recovery of Constantinople, when it became clear just how difficult it was to preserve the balance between imperial and aristocratic interests. It had already been weighted too heavily in the aristocracy's favour by the lavish grants of lands, revenues, and privileges made by the Emperor John Vatatzes to the great magnate families. After 1261 it became increasingly apparent that both at home and abroad imperial aspirations rested on far too weak a base.

PART I

THE EMPIRE OF NICAEA AND BYZANTIUM

I

THE PROBLEM OF THE UNITY OF THE BYZANTINE WORLD AFTER 1204

Ever since the death of Manuel I Komnenos in 1180 the weaknesses of the Byzantine Empire had become increasingly apparent. By the end of the century there was an atmosphere of complete demoralization. There was vicious intrigue and corruption in the capital, anarchy in the provinces, and growing external pressure on the boundaries of the Empire. The Fourth Crusade was sucked into this whirlpool with terrible consequences for the Empire.

From one point of view the conquest of Constantinople by the Venetians and the soldiers of the Fourth Crusade in April 1204 simply completed a process of disintegration long begun; from another there can be little doubt that it turned what was only a very threatening situation into a catastrophe. Yet such was the resilience of the Byzantines that Constantinople was restored to the Empire in 1261, and for a short while it regained much of its prestige and influence. It was then to decline rapidly as a result of the loss of its provinces in western Asia Minor to the Turks in the early years of the fourteenth century. The great effort mounted to save these provinces had been to no avail and the reserves of strength left to the Empire were largely squandered in a series of civil wars that dominate the internal history of fourteenth-century Byzantium. It was reduced to the level of a vassal state of the Ottoman Turks, but it still clung tenaciously to Constantinople until the final fall of the city in 1453.

In this history of decline and fall the Empire of Nicaea, the Byzantine successor state that came into existence in western Asia Minor after 1204, holds a place of unique interest. This is not simply because its emperors succeeded in winning back Constantinople or because it preserved and passed on Byzantine traditions. It is also because the fall of Constantinople was an unprecedented disaster, a 'cosmic cataclysm', as one contemporary put it.[1] The loss of the capital, a city under the special protection of the Mother of God,[2] was almost unthinkable. The principles, as well as the central institutions, upon which the Empire was based, were overturned. The interest of the history of the Nicaean Empire is partly how these were rebuilt and how they were adapted to the new conditions that exile brought. In the process, not only was a new political system established,[3] but a new administrative structure evolved. Trends in the administration and changes in the shape of society that can be traced back well before 1204 crystallized under the pressures produced by the fall of Constantinople. This helps to explain much of the vitality of the Byzantine Empire in the thirteenth century, but from the start there were flaws that contained the seeds of decay.

The administrative system was one of the great strengths of the Byzantine Empire, providing much of its internal cohesion. It is probably going too far to say that it shaped society, for it could not hold in check long-term social changes, but it was surprisingly successful in adapting itself to them and harnessing them to the needs of government. Consequently, any examination of the Byzantine administrative system has to be carried out within a rather wide framework. Not only must the underlying social structure be considered, but also the constitutional ideas that gave it direction; still less should the over-all political situation be neglected, for the way in which the administration evolved was in part in answer to the burdens that imperial aspirations placed upon it.

The fall of Constantinople brought utter confusion and despair to the Byzantines. They accepted that it was a sign of God's wrath and a punishment for their sins and factiousness. There was no acknowledged emperor to whom they

[1] J. Darrouzès, 'Les Discours d'Euthyme Tornikès (1200–1205)', *REB* 26 (1968), 82–3.

[2] See N. H. Baynes, *Byzantine Studies and Other Essays*, London, 1955, pp. 240–60; P. J. Alexander, 'The Strength of Empire and Capital as seen through Byzantine Eyes', *Speculum*, 37 (1962), 339–57.

[3] See G. Ostrogorsky, *History of the Byzantine State* (translated by J. Hussey), 2nd edn., Oxford, 1968, pp. 422–34.

could turn for guidance. Most of the aristocrats fled from the sack of the city to Asia Minor or even further afield,[4] while the Patriarch along with members of the bureaucracy and the clergy of St. Sophia left the capital to seek refuge at Selymvria.[5] Several bureaucrats sought safety and solace in the monastic life.[6] Others after great hardships regained their native cities.[7]

Provincials scoffed at the misfortunes of the refugees from Constantinople,[8] but the Latin conquest was to bring the provinces their share of suffering and dislocation of everyday life, as is only too clear from the letters of Michael Choniates, the Archbishop of Athens. After the fall of Constantinople he set out from Athens for Thessalonica, only to retrace his steps to Euboea and finally to seek refuge from Latin rule on the island of Keos, penniless.[9] From this island he did his best to see to the needs of his flock and to discover the whereabouts of his many acquaintances. He was remarkably successful, but he could lament that the Archbishop of Patras had disappeared without trace.[10]

In an atmosphere of recrimination and despair, the Byzantines were at first inclined to accept the rule of their Latin conquerors. Within less than a year the Latins were able to extend their authority over many of the cities of Thrace, the littoral of the Sea of Marmara, and most of the European coastlands of the Aegean. A Latin emperor and a Latin patriarch had been set up at Constantinople; and there seemed to be every danger that Byzantium might be recreated in a Latin image.

That this spectre did not materialize was due to a combination of factors. The quarrel between the Latin Emperor Baldwin I and Boniface of Montferrat, the original leader of the

[4] Miklosich and Müller IV, p. 345, ll. 12–31; Heisenberg, 'Neue Quellen' I, pp. 62, ll. 9–32.

[5] Nicetas Choniates, p. 784, ll. 15–20.

[6] e.g. the brothers Michael and John Belissariotes (see *Nicetae Choniatae Orationes et Epistulae*, ed. J. A. Van Dieten (Corpus Fontium Historiae Byzantinae, III), Berlin/New York, 1972, pp. 161–2.

[7] e.g. Euthymios Tornikes, a member of the clergy of St. Sophia (see Darrouzès in *REB* 23 (1965), 153–4 and in ibid. 26 (1968), 77–83).

[8] Nicetas Choniates, p. 785, ll. 7–17.

[9] Michael Choniates II, p. 312, ll. 12–19.

[10] Ibid., pp. 356–7; cf. ibid., pp. 292–4.

crusade, over Thessalonica revealed divisions among the crusaders; the full horror of the sack of Constantinople began to be appreciated,[11] but most of all the harshness of Latin rule and their general disregard for the Orthodox Church and its customs brought home the fact that a conquest by an alien people had been affected, not simply the substitution of a Latin emperor for the Byzantine.

The Greeks in Thrace turned for help to the Bulgarian Tsar Kalojan. In April 1205 he inflicted a severe defeat upon the main body of the Latin army near Adrianople. The Latin Emperor Baldwin was captured and presumably put to death. This disaster was followed two years later by the death of Boniface of Montferrat, again at the hands of the Bulgarians. The very existence of the Latin Empire was in the balance; and the Greek leaders were given a breathing space in which to transform what had simply been centres of resistance to the Latins into veritable states.

Already, shortly before the fall of Constantinople in 1204, scions of the house of Komnenos had set up the Empire of Trebizond, but its history lies slightly outside the mainstream of Byzantine history. The two most important Byzantine successor states were set up by men related to the ruling house of Angelos. Behind the Pindos mountains around Arta Michael Angelos was laying the foundations of what has come to be known as the despotate of Epiros, while a son-in-law of Alexios III Angelos (1195–1203), the Despot Theodore Laskaris, escaped to Asia Minor and immediately began to organize local resistance to the Latins. Out of this was to grow the Empire of Nicaea.

In the spring of 1205 the Latin forces in Asia Minor were withdrawn to counter the Bulgarian threat,[12] and Theodore Laskaris was able to bring under his control various local rulers who had made themselves independent in the confusion that followed the fall of Constantinople.[13] He was then acting in his capacity as despot,[14] the highest-ranking

[11] e.g. J. Darrouzès, 'Le Mémoire de Constantin Stilbès contre les Latins', *REB* 21 (1963), 81–6.

[12] Nicetas Choniates, p. 814, ll. 15–22, p. 826, ll. 16–18.

[13] Ibid., p. 798, ll. 5–8, pp. 826–7; Acropolites I, p. 12, ll. 10–13; Sathas I, pp. 113–14.

[14] Acropolites I, p. 11, ll. 5–9, 17–18.

member of the Byzantine hierarchy beneath the emperor. He did not have himself proclaimed emperor at Nicaea until perhaps as late as 1206.[15] There still remained his two most dangerous Greek rivals in Asia Minor, Manuel Mavrozomes and David Komnenos, one of the founders of the Empire of Trebizond. Mavrozomes had Seljuq backing, but he was defeated by Laskaris; and the frontier with the Seljuqs was restored.[16] Two invasions mounted by David Komnenos against Nicaea were beaten off, probably in 1206 and 1207.[17]

Theodore Laskaris's position was anomalous. His father-in-law was still alive; he was only recognized as emperor by the Greeks of western Asia Minor, and he had not been crowned. He hoped to strengthen his claims by inviting to his court the Greek Patriarch of Constantinople John Kamateros, then in exile among the Bulgarians. The patriarch refused and died shortly afterwards in 1206.[18] It was not until two years later in March 1208 that Laskaris took the decisive step of assembling a synod at Nicaea which was enjoined to elect a new patriarch. Its choice fell upon Michael Autoreianos. His first act was an event of great symbolic importance, the coronation of Theodore I Laskaris.[19] It demonstrated that the twin pillars upon which the Byzantine Empire was built, the imperial office and the patriarchate, had been re-erected, if only in exile.

Theodore Laskaris and his patriarch laid claim to all the prerogatives that the emperors and patriarchs had enjoyed before 1204. Almost from the first it was maintained that though Constantinople had fallen its imperial traditions had passed to Nicaea, where God, in his mercy, had set up an emperor. It was the duty of the emperor, like Moses or Zorobabel before him, to lead his people out of captivity and to restore the integrity of the Empire.[20] This meant above all

[15] Sathas I, pp. 113–14; Nicetas Choniates, p. 828, ll. 1–4; Acropolites I, p. 11, l. 5. Acropolites is the only independent source to give a date. He is followed by the Short Chronicle of 1352: see R.-J. Loenertz, 'La Chronique brève de 1352', *OCP* 29 (1963), 332, 366–8.

[16] Nicetas Choniates, p. 827, ll. 14–21, p. 828, ll. 19–23, p. 842, ll. 8–13.

[17] Ibid., p. 828, ll. 4–19, pp. 844–5.

[18] Ibid., p. 837, ll. 2–5; Acropolites I, p. 11, l. 13; Dölger, *Reg.* 1671.

[19] Heisenberg, 'Neue Quellen' II, pp. 5–12; Laurent in *REB* 27 (1969), 129–33.

[20] Michael Choniates I, pp. 354–5; II, pp. 257–61, 276–7, 336–7; Sathas I, pp. 104–5, 106–7, 128–9.

the recovery of Constantinople. Hopes ran very high that it would soon be restored after Theodore Laskaris's great victory in 1211 over the Seljuqs at the battle of Antioch-on-the-Maiander[21] but quickly receded after his defeat in the autumn of that year by the Latin Emperor Henry.[22] The recovery of the capital remained the ultimate aim of the emperors of Nicaea, but in practice it had to be adapted to the very complicated political and ecclesiastical situation that had come into being since 1204 in the lands that had formerly constituted the Byzantine Empire.

It is a tangled history dominated by contradictory themes: the emperors of Nicaea had to temporize with the papacy, at first in order to draw off the full weight of the Latin offensive,[23] and then because it seemed to open up an easier path to the recovery of the capital. This ran almost directly counter to their struggle to preserve the unity and the purity of Orthodoxy in the face of papal claims of supremacy.

These contradictions set up pressures that ruffled the internal history of the Nicaean Empire. The clergy was for the most part and on most occasions opposed to an imperial policy of negotiating with the papacy over the question of the Union of Churches. In 1234 a debate at the Nicaean court between representatives of the two churches broke up in confusion with the Greeks yelling after the departing Latins: 'It is you who are the heretics.'[24]

The points of doctrine that separated the Greeks and Latins were those that had been at issue at the time of the 1054 Schism and even before. Most important was the dispute over the procession of the Holy Spirit; less important was the disagreement over the use of unleavened bread in the communion service. From a practical point of view, perhaps most important of all was the problem of papal primacy. How valid were the papal claims to supreme jurisdiction over all the bishops of the church? The Greeks were

[21] Michael Choniates II, pp. 353–6; Sathas I, pp. 129–36, esp. p. 136, ll. 19–20. Cf. Heisenberg, 'Neue Quellen' III, p. 10, ll. 21–3.

[22] Acropolites I, p. 27, ll. 13–21.

[23] e.g. Migne, *P.L.* 215, cols. 1372–5: Letter of Innocent III to Theodore I Laskaris (Mar. 1208).

[24] J. D. Mansi, *Sacrorum Conciliorum nova et amplissima collectio*, XXIII, col. 305, ll. 51–3.

willing to admit a primacy of honour but insisted that it could only be exercised in harmony with the other patriarchs. The pope certainly did not have the right to appoint bishops or a patriarch outside his own territories. If he tried to do so, he was infringing the canons of the church.[25]

The disputed points of doctrine, the very different concepts that the Greeks and Latins held of the principles of church organization, meant that at this level negotiations over the Union of Churches were doomed from the start. The practical basis for negotiation was political, as can be seen from the two occasions during the period of exile that talks over the Union of Churches appeared to have some real hope of success. The first occurred towards the end of Theodore I Laskaris's reign. He was scheming to obtain the regency of the Latin Empire. Since the death of Henry of Hainault in 1216 it had been virtually without a ruler. Laskaris hoped to establish his claims to the regency by a complicated series of marriage alliances. In 1219 he married the late emperor's niece, and her brother, the heir to the throne, was betrothed to one of Theodore's daughters. In 1220, in order to strengthen his claims still further, he convened a council at Nicaea to discuss whether an approach should be made to the papacy over the Union of Churches. The whole plan fell through as a result of the intransigence of the Latins of Constantinople and the opposition it provoked both from the Greek patriarch and from the Orthodox Church in Epiros.[26]

The second occasion occurred at the very end of the reign of Laskaris's son-in-law and successor, John III Doukas Vatatzes (1222–54). In the early years of his reign he followed an anti-Latin policy which had the whole-hearted approval of the Patriarch Germanos II.[27] But increasingly he found himself drawn into the great struggle between the papacy and the Hohenstaufen. Alliance with Frederick II seemed to hold out the best hope of tangible rewards. There was a promise that Constantinople might be returned. The alliance was

[25] e.g. Heisenberg, 'Neue Quellen' I, pp. 52–63; A. Papadopoulos-Kerameus, '*Θεόδωρος Εἰρηνικὸς Πατριάρχης οἰκουμενικός*', *BZ* 10 (1901), 187–92.

[26] Norden, *Das Papsttum und Byzanz*, pp. 341–7.

[27] J. Nicole, 'Bref inédit de Germain II, patriarche de Constantinople (Année 1230) avec une recension nouvelle du chrysobulle de l'empereur Jean Ducas Vatacès', *REG* 7 (1894), 74–80.

sealed by the marriage, probably in 1244, of the widower John Vatatzes to a bastard daughter of Frederick II. In general, Vatatzes remained true to his father-in-law helping him with both men and money,[28] but he gained nothing in return and carried on intermittent negotiations with Pope Innocent IV.

The pope, for his part, came to see that the establishment of the Latin Empire, far from solving the problem of the Greek Church, had made actual what was only a potential schism. In order to achieve a restoration of the unity of the two churches, he was willing to abandon Constantinople to Vatatzes. By 1254 terms acceptable to both sides had been set out. Vatatzes was able to secure synodical approval for his proposals.[29] The Patriarch Manuel II even put forward what might have been a satisfactory solution to the problem of the procession of the Holy Spirit.[30] But within the year Pope, Emperor, and Patriarch were all dead; and both at Rome and at Nicaea other policies prevailed.

John Vatatzes's son and successor Theodore II Laskaris (1254–8) certainly proposed that a general council should be held to decide questions of dogma and organization that separated the two churches, but he maintained that in cases where no agreement had been reached it was the imperial prerogative to decide the points at issue.[31] This lofty concept of the imperial office left little room for negotiation; and in 1256 papal envoys were expelled from his territories.[32]

These negotiations over the Union of Churches form an important, but barren chapter in the diplomatic history of the Nicaean Empire. For the patriarchs of Nicaea a more pressing problem was protecting and giving guidance to those members of the Orthodox Church who found themselves under Latin rule. In the years immediately following the fall of Constantinople the latter looked to the Nicaean

[28] See S. Borsari, 'Federigo II e l'Oriente bizantino', *RSI* 63 (1951), 279–91.

[29] Pachymeres I, pp. 366–7, 374–5; and, in general, Norden, *Das Papsttum und Byzanz*, pp. 368–78.

[30] Norden, *Das Papsttum und Byzanz*, pp. 756–9.

[31] J. Draeseke, 'Theodoros Laskaris', *BZ* 3 (1894), 512–13; Norden, *Das Papsttum und Byzanz*, pp. 378–83; V. Laurent, 'Le Pape Aléxandre IV (1254–1261) et l'Empire de Nicée', *EO* 34 (1935), 34–55.

[32] Acropolites I, pp. 139–40.

Empire as their hope of salvation;[33] and many sought refuge there.[34] It was partly under pressure from the Greeks of Constantinople that Theodore I Laskaris proceeded to have a patriarch elected at Nicaea.[35] When they were being persecuted by the Latins, the patriarchs of Nicaea encouraged and sustained them in their resistance.[36] But under the beneficent rule of Henry of Hainault the Greeks of Constantinople became increasingly resigned to the Latin yoke.[37]

Analogous to their position was that of the Orthodox in Cyprus who had been under Latin rule since 1191, but there were differences; these stemmed from the status of the church of Cyprus. It was an autocephalous church. This meant that, although the Archbishop of Cyprus was elected by the bishops of his church, final approval lay with the emperor.[38] The last archbishop appointed before 1204 died soon afterwards; and the church of Cyprus was left without a shepherd. There was now no fully acknowledged Byzantine emperor to carry out the traditional imperial role in the making of a new archbishop. In the year 1209 or shortly before, the Cypriot clergy and people met under the auspices of the Latin king of the island to break this deadlock. They chose as archbishop Esaias, the exiled Orthodox Archbishop of Lydda. There were doubts in general about the validity of the procedure and in particular about the archbishop's translation. The Bishop of Paphos was therefore sent to Nicaea to obtain from the patriarch recognition of the validity of the election and confirmation that the translation was in no way uncanonical. The patriarch called together a synod at Nicaea and together they provided the assurances that were sought.[39] There are no indications that the election was put before the emperor for his approval, but the traditional

[33] Michael Choniates I, pp. 346–7; II, pp. 257–61, 276–8, 278–9, 336–7.

[34] e.g. Heisenberg, 'Neue Quellen' I, p. 62, ll. 9–32; Nicetas Choniates, p. 830, ll. 2–4; Michael Choniates II, pp. 276–80.

[35] Heisenberg, 'Neue Quellen' II, p. 28, ll. 9–19. Cf. ibid. I, pp. 63–4.

[36] e.g. Papadopoulos-Kerameus in *BZ* 10 (1901), 182–92.

[37] Acropolites I, p. 30, ll. 2–12.

[38] Migne, *P.G.* 132, col. 1097.

[39] K. Chatzepsaltes, *'Η ἐκκλησία Κύπρου καὶ τὸ ἐν Νικαίᾳ οἰκουμενικὸν Πατριαρχεῖον τοῦ ιγ' μ.χ.αἰῶνος. συνοδικὴ πρᾶξις τοῦ πατριαρχείου Κωνσταντινουπόλεως σχετικῶς πρὸς τὴν ἐκλογὴν καὶ τὴν ἀναγνώρισιν τοῦ Ἀρχιεπισκόπου Κύπρου 'Ησαίου'*, *Κυπριακαὶ Σπουδαί*, 28 (1964), 137–78, text pp. 141–4.

procedure was in large measure restored towards the end of Theodore I Laskaris's reign when Neophytos, the newly elected Archbishop of Cyprus, came to Nicaea to be formally instituted into his office by the emperor.[40]

Archbishop Neophytos gave full expression of his loyalty to the emperor of Nicaea when he wrote that he and his flock recognized the Emperor John Vatatzes as their true lord;[41] and it was natural that Neophytos and his bishops should have found refuge in the 1240s at the Nicaean court from Latin persecution.[42] But this is all rather deceptive.

Neophytos appears to have turned a blind eye to the Patriarch Germanos II's instructions of 1223 that there should be no submission to the Latin Church;[43] and the patriarch's letter to the Cypriot church warning of the dangers of submission[44] only brought forth from Neophytos a succinct statement and defence of the autocephalous status of his church and an appeal to John Vatatzes that he should stop the patriarch meddling in the internal affairs of his church.[45] This defence of the traditional rights of the church of Cyprus was perhaps only to be expected, but it marks the beginning of a deep rift between the Empire of Nicaea and the Cypriot church. By 1250 it was rapidly moving out of the Nicaean orbit. In that year Neophytos proposed that his church should become directly dependent upon the papacy, as it had once been upon the Byzantine emperor, and that Rome should be the final court of appeal for all cases coming before the Greek ecclesiastical courts.[46] These proposals were enshrined ten years later in Pope Alexander IV's *Constitutio Cypria*.[47]

The status of the Cypriot church no doubt pointed to-

[40] K. Chatzepsaltes, '*Σχέσεις τῆς Κύπρου πρὸς τὸ ἐν Νικαίᾳ βυζαντινὸν κράτος*', *Κυπριακαὶ Σπουδαί*, 15 (1951), 76, ll. 30–2; Sp. Lampros, '*Κυπριακὰ καὶ ἄλλα ἔγγραφα ἐκ τοῦ παλατίνου κώδικος* 367 *τῆς βιβλιοθήκης τοῦ Βατικάνου*', *NH* 14 (1917), No. 28, p. 43, ll. 5–7.

[41] Lampros in *NH* 14 (1917), p. 42, ll. 24–8; p. 43, ll. 7–9; Chatzepsaltes in *Κυπριακαὶ Σπουδαί*, 15 (1951), 76, ll. 21–5, 32–4.

[42] Lampros in *NH* 14 (1917), No. 25, p. 39, ll. 12–17; Chatzepsaltes in *Κυπριακαὶ Σπουδαί*, 15 (1951), p. 66, ll. 10–14, pp. 66–75.

[43] Sathas II, pp. 5–14; Migne, *P.G.* 140, cols. 601–13.

[44] Sathas II, pp. 14–19; Migne, *P.G.* 140, cols. 613–21.

[45] Lampros in *NH* 14 (1917), No. 28, pp. 41–3.

[46] E. Berger, *Les Registres d'Innocent IV*, II, Paris, 1887, Reg. 4769.

[47] J. Hackett, *A History of the Orthodox Church of Cyprus*, London, 1901, pp. 114–23.

wards the independent stand that Archbishop Neophytos was finally to take in his relations with the Nicaean Empire, but these relations do illustrate the great difficulty that the emperors of Nicaea had in giving substance to their imperial claims. Where they lacked political power, the ecclesiastical ties that held together the different members of the Orthodox Church weakened. Yet other bonds remained surprisingly durable. The martyrdom of the thirteen monks of Kantariotissa in 1231 bears witness to the strength of Cypriot Orthodoxy,[48] while the future Patriarch Gregory of Cyprus (1283–1289) ran away from his native land in 1259 in order to seek a more congenial education at Nicaea. He could not abide the Latin education that was forced upon him in Cyprus.[49]

This contrast between the need to accept the existing political situation and deep-rooted currents of sentiment and tradition can also be seen in Nicaean relations with the Russian and Oriental churches. To a large extent they were a matter of form, though there was some substance to the Patriarch Germanos II's boast that his pastoral authority had borne fruit among the inhabitants of the Crimea, the Armenians and the Georgians, the Russians, and the Melkites of Jerusalem.[50] There were long-drawn-out and ultimately unsuccessful negotiations during his patriarchate over the union of the Greek and Armenian churches.[51] He was in touch with Theodore, the Bishop of Alania, whose see stretched from the Crimea to the Caucasus.[52] Possibly, too, the agreement by which the primate of the Russian church was to be appointed in turn from among the Greeks and from among the native Russians was concluded during this period.[53] The Oriental Patriarchs were invited to send representatives to the council

[48] Sathas II, pp. 20–39.

[49] Gregory of Cyprus, pp. 177–81.

[50] R. Loenertz, 'Lettre de Georges Bardanès, métropolite de Corcyre, au patriarche oecuménique Germain II 1226–1227c.', *EEBS* 33 (1964), 96–7. Cf. Laurent, *Regestes*, No. 1257.

[51] R. Devréesse, 'Négociations ecclésiastiques arméno-byzantines au XIIIe siècle', *Studi bizantini e neoellenici*, 5 (1939), 146–51; Laurent, *Regestes*, Nos. 1290, 1309.'

[52] Migne, *P.G.* 140, cols. 387–414; M. Nystazopoulou, *"Ο "Αλανικὸς" τοῦ ἐπισκόπου Ἀλανίας Θεοδώρου καὶ ἡ εἰς τὸν πατριαρχικὸν θρόνον ἀνάρρησις Γερμανοῦ τοῦ β'"*, *EBBS* 33 (1964), 270–8.

[53] See D. Obolensky, 'Byzantium, Kiev and Moscow: a Study in Ecclesiastical Relations', *DOP* 11 (1957), 34.

convened by Theodore I Laskaris in 1220.[54] They were consulted in 1234 about the elevation of the archbishopric of Trnovo to patriarchal standing.[55] The Emperor John Vatatzes distributed his largess in traditional manner both to the Oriental Patriarchates and to the monastery of St. Catherine on Mount Sinai.[56] One suspects that the emperors and patriarchs derived great prestige from acting out traditional roles; a possible sign of this is the way the church in Trezibond finally came to recognize the authority of the Nicaean Patriarch in January 1261.[57]

In the East, in Cyprus, and in Russia they were dealing with areas which were not of vital political importance for the Nicaean Empire. Increasingly their eyes turned beyond Constantinople to the Balkans where their claims were coming under scrutiny from Theodore I Angelos, the ruler of Epiros, who was going from strength to strength. In the autumn of 1224 Thessalonica fell to him. He was proclaimed emperor shortly afterwards, though he was not crowned until much later, probably towards the end of 1227.[58] A rival Greek Empire had been established. Even before 1224 the rulers of Epiros had been appointing bishops without reference to Nicaea. Theodore Angelos complained that if he accepted Nicaean nominees he would not be able to trust them,[59] a point of view that is readily understandable if the great power wielded by bishops in local affairs is borne in mind.

Theodore Angelos may have toyed with the idea of establishing a rival patriarchate,[60] but he never did. In a sense he had no need to; for within his dominions lay the see of Ohrid. This church was of exactly the same autocephalous status as the church of Cyprus.[61] Its incumbent, the Arch-

[54] Dölger, *Reg.* 1704; Laurent, *Regestes*, No. 1224.

[55] Dölger, *Reg.* 1744; Laurent, *Regestes*, Nos. 1278, 1282.

[56] Scutariotes, pp. 287–8.

[57] Laurent, *Regestes*, No. 1351.

[58] L. Stiernon, 'Les Origines du despotat d'Épire (suite)', *Actes du XIIe Congrès d'Études Byzantines. Ochride 1961*, II, Belgrade, 1964, pp. 197–202.

[59] D. M. Nicol, 'Ecclesiastical Relations between the Despotate of Epiros and the Kingdom of Nicaea in the years 1215 to 1230', *B* 22 (1952), 208–13; Loenertz in *EEBS* 33 (1964), 99–100.

[60] Blemmydes, p. 14, ll. 17–23.

[61] Migne, *P.G.* 132, col. 1097; B. Granić, 'Kirchenrechtliche Glossen zu den vom Kaiser Basileios II dem autokephalen Erzbistum von Achrida verliehenen Privilegien', *B* 12 (1937), 395–415, esp. pp. 402–7.

bishop of Bulgaria, in theory had jurisdiction over the majority of Balkan sees. He was subject to the will of the emperor and not to the Patriarch of Constantinople. In 1217 Theodore Angelos appointed Demetrios Chomatianos to this see; and the latter set about defending the privileges of his church and using them to establish it as the centre of an independent Epirot church.[62] After he had been crowned emperor by Chomatianos, Theodore Angelos called together a synod at Arta, proposing to the assembled prelates that they should set up an autocephalous church. They demurred out of respect for the rights of the Patriarch at Nicaea. A compromise was reached. The prelates were authorized to seek from the Nicaean Patriarch recognition of the autonomy of the Epirot church. He was to be reassured that his name would continue to be commemorated in its prayers.[63] At Nicaea there was indignation and suspicion.[64] The Patriarch Germanos II was in no mood to accede to this request. A mission led by the Metropolitan of Amastris was sent with instructions to examine the state of the western churches and to find out how genuine was their desire for union. With such terms of reference it was no wonder that the mission utterly failed and that canonical relations between the two churches were broken off.[65]

The claims of the church of Ohrid also brought Epiros into conflict with Serbia and Bulgaria. With some justification Demetrios Chomatianos maintained that the churches within those states were subject to his authority. In the early thirteenth century the church both in Serbia and in Bulgaria appeared at different times to be on the brink of falling under Roman supremacy. In November 1204 a papal legate crowned the Bulgarian ruler Kalojan king and raised the Archbishop of Trnovo to the rank of primate.[66] In 1217 Stefan, the Grand Župan of Serbia, similarly received a crown from a papal legate.[67] Serbia wavered between the

[62] Nicol in *B* 22 (1952), 212, 217–18, 221–8.

[63] Ibid., pp. 225–7; Loenertz in *EEBS* 33 (1964), 90–3.

[64] Blemmydes, p. 14, ll. 17–23.

[65] Loenertz in *EEBS* 33 (1964), 92–3.

[66] Norden, *Das Papsttum und Byzanz*, p. 231; R. L. Wolff, 'The "Second Bulgarian Empire". Its Origin and History to 1204', *Speculum*, 24 (1949), 190–8.

[67] C. Jireček, *Geschichte der Serben*, Amsterdam, 1967, pp. 296–9.

papacy and Orthodoxy. In the face of the claims of the see of Ohrid, St. Sava, the brother of the Grand Župan, turned to Nicaea for recognition of the independence of the church in Serbia. In 1220 the Patriarch Manuel I consecrated St. Sava autocephalous Archbishop of Serbia. It is possible that it was also agreed that St. Sava's successors should be chosen and consecrated in Serbia and need not seek either imperial or patriarchal confirmation of their appointment. The name of the Orthodox Patriarch was still to stand first in the list of those commemorated in the prayers of the church in Serbia. In this way the Patriarch of Nicaea was at least able to preserve a primacy of honour.[68]

Because of the hostility that existed between the Bulgarians and the Latins of Constantinople the subjection of the Bulgarian church to the papacy was purely nominal. Shortly before 1232 negotiations were begun that were to lead to the recognition of the authority of the Nicaean Patriarch by the Bulgarian church. In 1233 the Bulgarian Tsar John II Asen (1218–41) was instructed to send his nominee as Archbishop of Trnovo for ordination either by the Patriarch himself at Nicaea or by his exarch who happened to be in Bulgaria.[69] The exact details of this settlement are not known, but this is not a matter of great importance, as they were soon superseded. In the following year negotiations were begun between John Asen and John Vatatzes for an alliance against the Latin Empire. As his part of the bargain Vatatzes was able to secure the recognition of the independence of the Bulgarian church and the elevation of the archbishopric of Trnovo to patriarchal status. Again, the Patriarch of Nicaea was able to preserve a primacy of honour, by insisting that his name should be commemorated by the new patriarch, just as it would be by any other metropolitan.[70]

The emperors and patriarchs of Nicaea were forced to recognize the realities of the political situation and to accede

[68] Dölger, *Reg.* 1705; Laurent, *Regestes*, Nos. 1225–6; Ostrogorsky, *History of the Byzantine State,* 2nd edn., p. 431; Jireček, op. cit., pp. 296–9.

[69] E. Kurtz, 'Christophoros von Ankyra als Exarch des Patriarchen Germanos II', *BZ* 16 (1907), 128–30, 141–2.

[70] Acropolites I, pp. 50–1; Gregoras I, p. 30, ll. 3–6; Miklosich and Müller I, pp. 438–9; Dölger, *Reg.* 1746; Laurent, *Regestes*, Nos. 1282, 1285.

to the division of the Orthodox patriarchate of Constantinople into a series of independent churches owing them but the slightest allegiance. In the case of Serbia and Bulgaria very little could be done. Their churches were not to be reunited with that of Constantinople until the time of the Ottoman conquests, but the church in Epiros was quickly brought back into the Nicaean orbit.

In the course of the 1230s the political situation in the Balkans changed in a way that favoured the Nicaean Empire. Its most dangerous rival, Theodore I Angelos, the Emperor of Thessalonica, was defeated and captured in 1230 by the Bulgarians. The Empire of Thessalonica was stripped of its territories in Thrace and Macedonia and broke up into three distinct parts, Epiros, Thessaly, and Thessalonica. There followed a series of quarrels between the members of Theodore's family. John Vatatzes was soon in a good position to exploit these family squabbles. The alliance of 1234 with the Bulgarians enabled him to seize the whole of southern Thrace as far west as the Maritsa river.[71] After the death of the great Tsar John Asen in 1241 the Bulgarian state grew weaker under the rule of a succession of child kings. In 1246, taking advantage of this situation, John Vatatzes annexed the Bulgarian territories in Macedonia. At the same time leading citizens of Thessalonica were engineering a plot against its ruler Demetrios Angelos. By the end of November the city and its surrounding region had passed into Nicaean hands.[72]

These were huge conquests made within the space of a few months. They had been prepared by the work of the Patriarch Germanos II. After the defeat of 1230 the new emperor of Thessalonica, Manuel Angelos, was in an extremely precarious position, even turning to the papacy for support.[73] John Vatatzes demanded that he renounce his imperial pretensions.[74] Manuel hoped that Germanos II might act as a mediator between Vatatzes and himself and

[71] Acropolites I, p. 51, ll. 13–18; Gregoras I, p. 30, ll. 7–12.

[72] Acropolites I, pp. 72–83.

[73] Norden, *Das Papsttum und Byzanz*, pp. 320, 349; J. M. Hoeck and R.-J. Loenertz, *Nikolaos-Nektarios von Otranto, Abt von Casole: Beiträge zur Geschichte der ost-westlichen Beziehungen unter Innozenz III. und Friederich II.* (Studia Patristica et Byzantina 11), Ettal, 1965, pp. 154–5.

[74] Acropolites I, pp. 43–4; Hoeck and Loenertz, op.cit., pp. 156–8.

entered into negotiations with the patriarch over the restoration of eccesiastical relations. In August 1232 the patriarch sent his exarch to the western church and unity was formally restored.[75] Thereafter Germanos II took an active part in its affairs, even, it seems, going in person to supervise its organization. Particular attention was paid to the status of monasteries, many of which were brought under direct patriarchal control.[76]

Succeeding patriarchs continued to concern themselves with problems arising within the church in Epiros.[77] The emperor too appears to have intervened in its internal affairs, but it does seem that some sort of understanding was reached between John Vatatzes and Michael Angelos, since about 1237 the ruler of Epiros.[78] Towards the end of his reign Vatatzes confirmed the rights of the metropolitan of Larissa over a monastery within his diocese, but soon afterwards rescinded the grant at the request of Michael Angelos.[79] This suggests that the latter preserved a large measure of control over the church within his territories, even if nominally he was subject to the Nicaean emperor.

Both before and after the conquest of Thessalonica in 1246 it was part of John Vatatzes's policy to bring the leading members of the house of Angelos under his suzerainty. This was achieved by forcing them to renounce any imperial pretensions they might still have had and by granting them the title of despot.[80] This certainly placed them at the head of the Nicaean court hierarchy, but it meant that they recognized the validity of the imperial claims of the Nicaean emperor and that they owed him allegiance.[81] It had the

[75] Miklosich and Müller III, pp. 62–3; Kurtz in *BZ* 16 (1907), 121–8; Loenertz in *EEBS* 33 (1964), 94–5; Hoeck and Loenertz, op.cit., pp. 158–9.

[76] Kurtz in *BZ* 16 (1907), No. 4, pp. 137–9; Rhalles and Potles V, pp. 106–9; V. Laurent, 'Charisticariat et commende à Byzance. Deux fondations patriarchales en Épire aux XIIe et XIIIe siècles', *REB* 12 (1954), 100–13, esp. 108–9.

[77] Rhalles and Potles V, pp. 114–20.

[78] Acropolites I, pp. 64–5; Hoeck and Loenertz, op.cit., pp. 168–71.

[79] Dölger, *Reg.* 1807–8.

[80] e.g. the following emperors of Thessalonica:
Manuel Angelos (1230–*c.* 1237) in 1237: Acropolites I, p. 61, ll. 23–4.
John Angelos (*c.* 1237–44) in 1242: ibid., p. 67. ll. 15–20.
Demetrios Angelos (1244–6) in 1244: ibid., p. 70, ll. 15–18.

[81] Cf. G. Ostrogorsky, 'Observations on the Aristrocracy in Byzantium', *DOP* 25 (1971), 21–2.

additional advantage of devaluing the court titles that had been granted by the emperors of Thessalonica.

After 1246 John Vatatzes's most ambitious project was to negotiate a marriage between one of his grand-daughters and Nikephoros, the eldest son of Michael Angelos. Terms were not finally agreed until the peace treaty concluded in 1252 between the Nicaean Empire and Epiros. Nikephoros was to be raised to the dignity of despot by John Vatatzes;[82] and so, too, it seems, was his father.[83] The marriage was celebrated in 1256 at Thessalonica; and to give it greater solemnity the patriarch came from Nicaea to officiate.[84] At the same time the Epirots agreed to surrender the important cities of Servia in Thessaly and Dyrrhachion.[85]

Vatatzes also tried to win over to the Nicaean side members of the Epirot nobility. An important Albanian chieftain, Goulamos, was enticed over and so was Theodore Petraliphas, Michael Angelos's brother-in-law. The former was married to a distant relative of the Nicaean imperial house; the latter to a daughter of Demetrios Tornikes, Vatatzes's chief minister.[86] This complicated network of marriage alliances among the Byzantine aristocracy gave a degree of unity to the shattered fragments of the Byzantine Empire that transcended the new political divisions, but it would be wrong to suppose that they necessarily provided a means through which the Nicaean emperors could extend their political power. Petraliphas soon returned to his allegiance to Michael Angelos.[87]

Nor did marriage alliances always produce the results intended. The marriage of Nikephoros Angelos to a Nicaean

[82] Acropolites I, p. 88, ll. 17–19, p. 92, ll. 9–10; Pachymeres I, p. 36, ll. 2–3, p. 243, ll. 7–12; Gregoras I, 48–9; Dölger, *Reg.* 1806.

[83] Gregoras I, p. 49, ll. 1–2. Gregoras is the only source to give this information. Though trustworthy, he was not a contemporary. George Akropolites who actually took part in the negotiations in question has nothing to say on this subject. Even before 1252 Akropolites consistently entitles Michael Angelos despot, the first occasion being in 1247 (Acropolites I, p. 84, l. 18). Consequently, it is very likely that he had first received this dignity at the hands of one of the emperors of Thessalonica. He most probably received the title in 1237 following the death of Manuel Angelos (see Acropolites I, p. 65, ll, 2–3).

[84] Acropolites I, p. 134, ll. 3–6; Sathas VII, p. 527, ll. 4–7.

[85] Acropolites I, pp. 132–3.

[86] Ibid., p. 90, ll. 17–20, p. 91, ll. 6–16.

[87] Ibid., p. 166, ll. 1–4.

princess at first sight appears to have been a great diplomatic coup for the Nicaeans, but Dyrrhachion was never properly secured and within a year Michael Angelos had invaded the Macedonian territories of the Nicaean Empire.[88] But one marriage alliance brought unexpected windfalls to the Nicaean Empire. To cement the Nicaeo-Bulgarian alliance of 1234 Vatatzes's son and heir Theodore Laskaris was married to a daughter of the Bulgarian tsar.[89] This marriage was to provide one of the grounds on which the citizens of Melnik in Macedonia took their decision in 1246 to surrender their city, then under Bulgarian control, to John Vatatzes. It was argued a little ingenuously that his son had a strong claim to the city in his wife's right.[90]

At the beginning of his reign Theodore II Laskaris was faced with a Bulgarian invasion that threatened to undo the very conquests that his marriage had helped to secure. With great energy the Bulgarians were thrown back and by the summer of 1256 the former frontiers had been restored.[91] He was then called back to Asia Minor by the flight of the future Emperor Michael Palaiologos to the Seljuq Turks.[92] It was at this point that Michael Angelos chose to invade the Nicaean provinces in Europe. By the end of Theodore's reign their conquest seemed almost within his grasp.

Theodore left only a young son John IV Laskaris; his rights were put aside and the throne passed to Michael Palaiologos (1259–82). Palaiologos's usurpation momentarily revealed deep divisions within the Nicean Empire. These seemed to offer Michael Angelos still greater hopes that the Nicaeans might be driven out of Europe and the way opened to Constantinople.[93] He concluded alliances with the rulers of Sicily and of the Frankish principality of Achaea, but in the late summer of 1259 the allied forces were completely defeated by a Nicaean army at the battle of Pelagonia. The Nicaean conquests in Europe were at last secure. The next year Michael

[88] Acropolites I, pp. 140–3, 149–50.

[89] Ibid., pp. 48–9, 50–1; Dölger, *Reg.* 1745.

[90] Acropolites I, p. 77, ll. 1–5.

[91] Ibid., pp. 107–27, esp. p. 127, ll. 12–16; Theodore Lascaris, pp. 279–82, esp. p. 281, ll. 68–73; Dölger, *Reg.* 1883.

[92] Acropolites I, pp. 134–5.

[93] See Pachymeres I, pp. 81–3.

Palaiologos launched a great assault on Constantinople and failed ignominiously. But on 25 July 1261 a small Nicaean force penetrated the great walls of the city while the Latin garrison was absent. Constantinople was restored to the Empire, as it seemed to men of the time by the workings of Divine Providence.

In the great speech that Michael Palaiologos made on hearing the wonderful tidings, he proclaimed that just as the capital had fallen into his hands through God's mercy, so would the remaining parts of the Empire that lay outside his dominion.[94] His reign saw a vast effort mounted towards their reconquest. It had its successes but must in the long term be accounted a failure.

This failure stemmed in part from the Nicaean legacy. The opposition of the people of Bithynia to Michael Palaiologos's usurpation had its roots in their devotion to the Laskarid dynasty.[95] Much more serious than this was the deep resentment felt throughout all sections of Byzantine society at Palaiologos's policy of church union with Rome. It was a policy that deliberately took as its precedent John Vatatzes's negotiations with the papacy.[96]

It was ironic, too, that the recovery of Constantinople should have emphasized the weakness of what at first sight appears to have been one of the great Nicaean achievements: to have kept alive the Byzantine imperial tradition at a time when it might have been destroyed for all time. The continuity of Byzantine civilization was ensured and a semblance of unity was preserved for the Byzantine 'Commonwealth', but it did not provide an adequate basis for Michael Palaiologos's plan of reconquest. In reality, this unity was weak and compromised, based on sentiment and common traditions rather than anything more concrete. The independence of Serbia and Bulgaria was firmly established both politically and ecclesiastically. The rulers of Epiros were subject to the emperors of Nicaea in name only, a state of affairs that exacerbated mutual distrust and increased Epirot resentment of Nicaean claims. The church in Epiros certainly came under

[94] Ibid., pp. 153–7, esp. p. 155, ll. 10–11.
[95] Ibid., pp. 193–4.
[96] Ibid., pp. 366–7, 374–5.

the authority of the Nicaean patriarch. Theodore II Laskaris saw that this ecclesiastical dependence might provide him with a political lever. Faced with a Epirot invasion, he called together in 1257 a synod which at his prompting placed the ruler of Epiros, Michael Angelos, and his people under an interdict.[97] There are no signs that this move had any success. At home it only brought forth opposition from Nikephoros Blemmydes, the emperor's former tutor, who bitterly objected to this use of the church for political ends.[98]

Blemmydes's attitude to Epiros, and for that matter to Rhodes, went directly against the official view. The Nicaean government considered Michael Angelos a rebel.[99] In general Nicaean opinion of the Epirots was low. They were not to be trusted; their submission brought with it no loyalty.[100] Much the same can be said about the Nicaean attitude to the Gavalas family that had held the island of Rhodes since the fall of Constantinople.[101] In the Nicaean view they had usurped imperial rights. In contrast, Blemmydes accepted that it was quite natural that the Gavalas family should consider it their hereditary possession and that they held it quite independently of the Nicaean Empire.[102] He adopted a similar attitude towards the authority of the rulers of Epiros.[103] Blemmydes, a renowned and cantankerous scholar, twice a candidate for the patriarchal throne,[104] was a man whose opinion counted at the Nicaean court.[105] These differing attitudes show what difficulty there was even in Nicaean court circles in adapting imperial aspirations to the political fragmentation of the lands that had formerly constituted the Byzantine Empire. Perhaps they also point to a paradox that lies at

[97] Blemmydes, pp. 45–6.

[98] Ibid., pp. 46–7.

[99] e.g. Acropolites I, p. 143, ll. 8–9, 13, p. 145, ll. 16–17, p. 150, l. 17, p. 157, l. 16, p. 160, ll. 19–20, p. 163, ll. 8, 24, p. 165, ll. 8, 20, p. 166, l. 16, p. 167, l. 25, p. 169, ll. 17, 25, p. 171, ll. 11, 27, p. 172, l. 5.

[100] Acropolites I, p. 167, ll. 20–3; Pachymeres I, p. 137, ll. 10–15.

[101] Nicetas Choniates, p. 842, ll. 20–1; Tafel and Thomas II, p. 320, ll. 9–11, ll. 17–18. Two Nicaean invasions were mounted against the island, the second in 1249 being successful: Acropolites I, pp. 45–6, 86–8.

[102] Blemmydes, p. 62, ll. 11–21.

[103] Ibid., p. 36, ll. 16–19; cf. Theodore Lascaris, pp. 320–4.

[104] Blemmydes, pp. 38–9, 41–5; Acropolites I, pp. 106–7.

[105] Cf. Blemmydes, pp. 31–2, 33, ll. 12–24, 46–7, 48–50, 50, ll. 17–25, 89, ll. 19–25.

the heart of the history of the Nicaean Empire. Its imperial aspirations were its *raison d'être*, but they now rested, both in terms of ideas and resources, on foundations too narrow to support them. That the Nicaean Empire had at its disposal fewer resources than the Byzantine Empire in the twelfth century is obvious enough. But a narrowing of its ideological basis needs some explanation.

The fall of Constantinople and the period of exile at Nicaea served to emphasize the parallel that the Byzantines liked to draw between themselves and the Jews.[106] Nicaea was their Babylon.[107] In exile they would atone for their sins; with the purity of their faith renewed they would be led back in triumph to their Sion—Constantinople.[108] In this way their claims to be a chosen people were enhanced.

Another parallel that had played a vital part in shaping the view that the Byzantines had of themselves was also reinforced. They, like the ancient Hellenes before them, were now in danger of being overwhelmed by the Barbarian sea. Thus, Nicetas Choniates compares the boastfulness of the Seljuq Sultan killed by Theodore I Laskaris at the battle of Antioch with that of Xerxes;[109] and the deeds of Laskaris are set beside those of Alexander.[110] Thus, too, the Patriarch Germanos II likens John Vatatzes's great victory over the Latins in 1224 at Poimanenon to those of Marathon and Salamis.[111]

With this parallel in mind Nicaean scholars generalized a usage only rarely found in the twelfth century.[112] Before 1204 the Byzantines normally used the word 'Roman', when they referred to themselves. This continued to be the case after the fall of Constantinople, but it became increasingly common for scholars to use the word 'Hellene', as well. Previously, it had practically always been synonymous with pagan. It must be emphasized that, although all the major

[106] See Alexander in *Speculum*, 37 (1962), 339–57.

[107] Michael Choniates I, pp. 354–5; Sathas I, p. 129, ll. 3–7; E. Miller, *Recueil des historiens des croisades. Historiens grecs*, II (Paris, 1881), pp. 662–3.

[108] Papadopoulos-Kerameus in *BZ* 10 (1901), 191, ll. 8–35; Sathas I, p. 106, ll. 1–9, p. 129, ll. 3–7; Michael Choniates I, pp. 354–5; II, pp. 257–61; 353–6.

[109] Sathas I, p. 131, ll. 16–17.

[110] Ibid., pp. 107–8.

[111] Nicole in *REG* 7 (1894), p. 77, l. 12.

[112] See R. Browning, *Greece—Ancient and Mediaeval*, London, 1966, p. 16; and in *Journal of Hellenic Studies*, 91 (1971), pp. 214–15.

Nicaean scholars used this word to mean Byzantine, it was a usage limited almost entirely to *Belles-Lettres*. It became part and parcel of rhetorical convention. Otherwise, there seems to have been little consistency about this new usage. In some contexts it retained its old meaning of pagan,[113] while the historian George Pachymeres even identified the Vlachs with the 'Hellenes'.[114]

At the same time this new usage seems to denote a new awareness on the part of Nicaean scholars of the unique value of their 'Hellenic' past. This is perhaps best explained as a reaction to the threat posed by the Latins not only politically and ecclesiastically, but also intellectually. It was only during the period of exile that Byzantine scholars became fully aware of the great strides made by western learning during the twelfth century.[115] Theodore II Laskaris feared that philosophy would desert the Byzantines and find a new home among the Barbarians. He regarded it as part of his duty to lead the fight against this threat.[116] In 1254 a disputation took place at the Nicaean court between its scholars and members of a Hohenstaufen embassy. Laskaris claimed victory and believed that it reflected great glory on the 'Hellenes'.[117]

There is possibly another, rather ironic, reason why Nicaean scholars should use the term 'Hellene', where before 1204 'Roman' would have been more usual. 'Roman' now became a term that might be applied to the Latins as well as the Byzantines. George Akropolites ended a tract on the procession of the Holy Spirit with the point that the name 'Roman' was common to both peoples.[118] Such a usage would have given rise to obvious difficulties. It was perhaps to overcome them that the Emperor John Vatatzes referred, in his letter of 1237 to Pope Gregory IX, to his imperial predecessors as 'Hellenes' and to his forbears as being 'of Hellenic stock'.[119]

[113] e.g. Oikonomides in *REB* 25 (1967), 117, ll. 20–1.

[114] Pachymeres I, p. 83, ll. 10–11.

[115] Cf. P. Tannery, *Quadrivium de Georges Pachymère* (Studi e Testi 94), The Vatican, 1940, pp. xvii–xxiv.

[116] Theodore Lascaris, pp. 8–10; Andreeva, *Očerki*, pp. 147–8.

[117] Theodore Lascaris, pp. 174–5; Andreeva, *Očerki*, pp. 144–6.

[118] Acropolites II, p. 64, l. 12; Andreeva, *Očerki*, pp. 165–6.

[119] A. Meliarakes, *'Ιστορία τοῦ Βασιλείου τῆς Νικαίας καὶ τοῦ Δεσποτάτου τῆς 'Ηπείρου* (*1204–1261*), Athens, 1898, pp. 276–9.

The new usage of the word 'Hellene' has its parallel in the way in which Theodore II Laskaris calls the Anatolian provinces of the Nicaean Empire the *Hellenikon* or even *Hellas*;[120] and George Akropolites describes the Pindos mountains as the frontier between Epiros and 'our Hellenic Land' (*Hellenis*).[121] In similar vein, it became almost a commonplace of Nicaean letters to consider Nicaea a latter-day Athens.[122]

It has been argued very largely on the basis of these new usages that the Nicaean Empire must be considered one of the cradles of Greek nationalism.[123] This is a point of view hard to sustain, since it assumes that the 'Hellenic' element was becoming divorced from the Biblical and Christian Roman strands that were equally important in the forging of Byzantine civilization. This was certainly not the case under the emperors of Nicaea. If Theodore I Laskaris is compared with Alexander and Achilles, he is also compared with David and Moses.[124] At the battle of Antioch he and his men wore the sign of the cross in imitation of Constantine the Great and his army at the battle of Milvian Bridge.[125] Michael Palaiologos's proudest epithet was the 'New Constantine'.[126]

A simpler explanation perhaps comes rather nearer the truth.[127] The new meaning attached to the word 'Hellene' reflects the intensity with which the Greeks of Nicaea clung to Byzantine traditions in the face of an unprecedented calamity. It was not a question that just one strand in Byzantine civilization was exaggerated; the same can be said of all of them. This can be seen in the great devotion to the imperial office that stood at its centre. A clear sign of this is the way

[120] Theodore Lascaris, p. 165, ll. 23–4, p. 176, ll. 52–3. Cf. Blemmydes, p. 4, ll. 17–18.

[121] Acropolites I, p. 166, ll. 5–7.

[122] Gregory of Cyprus, p. 179, ll. 26–8; H. Hunger, 'Von Wissenschaft und Kunst der frühen Palaiologenzeit', *JOBG* 8 (1959), 128.

[123] e.g. A. E. Vacalopoulos, *The Origins of the Greek Nation: The Byzantine Period, 1204–1461*, New Brunswick, N.J., 1970.

[124] Sathas I, p. 131, ll. 6–13.

[125] Ibid., p. 135, ll. 18–22.

[126] Pachymeres I, pp. 300–1.

[127] Cf. J. Irmscher, 'Nikäa als "Zentrum des griechischen Patriotismus"', *Revue des Études Sud-Est Européennes*, 8 (1970), 33–47.

John Vatatzes came to be venerated as a saint by the people of Asia Minor soon after his death.[128]

There is, it is true, a 'nationalist' tinge to the Empire of Nicaea. There was a deep devotion to the land of Asia Minor which is best expressed in an official letter that Theodore II Laskaris sent to its cities at the end of his successful war with the Bulgarians. He proclaimed that he was offering his victories as a gift for 'my mother, the Holy Land of Anatolia'.[129] The other side of this was the growing xenophobia of the Greeks of the Nicaean Empire. The Armenians of the Troad were massacred in 1205 in retaliation for the help they had given the Latins.[130] Shortly before his death in 1254 John Vatatzes ordered the forcible conversion to Christianity of the Jews within his dominions.[131] His protectionist economic policies stemmed from his desire to prevent the wealth of his people passing into the hands of foreigners.[132] It was a similar desire that led his son to dream of creating an army from which foreigners were to be excluded.[133] At a more personal level, Nikephoros Blemmydes turned down Gregory of Cyprus as a student not only because he was poor, but also because he was a foreigner.[134]

These attitudes hardly stem from a consciousness of a 'Hellenic' past. They were much more the result of the transfer of the imperial and oecumenical claims of Constantinople to Nicaea.[135] Associated with this was the conviction that only subjects of the emperor of Nicaea had the right to consider themselves Byzantine. This gained currency even outside Asia Minor and was not without its political advantages. The main reason why the people of Melnik decided to surrender their city to John Vatatzes in 1246 was their belief that they were true Byzantines (*Rhomaioi*) and not Bulgarians and that, consequently, they should submit to the rule of the Nicaean

[128] Pachymeres II, pp. 400–2; A. Heisenberg, 'Kaiser Johannes Batatzes der Barmherzige', *BZ* 14 (1905), 193–235.

[129] Theodore Lascaris, p. 281, ll. 73–4.

[130] Nicetas Choniates, pp. 796–7, p. 814, ll. 16–19.

[131] Dölger, *Reg.* 1817; P. Charanis, 'The Jews in the Byzantine Empire under the First Palaeologi', *Speculum*, 22 (1947), 75.

[132] Gregoras I, pp. 43–4. Cf. Pachymeres I, pp. 38–9.

[133] Theodore Lascaris, pp. 58–9.

[134] Gregory of Cyprus, p. 181, ll. 15–23.

[135] See Michael Choniates I, p. 355, ll. 6–10; Sathas I, pp. 104–5.

emperor.[136] The negative side of this, as we have seen, was the distrust and resentment that Nicaean claims engendered among the Greeks of Epiros. Thus, the conditions of exile exaggerated a contradiction that had been present throughout the history of the Byzantine Empire: the contrast between its oecumenical claims and a deeply held feeling of exclusivity. As a result, the foundations of its imperial aspirations were ever more rapidly undermined.

The history of Byzantium during the period of exile displays conflicting patterns of development. There is the great resilience shown by the Greeks of Nicaea. Thrace and Macedonia were reconquered and Constantinople finally recovered. The emperors and patriarchs of Nicaea established, at least nominally, the validity of their claims to be the heirs of their predecessors at Constantinople; and Nicaea became the temporary centre of the Byzantine 'Commonwealth'. On the other hand, the bonds holding together these diverse lands became weaker.

The imperial and oecumenical claims preserved in the Nicaean Empire were given a new vitality by changes that took place in the structure of government and society during the period of exile, but the momentum these generated was never strong enough to restore the Byzantine Empire to the bounds it had enjoyed before 1204. As this momentum began to fail, the dangers that these changes held for imperial authority and for the integrity of the state became increasingly obvious.

[136] Acropolites I, p. 76, ll. 11–20.

PART II

POLITICS AND THE CONSTITUTION

II

THE BYZANTINE CONSITUTION: THEORY AND PRACTICE

As we have seen, Theodore I Laskaris, the founder of the Nicaean Empire, had been raised to the rank of despot before the fall of Constantinople by his father-in-law, the Emperor Alexios III Angelos (1195–1203), and had thus been officially designated his heir apparent. This did not, however, form the basis of his claim to the imperial office. Instead, he maintained that it had been bestowed upon him directly by God as a reward for his exertions on behalf of the Byzantine people.[1] At his proclamation which probably took place in 1206 he assumed the imperial purple and put on the red sandals of office.[2] He laid claim to the prerogatives exercised by the emperors of Byzantium before the fall of the City to the crusaders. He signed himself in red ink with the hallowed title of the emperors of Byzantium: *Ὁ ἐν Χριστῷ τῷ Θεῷ πιστὸς Βασιλεὺς καὶ Αὐτοκράτωρ Ῥωμαίων*.[3] He minted his own coinage.[4] He strove to recreate in exile the fallen Empire.[5] A patriarch was elected at Nicaea in March 1208 and, as we have seen, his first action was to crown Theodore. The imperial court with its attendant ceremonial and hierarchy was re-established;[6] and the senate restored.[7]

The Byzantine theory of Empire was preserved unchanged, as the following passage makes plain. It comes from a letter of the Patriarch Michael Autoreianos, written most probably soon after his election in March 1208.

[1] Sathas I, p. 98, l. 24, p. 109, ll. 18–23, p. 110, ll. 1–4.

[2] Ibid., pp. 113–14; Nicetas Choniates, p. 828, ll. 2–4.

[3] The earliest example of Theodore's imperial signature is found in a document dated June 1207: Miklosich and Müller IV, pp. 217–18; Dölger, *Reg.* 1676.

[4] Hendy, *Coinage and Money*, pp. 227–36.

[5] Michael Choniates I, p. 355, ll. 6–10; II, pp. 149–52.

[6] See Andreeva, *Očerki*, pp. 55–80; Heisenberg, 'Palaiologenzeit', pp. 82–97.

[7] Scutariotes, p. 282, l. 10.

God gave us the Empire as a monarchical institution in the likeness of his own government, thus setting aside for all time the disorder that results from polyarchy. He established it at the time of his incarnation, so that those who believed in him should not behave towards one another in a heedless and foolish fashion and should not in their wickedness destroy both themselves and their faith. You know how God has punished us for our sins so that we were almost in danger of being handed over to the barbarians, but He took pity on us again and restored our first boon, the Empire, and raised up for us an emperor both industrious and painstaking, such as the time required . . .[8]

The first part of this passage echoes very closely the ideas of Eusebius of Caesarea on the origin and function of the Christian monarchy. Constantine the Great's conversion to Christianity made necessary the formulation of a theory of empire that reconciled the idea of kingship with the Christian faith; and this is what Eusebius achieved by building very largely on Hellenistic concepts of kingship.

His formulations were to remain the basis of the Byzantine view of the state and of the imperial office. The emperor was God's vice-gerent upon earth, deriving his authority directly from God and mirroring His perfection. It was no accident that the establishment of the Roman Empire by Augustus should have coincided with Christ's incarnation, for the imperial office had been created by God to protect and foster the Church. This was the main task devolving upon the emperor and the end to which his absolute authority was to be directed.[9]

How this theory of the Divine Right of Kings was to work in practice was much less clear. It conflicted with the vestiges of Roman republican tradition which held that the Law was the true master of the state, and the emperor only its guardian and interpreter. It left unresolved the exact nature of the relationship between the Church and the Empire which Constantine's conversion had imperfectly fused. The Emperor Justinian tried to provide the necessary solutions to these problems. Church and Empire were simply different, but mutually supporting, aspects of a single unity presided

[8] N. Oikonomides, 'Cinq actes inédits du patriarche Michel Autôreianos', *REB* 25 (1967), 118, ll. 37–46.

[9] See N. H. Baynes, *Byzantine Studies and other Essays*, pp. 168–72; F. Dvornik, *Early Christian and Byzantine Political Philosophy*, II, pp. 614–22.

over by the emperor by virtue of the power he derived from God. God was the only source of law, but Justinian maintained that the emperor was sent by God as 'incarnate law' and was therefore above the Law.[10] Thus was the theory of Divine Right further elucidated and strengthened.

The theory of Divine Right was hardly if ever called in question by the Byzantines. It was gratefully accepted that the imperial office was the chief principle of unity and order in the world and that the emperor's authority was absolute. This was to have two very important implications for the internal history of the Byzantine Empire. On the one hand, much of its internal history was simply concerned with the exercise of imperial authority through the administration; on the other hand, Byzantine politics turned to a very large extent on two issues that were central to the theory of Divine Right but had never been resolved. In the first place, there was the question of the succession. No law of succession was ever established. In theory, and often in practice, the throne might pass to anybody, who simply by seizing it, proved that he was the elect of God. But whether the emperor was a usurper or, as was more likely, had been designated by the previous emperor and associated in the imperial office, certain formalities had to be gone through before his claims were recognized. The emperor was only elected in exceptional circumstances, but the wishes of the aristocracy, army, and people were made known through acclamation; and this remained an essential element in the making of an emperor. It was followed by the other essential element—his coronation by the patriarch. It was never completely clear whether the patriarch was thus only approving the choice made through acclamation or was giving divine sanction to this choice.[11]

This illustrates the uncertainties that in practice accompanied the ideal relationship between church and empire formulated by Justinian. These provided a second area of

[10] See Dvornik, op.cit. II, pp. 716–23, 815–24; J. Meyendorff, 'Justinian, the Empire and the Church', *DOP* 22 (1968), 43–60.

[11] See J. B. Bury, 'The Constitution of the Later Roman Empire', in *Selected Essays of J. B. Bury* (ed. Harold Temperley), Cambridge, 1930, pp. 99–125; P. Charanis, 'Coronation and its Constitutional Significance in the Later Roman Empire', *B* 15 (1940–1), 49–66.

dispute around which Byzantine politics revolved. It was partly a question of defining the limits of imperial authority in ecclesiastical affairs. It was generally agreed that the emperor had complete authority in matters of organization, but no authority to alter the dogma of the Church. Any such attempt was bound to call forth the bitter opposition of at least a section of the Church.

It was also a question of determining what rights the patriarch had over the emperor. He could refuse to crown an emperor whose confession of faith he found unsatisfactory; he could excommunicate an emperor who, in his judgement, was failing to carry out the duties of his office properly. But what this amounted to is much less clear. Did the patriarch have a right and a duty to supervise the emperor's conduct of his office?

The uncertainties that existed both in this case and over the succession were never resolved. As we shall see, they were at the bottom of the constitutional crisis that accompanied Michael Palaiologos's usurpation. This episode also shows the way in which constitutional questions provided an outlet for the contradictions existing within the Byzantine Empire. One of the most important of these was the contrast between the supreme legal, judicial, and executive powers vested in the emperor by virtue of the theory of Divine Right and a society and government increasingly dominated by the aristocracy.

The relations between the emperor and the aristocracy undoubtedly constitute one of the most important elements of Byzantine politics, but they were often cloaked by other issues, such as the question of succession. As before the fall of the City in 1204, so during the period of exile at Nicaea each succession brought a crisis of varying intensity. Theodore I Laskaris's successor, his son-in-law John III Doukas Vatatzes (1222–54), was faced at the beginning of his reign with opposition from the late emperor's brothers and then from some of the most influential families.[12] At the end of his reign he again came into conflict with the aristocracy. The reasons for this are nowhere made clear, but the most probable explanation is that he was trying to ensure the succession

[12] Acropolites I, pp. 34–7; Gregoras I, p. 25, ll. 3–7.

of his son Theodore II Laskaris (1254–8) who was unpopular with certain sections of the aristocracy.[13] These crises culminated in the usurpation of Michael VIII Palaiologos and the setting aside of the rights of Theodore II's only son John IV Laskaris.

Succession under the Lascarids was by and large hereditary. It is true that Theodore I Laskaris's son by his second marriage to an Armenian princess was passed over in favour of Theodore's son-in-law on the grounds that he was still a child.[14] It had become the practice in Byzantium for the throne to pass, in the absence of acceptable male heirs, to the emperor's son-in-law.[15]

Something of a mystery surrounds John Vatatzes's succession. It was claimed that he had been designated heir apparent by his father-in-law and that he had received the throne as his just and rightful inheritance and not by force,[16] but he only held the rather lowly office of *protovestiarites*[17] or just possibly the rather higher dignity of *protovestiarios*,[18] when it would have been more usual for him to be honoured with the rank of despot. As has already been remarked, this rank was reserved in this period for the emperor's son-in-law and heir apparent. Earlier in his reign Theodore Laskaris raised Constantine Palaiologos to this rank and married him to one of his daughters.[19] Palaiologos was thus designated heir apparent but he died soon afterwards.[20] Whether or not Theodore Laskaris formally designated his next son-in-law, John Vatatzes, as his successor, the fact remains that in the eyes of contemporaries their relationship gave Vatatzes a very strong claim to the imperial throne.[21]

It was one thing to designate a successor, but, as the fate of John IV Laskaris shows, another to ensure his succession,

[13] Acropolites I, p. 105, ll. 3–6, p. 131, ll. 3–9; Andreeva, *Očerki*, pp. 156–9.

[14] Acropolites I, p. 31, ll. 15–19.

[15] See Gregoras I, p. 69, ll. 2–9.

[16] Acropolites II, p. 15, ll. 12–22; Gregoras I, pp. 24–5.

[17] Acropolites I, p. 26, l. 22.

[18] Ibid., p. 26, l. 37; Sathas VII, p. 462, ll. 2–4.

[19] Acropolites I, p. 26, ll. 16–17, p. 29, ll. 5–7; A. Heisenberg, *Nikolaos Mesarites. Die Palastrevolution des Johannes Komnenos*, Würzburg, 1907, p. 10; see Polemis, *The Doukai*, No. 140, p. 156.

[20] Acropolites I, p. 26, l. 18.

[21] See ibid. II, p. 28, ll. 11–14.

particularly if he was still a child. Theodore I Laskaris was faced with this problem in the case of his young son by his first marriage, Nicholas, who was in the event to die before him. All sections of lay society were required to take an oath of loyalty both to Theodore and to his son, while the Church, for its part, affirmed its loyalty and obedience to the emperor, the empress, and their son. Should Theodore die, it undertook to guarantee his son's succession and to support the empress in any actions she might take on behalf of her son. In addition, it would respect the rights of any guardians and ministers appointed either by her or by Theodore to manage the affairs of state while Nicholas was still a minor.[22] Nicholas was already designated emperor, but he is not given the full titulature of the imperial office.[23] This may mean that Theodore followed the Byzantine practice of formally associating his son in the imperial office, or the prince's position may have been analogous to that of Theodore II Laskaris who was never formally invested with the imperial office in his father's lifetime,[24] but was the acknowledged heir apparent and was occasionally unofficially termed emperor.[25]

The steps that Theodore II took to ensure the succession of his young son John recall those of his grandfather outlined above. He drew up a will appointing his son as his successor and his favourite George Mouzalon as regent. All sections of society both lay and ecclesiastical were then made to swear that they would observe these terms.[26] With one possible exception, therefore, the emperors of Nicaea do not appear to have had their heir apparent proclaimed emperor in their lifetime. This was in marked contrast, as the historians of the fourteenth century observed, to the practice prevailing under the Palaiologoi.[27]

As was to be expected, the emperors of Nicaea maintained the traditional ceremonies of the proclamation and acclama-

[22] Oikonomides in *REB* 1967, pp. 122–4.

[23] e.g. *τὸν κληρονόμον καὶ διάδοχον τῆς Βασιλείας αὐτῶν τὸν περιπόθητον υἱὸν τῆς ἁγίας αὐτῶν Βασιλείας, τὸν Βασιλέα κῦρ Νικόλαον*.

[24] Pachymeres I, p. 38, l. 10; Gregoras I, pp. 53–4.

[25] Theodore Lascaris, pp. 117, 140, 150, 159, 162, 172, 177, 186.

[26] Acropolites I, p. 154, ll. 15–20; Arsenios Autoreianos in Migne, *P.G.* 140, col. 949, ll. 33–9.

[27] Gregoras I, pp. 53–4; Cantacuzenus I, pp. 16–17. Cf. Acropolites I, pp. 188–9.

tion and of the coronation,[28] but it has been argued very plausibly that the period of exile saw the revival of the ceremony of hoisting the emperor aloft on a shield to receive his acclamation and that the rite of anointing was introduced into the coronation service, apparently in emulation of the Latin emperors of Constantinople.[29] Attractive as this thesis is, it must be pointed out that the evidence for it is not conclusive.

The ceremony of raising the emperor aloft on a shield appears to have lapsed at the beginning of the seventh century. It is not clearly attested again until the proclamation of Theodore II Laskaris in November 1254.[30] Nikephoros Gregoras, who records it, simply remarks that it was customary.

The question of the introduction of the rite of anointing is altogether more complicated. By analogy with King David, the Byzantine emperor was often called the Lord's anointed. It is usually assumed that this usage was metaphorical. It did not mean that the emperor had actually been anointed by the patriarch. It is argued that before 1204 the word, 'to anoint' (*χρίειν*), in connection with the making of an emperor or patriarch, only meant to institute.[31]

As we know, Theodore I Laskaris assembled a synod of the Church in March 1208 to elect a patriarch. It was to meet in the third week of Lent. The reason given for this was that the patriarch ought to be invested with his office before Holy Week, 'since it was the custom during that week for the patriarch to consecrate the holy oil'.[32] This has consistently been taken to mean that the emperor was to be anointed in the course of the coronation ceremony. In fact, it simply refers to the customary consecration of the holy oil by the patriarch which takes place each year in Holy Week.

There is, however, other evidence that Theodore I Laskaris

[28] Andreeva, *Očerki*, pp. 60–6.

[29] G. Ostrogorsky, 'Zur Kaisersalbung und Schilderhebung im spätbyzantinischen Krönungszeremoniell', *Historia*, 4 (1955), 246–56.

[30] Gregoras I, p. 55, ll. 1–3.

[31] See Ostrogorsky in *Historia* 1955, pp. 246–9.

[32] Heisenberg, 'Neue Quellen', II, pp. 34–5: '*καθ'ἣν εἰώθει τὸ θεῖον τοῦ μύρου χρῖσμα διὰ τῶν πατριαρχικῶν τελεσιουργεῖσθαι χειρῶν τε καὶ προσευχῶν*'. See F. Dölger in *BZ* 49 (1956), 201–2.

was anointed. Theodore himself claimed that God had anointed him after the fashion of David,[33] while Michael Choniates, the exiled Archbishop of Athens, wrote to Basil Kamateros, probably the most powerful man at Theodore Laskaris's court, to congratulate him: he had been able to persuade Theodore 'to impose a head upon our order of priesthood [i.e. to set up a patriarch] and not to disregard the priestly unction that he was in danger of omitting, but to enjoy the imperial priesthood through the fragrance of the double myrrh'.[34]

This passage is not conclusive proof that Theodore I Laskaris was anointed, since elsewhere Michael Choniates uses unction in a metaphorical sense.[35] But the probability that he was is strengthened by the decisive evidence for the anointing of his grandson Theodore II. At the time of his accession, there was no patriarch; the last one had died at almost exactly the same time as the previous emperor. Nikephoros Blemmydes who was intimately involved in these events records that Theodore was in great haste to have a new patriarch installed, so that he could carry out the anointing of the emperor.[36] Only then would he be able to set out from Nicaea to deal with the very disturbing situation that was developing in the European provinces of the Empire.

Whether the rite of anointing had formed part of the coronation service before 1204—perhaps long before—or whether it was only introduced during the period of exile must remain an open question. Despite the strong presumption that Theodore I Laskaris was anointed, there is no hint that his coronation witnessed any innovations. Michael Choniates appears to suggest that it was entirely traditional. It is nevertheless strange that no trace of the rite of anointing the emperor has been preserved in the various handbooks of Byzantine court ceremonial.

[33] Sathas I, pp. 105–6: '*δαυΐδειον τὸ χρῖσμα καὶ τὴν ἀρχαιρεσίαν ταὐτίζουσαν*'.

[34] Michael Choniates II, p. 258, ll. 20–4: '*τὸ ὑποθέσθαι τῷ βασιλεῖ κεφαλὴν ἐπιθεῖναι τῇ καθ' ἡμᾶς ἱερωσυνῇ καὶ μηκέτι περιορᾶν τὸ ἱερατικὸν χρῖσμα κινδυνεῦον ἐκλιπὲς γενέσθαι, ἀλλὰ τῆς ἐκ τοῦ διπλοῦ μύρου εὐοδμίας ἀπολαύειν τὸ βασίλειον ἱεράτευμα*'.

[35] e.g. Michael Choniates II, pp. 336–7.

[36] Blemmydes, pp. 41–2: '*τὴν τοῦ τῆς βασιλείας χρίσματος τελεσιουργίαν*'. Cf. Gregoras I, p. 55, ll. 21–3; Acropolites I, pp. 106–7.

Two lines of some verses that Nikephoros Blemmydes composed in honour of the birth of Theodore II's son John IV Laskaris[37] have been interpreted as showing that the ceremony of anointing strengthened the principle of hereditary succession.[38] As we have seen, hereditary succession was the general rule under the Laskarids; this was anyway the case almost throughout Byzantine history. But there was always the countervailing sentiment that the emperor ought also to be the man best-fitted to carry out the duties of the imperial office. Under the Laskarids great stress was laid not only on hereditary succession, but perhaps even more on the emperor as a philosopher king, for only love of philosophy was thought to equip an emperor with the wisdom necessary to carry out the onerous burdens of his office.[39] This can perhaps be seen as an attempt to reconcile the two conflicting views on the principles of succession.

It was natural that at the time of Michael Palaiologos's usurpation his supporters should have argued against hereditary succession and in favour of the throne passing to the man best-fitted for the office. Michael Palaiologos even proclaimed himself willing to pass over his son if he did not prove himself competent to be emperor.[40] This was sheer hypocrisy, but it does illustrate the tension which always existed in Byzantium between the two principles of succession.

[37] Blemmydes, p. 110, vv. 8–9:

χριστοῦ πατὴρ κληρουχικῶς αὐτάναξ, αὐτοκράτωρ,
ἐκ γὰρ χριστοῦ χριστός ἐστι, καὶ σὺ χριστὸς ἐκ τούτου.

[38] Andreeva, *Očerki*, p. 153.

[39] E. Barker, *Social and Political Thought in Byzantium from Justinian to the Last Palaeologus*, Oxford, 1957, pp. 151–61.

[40] Pachymeres I, pp. 90–1.

III

THE EMPEROR AND THE CHURCH

'For the Priesthood and the Empire, as it seems to me, are sisters, linked together like soul and body. The one is akin to the divine—the other is material.' This view of the relationship between Church and state was put forward by the future Emperor Theodore II Laskaris in a letter to the Patriarch Manuel II.[1] He is expressing the typical Byzantine conviction that Church and state were only different aspects of a single unity. Ideally, harmony should always prevail between them; in practice, this was not always the case.

Patriarchs of Constantinople were made and sometimes unmade by the emperor, while emperors might be excommunicated by the patriarch. The emperor had a duty to supervise the organization of the Church and to protect the purity of the Christian faith. He presided over the councils of the Orthodox Church, but had no authority to alter the dogma of the Church. The Church, for its part, took upon itself the task of supporting the emperor in the execution of the duties that the imperial office thrust upon him.

It would be fair to say that under the emperors of Nicaea both parties carried out their obligations. The creation of an empire in exile naturally demanded the closest co-operation of emperor and patriarch. The Patriarch Michael Autoreianos took the unprecedented step of pardoning the sins of all Theodore's troops who fell in battle. He urged them to fight on behalf of their emperor; they must protect the head that God had given them, for the monarchy was divinely instituted to save them all from the perils of anarchy.[2] He also pardoned the emperor his sins.[3] The patriarch and the bishops further undertook to persuade the people of their

[1] Theodore Laskaris, p. 138, ll. 17–19, translated in A. Gardner, *The Lascarids of Nicaea. The Story of an Empire in Exile,* London, 1912, p. 305.

[2] Oikonomides in *REB* 1967, pp. 117–19.

[3] Ibid., p. 120.

dioceses to honour and respect their emperor.[4] Theodore I Laskaris, for his part, took firm action to prevent the spread of heresy. Scholars from Constantinople came to Nicaea and began to dispute over the character of the eucharistic elements. Theodore threatened that, unless they returned to the traditions and dogma of the Church, he would leave off fighting against the Turks and Latins and would persecute them until he had utterly destroyed them.[5]

Both Theodore and his successor John Vatatzes encountered some opposition from the Church to their unionist policies, but they were careful to consult its opinion and strove to obtain its approval.[6] John Vatatzes relied very heavily on the support of the Patriarch Germanos II in his conduct of foreign affairs, and at the end of his reign the Patriarch Manuel II aided him in the growing difficulties he was experiencing in his relations with the aristocracy. Vatatzes failed to have Michael Palaiologos, who was even then suspected of having designs upon the throne, convicted on a charge of treason. He therefore requested that the patriarch should demand from Palaiologos an undertaking on oath that he would remain loyal to the emperor and his successors.[7] Another example of Vatatzes's need for the moral support of the Church can be quoted. Soon after the death of his first wife Eirene, John Vatatzes too appeared to be on the point of dying. He distributed vast sums of money in alms to the poor. Happily, he recovered, but he was extremely worried lest it be thought that he had thus wasted public funds; and so he took an oath before the Patriarch Manuel II that this was not the case, since the money expended had accrued from his careful management of the imperial demesne.[8]

Both John Vatatzes and his Empress Eirene were renowned for their lavish benefactions to the Church.[9] Their piety was expressed in the endowment of new churches, monasteries, hospitals, and almshouses.[10] The most famous of these new

[4] Ibid., p. 123, ll. 36–40.

[5] Scutariotes, pp. 280–1. Cf. Heisenberg, 'Neue Quellen', III, pp. 12–13. On the twelfth-century origins of this dispute, see C. M. Brand, *Byzantium confronts the West 1180–1204*, Cambridge, Mass., 1968, pp. 141–2, 351, n. 43.

[6] See above, pp. 15–16.

[7] Acropolites I, p. 101, ll. 2–6; Pachymeres I, p. 95, ll. 5–10; Dölger, *Reg.* 1814.

[8] Pachymeres I, pp. 70–1.

[9] Scutariotes, pp. 287–8; Gregoras I, pp. 44–5.

[10] Gregoras I, pp. 44–5.

foundations were perhaps the monasteries of St. Anthony the Great at Nicaea[11] and of Sosandra near the imperial residence of Nymphaion close to Smyrna.[12] The emperor also helped restore monasteries that had fallen into decay[13] and he gave extensive properties to the patriarchate which had previously only enjoyed the rather meagre revenues of the metropolis of Nicaea.[14] His piety was shown at another level in the conversion to Christianity of the Koumans, Turkic tribesmen that he had settled in his dominions. George Akropolites singled this out as an act of special merit.[15]

The emperors of Nicaea attacked the spread of heresy and tried to extend the Christian faith through missionary work; they were generous in their grants of estates, revenues, and privileges to the Church and, in general, respected the rights and the traditions of the Church. There is no need to minimize this achievement, but just as important was the way they exercised control over the organization of the Church.

The emperors of Byzantium possessed the right to make alterations in the diocesan organization of the Church. As far as one can see, the emperors of Nicaea made few changes, and the diocesan organization of the Church in Asia Minor remained close to that existing before 1204 under Isaac II Angelos (1185–95).[16] Only two changes should be noted. The church of Philadelphia formerly subject to the Metropolitan of Sardis was now raised to metropolitan status and given thirteenth position in the hierarchy in place of the church of Syracuse.[17] Likewise, the church of Pontic Heraklea was given metropolitan status and received seventeenth position in place of its former superior, the metropolitan church of

[11] Gregoras I, p. 44, l. 19.

[12] Ibid., p. 44, ll. 17–18; Scutariotes, pp. 287–8; A. Heisenberg, 'Kaiser Johannes Batatzes der Barmherzige', *BZ* 14 (1905), 166–71; Andreeva, *Očerki*, pp. 24–7; Ahrweiler, 'Smyrne', pp. 89–91, 94–6.

[13] e.g. the monastery of Lemviotissa near Smyrna: Miklosich and Müller IV, pp. 1–4; Dölger, *Reg.* 1718; the monastery of Rouphianon: Miklosich and Müller IV, pp. 303–5; Dölger, *Reg.* 1754.

[14] Zepos, *Ius*, I, pp. 661–2; Dölger, *Reg.* 1956.

[15] Acropolites II, p. 24, ll. 15–17. Cf. Cantacuzenus I, p. 18, ll. 14–16.

[16] See H. Gelzer, 'Ungedruckte und ungenügend veröffentlichte Texte der Notitiae episcopatum, ein Beitrag zur byzantinischen Kirchen- und Verwaltungsgeschichte', *Abhandlungen der königlich bayer. Akad. d. Wiss.*, philos.-philol. Classe, 21 (1901), pp. 590–5.

[17] Dölger, *Reg.* 1700.

Klaudiopolis.[18] The exact date of these promotions is not known, but they most probably took place in the reign of Theodore I Laskaris. Both Philadelphia and Pontic Heraklea were places of great importance under the Laskarids; and these promotions brought the diocesan organization closer to the political realities of the time.

This is one aspect of imperial control over ecclesiastical administration. Another much more vital one was the question of ecclesiastical appointments and above all that of the patriarch. One of the emperor's most powerful weapons in his dealings with the Church was his right to make and unmake patriarchs. The procedure for the election of the patriarch of Constantinople had long been established. A synod of the church of Constantinople forwarded the names of three candidates to the emperor who selected the one who pleased him best. If none of the candidates seemed suitable, the emperor had the right to make an independent choice.[19] In practice, the election of a patriarch was more complicated than this suggests. As we shall see, the emperors of Nicaea were forced to adapt this procedure to their own needs and to the pressures of the time.

The election of Michael Autoreianos was quite exceptional. For this reason alone, it was necessary to vest it with every sign of legality. The synod that elected him was composed not only of the metropolitans and their suffragans who resided in the emperor's dominions, but also the clergy of St. Sophia and the abbots of the monasteries of Constantinople.[20] But, as far as Theodore was concerned, the main reason for assembling all these prelates at Nicaea was not so much the election of a patriarch; it was more so that they could witness the institution of the patriarch into his office by the emperor.[21]

A serious departure from the normal procedure occurred after the death of the Patriarch Theodore II Eirenikos (1214–16)[22] in January 1216. Theodore Laskaris was at that

[18] Dölger, *Reg.* 1805.

[19] See Beck, *Kirche und theologische Literatur*, pp. 60–2.

[20] Heisenberg, 'Neue Quellen', II, pp. 34–5; Dölger, *Reg.* 1678–9.

[21] Heisenberg, 'Neue Quellen', II, p. 35, ll. 9–10.

[22] Eirenikos's election followed traditional procedure: Heisenberg, 'Neue Quellen', III, pp. 18–19.

time away from Nicaea campaigning on the Turkish frontier. He called together two synods, one consisting of the prelates of Bithynia and Paphlagonia, the other of those of western Asia Minor. They were to decide whether it was lawful for an emperor to invest the patriarch with his office while away from Nicaea. Laskaris stressed that a patriarch would only be chosen after listening to their advice.[23] Consent was obtained; and Laskaris proceeded to invest his confessor, Maximos,[24] the abbot of the monastery of Akoimetos, with the patriarchal office. A second investiture took place, it should be noted, once the emperor and the patriarch had returned to Nicaea.[25]

His successor, John Vatatzes, was less considerate of ecclesiastical opinion. His control over appointments to the patriarchal throne was more blatant. He tried to ensure that the patriarchs would be amenable to imperial control. As the Patriarch Germanos II (1223–40) lay dying, he discussed the succession with the emperor. The patriarch put forward the claims of his protégé, Nikephoros Blemmydes; the emperor, for his part, preferred either Methodios, the abbot of the monastery of Hyakinthos at Nicaea, or the head of the palace clergy. It was Methodios who became patriarch, while Blemmydes was only chosen to instruct him in his duties. He turned this down in disgust.[26]

Methodios died after a reign of only three months. Vatatzes then left the office vacant for two years because he could find no candidate acceptable to him.[27] It was at this time that he rejected the synod's choice of Nikephoros, the Metropolitan of Ephesus, as patriarch, because he feared 'the man's zeal'.[28]

John Vatatzes and the last patriarch of his reign, Manuel II, died at almost exactly the same time. For reasons that have already been underlined, the election of a new patriarch was a matter of the utmost urgency for the new Emperor, Theo-

[23] E. Kurtz, 'Tri sinodalnykh gramoty mitropolita Ephesskago Nikolaja Mesarita' ('Three Synodal Letters of the Metropolitan of Ephesus, Nicholas Mesarites'), *VV* 12 (1906), No. 1, pp. 103–5; Dölger, *Reg.* 1698.

[24] Oikonomides in *REB* 1967, p. 115, ll. 1–20, p. 125, ll. 1–3.

[25] Nicephorus Callistus Xanthopoulos, *Enarratio de episcopis Byzantii*, in Migne, *P.G.* 147, col. 464; Dölger, *Reg.* 1699; Laurent in *REB* 1969, pp. 134–5.

[26] Blemmydes, pp. 38–9; Acropolites I, pp. 71–2.

[27] Acropolites I, p. 72, ll. 2–8.

[28] Pachymeres I, p. 117, ll. 7–13.

dore II Laskaris. The emperor entrusted the election of a new patriarch to a synod of bishops. Their unanimous choice fell upon Nikephoros Blemmydes, the emperor's former tutor. The day appointed by the emperor for his investiture came, but Blemmydes refused to accept office. The emperor tried to persuade him to change his mind, pointing out that not only was he elected unanimously by the synod, but that the monks and people, the army and all the nobility preferred him to anybody else. This argument appears to reflect some of the hidden pressures involved in the choice of a patriarch. Blemmydes remained adamant. He distrusted his former pupil's headstrong temperament. He did not want to act as the emperor's 'minister of religion'.[29] Theodore could wait no longer and such was his haste that he had the monk Arsenios Autoreianos 'made deacon, priest, and patriarch within a week'.[30]

Imperial intervention was necessarily less obvious in other ecclesiastical appointments, but it did exist. In 1216, for example, Nicholas Mesarites, the Metropolitan of Ephesus, assembled the synod of his province to fill a vacant bishopric. Unknown to Mesarites, Theodore I Laskaris had already promised the see to the Metropolitan of Mitylene who had found refuge from the Latins at the Nicaean court. As soon as he learnt of this, the Metropolitan of Ephesus quashed the election made by his synod and put the exiled Metropolitan of Mitylene into possession of the bishopric.[31]

The emperors had the right to appoint abbots to certain monasteries. These were called imperial monasteries. They were either imperial foundations or they had been placed under imperial protection. In 1227 John Vatatzes appointed Gerasimos Opsikianos, a monk of the monastery of St. Paul in Latros, to the abbacy of the monastery of Lemviotissa which he was in the process of refounding.[32] A more instructive

[29] Blemmydes, pp. 41–5; Acropolites I, pp. 106–7.

[30] Acropolites I, p. 107, ll. 4–14; Blemmydes, p. 45, ll. 1–6; Pachymeres I, p. 116, pp. 2–7. Scutariotes (pp. 288–91) gives a garbled version of these events. He was close to Arsenios, but it does not seem that much reliance can be placed on his account which completely passes over Blemmydes's election.

[31] Kurtz in *VV* 1906, pp. 110–11; Dölger, *Reg.* 1701.

[32] Miklosich and Müller IV, p. 36, ll. 5–9. Cf. ibid., pp. 145–6, 240–1; Dölger, *Reg.* 1713–14.

example comes from the closing months of the emperor's reign. Phokas, the Metropolitan of Philadelphia, was forced to accept an imperial nominee as the abbot of the imperial monastery of Kouzenas near Magnesia. Theodore Laskaris who was acting for his father informed the metropolitan that, though he might have spiritual jurisdiction over the monastery, the emperor had direction of its secular affairs.[33] About the same time, Theodore demanded as part of the imperial prerogative (*τῇ βασιλείῳ ὑπεροχῇ*) that the monastery of St. Andreas which came under Phokas's authority should be converted into the dormitory of a hostel that was being built; adding that the bathroom was not to be taken away.[34] Both these examples suggest that the jurisdiction over monasteries and the appointment of abbots to imperial monasteries were a possible cause of friction between the emperor and the Church.

The question of the jurisdiction over the monasteries was to be one of the major concerns of the patriarchs of Nicaea. As a rule a monastery came under the authority of the local bishop, but if it was an imperial or patriarchal foundation, it would come under the direct control of the emperor or patriarch. In the confusion that surrounded the fall of Constantinople to the Latins many monasteries were withdrawn from the oversight of the local bishop either by the family of the founder or by some local magnate on the pretext that it was an imperial monastery. The situation was worst in Epiros,[35] and, as far as it is possible to tell, much less serious in western Asia Minor, with the possible exception of Paphlagonia.[36] The Patriarch Germanos II was particularly concerned to bring imperial monasteries in Epiros under the control of the local bishop or failing this under direct patriarchal control.[37] But in Asia Minor the patriarchs of Nicaea were mainly interested in regulating the respective rights that the patriarchal administration and local bishops had over monasteries.[38] Hardly ever was it a question of a clash of imperial and ecclesiastical jurisdictions.

[33] Theodore Lascaris, pp. 162–3.
[34] Ibid., pp. 164–5.
[35] See Laurent in *REB* 1954, pp. 109–13.
[36] Rhalles and Potles, V, pp. 112–13; Laurent, *Regestes*, No. 1260.
[37] Kurz in *BZ* 1907, pp. 137–9; Laurent in *REB* 1954, pp. 108–13.
[38] Rhalles and Potles, V, pp. 112–13; Miklosich and Müller I, pp. 118–25; IV, pp. 302–3; VI, pp. 193–5, 205–6.

This is not to say that imperial and ecclesiastical jurisdictions did not overlap, sometimes bewilderingly, but co-operation rather than competition appears to have been the rule. Disputes over the ownership of property bulk largest in the sources and these usually came before the imperial authorities, but against this it is possible to cite a quarrel between the monastery of Lemviotissa and another monastery, that of St. Nicholas of Kalyphas, over some houses in the city of Smyrna; judgement was given by the Metropolitan of Smyrna, even though both parties were imperial monasteries.[39]

Disputed appointments might also come before the imperial authorities. The Emperor John Vatatzes reversed a verdict of the Metropolitan of Ephesus, Constantine Klaudiopolites, and ordered that Nikephoros Blemmydes should be reinstated as abbot of the monastery of St. Gregory the Wonder-worker near Ephesus.[40] The emperors do not seem to have interfered in matters coming within the spiritual jurisdiction of the Church. One of the monks of the monastery of Hieras, popularly known as Xerochoraphiou, complained to Theodore I Laskaris of the conduct of the abbot of the monastery. Laskaris did not deal with the matter himself, but ordered that the monk's allegations should be examined by Nicholas Mesarites who was then Metropolitan of Ephesus and under whose jurisdiction the monastery came.[41]

As we have already seen in the case of the appointment of an abbot to the monastery of Kouzenas, a clear distinction seems to have been made, at least in the case of the monasteries, between secular and spiritual jurisdiction. Secular jurisdiction over a monastery (*ἡ χρηματικὴ . . . δεσποτεία*, as it is called in one instance)[42] might be exercised by the emperor, or by a layman. This immediately prompts the question—does this indicate the survival after 1204 of the institution of *charistike*?

Charistike was the grant either by the emperor or by a bishop of the administration of monastic estates. The recipients of these grants were normally members of the aristocracy.

[39] Miklosich and Müller IV, pp. 55–6.
[40] Blemmydes, p. 33, ll. 8–24; Dölger, *Reg.* 1760A.
[41] Kurtz in *VV* 1906, pp. 106–10; Dölger, *Reg.* 1698.
[42] Rhalles and Potles V, pp. 120, ll. 18–19.

In theory, they were to protect the monastery's best interests. Of course, they often used their authority to line their own pockets. It was an institution that must have had its advantages for the Church, since ecclesiastical reaction to it was by no means completely hostile. As far as the emperor was concerned, it provided a rich source of rewards.[43]

It is therefore rather surprising to find virtually no traces of *charistike* after 1204. This is possibly to be explained by the massive appropriation of monastic properties both by the emperor and by landowners that took place after 1204.[44] It is to be supposed that temporary rights held in *charistike* were made permanent.[45] As we have seen, at the same time monasteries were being withdrawn from the jurisdiction of the local bishop. It was this that most concerned the patriarchs of Nicaea, not the administration of monastic estates and revenues.

The distinction drawn between spiritual and secular jurisdiction makes plain that the administration of monastic estates by laymen continued. In July 1252 the Bishop of Monoikos near Smyrna granted the monastery of Amanariotissa to Constantine Monomachos, a member of a powerful local family,[46] and to his brother, the monk Chariton. The monastery was falling down, and the brothers undertook its restoration.[47] It was also possible to seek help from a more

[43] See E. Herman, 'Ricerche sulle istituzione monastiche bizantine: typika ktetorika, caristicarii e monasteri "liberi"', *OCP* 6 (1940), 315–19; P. Charanis, 'Monastic Properties and the State', *DOP* 4 (1948), 71–81; Ostrogorskij, *Féodalité*, pp. 17–19.

[44] See H. Glykatzi-Ahrweiler, 'La Politique agraire des empereurs de Nicée', *B* 28 (1958), 57.

[45] Miklosich and Müller IV, p. 33, ll. 1–3.

[46] See Ahrweiler, 'Smyrne', p. 156.

[47] Miklosich and Müller IV, pp. 262–3. Cf. ibid. IV, pp. 263–5. In this context it should be noted that there survive two very interesting documents that were produced in a case heard by the Patriarch Arsenios in Nov. 1261. (ibid. I, pp. 124–6; Laurent, *Regestes*, Nos. 1331, 1358).

The first is dated May Indiction 13, the second February Indiction 10. They concern the monastery of Kato Ptomaion on the island of Mitylene. According to the first document, the monastery had been given for two lives to one Manuel Xeros by the metropolitan of the island. In return, the former was to pay 20 *nomismata* per annum—apparently the sum owed annually in taxes by the monastery. Half of this sum was to be paid to the metropolitan and the other half to his son-in-law. After Xeros's death this agreement was confirmed in the second document by his son. These documents cannot be firmly dated to the thirteenth century; and since the agreements no longer seemed to be in force in 1261, the likelihood is that they should be dated to before 1204.

powerful monastery, as the example of the monastery of St. Panteleemon near Smyrna shows. The son of the monastery's founder, harassed by local men, turned for protection to the monastery of Lemviotissa which had recently been refounded by the Emperor John Vatatzes. It was agreed that the ownership (*despotikon dikaion*)[48] of the former's estates should pass to Lemviotissa, but spiritual jurisdiction (*anaphora*) was to remain with the metropolitan of Smyrna.[49]

It seems that, at least in name, the institution of *charistike* disappeared after 1204, but this does not mean that lay control of monastic properties was completely eradicated. In the first place, the founder's family retained, if not outright possession, at least an interest in the property with which the monastery had been endowed; and this interest could be handed on. In the second place, a bishop valued the support of the local landowning families. It was from these families that many members of the bishop's administration were recruited and sometimes the bishop himself.[50]

The loser would seem to be the emperor who with the disappearance of *charistike* no longer had at his disposal an extremely convenient source of patronage. Some compensation was perhaps to be found in another practice similar to *charistike* which survived the fall of Constantinople. The emperor might place an imperial monastery under the superintendence of a guardian (*epitropos, ephoros*).[51] In 1226 Michael Kadianos was appointed *epitropos* of the monastery of Lemviotissa which the Emperor John Vatatzes was in the process of refounding. He was to see to it that all its former properties were restored to it.[52] Once the monastery had been formally restored by the chrysobull of 1228, there is no further mention of an *epitropos*. In 1273 the holder of the important chancery office of *epi tou kanikleiou* was appointed guardian of the monastery of St. John the Theologian on the island of Patmos by the emperor. He was responsible for protecting the monastery's interests against local officials and landowners.

[48] Miklosich and Müller IV, p. 139, l. 1.
[49] Ibid., pp. 56–60.
[50] See below, p. 269.
[51] See Sathas VI, p. 648, ll. 1–18: the formula of an imperial grant of an *ephoria*.
[52] Miklosich and Müller IV, p. 36, pp. 145–6; Dölger, *Reg.* 1713. Cf. Miklosich and Müller IV, pp. 240–1; Dölger, *Reg.* 1714.

His activities are limited to the single year of 1273. His appointment appears to be connected with the death of the abbot of the monastery in the previous year.[53]

At first sight, the appointment of an *epitropos* seems to be very close to a grant of *charistike*. The difference appears to be that it was an appointment only made in exceptional circumstances and for a very brief period. A grant of *charistike* was normally made for life.

Vacant sees might be a source of profit, if not for the emperor, at least for his administration. This was the subject of a chrysobull issued by John Vatatzes in December 1228. It safeguarded the property of dead bishops from the rapacity of the provincial authorities.[54] Such property was to be handed over to the safekeeping of the financial officer (*oikonomos*) of the church. Yet in 1260, when the Patriarch Nikephoros lay dying, the Emperor Michael Palaiologos was to appoint an *epitropos,* responsible for the administration of the patriarch's private fortune. The man appointed was a monk called Theodosios. He apparently came from the Villehardouin family and was a favourite of the emperor.[55] This seems to reveal another side to the appointment of an *epitropos*. Though more restricted than a grant of *charistike,* it still retained an element of patronage.

Despite both imperial and lay involvement in ecclesiastical and monastic affairs, there is surprisingly little evidence during the period of exile of any conflict between imperial and ecclesiastical jurisdictions or of competition for ecclesiastical patronage. The reason for this was perhaps not that Church and state were more rigidly separated then in western Europe, but the very opposite; they were inextricably bound together.

Because the Church was part of the fabric of the Byzantine state, any conflict that set the Church against the imperial government was likely to have the most serious consequences. The long and bitter struggle between the Emperor Michael Palaiologos and the partisans of the Patriarch Arsenios shows

[53] M. G. Nystazopoulou, '*Ὁ ἐπὶ τοῦ κανικλείου καὶ ἡ ἐφορεία τῆς ἐν Πάτμῳ μονῆς*', in *Σύμμεικτα*, I (*Βασιλικὸν Ἵδρυμα Ἐρευνῶν—Κέντρον Βυζαντινῶν Ἐρευνῶν*), Athens, 1966, pp. 76–94.

[54] Zepos, *Ius*, I, pp. 387–9; Dölger, *Reg.* 1720.

[55] Pachymeres I, pp. 126–7.

this only too well. It completely divided the Empire.[56] The immediate cause of this conflict was the usurpation of Michael Palaiologos, but increasing tension between the emperor and the Church can be detected before this. The annoyance felt by some of the clergy at John Vatatzes's insistence on a subservient patriarch may be reflected at the beginning of his son's reign in Nikephoros Blemmydes's refusal to accept the patriarchal throne. This does not necessarily mean that within the Church parties were beginning to form along the traditional division between 'Zealots' and 'Politicians'. Blemmydes's autobiographies contain many instances of the infighting that went on among the higher clergy, but it seems to have been compounded of pique and personal rivalry.[57]

Nikephoros Blemmydes was very suspicious of his former pupil Theodore II Laskaris.[58] His suspicions appear to have been justified by Theodore's exaggerated claims for the imperial prerogative. He maintained, at least over the question of the union of churches, that the emperor had a right to decide issues which a General Council had failed to resolve.[59] This was an extreme interpretation of the emperor's powers as president of a council. It contrasts with the actions of his father when presiding over a council held in 1234. The question of the union of churches was being debated between representatives of the Catholic and Orthodox Churches. John Vatatzes put forward a possible solution that might bridge the gap between the two sides. It was not acceptable; and he did not try to impose it upon the council.[60] Theodore's apparent lack of respect for the Church and his insistence upon the imperial prerogative were, ironically, to be exploited by Michael Palaiologos in his bid for the crown.[61]

There is a final aspect of the origins of the Arsenite controversy that must be considered, even though it did not contribute directly to widening the gulf between the emperor and

[56] See I. Sykoutres, *Περὶ τὸ σχίσμα τῶν Ἀρσενιατῶν*', '*Ελληνικά*, 2 (1929), 267–332; 3 (1930), 15–44.

[57] See Blemmydes, pp. 6–16, esp. pp. 7–8.

[58] See Theodore Laskaris, pp. 56ff., where Laskaris appears to be trying to justify his rule to Blemmydes.

[59] Draeseke in *BZ* 1894, pp. 512–13.

[60] Norden, *Das Papsttum und Byzanz*, pp. 352–5.

[61] Pachymeres I, p. 93, ll. 4–8.

the Church. This is the question of the patriarchal administration. The patriarchs, no less than the emperors, were faced with the task of rebuilding an administration. This seems to have been completed during the reign of the Patriarch Germanos II (1223–40) in such a way that direct patriarchal control over the organization of the Church was strengthened. This was achieved by the greater use made of patriarchal exarchs. Patriarchal authority might be formally delegated to certain metropolitans, who were styled exarch,[62] or the patriarch might dispatch special representatives who investigated questions of discipline and ecclesiastical organization, but above all, as their title, 'Exarch of the Patriarchal Rights', suggests, they were responsible for upholding patriarchal interests.[63] Their activities brought them into contact and often into conflict, not with the imperial administration, but with the episcopal. Their work was part of a patriarchal plan aimed at regulating the respective rights and jurisdiction of bishop and patriarch.

It may simply be an accident of survival that the sources show increasing activity on the part of the patriarchal administration under Arsenios. This patriarch also issued a number of documents confirming monasteries in possession of their privileges and their property.[64] Most come from the period of Michael Palaiologos's usurpation when the patriarch must have represented the one stable authority in the state, but there are earlier examples. It is interesting that the monasteries are not only protected against the claims of their local bishops, but also against the excess of imperial officials.[65]

The manner of the creation of the patriarchate at Nicaea meant that the patriarchs were heavily dependent upon the emperor. John Vatatzes was able to ensure that this state of affairs continued: on the one hand, he was lavish in his benefactions to the Church; on the other, he kept a very tight

[62] Thus the metropolitan of Ephesos was the exarch of All Asia; that of Kyzikos exarch of All the Hellespont; that of Sardis exarch of All Lydia; that of Nikomedia exarch of All Bithynia.

[63] Miklosich and Müller I, pp. 118–22 (Mar. 1256); ibid. I, pp. 122–4 (Nov. 1261); ibid. IV, pp. 34–6 (July 1235); ibid. IV, pp. 353–7 (Oct. 1256).

[64] Laurent, *Regestes*, Nos. 1330, 1333, 1337, 1346.

[65] e.g. Miklosich and Müller IV, p. 355, ll. 22–3; ibid. VI, pp. 193–5.

control over appointments to the patriarchal office. Apart from Nikephoros Blemmydes's refusal to accept this office at the beginning of his reign, Theodore II Laskaris appeared to meet with little opposition from the Church. But this calm was deceptive. There was after all a serious contradiction between the increasing effectiveness of the patriarchal administration and the exaggerated claims that Theodore II made for imperial authority. Nikephoros Blemmydes's refusal to absolve the dying emperor[66] indicated that tension had been mounting between the emperor and the Church. This contributed to the crisis that followed the emperor's death. In its later stages it came to centre upon the question of the relations of patriarch and emperor, but its origins must be sought in the precarious compromise that existed between imperial authority and aristocratic privilege.

[66] Blemmydes, pp. 47–8.

IV

THE EMPEROR AND THE ARISTOCRACY

One of the chief problems that faced the emperors of Nicaea was how to maintain central authority while at the same time retaining the support of the aristocracy. It was a dilemma that runs right through Byzantine history: how could an autocratic system of government be reconciled with a social structure increasingly dominated by an aristocracy? By the eleventh century this problem had become acute and produced a series of grave political crises. A more or less satisfactory solution was found by the emperors of the House of Komnenos.

The Komnenoi did not renounce any of the imperial prerogatives, nor was government decentralized. If anything, it was centralized still further, but at the same time they tried to ensure that the interests of the aristocracy coincided with those of the imperial government. Great emphasis was placed on the role of the imperial family. The most influential families were bound to the imperial dynasty by the ties of blood and marriage. A man's place in the court hierarchy came to depend upon the closeness of his relationship to the emperor. Members of the great families could normally expect to be rewarded with the highest dignities. They also received grants of land and immunities for their estates from the emperor. There was another side to this apparently generous policy: these grants were often conditional and sometimes for a single life only; they were carefully supervised by the imperial administration. The merits of this system were that the place of the aristocracy in government was recognized, while their landed property came under increasingly close imperial supervision.

The balance that the Komnenoi were able to preserve between central authority and aristocratic pretensions was always a precarious one. By the end of Manuel I Komnenos's reign it had been undermined by the great strain that his foreign policy placed upon the Empire and it was then destroyed by Andronikos I Komnenos's attempt to eradicate the power of the aristocracy. The emperors of the house of Angelos rose on aristocratic dislike of strong government; and they were in no position to check the renewed usurpation of imperial authority in the provinces.

The conquest of Constantinople by the soldiers of the fourth crusade intensified the anarchy which already existed in the provinces. We have seen that one of the most urgent tasks facing Theodore I Laskaris was to put an end to the disorder in western Asia Minor. And this meant above all coming to some sort of compromise with the local magnates.

Theodore Laskaris used force against his chief rivals, David Komnenos of Paphlagonia and Manuel Mavrozomes, the father-in-law of the Seljuq sultan, but this was only possible because he had compromised with his lesser rivals. By the spring of 1205 Theodore Mangaphas who had seized Philadelphia was co-operating with Theodore's brother Constantine against the Latins.[1] Savvas Asidenos was another local magnate who had seized power in the aftermath of the fall of the City. From the town of Sampson (the ancient Priene)[2] he controlled the lower Maiander valley. He is found later in Theodore's reign still in possession of Sampson and exerting considerable influence in local government. He had married into the imperial family and had been honoured with the high court title of *sevastokrator* which was normally reserved at that time for the brothers of the reigning emperor.[3] Theodore also conferred the same dignity upon Nikephoros Kontostephanos. Before 1204 his family had possessed extensive estates along the Maiander valley. He too exercised considerable authority in the government of that region.[4] These two examples suggest that to win the support

[1] Nicetas Choniates, pp. 798–9; Acropolites I, p. 12, ll. 10–11.

[2] See W. Tomaschek, 'Zur historischen Topographie von Kleinasien im Mittelalter', *Sitzungsberichte der kaiserlichen Akademie der Wissenschaften in Wien*, philos.-hist. Classe, 124 (1891), Abh. 8, p. 35; G. de Jerphanion, '*ΣΑΜΨΩΝ* et '*ΑΜΙΣΟΣ*. Une ville à déplacer de neuf cent kilomètres', *OCP* 1 (1935), 257–67.

[3] SP. Lampros, '*Ἀνέκδοτα ἔγγραφα τῆς μονῆς Ξηροχωραφίου ἢ Ἱερᾶς*', *NH* 11 (1914), 402–3; N. Wilson and J. Darrouzès, 'Restes du cartulaire de Hiera-Xerochoraphion', *REB* 26 (1968), 14–15; Dölger, *Reg.* 1688; P. Orgels, 'Sabas Asidénos, dynaste de Sampson', *B* 10 (1935), 67–80.

[4] Miklosich and Müller IV, p. 291, ll. 8–13; Dölger, *Reg.* 1694–5; Tafel and Thomas I, p. 479, ll. 3–4.

of the local magnates, Theodore Laskaris confirmed them in possession of their estates, accepted their influence in local government, and in some cases was even prepared to work through them. Their loyalty was further ensured by the grant of high court titles.

To balance the power of these magnates, Theodore turned to his immediate family. Important military commands were given to his brothers.[5] An uncle, Theodotos Phokas, was given the office of Grand Duke and made governor of the district of Palatia (the ancient Miletos).[6] In the early part of Theodore's reign his wife's uncle, Basil Kamateros, was the most powerful man at the Nicaean court.[7]

Not all the great Constantinopolitan families who fled to Nicaea can have been as fortunate as the Kontostephanoi who already possessed great estates in Asia Minor. They must have been heavily dependent upon Theodore Laskaris's well-known generosity.[8] Imperial service provided a means of restoring a family's fortunes.[9] Their loyalty to the throne might be further strengthened by the ties of marriage. Theodore chose as his son-in-law Constantine Palaiologos who came from a family already distinguished before 1204. We have already seen how he was given the title of despot and designated Theodore's heir apparent. Another son-in-law, Theodore's eventual successor, John Doukas Vatatzes, came from a family that was already beginning to make its mark in the last decades of the twelfth century.[10]

John Vatatzes encountered difficulties in his relations with the aristocracy both at the beginning and at the end of his

[5] Acropolites I, p. 29, l. 3; Miklosich and Müller IV, pp. 35–40, 217, l. 24.

[6] Miklosich and Müller VI, pp. 153–6. For the site of Palatia, see Tomaschek, 'Topographie', p. 36.

[7] Michael Choniates II, pp. 257–61; E. Miller, *Recueil des Historiens des Croisades. Historiens Grecs II*, Paris, 1881, pp. 664–5. See Polemis, *The Doukai*, No. 100, p. 130.

[8] Sathas I, p. 115, ll. 2–4; Acropolites I, p. 32, ll. 3–5; Scutariotes, p. 282, ll. 14–21.

[9] e.g. Demetrios Tornikes became Theodore I Laskaris's chief minister towards the end of his reign. This ushered in a new period of prosperity in the family's long history: see G. Schmalzbauer, 'Die Torkikioi in der Palaiologenzeit', *JOB* 18 (1969), 115–35.

[10] See Polemis, *The Doukai*, pp. 106–8.

reign. Nevertheless, he was able to maintain the balance of interests which his father-in-law had established between emperor and aristocracy. This balance of interests was based on material considerations, but it was also connected with the traditional veneration for the imperial office which lay at the heart of the ceremonial of the imperial court.

Theodore I Laskaris established his court in the city of Nicaea, but his successor John Vatatzes moved the imperial residence to Nymphaion near the city of Smyrna.[11] As far as can be judged, the emperors of Nicaea preserved the court ceremonial much as it had existed before 1204 at Constantinople, within the limits dictated by the smaller size and less permanent nature of their court. The great festivals of the year were frequently celebrated away from the imperial palace because of the pressures of the campaigning season.[12]

For the purposes of court ceremonial the members of the court were arranged in a hierarchy. Between the tenth and the fourteenth centuries the hierarchy of the Byzantine court was completely transformed. In the tenth century there existed two sharply distinguished hierarchies: there was a hierarchy of office and a hierarchy of rank. It was rank that bestowed nobility and precedence at court upon its holder. Normally, a man would hold a rank corresponding to the importance of his office.[13] By the middle of the fourteenth century there was no longer any sharp division between rank and office, but only a single hierarchy in which the titles of both were included.[14]

There is enough evidence to suggest that the final stages of this transformation were accomplished under the emperors of Nicaea. Under the Komnenoi precedence at court depended in the first place on a man's degree of kinship

[11] Blemmydes, p. 7, ll. 6–7; Andreeva, *Očerki*, pp. 22–3; S. Eyice, 'Le Palais byzantin de Nymphaion près d'Izmir', *Akten des XI. Internationalen Byzantinisten-Kongresses*, Munich, 1958, pp. 150–3.

[12] Heisenberg, 'Palaiologenzeit', pp. 82–97; Andreeva, *Očerki*, pp. 55–80.

[13] Bury, *The Imperial Administrative System in the ninth century*, London, 1911, pp. 20–3, 36–9, 120–1; R. Guilland, 'Études sur l'histoire administrative de Byzance. Observations sur le Clétorologe de Philothée', *REB* 20 (1962), 156–70.

[14] Pseudo-Kodinos, pp. 133–40; R. Guilland, 'Observations sur la liste des dignitaires du Pseudo-Codinos', *REB* 12 (1954), 58–68.

to the emperor and, failing that, on rank.[15] Both of these retained some importance at the Nicaean court. A man's relationship to the emperor, however distant, formed part of his official title, while an office holder normally held a rank or received an honorific appellation as well. As a mark of special distinction, the Emperor John Vatatzes bestowed upon his chief minister, Demetrios Tornikes, the honorific title of 'Brother of the Emperor'. This appears to have placed him at or near the head of the Nicaean hierarchy.[16] But these are only vestiges of an older hierarchical system. As the following lists show, the upper ranks of the Byzantine court hierarchy during the period of exile were very close to those of the mid-fourteenth century:

c. 1226[17]	1259[18]	*c.* 1350[19]
Despot	Despot	Despot
Sevastokrator	*Sevastokrator*	*Sevastokrator*
Grand Domestic	Caesar	Caesar
Protovestiarios	Grand Duke	Grand Domestic
	Protovestiarios	*Panhypersevastos*
	Grand Domestic	*Protovestiarios*
	Grand Stratopedarch	Grand Duke
	Protostrator	*Protostrator*
	Grand *Primikerios*	Grand Stratopedarch
	Protosevastos	Grand *Primikerios*
		Protosevastos

This change in the nature of the court hierarchy took place over a period of time that saw the formation for the first time at Byzantium of a hereditary aristocracy. Does this change therefore mirror the aristocracy's struggle to win for itself a definite place in the government of the Empire? It is an obvious question, but there is no clear answer. On the one hand, it does appear to reflect a change in the nature of government and of the relations between the emperor and the

[15] Nicetas Choniates, *Thesaurus Orthodoxae Fidei*, in Migne, *P.G.* 140, pp. 177–80, 236–7, 252–3; L. Petit, 'Documents inédits sur le concile de 1166 et ses derniers adversaires', *VV* 11 (1904), 490–1.

[16] Acropolites I, p. 66, ll. 14–16, p. 90, ll. 22–3; Pachymeres I, p. 64, ll. 15–17; Miklosich and Müller IV, p. 41, ll. 19–20, p. 99, ll. 17–19, p. 147, ll. 10–11.

[17] Acropolites I, p. 34, ll. 5–8.

[18] Pachymeres I, pp. 108–9.

[19] Pseudo-Kodinos, pp. 133–7.

aristocracy as an order of society. The distinction made between rank and office had allowed the emperors of Byzantium to keep separate the ritual of the court and the administration. This provided a means of excluding the aristocracy from central government, but this became more difficult once the two hierarchies coalesced. Rank now almost of right brought with it real authority within the central government.

On the other hand, the transformation of the court hierarchy only reflected the simplification of the ceremonial which had begun before 1204 when the Emperor Manuel I Komnenos moved his residence from the Great Palace to the smaller palace of the Vlachernai.[20] It could be argued that no appreciable change had taken place at an individual level between the emperor and the members of the aristocracy. They owed their office and their rank to the emperor; they were the emperor's servants. The emperor, in other words, continued to control patronage and the conferment of status. This was one of his great strengths and helps to explain why it was that the aristocracy as an order always held faithfully to the Byzantine imperial idea.

The bonds uniting emperor and aristocracy at Byzantium were a mixture of personal loyalty, tradition, and self-interest. The emperor granted offices and rank; he controlled the grants of land and revenues upon which the aristocracy were so dependent. The loyalty of the aristocracy was further ensured by the use of oath. Every office holder or member of the imperial court was required to take an oath of allegiance to the emperor. The historians George Akropolites and George Pachymeres both describe it as an oath of servitude (*ὅρκος δουλείας*).[21] This suggests that the formula, 'Servant of our most mighty and holy Lord and Emperor' (*ὁ δοῦλος τοῦ κραταιοῦ καὶ ἁγίου ἡμῶν Αὐθεντοῦ καὶ Βασιλέως*), with which all dignitaries and officials from the highest to the lowest signed themselves, indicated a man who had sworn allegiance to the emperor. This oath was taken on the assumption of office and was renewed on the accession of each new

[20] Nicetas Choniates, p. 269, ll. 1–11, p. 351, ll. 11–14; R. Janin, *Constantinople byzantine: développement urbain et répertoire topographique* (Archives de l'Orient chrétien 4), Paris, 1950, pp. 126–7.

[21] Acropolites I, pp. 24–5; Pachymeres I, p. 96, ll. 4–6.

emperor.[22] An official or a dignitary of the imperial court whose loyalty was in doubt might be compelled to renew his oath of allegiance to the emperor. Michael Palaiologos was forced to do so both after his inconclusive trial for treason and after his return in 1257 from exile among the Seljuqs.[23]

As we have seen, the oath of allegiance had an important role to play in relations between the emperors of Nicaea and the various Epirot rulers as well as in those of emperor and aristocracy, but it was no new departure in the history of Byzantium. Its origins go back to the late Roman period. Possibly, as has been argued,[24] it received greater emphasis in the later Byzantine period. It must of course be stressed that it does not contain those reciprocal undertakings of lord and vassal that are so characteristic of the oath of allegiance in medieval Europe. It merely binds the taker in loyalty to the emperor. It imposes no specific obligations upon the emperor.[25]

The aristocracy might be bound in another slightly less formal way to the emperor. They were often married into the imperial family, which brought with it considerable prestige. It seems that the emperors of Nicaea exercised a right to arrange the marriages of the aristocracy. John Vatatzes was even able to set aside the prohibited degrees.[26] It was a useful means of rewarding the services of ministers, generals, or favourites, or it could be used to bind a man whose loyalty was suspect more closely to the emperor. After his trial on a charge of treason Michael Palaiologos was not only compelled to renew his oath of allegiance to the Emperor John Vatatzes. He was also married into the imperial family. The emperor first contemplated a marriage between his eldest grand-daughter Theodora and Palaiologos. He changed his mind and, instead, gave him as a bride one of his great-nieces who was also called Theodora.[27]

[22] Pachymeres I, pp. 53–4; Cantacuzenus I, p. 16, ll. 8–13 Cf. *Τὸ Χρονικὸν τοῦ Μορέως*, ed. P. P. Kalonaros, Athens, 1940, ll. 1237–8.

[23] Acropolites I, p. 101, ll. 3–5, p. 144, ll. 20–3; Pachymeres I, p. 21, ll. 7–11.

[24] See N. G. Svoronos, 'Le Serment de fidélité à l'empereur byzantin et sa signification constitutionelle', *REB* 9 (1951), 106–42.

[25] See Sathas VI, pp. 652–3, where the formula of the Byzantine oath of allegiance is preserved.

[26] Acropolites I, p. 100, ll. 5–14.

[27] Ibid., pp. 100–1.

We have so far been largely concerned with the formal relations existing between the emperor and the aristocracy. Their framework was provided by the protocol of the imperial court. A member of the aristocracy as the holder of a court rank or of an office was the emperor's servant and subject to his will. There is no need to minimize the power that this gave the emperor in his dealings with individual members of the aristocracy. On the other hand, the aristocracy was beginning to form a definite order of society. Naturally, the emperor's relations with the aristocracy as a body tended to modify his relations with the aristocracy as individuals. For instance, after Michael Palaiologos had been acquitted on a charge of treason, he still remained under suspicion, but John Vatatzes dared not proceed any further against him, because of the prestige and influence of his family.[28]

Aristocracy is of course an extremely loose term. An examination of the terminology employed in our sources may perhaps give us a more precise idea of its meaning in a Byzantine context. The terminology is mostly borrowed from classical usage. Despite this, it defines the members of the upper ranks of society in relation to their position in the imperial court and administration. Since these were the yardsticks of status, it does allow us a fairly clear idea of the social divisions among the upper ranks of society. George Akropolites is normally content to contrast the chief magistrates and the military (e.g. *οἱ τῶν ἐν τέλει* and *οἱ τῶν στρατιωτικῶν ταγμάτων*).[29] It is a distinction that is also drawn by other contemporaries, such as Nikephoros Blemmydes[30] and George Pachymeres.[31] On two occasions, the latter provides us with a much more precise analysis of the upper ranks of Nicaean society. They are divided on the first occasion into senators, members of the imperial family, *archontes*, and the military (*ὅσον ἦν τὸ τῆς γερουσίας καὶ ὅσον τοῦ βασιλείου γένους ὅσον τε τῶν ἀρχόντων καὶ ὅσον τῆς στρατιωτικῆς τάξεως*),[32] and on the second into senators, chief magistrates, and

[28] Ibid., p. 100, ll. 17–20.

[29] Ibid., p. 99, ll. 14–15, p. 105, ll. 1–2, p. 109, ll. 8–11, p. 156, ll. 19–21, p. 159, ll. 13–14.

[30] Blemmydes, p. 43, ll. 9–10, p. 49, ll. 14–15.

[31] Pachymeres I, p. 105, l. 20.

[32] Ibid., p. 41, ll. 5–7.

blood relatives of the emperor (*τὸ δέ γε τῆς γερουσίας καὶ ὅσον ἦν τῶν ἐν τέλει καὶ τῷ βασιλεῖ πρὸς αἵματος*).[33] These divisions echo those made by the Patriarch Michael Autoreianos in a synodal letter issued soon after Theodore I Laskaris's coronation. He noted that members of the imperial family, the magnates and the remaining *archontes*, all the civil and military, together with the inhabitants of the cities and provinces of the Empire, had already taken an oath of allegiance to the Emperor Theodore I Laskaris and his son Nicholas.[34]

All three lists agree that the imperial family enjoyed a distinct position in the state. We have already seen how heavily Theodore I Laskaris relied upon his immediate family. His successor John Vatatzes does not appear to have allowed his brothers any prominent position in government, but one of them, Isaac Doukas, held the rank of *sevastokrator*[35] which was traditionally accorded to the brothers of the reigning emperor and which placed them second in the court hierarchy.[36] On the other hand, the lists show some confusion in the use of the terms, 'magnates' (*megistanes*), 'chief magistrates' (*οἱ τῶν ἐν τέλει*), and '*archontes*'. Were they simply interchangeable? 'Magnates' is a term that George Pachymeres uses frequently to describe the holders of the highest ranks of the hierarchy; his use of it seems to be equivalent to George Akropolites's use of the term 'chief magistrates'. Both are distinguished from the '*archontes*'.[37]

By the beginning of the reign of Andronikos II Palaiologos (1282–1328) magnates were marked off from other notables of the Byzantine court by their special golden-red headdress.[38] They were also distinguished by the nobility of their birth. Their families are usually described as being 'noble' (*eugeneis*). The association of noble birth and the holding of high court rank can be seen in George Akropolites's descrip-

[33] Pachymeres I, pp. 135–6.

[34] Oikonomidés in *REB* 1967, p. 123, ll. 8–11, i.e. *τοὺς καθ' αἷμα προσῳκειωμένους τῷ κραταιῷ καὶ ἁγίῳ ἡμῶν βασιλεῖ, εἶτα τοὺς μεγιστάνας καὶ λοιποὺς ἄρχοντας, καὶ ἐπὶ τούτοις, τὸ πολιτικόν τε ἅπαν καὶ τὸ στρατιωτικὸν καὶ τοὺς κατὰ τὴν ῥωμαϊκὴν [τήν] δε ἐπικράτειαν τῶν τε πόλεων καὶ χωρῶν οἰκήτορας.*

[35] Acropolites I, p. 101.

[36] Pseudo-Kodinos, p. 133, pp. 12–22; Bréhier, *Institutions*, pp. 138–40.

[37] Acropolites I, p. 188, ll. 12–14.

[38] Pachymeres II, p. 59, ll. 10–12.

tion of certain members of the Nicaean aristocracy as 'nobles and of the first rank' (*εὐγενεῖς καὶ τῆς πρώτης . . . τάξεως*).[39]

The magnates or chief magistrates were simply the most prominent representatives of the hereditary aristocracy that had come into being at Byzantium in the course of the eleventh century. By the end of the period of exile they had emerged as a tightly knit group restricted to about twenty families. It was these that disputed among themselves the regency after the murder of George Mouzalon. George Pachymeres gives the following list:[40]

Tzamantouroi or Laskarids
Tornikioi
Strategopouloi
Raoul
Palaiologoi
Vatatzai
Philai
Kavallarioi
Nestongoi
Kamytzai
Aprenoi
Angeloi
Livadarioi
Tarchaneiotai
Philanthropenoi
Kantakouzenoi

This is not quite a complete list of the noble families of the Nicaean Empire. The Petraliphas, Vranas, and Synadenoi families should be added. Pachymeres in fact closes his list with the words: 'and as many others as possess a golden ancestry'.[41] The very phrasing emphasizes the exclusiveness of the Byzantine nobility.

They were allied by marriage both among themselves and to the ruling dynasty. They took great pride in their descent from the earlier imperial houses of Doukai, Komnenoi, and Angeloi. Marriage with non-noble families was frowned on,

[39] Acropolites I, p. 154, ll. 25–6.

[40] Pachymeres I, pp. 64–5.

[41] Ibid., p. 65, ll. 11–12: *καὶ ὅσοι ἄλλοι οἷς ἡ μεγαλογενὴς σειρὰ καὶ χρυσὴ συγκεκρότητο.*

but certainly not unknown. They set great store by their ancestry and the deeds of their forbears which they held up as an example to be emulated. They were great landowners. A family that was noble was expected to be self-sufficient (*autarkes*). The two ideas went together.[42] It was assumed that the emperor would grant members of these noble families lands and revenues and that they would hold the chief positions at court, even that some of the great offices of state (*axiomata*) would be hereditary in a particular family.[43] Nobility naturally brought with it certain obligations, since the ordinary people were supposed to be guided by their example.[44]

The Byzantine nobility never became a closed caste. There was always some movement of new families into their ranks, while some noble families disappeared; and, of course, within the nobility there were gradations. Some noble families were much more prominent, wealthy, and influential than others. It was these that provided the nucleus of the nobility. Families, such as the Tornikioi, Raoul, and Palaiologoi, which were among the most prominent at the Nicaean court, could boast men who had distinguished themselves at the court of the Komnenoi and had played an important political role under the Angeloi.[45] The majority of the Nicaean nobility could trace their ancestry back to the late eleventh century and some even earlier. But other families, the Philai, Philanthropenoi, and the Kavallarioi, for instance, seem only to have joined the ranks of the nobility under the emperors of Nicaea. It is a very great pity that absolutely nothing is known of their origins. They replaced families that had died out. The Kamateroi provide a good example. Before 1204 they were one of the most powerful Byzantine families.[46] We have already seen how much the creation of the Nicaean Empire owed to Basil Kamateros, the uncle of Theodore Las-

[42] One of the qualifications that Michael Palaiologos was thought to possess for the regency was: *καὶ οἱ ἐκ παλαιοῦ αὐτάρκες εἶναι τὸ εὐγενές*. (Pachymeres I, p. 66, l. 16. Cf. ibid., p. 82, l. 20.)

[43] Miklosich and Müller IV, p. 345, ll. 29–31.

[44] Gregoras I, pp. 43–4. Cf. Acropolites I, p. 97, pp. 7–14.

[45] See Nicetas Choniates, p. 593, ll. 15–18.

[46] See V. Laurent, 'Un Sceau inédit du protonotaire Basile Kamateros', *B* 6 (1931), 253–72; G. Stadtmüller, 'Zur Geschichte der Familie Kamateros', *BZ* 34 (1934), 352–8; Polemis, *The Doukai*, pp. 125–33.

karis's empress, but, as Michael Choniates lamented, he was the only one of his 'Golden Race' to have survived the fall of Constantinople.[47] After his death the Kamateroi simply disappear. The Kontostephanoi were another family that had distinguished itself during the twelfth century. As we have seen, they had estates in Asia Minor and possessed great influence in the Maiander valley during the reign of Theodore I Laskaris. Theodore Kontostephanos held the high rank of *protosevastos*[48] at the court of John Vatatzes, but after his death the family seems to disappear.

The members of the great noble families almost never held routine administrative functions. They enjoyed almost as of right the highest ranks of the court hierarchy which consisted of court dignities, military offices, and household offices. Below these came the administrative offices, such as those of the various logothetes, together with the less important household offices and military posts. The holders of these positions were called *archontes*.

Strictly speaking, *archon* meant little more than the holder of an imperial commission. There were also provincial *archontes*, local landowners who played an important part in local government and military organization. They were sometimes described as 'thematic *archontes*'.[49] The term *archontes* was therefore applied to a very broad social grouping, ranging from members of the imperial court to quite modest landowners. At the head of this group, and distinguished from it, were the chief bureaucrats[50] who formed a *noblesse de robe*. They were a less well-defined body than the upper nobility, since education and ability were as much a qualification for high administrative office as birth. None the less, family connections and a tradition of service all counted for a great deal when it came to an administrative career. It is not at all

[47] Michael Choniates II, p. 257, ll. 10–11. The mother of the future Patriarch Arsenios came from the Kamateros family (Scutariotes, p. 290, ll. 1–4).

[48] Acropolites I, p. 66, ll. 21–2, p. 87, ll. 17–19.

[49] Michael Choniates II, p. 277, l. 2, p. 278, ll. 10–12, p. 280, ll. 1–2. One Chalkoutzes is described as *τὰ πρῶτα ὢν τῶν ἐκεῖσε* [i.e. Euboea] *θεματικῶν καὶ κτηματικῶν ἀρχόντων*.

[50] Acropolites I, p. 188, ll. 13–14. Michael VIII Palaiologos was accompanied on his triumphal entrance into Constantinople in 1261 by *τῶν ἐν τέλει πάντες καὶ τῶν ἀρχόντων οἱ πρόκριτοι*.

surprising that members of the Hagiotheodorites,[51] Alyates,[52] Mesopotamites,[53] and Balsamon[54] families should have been just as prominently represented in the Nicaean administration, as they had been in that of the twelfth century.

There was no clear-cut line dividing the administrative aristocracy from the upper nobility. George Akropolites, who had a very distinguished career in the Nicaean administration, married into a noble family connected with the Palaiologoi.[55] Nikephoros Alyates, who was promoted to the important chancery post of *epi tou kanikleiou* at the beginning of Theodore II Laskaris's reign is included at the foot of a list of men whom George Akropolites considered to be 'noble and of the first rank'.[56] There is no real sign that the period of exile saw a resurrection of that enmity which in the eleventh century divided the civil aristocracy from the military aristocracy.

At that time the senate and the senatorial order[57] were the preserve of the civil aristocracy. They were to lose much of their political influence with the accession of Alexios I Komnenos (1081–1118), but the senate continued to be dominated by bureaucrats. The presidency still brought with it considerable prestige.[58] After the recovery of Constantinople the senate had little but formal importance, but the senators or senatorial *archontes,* as they were called, were men who exercised considerable influence in the affairs of state. They were sent on important embassies;[59] they acted as assessors in cases that came before the patriarchal synod;[60] they assisted along-

[51] A member of this family was logothete of the flocks and was then promoted in 1259 to logothete *ton oikeiakon* (Pachymeres I, p. 109, ll. 21–2).

[52] See below, n. 56 and pp. 163–4.

[53] Joseph Mesopotamites was a secretary of John Vatatzes (Acropolites I, p. 91, ll. 2–5).

[54] A member of this family was a secretary of Theodore II Laskaris (Theodore Lascaris, pp. 159–61).

[55] Acropolites I, p. 164, ll. 15–21. Cf. Pachymeres I, p. 109–10, 495–6.

[56] Acropolites I, pp. 154–5.

[57] On the senate, see A. A. Christophilopoulou, *"Η σύγκλητος εἰς τὸ Βυζαντινὸν Κράτος'*, *'Επετηρὶς τοῦ Ἀρχείου τῆς Ἱστορίας τοῦ Ἑλληνικοῦ Δικαίου*, 7 (1949), fasc. 2; L.-P. Raybaud, *Le Gouvernement et l'administration centrale de l'Empire byzantin sous les premiers Paléologues* (1258–1354), Paris, 1968, pp. 112–39; H.-G. Beck, 'Senat und Volk von Konstantinopel. Probleme der byzantinischen Verfassungsgeschichte', *Sitzungsberichte der bayer. Akad. der Wiss.*, philos. hist. Kl., 1966, heft 6, esp. pp. 63–75.

[58] Nicetas Choniates, p. 749, ll. 4–7.

[59] Pachymeres I, p. 384, ll. 15–17.

[60] Ibid., pp. 376–7.

side members of the imperial household in the judgements given by the imperial tribunal (*sekreton*).[61] In Michael VIII Palaiologos's reign the senators all appear to have been the holders of high administrative office.[62] Promotion to senatorial rank may indeed have automatically accompanied a man's appointment to such an office.[63]

It therefore seems that after 1261 the civil aristocracy came to be identified with the senatorial *archontes* and that the formal qualification for entry into their ranks was the holding of office. It may be that this was already the case before the recovery of the City, for we have seen how the civil aristocracy formed a distinct group. Its members must have been identical with the senators who were singled out by George Pachymeres as forming an order among the upper ranks of society.

Virtually no evidence has survived that will illuminate the history of the senate and senators during the period of exile. In his history George Akropolites scrupulously avoids using the term 'senate'. On the other hand, he did address his funeral oration over the Emperor John Vatatzes to the senate;[64] and there are other stray references to the senate at Nicaea.[65] Theodore I Laskaris is said to have re-established it at Nicaea parallel to the ecclesiastical hierarchy.[66] Together with the army it was responsible for trying Alexios III Angelos, who had fallen into the hands of Theodore I Laskaris after the battle of Antioch (1211).[67]

It is to be supposed that 'senate' was simply used as another term for the imperial court, as was the case in the

[61] Miklosich and Müller IV, 276–8.

[62] e.g. George Akropolites—Grand Logothete (Pachymeres I, p. 377, ll. 8–9, p. 384, ll. 15–16); Demetrios Iatropoulos—logothete *ton oikeiakon* (ibid., p. 377, l. 10); Panaretos—*prokathemenos tou vestiariou* (ibid., p. 384, ll. 16–17); Verroiotes—*megas diermeneutes* (ibid., p. 384, l. 17), Theodore Skoutariotes—*dikaiophylax* (Miklosich and Müller V, pp. 246–8).

[63] Miklosich and Müller V, pp. 246–8.

[64] Acropolites II, p. 14, l. 1.

[65] There is a single reference to the senatorial order (*synkletikos*). In a document issued in Oct. 1256 for the monastery of Makrinitissa in Thessaly by the Patriarch Arsenios, the Patriarch protected the monastery from the interference of members of the clergy, officials, *synkletikoi*, and private individuals (Miklosich and Müller IV, p. 355, ll. 21–2).

[66] Scutariotes, p. 282, l. 10. Cf. Heisenberg in *BZ* 1905, p. 214, ll. 3–4.

[67] Scutariotes, p. 278, ll. 6–10.

mid-fourteenth century.[68] It seems likely that it was applied to the Nicaean court, when it met as the highest tribunal of the Empire or as an imperial council.[69] The simplification of the machinery of government after the fall of Constantinople meant that the consultative and judicial aspects of the imperial court became as important as its ceremonial. It provided a setting in which the aristocracy as an order could be associated in some of the decisions of government.

It might be thought that at last the aristocracy were beginning to win for themselves constitutional powers, but this is deceptive. The traditional concept of the imperial office was too deeply ingrained to allow any limitations upon the emperor's absolute authority. It was a problem that at another level attracted the attention of the Emperor Theodore II Laskaris. He wanted to find a theoretical basis to reconcile absolute imperial authority and the natural aspirations of the aristocracy. He suggested that, in return for complete loyalty and obedience, a subject might expect his sovereign's friendship; and from this all the benefits he desired were likely to spring.[70]

It has been urged that Theodore's concept of the relations between emperor and subject comes very close to the feudal contract between lord and vassal and that, consequently, it marks a stage further in the 'feudalization' of the Byzantine Empire.[71] On the face of it, there seems to be little to support this view. Theodore Laskaris was after all very conscious of his imperial prerogatives. The most that can be said is that he was aware of the problem of the emperor's obligations to his servants. Though disguised by the idea of friendship, relations between the emperor and the aristocracy still depended upon the imperial will. It remained a very one-sided contract.

Ironically, Theodore's reign witnessed a very bitter conflict between the emperor and members of the aristocracy. The

[68] Pseudo-Kodinos, p. 130, ll. 15–16.

[69] A. Dmitrievskij, *Opisanie liturgičeskikh rukopisej*, I. 1, Kiev, 1895, p. 790, ll. 29–35. Cf. Pachymeres II, p. 610, ll. 7–8. See below, pp. 85–6, 153.

[70] E. Lappa-Zizicas, 'Un Traité inédit de Théodore II Lascaris', *Actes du VIe Congrès International d'Études Byzantines*, I. Paris, 1948, pp. 119–26.

[71] N. Svoronos, 'Le Serment de fidélité à l'empereur byzantin et sa signification constitutionelle', ibid., pp. 195–6.

roots of this quarrel go back to his father's reign. In one important respect, the arbitrary authority of the emperor increased. It seems to have been during the period of exile that the ordeal was introduced into Byzantine judicial procedure.[72] It was employed in cases of high treason and could only be used at the express order of the emperor.[73] John Vatatzes resorted to its use at Michael Palaiologos's trial for treason.[74] His son employed the ordeal by hot iron to try cases involving men suspected of trying to harm the emperor by sorcery.[75] Its use was not only resented by the aristocracy, but by all ranks of society. It was considered to be contrary to Byzantine traditions of justice and ecclesiastical practice.[76] It was abolished by Michael Palaiologos as soon as he became emperor.[77]

The ordeal was an irksome innovation that aggravated the aristocracy. It did not undermine their privileged position within the state. The use of imperial patronage to promote men of humble origin to the highest offices of state did do so. Imperial service was always at Byzantium the main channel of social mobility. It remained, especially in its lower reaches, a career open to talents. John Vatatzes welcomed foreigners into Nicaean service;[78] and not all of his officers came from the upper ranks of society.[79] The career of Constantine Margarites is a case in point. He came of peasant stock and began his career by serving in the army of his native theme of Neokastra. He attracted the attention of John Vatatzes who took him into his own service and promoted him to the office of Grand *Tzaousios*. This was one of the lesser household offices and brought with it responsibility for maintaining proper order in the court ceremonies.[80] His career continued to prosper under Theòdore II Laskaris. He

[72] See J. B. Pitra, *Analecta sacra et classica spicilegio Solesmensi parata*, VII, Paris, 1891, No. 127, cols. 525–8.

[73] Acropolites I, p. 99, ll. 8–9.

[74] Ibid., pp. 92–100.

[75] Pachymeres I, pp. 32–3.

[76] Acropolites I, p. 98, ll. 4–9; Pachymeres I, p. 33, ll. 3–6.

[77] Pachymeres I, p. 92, ll. 14–17.

[78] Pachymeres II, p. 546, ll. 13–14; Acropolites I, p. 59; Wilson & Darrouzès in *REB* 26 (1968) 20, l. 4.

[79] e.g. the *mystikos* John Mouzalon (Acropolites I, p. 67, ll. 6–9).

[80] Pseudo-Kodinos, p. 182, ll. 18–21.

was made commander of the household troops and the new office of Grand Archon was created for him.[81] He was for a time among the emperor's close advisers[82] and received joint-command of the Nicaean forces in Thrace. The office of Grand Archon did not place him very high in the court hierarchy. It only comes thirty-fifth in the list of the Pseudo-Kodinos.[83] But the advancement of a man of lowly birth to relatively high office and into the emperor's confidence caused some resentment among the aristocracy. George Akropolites, who married into the upper ranks of the nobility, reflects aristocratic feeling when he pours scorn on Margarites's rustic manners and speech.[84]

Theodore II Laskaris embarked upon a deliberate policy of advancing commoners to the chief offices of state. It was partly a matter of temperament. He was happier in the company of a cultivated circle of friends, some of whom had been his childhood companions (*paidopoula*). He clearly disliked what he considered the philistinism prevalent among a section of the young men at his father's court.[85] His opponents at court seem to have been lead by Theodore Philes with whom he had quarrelled bitterly even before he came to the throne.[86] Judging by his later actions, his enemies were the young commanders, such as Michael Palaiologos and Alexios Strategopoulos, who distinguished themselves campaigning in Europe with John Vatatzes, while Theodore was left behind as viceroy in Asia Minor.

It is also true, as the historian George Pachymeres emphasizes, that Theodore intended to find the men most capable of filling the great offices of state.[87] He was at the same time completely unsympathetic to aristocratic aspirations and showed a complete lack of tact in his dealings with the aristocracy.

As soon as he became emperor, he raised his childhood friend George Mouzalon to the office of Grand Domestic

[81] Acropolites I, pp. 122–3.
[82] Ibid., p. 122, ll. 1–10.
[83] Pseudo-Kodinos, p. 138, l. 16.
[84] Acropolites I, p. 123, ll. 6–7.
[85] Andreeva, *Očerki*, pp. 147–9, 160–70.
[86] Ibid., pp. 102, 158–9.
[87] Pachymeres I, pp. 37–8.

which brought with it command of the army. He did not come from a noble family, but had been brought up with the emperor.[88] Then in the autumn of 1255 Theodore created for his favourite a new combination of titles. He was made *protovestiarios, protosevastos,* and Grand Stratopedarch which placed him at the head of the court hierarchy.[89] The dignity of *protovestiarios* was then held by Alexios Raoul. Theodore simply dismissed him; and this created deep bitterness between the emperor and the powerful Raoul family.[90] The magnates' resentment against Mouzalon was further increased by the favour the emperor showed his brothers. Andronikos Mouzalon was first made *protovestiarites* and then Grand Domestic. Another brother, Theodore, was made *protokynegos.*[91]

Opportunities open to the magnates of high office or command became even more restricted when at the beginning of his reign Theodore recalled from exile his great-uncles, Michael and Manuel Laskaris. Manuel was honoured with the rank of *protosevastos* and both were given important military commands.[92] George Akropolites, again reflecting the opinion of the circle opposed to Theodore II, is very scathing about their characters and abilities.[93]

Theodore decided that he could not rely upon the upper nobility in the course of his desperate winter campaign against the Bulgarians. Two aristocratic generals, Alexios Strategopoulos and Constantine Tornikes, were relieved of their commands for cowardice and incompetence.[94] Strategopoulos was thrown into prison,[95] and his son Constantine was blinded, ostensibly for disparaging the emperor.[96] Theodore's

[88] Ibid., p. 24, ll. 5–6, pp. 41–2.

[89] Acropolites I, p. 124, ll. 4–7, p. 160, ll. 6–8; Andreeva, *Očerki*, p. 36.

[90] Acropolites I, p. 66, ll. 19–20, p. 92, ll. 17–18, p. 155, l. 6; Pachymeres I, p. 23, ll. 18–20.

[91] Acropolites I, p. 124, ll. 7–8, p. 155, ll. 18–19; Gregoras I, p. 66, l. 2; Pachymeres I, p. 24, ll. 4–5, where Theodore is entitled *protoierakaris.*

[92] Acropolites I, pp. 109–10, pp. 122–3.

[93] Ibid., pp. 109–10.

[94] Ibid., pp. 113–14; Theodore Lascaris, pp. 252–3.

[95] Acropolites I, p. 154, l. 26.

[96] Ibid., p. 154, l. 27; Pachymeres I, p. 24, ll. 6–11, pp. 64–5; II, p. 154, ll. 17–20.

great enemy Theodore Philes was also blinded;[97] and other members of the nobility were removed from their offices.[98] Michael Palaiologos was warned that the emperor intended something against him and fled to the Seljuqs.[99]

There was one thing that the great noble families resented far more than the loss of office and of imperial favour. This was Theodore's deliberate policy of giving noble brides to his favourites who were often commoners. He imagined that their claims to nobility would thus be enhanced while their brides would share in the honour attached to the great offices of state.[100] The nobility construed this as an attack upon their privileged position within the state.

George Mouzalon married a niece of Michael Palaiologos from the Kantakouzenos family and his brother Andonikos was given to wife a daughter of Alexios Raoul.[101] Far worse was the emperor's treatment of another of Michael Palaiologos's nieces, the daughter of his sister Maria and the Grand Domestic Nikephoros Tarchaneiotes. The emperor ordered her to be married to one of his childhood companions called Valaneidiotes, but before this could take place, he changed his mind and insisted that she should marry Basil Kavallarios, a man of noble birth. The bride and her mother tried to put off the marriage, but the emperor overruled them. The marriage was never consummated; and Theodore II Laskaris suspected sorcery. The bride's mother was thrown naked into a sack with some cats in order to extract a confession.[102]

What was at issue in this instance was not Theodore's policy of giving noble brides to commoners. Theodore obviously could not follow it out consistently. It was rather his disregard for natural proprieties. The bride's family had already accepted the emperor's first choice into their house as a son-in-law.[103] His inhuman treatment of a woman of noble family must also have left a deep impression. Theodore

[97] Acropolites I, p. 155, ll. 2–3, pp. 163–4; Pachymeres I, p. 24, ll. 10–11, p. 41, ll. 10–11.

[98] Acropolites I, pp. 154–5.

[99] Ibid., p. 134, ll. 10–14, pp. 136–8; Pachymeres I, pp. 24–5.

[100] Pachymeres I, p. 37, ll. 11–16.

[101] Ibid., pp. 23–4.

[102] Ibid., pp. 33–5.

[103] Ibid., p. 34, ll. 2–5.

realized that he had gone much too far.[104] He was close to death; and his excesses towards the end of his reign can be attributed in some measure to ill health. Increasingly severe bouts of epilepsy aggravated an unstable and pathologically suspicious temperament. He became convinced that his ill health was due to sorcery.[105]

Theodore's attack upon the aristocracy stemmed from his upbringing and his personality, but it also brought to the surface the incompatibility that existed within Byzantium between imperial autocracy and aristocratic privilege. It created a bitterness, the fruits of which were reaped after his death by the usurper Michael Palaiologos. Theodore tried to ensure the peaceful succession of his son John IV Laskaris. He appointed George Mouzalon as regent; and, as we have seen, extracted an oath from all sections of society, guaranteeing this settlement.[106] To counter any possible threat from Michael Palaiologos, he apparently entrusted to him the safe-keeping of his family.[107]

[104] Ibid., p. 35, ll. 5–15.
[105] Ibid., pp. 32–3; Blemmydes, pp. 47–8.
[106] See above p. 42, below, p. 81.
[107] Pachymeres I, p. 35, ll. 15–20.

V

THE USURPATION OF MICHAEL PALAIOLOGOS[1]

It was left to the regent George Mouzalon to face the bitterness produced by Theodore II Laskaris's attack upon the aristocracy. He knew that he was suspected of having designs upon the throne. One of his first acts was therefore to make his submission to the young emperor John IV Laskaris as a token of his good faith.[2] To calm the discontent of the aristocracy he called together a general assembly.[3] He admitted that injustice had been done under Theodore II and he tried to convince those who had been wronged of his own good intentions. With an emperor still too young to rule the business of government would now be in the hands of his guardians. These, he maintained, would be a guarantee against the arbitrary government that had previously existed.[4]

George Mouzalon owed his position as regent to Theodore Laskaris, but he was willing to submit to the choice of the assembly. He urged them, if they wished, to choose a new regent from the magnates. He would resign his offices and go and live as a private citizen, but whoever was chosen by the assembly as regent would be responsible to the assembly.[5]

The circumstances of this speech were of course exceptional. Mouzalon was in a very weak position. He was trying to win acceptance from the aristocracy. It was natural that he should be conciliatory. It is true that the powers that he was willing to see vested in the general assembly were only to last until John Laskaris attained his majority, but his initiative comes close to an attack upon the institution of monarchy. This is certainly

[1] See P. Wirth, 'Die Begründung der Kaisermacht Michaels VIII. Palaiologos', *JOBG* 10 (1961), 85–91; D. J. Geanakoplos, *Emperor Michael Palaeologus and the West 1258–1282. A Study in Byzantine-Latin Relations*, Cambridge, Mass., 1959, pp. 33–46.

[2] Pachymeres I, pp. 40–1.

[3] Ibid., p. 41, ll. 5–14.

[4] Ibid., pp. 42–6, esp. p. 45, l. 16–46, l. 6.

[5] Ibid., pp. 46–7.

how Michael Palaiologos construed it, in the reply he made on behalf of the assembly.

Palaiologos comes out as the champion of monarchy. He regretted the terror of Theodore II Laskaris's reign, but he had been emperor; and those who had bound themselves on oath to serve the emperor were completely subject to his will.[6] George Mouzalon had been appointed regent by imperial edict and there was no body that had the right to put this aside.[7] He then assured the regent that all of them would support him, adding 'not all of us can rule, not all of us can give orders, for the rule of the many is anarchy'.[8]

The regent now felt that his position was secure. He took pledges of good faith[9] and began to organize his administration. Imperial letters were drawn up and sent to all the cities of the Empire. They announced the death of Theodore II and ordered that all should take the usual oaths of allegiance to the new emperor.[10]

Michael Palaiologos was already plotting against the regent. Rumours were spread abroad that Mouzalon had brought about Theodore Laskaris's death by sorcery and that he was seeking to make himself emperor.[11] Theodore's favourites who now held the reins of government were slandered as singers and musicians.[12] The Latin mercenaries began to complain of the treatment that they had received under Theodore II and held Mouzalon responsible.[13] Their commander happened to be Michael Palaiologos and naturally it was assumed that he was the instigator of their discontent.[14]

At the beginning of September 1258 a memorial service was held for the late emperor at the monastery of Sosandra. The court and nobility were present, so too was the army. The soldiers and the Latin mercenaries began to demonstrate, demanding that the young emperor should be brought out

[6] Ibid., p. 50, ll. 2–5, ll. 12–14.
[7] Ibid., p. 52, l. 5.
[8] Ibid., p. 52, ll. 10–12.
[9] Ibid., p. 53, ll. 8–12.
[10] Ibid., pp. 53–4.
[11] Ibid., p. 54, ll. 7–15.
[12] Acropolites I, p. 156, ll. 10–15.
[13] Pachymeres I, pp. 54–5.
[14] Ibid., p. 55, ll. 3–11.

and shown to them. They claimed to have the boy's safety in mind and hinted that the Mouzalons were plotting against his life.[15]

The young emperor appeared on a balcony and waved to the troops. This was taken as a sign that he wished them to do away with the Mouzalon brothers.[16] The Latin mercenaries swept into the monastery where the service was already taking place and murdered the regent and his brothers.[17]

There followed days of uncertainty. All recognized the dangerous situation in which the Empire found itself. The threat posed by the Latins of Constantinople was not very great, but the alliance of Michael Angelos, the ruler of Epiros, and Manfred, the ruler of the *Regno*, left the Nicaean possessions in Europe exposed to attack. The eastern frontier too was, as always, under pressure from the Turks.

A new regent had to be chosen to put an end to the uncertainty. All the great families of the Empire had some member with a claim to be considered for the position of regent.[18] Two parties began to form. One grew up around Theodore Laskaris's great-uncles, Michael and Manuel Laskaris. It pressed the claims of George Nestongos. He held the office of Butler (*pinkernes*) and came from a family that had been much favoured by the Laskarids.[19] Theodore II Laskaris apparently intended that he should marry one of his daughters. This, he imagined, gave him a strong claim to the regency.[20] The other party was built up by Michael Palaiologos. Its nucleus was formed by his brothers, John and Constantine,[21] and by those who had suffered at the hands of Theodore II, men such as the Strategopouloi, Theodore Philes, and Constantine Tornikes.[22]

A general assembly was called to choose a new regent. Its first act was to summon the Patriarch Arsenios and the episcopal bench from Nicaea,[23] for it was agreed that any choice made by the assembly would have to receive the confirmation

[15] Pachymeres I, pp. 55–6.
[16] Ibid., p. 57, ll. 2–7.
[17] Ibid., pp. 57–61.
[18] Ibid., pp. 64–5.
[19] Scutariotes, p. 293, ll. 10–17; Polemis, *The Doukai*, pp. 150–1.
[20] Pachymeres I, pp. 65–6.
[21] Ibid., pp. 63–4.
[22] Ibid., p. 76, ll. 4–8; Acropolites I, pp. 154–5.
[23] Pachymeres I, p. 66, ll. 7–11.

of the Church. This did not prevent the assembly from electing Michael Palaiologos regent before the patriarch's arrival. It appears to have been satisfied by the assurance that he would seek the patriarch's approval and this would be a guarantee of whatever was decided.[24]

The patriarch did not arrive until after Palaiologos had been chosen regent and raised to the office of Grand Duke.[25] He probably approved of the choice. Apparently, when he heard of the death of Theodore Laskaris, he confided to one of his household that he thought Michael Palaiologos would make the best regent.[26] Palaiologos understood how valuable his support was and showed him every mark of respect. He went out to meet the patriarch and then, leading his mule by the bridle, conducted him into the palace of Nymphaion.[27] The patriarch was led to believe that real power in the state lay not with the new regent, but in his own hands.[28] Palaiologos assured him that he would only accept the regency at his command and with the consent of the patriarchal synod.[29]

On 13 November 1258[30] another general assembly met at Magnesia.[31] It consisted not only of members of the nobility and army, but also of the patriarch and prelates. Its purpose was to give full confirmation to Michael Palaiologos's earlier election as regent and to decide whether he should be raised to the position of *Basileopator* and to the rank of despot. This was being urged by his supporters who were found both among the aristocracy and among the higher clergy.[32]

They argued that his promotion to the despotate would give him a share in the imperial office.[33] This would have two advantages: he would be able to carry out his duties as regent properly and he would be able to uphold the institution of monarchy, while the emperor was still a minor. In

[24] Ibid., p. 67, ll. 1, 9–11.
[25] Arsenios Autoreianos, *Testamentum* in Migne, *P.G.* 140, col. 949, ll. 39–43.
[26] Pachymeres I, p. 79, ll. 5–13.
[27] Ibid., p. 72, ll. 12–18.
[28] Ibid., p. 73, ll. 3–15.
[29] Ibid., p. 73, ll. 1–3.
[30] Loenertz in *OCP* 1963, 341.
[31] Blemmydes, p. 89, ll. 19–25.
[32] Pachymeres I, pp. 73–4, p. 75, ll. 8–11, p. 76, ll. 4–10.
[33] Ibid., p. 74, l. 13.

such circumstances, imperial authority ought to be wielded by the man best-fitted. As it was, the regent was no more than a *primus inter pares* (τὶς τοῖς ἐξ ἴσου).[34]

Their opponents protested that the office of Grand Duke was of sufficient dignity for the regent. If he was raised any higher the court hierarchy would be upset. Theodore Laskaris was survived by unmarried daughters. Whoever married them would have a claim to the highest dignities of the Empire.[35]

Michael Palaiologos had the unanimous support of the army.[36] Most of the nobility and the upper clergy had been won over to his cause by his generosity.[37] Above all, his apparent humility had procured him the patriarch's whole-hearted backing.[38] It was agreed that he should be promoted to the rank of despot. The symbols of office were bestowed upon him by the young emperor with the assistance of the patriarch.[39] Opposition to Palaiologos among the aristocracy crumbled. Manuel Laskaris was imprisoned[40] and his estates confiscated.[41] The *protostrator* John Angelos, another of Theodore Laskaris's inner circle, was summoned from Europe where he had been in command of the army. He died apparently of fright on the journey home.[42] Other leading opponents of Palaiologos hastened to make their peace with him.[43] The first stage of his usurpation had been completed.

The struggle over the regency momentarily brought into the open two opposing views of how authority within the state was to be divided during a minority. The traditional view was put forward by Michael Palaiologos and his party. The rights of the emperor should be exercised by a regent who would share in the imperial office. The logic of this

[34] Pachymeres I, pp. 77–8.
[35] Ibid., pp. 75–6.
[36] Acropolites I, p. 158, ll. 15–21.
[37] Pachymeres I, p. 71, ll. 12–15, p. 73, ll. 7–15.
[38] Ibid., p. 79, ll. 1–5.
[39] Ibid., p. 79, ll. 11–16.
[40] Ibid., p. 80, ll. 16–18.
[41] Miklosich and Müller VI, pp. 201–2.
[42] Acropolites I, p. 160, ll. 3–15.
[43] Pachymeres I, p. 80, ll. 10–15. Michael Laskaris was promoted to the office of Grand Duke by Michael Palaiologos in 1259 (ibid., p. 108, ll. 16–18). George Mouzalon's brother-in-law, Hagiotheodorites, who was also a member of Theodore Laskaris's inner circle, received promotion at the same time (ibid., p. 109, ll. 21–2).

was usurpation. George Mouzalon, on the other hand, suggested that the regent ought to be responsible to a general assembly which would guarantee the rights of the young emperor.

Corresponding to these opposing views were different concepts of the relations between emperor and subject. Michael Palaiologos maintained that a man who had bound himself by oath to serve the emperor was completely subject to his will, whereas George Mouzalon emphasized the mutual relationship between emperor and subject. In return for loyalty and faithful service a subject could expect a just reward from the emperor. This was not the case under Theodore II Laskaris. His brutality and arbitrary government had destroyed the love that ought to provide the basis of the mutual obligations of emperor and subject. Mouzalon is, ironically, simply developing ideas already put forward by Theodore II Laskaris.[44]

George Mouzalon was not attacking the absolute authority of the monarchy nor was he enunciating a 'feudal relationship' between emperor and subject. His ideas did not have general application, but applied to a specific context only—the minority of John Laskaris. It was naturally assumed that once the emperor came of age he would exercise absolute authority. But in the intervening period authority within the state should be vested in a general assembly.

The crucial question is: what was the nature of this assembly? George Pachymeres describes the membership of the assembly called by George Mouzalon in great detail: 'He [George Mouzalon] then called together senators, members of the imperial family, *archontes*, and those of military rank. There were also present the brothers of the emperor's great-grandfather [Theodore I Laskaris] . . . nor were the blind ones missing—that is to say Strategopoulos and Philes. The assembly was completed by any other of the magnates.'[45] The second assembly is simply described as a meeting of the chief magistrates by both George Pachymeres[46] and Nikephoros Blemmydes.[47] The Patriarch Arsenios is more specific and clearly refers to it as a meeting of the senate with the addition

[44] Ibid., pp. 44–6. See above, p. 74.

[45] Ibid., p. 41, ll. 5–12.

[46] Ibid., p. 66, l. 7.

[47] Blemmydes, p. 89, ll. 19ff.

of some bishops.[48] 'Senate' is also the term that the patriarch appears to apply to the first assembly.[49]

There seems to be little doubt that these assemblies were considered to be meetings of the senate. Their membership to judge by the list given above was very close to that of the council of state and the imperial tribunal of the emperors of Nicaea. There is good reason to believe that these too might be referred to as meetings of the senate.[50] In reality, it is perhaps fairer to describe them as different facets of the imperial court, for membership seems to have consisted in the main of members of the court present with the emperor. It was not limited exclusively to those who held a place in the court hierarchy. Members of the magnate families, regardless of whether or not they held a court title, appear to have possessed the right of attendance.

The procedure adopted at these meetings seems to have been fairly rudimentary. Its main function was to enable the emperor to inform himself of the currents of opinion circulating among the aristocracy and to obtain some general assent for whatever course of action he framed on the basis of this opinion. The senate only met on extraordinary occasions either to debate some serious issue or to assist at a trial for high treason. Speeches were made and those present indicated the strength of their approval or disapproval. It was left to the emperor to interpret the feeling of the meeting. There does not seem to have been any clear-cut procedure that decided who it was who had the right to speak. Even to a contemporary it was something of a mystery why Michael Palaiologos should have taken it upon himself to reply on behalf of the assembly to George Mouzalon's speech.[51]

It was not unknown for a meeting of the senate to be reinforced by the attendance of the patriarch and his synod.[52] The third assembly, the one that approved Palaiologos's promotion to the despotate, was of this nature.[53] It was

[48] Arsenios Autoreianos, *Testamentum* in Migne, *P.G.* 140, col. 949, ll. 39–43.

[49] Ibid., col. 949, ll. 36–9.

[50] See above pp. 73–4, below p. 153.

[51] Pachymeres I, p. 49, ll. 7–11.

[52] Blemmydes, p. 49, ll. 10–16.

[53] Pachymeres I, p. 74, ll. 7–9; Acropolites I, p. 156, ll. 19–24.

presided over by the patriarch. The final verdict rested with him.[54]

In the months that followed George Mouzalon's murder the patriarch appears as possibly the most influential person in the Empire. His assent was needed to confirm Michael Palaiologos's election as regent. Together with the young emperor it was the patriarch who bestowed the symbols of the despotate upon the regent. Nikephoros Gregoras suggests that Arsenios had been made regent jointly with George Mouzalon by Theodore Laskaris[55] and that after the murder of Mouzalon it was the patriarch who took over the reins of government in his capacity as regent.[56] He then sought the co-operation of the chief magistrates and singled out Michael Palaiologos for special favour, even entrusting him with the keys of the treasury.[57]

According to Gregoras, it was only in November that an assembly came together, presided over by the patriarch who was persuaded by Palaiologos's supporters to make him regent. A few days later another assembly met at the insistence of the same people and Michael Palaiologos was raised to the despotate.[58]

Gregoras's account provides far and away the clearest narrative of the first stage of Michael Palaiologos's usurpation, but he was writing nearly a century after the events he is describing. His account conflicts with those of George Pachymeres, Nikephoros Blemmydes, and not least with that of the Patriarch Arsenios himself. They were all of course contemporaries. Arsenios's narrative has to be treated with caution, as it was an exercise in self-justification. Much that was embarrassing to the patriarch is omitted or glossed over, but there does not seem to be any deliberate falsification.

Nikephoros Blemmydes was not particularly interested in the politics of Michael Palaiologos's usurpation, but he was summoned to the assembly that raised him to the despotate and even offered a place of honour. He came, but with extreme

[54] Pachymeres, I, p. 79, l. 13.
[55] Gregoras I, p. 62, ll. 19–20.
[56] Ibid., p. 66, ll. 11–12.
[57] Ibid., pp. 69–70.
[58] Ibid., pp. 70–1.

reluctance.[59] The details that he gives of Michael Palaiologos's elevation to the despotate are only incidental to some private quarrel, but they are all the more valuable because he was an eye-witness and does not appear to have had any particular axe to grind. George Pachymeres was a young man at the time of Michael Palaiologos's ursurpation; he may not have been an eye-witness of the events he describes in such detail, but he certainly had access to people who were.[60]

There remains one more contemporary account, that of George Akropolites. He was confined in an Epirot gaol at the time. His narrative is not only rather thin and confused; it is also designed to justify Michael Palaiologos's rise to power.

There is no contemporary evidence to support Gregoras's contention that Arsenios had been made regent by Theodore Laskaris. The patriarch himself makes no such claim. He is also adamant that Palaiologos was elected regent in his absence.[61] This is supported by both George Pachymeres[62] and Nikephoros Blemmydes.[63] Arsenios's authority derived from his office, and not because he had been made regent.

He certainly acted as though it was his duty to safeguard the rights of the young emperor, but this was because he had taken an oath to the Emperor Theodore Laskaris to do so.[64] His main preoccupation seems to have been with the sanctity of oaths.[65] It was his responsibility to see that they were not broken; and it was he alone who could authorize dispensation from an oath already taken, as he seems to have done in the case of the oaths that Michael Palaiologos had taken both to John Vatatzes and to Theodore Laskaris that he would not seek to secure the throne.[66]

Arsenios acted on the assumption that the best safeguard of the young emperor's rights and the interests of the Empire

[59] Blemmydes, pp. 89–90.

[60] e.g. Pachymeres I, p. 59, l. 13, p. 79, ll. 7–9, p. 121, ll. 5–8.

[61] Arsenios Autoreianos, *Testamentum* in Migne, *P.G.* 140, col. 949, ll. 39–43.

[62] Pachymeres I, p. 66, ll. 7–9, p. 72, ll. 12–13.

[63] Blemmydes, p. 89, ll. 19ff.

[64] Arsenios Autoreianos, *Testamentum*, in Migne, *P.G.* 140, col. 949, ll. 33–9; Gregoras I, p. 63, ll. 10–15.

[65] See Arsenios Autoreianos, *Testamentum*, in Migne, *P.G.* 140, col. 949, ll. 43–4, 46–8, col. 952, ll. 6–22, ll. 36–41, col. 954, ll. 1–9.

[66] Acropolites I, pp. 158–9. Cf. Pachymeres I, p. 95, ll. 5–10.

was the election as regent of the man best-fitted to carry out the responsibilities of this position. It became more and more difficult to decide where the patriarch's responsibilities lay once Michael Palaiologos's supporters pressed that he should be made co-emperor. The regent himself threatened to resign on the grounds that unless he were made emperor his position would become untenable. The patriarch rather reluctantly agreed to Michael Palaiologos's proclamation as emperor.[67]

On New Year's Day 1259 Michael Palaiologos was raised aloft on a shield and acclaimed emperor at Nymphaion,[68] but only after the two emperors had exchanged mutual oaths of loyalty. This was done at the insistence of the patriarch who believed that it would be a guarantee of the young emperor's rights. It was also ordained that all the subjects of the Empire should take the usual oath of servitude to both of the emperors. In addition, should either emperor conspire against the other, the people were obliged to rise up and kill the usurper and elect a new emperor from the senate.[69] In a separate ceremony which occurred between Michael Palaiologos's proclamation as emperor and his raising aloft on a shield by the archbishops and the magnates, the magnates swore the normal oath of allegiance followed by a further oath to defend whichever emperor was the victim of the conspiracy of the other.[70] It was also agreed that in the ensuing coronation John Laskaris should be crowned first. This was thought to be a further guarantee that when he came of age he would receive his full rights as the senior emperor.[71] Michael Palaiologos saw this as a very serious barrier to his final usurpation. Great pressure was brought to bear upon the patriarch to allow Palaiologos to be crowned alone.[72] Even the safety of the young emperor was threatened, should the patriarch refuse to let Palaiologos have his way.[73]

[67] Pachymeres I, p. 81, ll. 4–19.

[68] Loenertz in *OCP* 1963, 342–4.

[69] Pachymeres I, p. 96, ll. 4–15; Arsenios Autoreianos, *Testamentum*, in Migne, *P.G.* 140, col. 952, ll. 10–22.

[70] Pachymeres I, pp. 96–7.

[71] Ibid., p. 100, ll. 4–10.

[72] Arsenios Autoreianos, *Testamentum*, in Migne, *P.G.* 140, col. 952, ll. 23–36.

[73] Pachymeres I, p. 101, ll. 18–20.

The patriarch refused to make any decision. Still nothing had been decided when the day appointed for the coronation came. The bishops with only two exceptions were of the opinion that Palaiologos had a right to be crowned first. They even agreed to take upon themselves responsibility for this breach of the oaths that had been sworn at Michael Palaiologos's proclamation as emperor. This overcame the opposition of the patriarch and the other dissenting bishops. Finally, all the bishops put their signature to a tome authorizing Palaiologos to be crowned first.[74] The patriarch then crowned him and his empress, while John Laskaris received nothing more than a special head-dress.[75] Michael Palaiologos departed almost at once from Nicaea and returned to Nymphaion, taking the young emperor with him.[76]

Completely disillusioned and with virtually no support among the bishops, Arsenios retired to the monastery of Paschasiou near Nicaea.[77] He refused to carry out the duties of his office; equally he refused to resign. The synod, frightened that the emperor might intervene, urged the patriarch to take up his duties again. There was nothing it could find in his conduct of office that would justify his dismissal.[78]

The emperor was planning an assault against Constantinople and wanted the affair cleared up as quickly as possible. He instructed the synod to deprive the patriarch of his office on the grounds that his ordination was irregular.[79] The synod complied with his wishes and dismissed the patriarch, but without giving any clear reason for its action.[80] At the turn of 1259[81] the bishops assembled at the emperor's camp at Lampsakos and proceeded on his orders to elect Nikephoros, Metropolitan of Ephesos, patriarch.[82] At least

[74] Pachymeres I, p. 102, ll. 14–15, p. 103, l. 12.

[75] Ibid., pp. 103–4.

[76] Ibid., p. 105, ll. 17–20.

[77] Ibid., pp. 111–12; Gregoras I, p. 80, ll. 11–14.

[78] Pachymeres I, pp. 112–15.

[79] Ibid., pp. 115–16.

[80] Ibid., pp. 116–17.

[81] See P. Wirth, 'Von der Schlacht von Pelagonia bis zur Wiedereroberung Konstantinopels. Zur äusseren Geschichte der Jahre 1259–1261', *BZ* 55 (1962), 33–4. Cf. Laurent in *REB* 1969, pp. 140–2.

[82] Acropolites I, pp. 179–80; Pachymeres I, pp. 116–18, esp. p. 118, ll. 13–16.

he had the reputation of being a worthy man who would defend the interests of the Church.[83]

The Bishops of Sardis and Thessalonica refused to recognize the legality of Nikephoros's election; and a schism developed within the Church.[84] The new patriarch found himself increasingly isolated at Nicaea. The prelates shunned him and the people were openly hostile.[85] The emperor refused to allow the Bishop of Sardis to return to his native Paphlagonia for fear that the bishop would rouse the people against him.[86] At court the claims of Arsenios were upheld with great insistence by the *sevastokrator* Constantine Tornikes.[87]

When Nikephoros of Ephesos died early in 1261,[88] the emperor gave in to Tornikes's demands and made it known that he would not oppose Arsenios's reinstatement as patriarch. He left the decision to the synod, as he thought it unwise to be involved personally.[89] Arsenios was extremely reluctant to resume the patriarchate. If one is to believe him, the price he was expected to pay for it was his agreement that John Laskaris should be reduced to the status of a private citizen.[90] He was not present at the triumphal entrance into Constantinople at the beginning of August 1261.[91] Negotiations were necessary before Arsenios was willing to take up the office of patriarch once again. He was not formally installed in the church of St. Sophia until the beginning of September 1261. He then proceeded to crown Palaiologos emperor a second time, as he had agreed to do.[92]

The rights of John Laskaris were passed over. Michael Palaiologos, secure in possession of the throne of Constantinople which he claimed was his by right of conquest,[93] felt strong enough to deprive John Laskaris of any claim that he

[83] Pachymeres I, p. 102, ll. 10–11, p. 117, ll. 7–13; Blemmydes, p. 38, ll. 16–27.

[84] Pachymeres I, pp. 118–19.

[85] Ibid., p. 119, ll. 3–7.

[86] Acropolites I, p. 179, ll. 4–15.

[87] Scutariotes, p. 300, ll. 19–23.

[88] See Laurent in *REB* 1969, pp. 140–2.

[89] Pachymeres I, pp. 165–6.

[90] Arsenios Autoreianos, *Testamentum*, in Migne, *P.G.* 140, col. 954, ll. 18–26.

[91] Acropolites I, p. 187, ll. 6–10.

[92] Pachymeres I, pp. 169–74; Arsenios Autoreianos, *Testamentum*, in Migne, *P.G.* 140, col. 954, ll. 36–9.

[93] Pachymeres I, p. 167, ll. 3–7.

still possessed to the imperial office. On Christmas Day 1261 the young emperor was blinded and then imprisoned in a fortress in Asia Minor.[94] As soon as the patriarch heard the news, he had the emperor excommunicated.[95] Palaiologos prayed forgiveness, expecting that the patriarch would relent.[96] He did not, even in 1264 formally driving the emperor out of the Church.[97] The emperor had no alternative but to have him removed from his office by force and sent into exile.[98]

The rights of the young emperor were always the main point at issue in the first phase of the struggle between Arsenios and Michael Palaiologos. But there were deeper implications for the position of the patriarch in the 'Byzantine constitution'. The patriarch acted as the guarantor of the constitution, in the sense that he saw it as his duty to uphold the oaths taken by all sections of society to protect the rights of the legitimate emperor. He possessed two sanctions that would enable him to carry out this task. He had the right of crowning the emperor. The importance attached to this ceremony is only too clear from Michael Palaiologos's insistence that he should be crowned emperor before John Laskaris. It set the final seal upon the emperor's legitimacy.

The second weapon that the patriarch possessed was the power of excommunication which Arsenios employed against Palaiologos. He also turned to the people as a whole as a further guarantee of the rights of the young emperor. In theory, an emperor ought to have been the choice of the people, but in practice they had little part to play in the making of an emperor. They might be called upon to take an oath of allegiance at the beginning of a reign, or even an oath guaranteeing the succession of an heir designated by the reigning emperor. In the uncertain days before he was proclaimed emperor, Theodore I Laskaris appears to have called together popular assemblies to win consent for his intended assumption of the imperial office.[99] There is furthermore

[94] Pachymeres I, pp. 191–2.
[95] Ibid., p. 203, ll. 5–6.
[96] Ibid., p. 204, ll. 5–13.
[97] Arsenios Autoreianos, *Testamentum*, in Migne, *P.G.* 140, col. 956, ll. 10–13.
[98] Pachymeres I, pp. 270–1.
[99] Sathas I, p. 110, l. 20.

a tradition that John Vatatzes refused to have his son Theodore Laskaris proclaimed emperor in his lifetime, because the people would not have been able to make their choice known.[100]

Lip-service continued to be paid to the popular basis of imperial sovereignty, but it was not of much consequence. The people did not rise up against the usurper Michael Palaiologos, except for some borderers near Nicaea.[101] These acted out of loyalty to the Laskarid dynasty under which they had enjoyed a period of great prosperity.[102] Their discontent must also have been increased by the measures taken by Michael Palaiologos to reduce the autonomy they had previously enjoyed.[103] The breach of the oaths provided a justification and an incentive for their actions.

In his struggle with Michael Palaiologos Arsenios was completely outmanœuvred. He had very little support among the aristocracy, while the upper clergy were inclined to bow before the demands of the emperor. Arsenios also displayed extreme indecision and was open to coercion. This was not only the nature of the man; it was also the nature of the situation, for a minority exposed some of the contradictions that lay behind the façade of an absolute monarchy: Did the patriarch as the guarantor of the rights of the legitimate heir have the right to dispose of imperial authority as he saw fit and, having disposed of it, was he responsible for seeing that this authority was not misused? The problem of exactly how far the emperor had to account for his actions to the patriarch was never resolved, nor was that of how far the aristocracy ought to be associated in the decisions of government. There could in fact be no solution. The usurpation of Michael Palaiologos demonstrates above all else the blind attachment that existed in Byzantium to the institution of an absolute monarchy. It was not felt necessary to adapt the theory of empire to the reality of increasing power of the aristocracy and the growing independence of the Church. As a result, in the years that followed the recovery of Constantinople, imperial authority came to have less and less substance.

[100] Gregoras I, p. 53, ll. 9–10, p. 54, ll. 18–23.

[101] Pachymeres I, pp. 193–4.

[102] Ibid., pp. 16–17.

[103] Ibid., p. 18, ll. 2–17.

PART III

THE ECONOMY AND SOCIETY OF THE NICAEAN EMPIRE

VI

THE NICAEAN ECONOMY

The history of the Nicaean Empire was determined by two main factors. The first we have already examined—its role as the guardian of the imperial traditions of Byzantium. The second was its situation in Asia Minor. This was decisive for its economic structure. It was decisive too for the realization of the imperial aspirations which provided the Nicaean Empire with its *raison d'être*. The Anatolian provinces provided the bulk of the resources that enabled the emperors of Nicaea to accomplish their European conquests and finally to restore the seat of empire to Constantinople.

When Theodore I Laskaris arrived in Asia Minor after the fall of Constantinople, such an achievement hardly seemed possible. The prospect that greeted him was not a happy one. This was not just because of the danger of a Latin invasion. It was also the general condition of the Anatolian provinces. They had been in a state of turmoil ever since the death of Manuel I Komnenos in 1180. There was deep disaffection. The people of these provinces showed their distrust of the government of Constantinople by supporting pretenders and rebels who were able to count on backing from the Seljuqs. The frontier defences began to give way; there was a succession of Turkish *razzias* that concentrated on plundering the rich lands and cities of the Maiander valley. The local inhabitants were rounded up and deported. In 1198 5,000 prisoners were taken by the Turks in one such raid. The Seljuq sultan settled them in his dominions near the city of Philomelion and exempted them from the payment of taxes for five years. This generous treatment attracted the settlement there of other Greeks.[1]

The devastation and depopulation of western Asia Minor at the turn of the twelfth century was aggravated by the

[1] Nicetas Choniates, pp. 656–7. See Sp. Vryonis Jr., 'The Byzantine Legacy and Ottoman Forms', *DOP* 23/4 (1969–70), 277.

oppression of local magnates.[2] The fall of Constantinople led to a further deterioration in the situation. Local rulers seized power, while peasants took advantage of the prevailing uncertainty to seize disputed property.[3] It was Theodore I Laskaris's great achievement to bring an end to the state of anarchy in these provinces and to restore a reasonably stable frontier with the Turks. This he did with surprisingly little loss of territory. The outlying posts that the Byzantines had held under the Komnenoi on the Anatolian plateau were never recovered, but after Theodore's victory over the Seljuqs at the battle of Antioch in 1211 the coastlands were secure from Turkish raids.

The eastern frontier of the Nicaean Empire[4] stretched in an arc along the edge of the Anatolian plateau. It began from a point on the Black Sea coast to the east of Amastris and ran south-eastwards to the south-western tip of Asia Minor. It was dictated to a large extent by natural features, by mountains and rivers. On the Nicaean side of the border there was a network of roads and frontier fortresses. On the Seljuq side there was a series of caravansarays along the roads that joined Antalya (Attalia) to Denizli (Laodikea) and Afyon Karahisar (Akroinon) to Kütahya (Kotyaion).[5] In between lay a tract of no man's land, the Turkish *Udj*, where Nicaean borderers and Turkoman tribesmen battled for control of the pastureland.

The Nicaean territories along the Black Sea were limited to a narrow coastal strip. This region known as Paphlagonia was only finally secured by Theodore I Laskaris in the autumn of 1214 after the death of its ruler David Komnenos.[6] The chief city of Paphlagonia was Pontic Heraklea which was refortified by Theodore I Laskaris.[7]

Connecting Paphlagonia and the region of Nicaea were the

[2] e.g. Miklosich and Müller IV, pp. 320–1, 327–9.

[3] e.g. ibid. IV, pp. 217–18; VI, p. 178, ll. 15–18.

[4] See P. Charanis, 'On the Asiatic Frontiers of Nicaea', *OCP* 13 (1947), 58–62; H. Glykatzi-Ahrweiler, 'Les Forteresses construites en Asie Mineure face à l'invasion seldjoucide', *Akten des XI. Internationalen Byzantinisten-Kongresses*, Munich, 1958, pp. 182–9; H. Ahrweiler, 'Choma-Aggélokastron', *REB* 24 (1966), 278–83.

[5] See K. Erdmann, *Das anatolische Karavansaray des 13. Jahrhunderts*, Berlin, 1961, 2 vols.

[6] Acropolites I, p. 18, ll. 3–4; Ephraim, v. 7535; Heisenberg, 'Neue Quellen', III, pp. 11, 66–73.

[7] *C.I.G.* No. 8748.

frontier districts of Plousiada,[8] Tarsia,[9] and Trikokkia,[10] which protected the exposed Sangarios border.[11] By the end of Michael Palaiologos's reign this frontier was well fortified,[12] and this was probably already the case under the emperors of Nicaea.[13] The last major town in Nicaean hands along the Sangarios was almost certainly Malagina, situated at the point where the river begins to emerge from the Anatolian plateau.[14] The Sangarios frontier was controlled by the city of Nicaea which was also refortified by Theodore I Laskaris.[15]

To the south-west the frontier was formed by Mount Olympos (Ulus Dağ). It was dominated by Prousa, another city refortified by Theodore I Laskaris,[16] and by Lopadion. Its fortress was constructed by John II Komnenos[17] who also fortified Achyraous (modern Balikesir) which controlled the middle reaches of the river Makestos (Simav).[18] The frontier to the south is in doubt. The main fortresses in this region were Pergamon,[19] Chliara,[20] and Kavallares.[21] One of the frontier fortresses protecting this section of the border was called Magidia. It is therefore very probable that the march of Magedon should be situated in this region.[22] The valley of the middle Hermos was controlled by the flourishing city

[8] Nicetas Choniates, p. 844, ll. 10–11.

[9] Acropolites I, p. 163, l. 8; Sir W. H. Ramsay, *The Historical Geography of Asia Minor* (Royal Geographical Society's Supplemental Papers IV), London, 1890, p. 191.

[10] Pachymeres I, pp. 193–4, p. 201, ll. 16–17; II, p. 638, ll. 1–2.

[11] Heisenberg, 'Neue Quellen', III, p. 33, ll. 18–20; Pachymeres I, p. 25, ll. 14–18.

[12] Pachymeres II, pp. 502–5. See ibid. I, p. 419, l. 8; II, p. 413, ll. 1–4.

[13] Acropolites I, p. 163, l. 8.

[14] Pachymeres II, p. 413, l. 3. It was refortified by Manuel I Komnenos (Nicetas Choniates, p. 71, ll. 1–5). The bishops of this city were reasonably prominent in the ecclesiastical affairs of the Nicaean Empire (Miklosich and Müller I, p. 119; Pachymeres I, p. 102, ll. 9–10).

[15] *C.I.G.* Nos. 8745–7; Oikonomides in *REB* 1967, p. 125, ll. 17–18.

[16] *C.I.G.* No. 8744.

[17] Cinnamus, p. 38, ll. 7–11.

[18] Nicetas Choniates, p. 44, ll. 12–14.

[19] Nicetas Choniates, p. 194, l. 24; Acropolites I, pp. 27–8; Theodore Lascaris, pp. 107–8, where it is described as *ἀνθρώπων εἰς δαιμόνας φυλακτήριον*.

[20] Nicetas Choniates, p. 194, l. 24; Acropolites I, pp. 27–8; Pachymeres II, p. 234, ll. 4–9.

[21] Scutariotes, p. 294, l. 23.

[22] Acropolites I, p. 28, ll. 6–8; Pachymeres I, p. 220, ll. 6–9, p. 311, l. 7, p. 468, l. 20; Doukas, p. 33, ll. 27–8; Ramsay, *Hist. Geography*, pp. 122, 211; Tomaschek, 'Topographie', p. 98; Pauly-Wissowa, 1A, cols. 1767–8, art. Saittai.

of Sardes.[23] To the south-east lay the city of Philadelphia. The historian George Akropolites described it as a great and populous city lying close to the Seljuq frontier. Its citizens were all capable of bearing arms and were skilled in the use of the bow. They were constantly at war with the Turks.[24] It was at the centre of a network of frontier fortresses. The most important of these was Tripolis, situated at the mouth of a gorge through which the river Maiander breaks out of the Anatolian plateau.[25] Its defences were put in order by John Vatatzes.[26] The river Maiander seems to have been recognized as the frontier at this point,[27] for a bridge had to be constructed across the river by Turkish workmen when the Seljuq sultan came to Tripolis to seek help from John Vatatzes.[28]

Further upstream stood the important cities of Laodikea (Denizli) and Chonai. They passed under the rule of Manuel Mavrozomes at the beginning of Theodore I Laskaris's reign and were only briefly recovered by Theodore II Laskaris in 1257 in return for aid sent to the Seljuqs.[29] South of the Maiander valley the coastal regions of Caria formed part of the Nicaean Empire.[30] The actual boundary seems to have been marked by a bridge over the river Indos (Dalaman Çay) which was raised during periods of war and lowered once peace returned.[31] The mountains to the north-east were settled by Turkoman shepherds. This south-western corner of Asia Minor was the most exposed part of the Anatolian provinces of the Nicaean Empire and caused John Vatatzes great anxiety.[32] It was to fall to the Turks soon after the recovery of Constantinople.[33]

[23] Theodore Lascaris, pp. 155–6; see M. F. Hendy, *Coinage and Money*, pp. 233–4.

[24] Acropolites I, p. 105, ll. 22–6. Cf. Pachymeres I, 99, ll. 6–16.

[25] See Sir W. M. Ramsay, *The Cities and Bishoprics of Phrygia, being an essay of the local history of Phrygia from the earliest times to the Turkish Conquest*, I, Oxford, 1895, pp. 3–6.

[26] Pachymeres II, p. 433, ll. 9–15.

[27] See Theodore Lascaris, p. 57, ll. 32–4.

[28] Acropolites I, pp. 69–70.

[29] Ibid., pp. 143–4; Scutariotes, pp. 294–5.

[30] The most southerly city held by the emperors of Nicaea was Stadia in the Knidian peninsula (Acropolites I, p. 45, l. 22).

[31] See P. Wittek, *Das Fürstentum Mentesche: Studie zur Geschichte Westkleinasiens im 13.–15. Jahrhundert* (Istanbuler Mitteilungen, 2). Istanbul, 1934, pp. 1–3.

[32] Theodore Lascaris, p. 57, ll. 32–4.

[33] Pachymeres I, p. 220, ll. 2–3, p. 311, ll. 8–11.

The pressure of the Turkomans upon the Nicaean frontier seems to have become more noticeable from the 1250s.[34] Theodore II Laskaris's first task once he had succeeded to the throne was to make a tour of inspection of the eastern frontiers from Philadelphia to Nicaea.[35] Michael Palaiologos did the same as soon as he had been proclaimed emperor.[36] He also sent his brother Constantine to secure the Paphlagonian frontier.[37] Even before this John Vatatzes had fought a number of engagements to hold back the Seljuqs,[38] and he took steps to see that the frontier was properly defended.[39] But there was little danger that the frontier would give way before Turkoman pressure, as long as the belt of no-man's-land continued to be dominated by the Nicaean borderers. The emperors of Nicaea understood how important they were for the defence of the frontiers. They granted them freedom from taxation and generous allowances. This encouraged them in their continuous border warfare with the Turkomans. They prospered and built up great flocks of sheep and cattle.[40] Their way of life resembled that of their opponents. Both were pastoralists; both, too, were skilled in the use of the bow.[41]

The Greeks of Cappadocia commemorated the reigns of the Nicaean emperors in inscriptions in their churches. This has been taken to mean that Nicaean authority extended as far inland as Cappadocia.[42] This seems most unlikely.[43] The

[34] Ibid., p. 133, ll. 2–15; Acropolites I, p. 136, ll. 11–16. Cf. Wirth in *BZ* 1962, pp. 33–4.

[35] Acropolites I, pp. 105–6.

[36] Pachymeres I, pp. 98–100.

[37] Acropolites I, pp. 160–1.

[38] Ibid. II, p. 13, l. 17, p. 18, ll. 14–19; Nicole in *REG* 1894, p. 77, ll. 14–15; C. Cahen, *Pre-Ottoman Turkey. A General Survey of the Material and Spiritual Culture and History c. 1071–1330*, London, 1968, p. 135. There is a sixteenth-century tradition that Caesar Alexios Strategopoulos's father was governor of Paphlagonia under John Vatatzes and won a victory against the Turks (Georgios Sphrantzes, *Memorii 1401–1477* (ed. V. Grecu, Scriptores Byzantini, V), Bucharest, 1966, p. 274, ll. 42–7).

[39] Pachymeres I, p. 69, ll. 5–11, p. 134, ll. 2–11.

[40] Ibid., pp. 16–18. See Wittek, *Das Fürstentum Mentesche*, pp. 3–14; Cahen, *Pre-Ottoman Turkey*, pp. 143ff.

[41] e.g. Nicetas Choniates, p. 844, l. 11; Pachymeres I, p. 122, ll. 11–12, p. 194, l. 1, p. 220, ll. 9–10.

[42] G. de Jerphanion, 'Les Inscriptions cappadociennes et l'histoire de l'Empire grec de Nicée', *OCP* 1 (1935), 239–41. Cf. Gregoras I, p. 16, ll. 18–25.

[43] See Cahen, *Pre-Ottoman Turkey*, p. 209.

emperors of Nicaea effectively controlled only the coastlands of western Asia Minor.

This is a very fertile area indeed. It is a region of river valleys, alluvial plains, and rolling hills. There are some mountains, such as Mount Sipylos. These form outliers of the Anatolian plateau which is increasingly broken up in the west by the rivers that flow off it. The most important of these are, in the north, the Sangarios (Sakarya), the Ryndakos (Atranos), and the Makestos (Simav), and, in the west, the Kaikos (Bakir), the Hermos (Gediz), the Kaystros (Küçük Menderes), and the Maiander (Büyük Menderes).

It is a well-wooded and a well-watered region, but otherwise it has few natural resources apart from the fertility of its soil. Some iron was still being mined in the thirteenth century on Mount Sipylos above the city of Magnesia.[44] There were of course rich alum deposits at Phokaia to the north of Smyrna, but they do not seem to have been properly exploited until the later thirteenth century when they were granted to the Genoese Benedetto Zaccaria by Michael VIII Palaiologos.[45]

Men writing after the recovery of Constantinople looked back on the period of the Nicaean Empire as one of great prosperity, while a contemporary, Theodore II Laskaris, praises the fertility of the Kaystros valley and of the regions surrounding Smyrna and Sardes.[46] The basis of this prosperity was a well-ordered agriculture. There seems to have been a good balance between animal husbandry, arable farming, and that other branch of farming that was so important in the Mediterranean—the cultivation of olive groves, vineyards, and orchards.

We have already seen how the Nicaean borderers built up large flocks. Large flocks of sheep and herds of cattle were also kept along the Maiander valley,[47] where winter pastures were to be found. Transhumance was a traditional feature of the economy of western Asia Minor.[48] Neighbouring land-

[44] Miklosich and Müller IV, p. 105, ll. 24–7.

[45] G. I. Bratianu, *Recherches sur le commerce génois dans la Mer Noire au XIIIe siècle*, Paris, 1929, p. 111.

[46] Theodore Lascaris, pp. 155–6, 239.

[47] Pachymeres I, p. 310, ll. 19–20.

[48] See A. P. Rudakov, *Očerki vizantijskoj kul'tury po dannym grečeskoj agiografii*, Moscow, 1917, p. 182.

owners made agreements about the use of common grazing lands. Care was taken to ensure that these were not converted into arable. In one instance, it was laid down that sheep were to be driven off the common pastures at the beginning of spring. This was to allow the grass to grow, presumably to be cut for hay which would provide winter fodder.[49] The importance of pastoral farming is underlined by the frequent appearance of demands for a pasturage tax (*ennomion*) in the monastic documents of the period. It was charged not only on animals but also on bees.[50] Honey must have been an important article of consumption. So too, were dairy products, such as eggs,[51] butter, cheese, and sour cream.[52]

Arable farming was equally important. Great stocks of corn were stored up both in the countryside and in the cities.[53] Corn was exported in large quantities to the territories of the Seljuq sultans.[54] Around the city of Smyrna the coastal plain of Memaniomenos was a centre of corn farming. Some of the great families of the Empire built up large estates here. In striking contrast, the hills behind Smyrna were given over to olive groves, fruit trees, and vineyards. It was much more a region of peasant proprietors, though great landowners can be seen buying their way in.[55] The standard of farming probably remained reasonably high in the region of Smyrna. Irrigation played an important part in the farming of the hilly districts, while mills are frequently mentioned.[56]

There are other signs that prosperity was returning to western Asia Minor. Villages were reconstructed[57] and new ones founded.[58] New olive trees and vineyards were planted.[59] New

[49] Miklosich and Müller IV, p. 181, ll. 8–25.

[50] Ibid., p. 223, l. 34. See ibid., p. 67, l. 31.

[51] Gregoras I, pp. 42–3.

[52] Theodore Lascaris, pp. 97–8; Miklosich and Müller IV, p. 257, l. 28.

[53] Scutariotes, pp. 285–6.

[54] Gregoras I, pp. 42–3.

[55] Ahrweiler, 'Smyrne', pp. 16–19; A. P. Každan, *Agrarnye otnošenija v Vizantii XIII–XIV vv.*, Moscow, 1952, p. 52.

[56] Každan, *Agrarnye otnošenija*, pp. 45–7; G. Rouillard, *La Vie rurale dans L'Empire byzantin,* Paris, 1953, pp. 175–7.

[57] Scutariotes, pp. 285–6.

[58] Pachymeres I, p. 69, ll. 5–11. Such a village may have been Neochorion near Smyrna (see Ahrweiler, 'Smyrne', pp. 32, 65–6).

[59] Miklosich and Müller IV, p. 8, ll. 19–20, p. 17, ll. 4–5, ll. 23–5, p. 20, ll. 29–30, p. 25, ll. 10–11, p. 64, ll. 30–2, p. 120, l. 20.

mills were built.[60] The reconstruction of the countryside presupposes a growing population. In addition to any natural increase,[61] the population of western Asia Minor was swollen by refugees from the areas conquered by the Latins. Theodore I Laskaris encouraged their settlement.[62] Immigration from the Aegean Islands was particularly marked.[63] Samians were found settled in the region of Ephesos.[64] The islands of Mitylene, Chios, Samos, Cos, and Ikaria were recovered from the Latins by John Vatatzes at the beginning of his reign,[65] but their inhabitants continued to suffer the effects of Latin piracy.[66] This is the most likely reason for their emigration to the mainland. The refugee problem appears to have been particularly acute under Theodore I Laskaris.[67] The solution adopted by the government seems to have been to settle them on the estates of the great landowners and presumably on the imperial demesne too. The restrictions that had existed before 1204 on the settlement of 'vagabonds' upon the great estates appear to have been lifted.[68] Of the 21 families living in 1235 on the Lemviotissa estate of Vari, just outside Smyrna, six are described as 'outsiders' (*xenoi*).[69] Twenty-five years later some of the 'outsiders' established on the Lemviotissa estates are described as islanders.[70]

[60] Miklosich and Müller IV, p. 3, ll. 10–17, p. 17, ll. 13–17, p. 21, ll. 2–4.

[61] The only detailed population figures that survive from the Nicaean period come from the village of Vari or Mela just outside Smyrna. It was granted in 1228 to the monastery of Lemviotissa. A survey was made in 1235. There were then 21 families with a total recorded population of 88. Of these 30 were stated to be under age. Only four of the families could be thought of as extended families. In three of these cases it was simply a question of a son-in-law present in the household. In only one case did the daughter and son-in-law have any children. These figures can therefore be taken as evidence that there was at least one village where the population was growing vigorously. If anything, they tend to minimize the rate of growth. Six families were newly settled and only contributed 19 people to the village's total population, while the 15 established families had no fewer than 69 members between them, that is an average of nearly 4 per household compared with 3 for the newcomers.

[62] Scutariotes, p. 282, ll. 14–18; Zepos, *Ius*, I, p. 661, pp. 25–7.

[63] Miklosich and Müller IV, p. 223, l. 6. See Ahrweiler, 'Smyrne', pp. 19–28.

[64] Theodore Lascaris, pp. 298–9.

[65] Gregoras I, pp. 28–9.

[66] Miklosich and Müller V, p. 12, l. 19; VI, pp. 229–30.

[67] Oikonomides in *REB* 1967, p. 125, ll. 14–17.

[68] See Ostrogorskij, *Paysannerie*, pp. 34–5.

[69] Miklosich and Müller IV, pp. 13–14.

[70] Ibid., p. 223.

The population was further increased by the settlement of a large body of Koumans along the Maiander valley and in Phrygia.[71] 'Phrygia', in the context of the Nicaean Empire, must mean the frontier region to the north and east of Sardes and Philadelphia. This settlement of foreigners—the Koumans were a Turkic people who had been infiltrating the Balkans from the steppes of southern Russia since the turn of the eleventh century—was carried out by John Vatatzes about the year 1241[72] and followed a traditional Byzantine expedient.[73] The Koumans were clearly a troublesome element in Nicaean society and were only slowly assimilated. It was their aid that a peasant from near Smyrna sought in the closing years of the Nicaean Empire when he had been illegally deprived of some property. They were clearly a quite distinct and rather lawless group.[74] Those serving in the army were most rapidly Hellenized. They were present at the assembly that elected Michael Palaiologos regent. Their opinion was consulted. It is recorded that they gave their answer in favour of Michael Palaiologos *in good Greek*.[75] Their chiefs were taken into imperial service. Syrgiannes, one of the leading figures at the court of Andronikos II, was the son of a Kouman chieftain who married into the imperial family.[76]

Foreigners settled in western Asia Minor in the course of the previous centuries appear to have been assimilated by the local Greek population.[77] Only the Armenians[78] and the Jews[79] still preserved their separate identities. There were of

[71] Gregoras I, p. 37, ll. 4–9; Acropolites I, p. 65, ll. 16–20.

[72] Acropolites I, p. 65, ll. 16–20.

[73] See P. Charanis, 'The Transfer of Population as a Policy in the Byzantine Empire', *Comparative Studies in Sociology and History*, 3 (1960–1), 140–54.

[74] Miklosich and Müller IV, pp. 165–8. The documents that relate this incident can be dated to the year 1271, but it is made clear that the events described took place many years previously.

[75] Acropolites I, p. 158, ll. 18–21.

[76] Gregoras I, p. 296, ll. 20–2; Cantacuzenus, I, p. 18, ll. 10–16.

[77] See P. Charanis, 'On the Ethnic Composition of Byzantine Asia Minor in the Thirteenth Century', *Προσφορὰ εἰς Σπ. Κυριακίδην*, Thessalonica, 1953, pp. 140–7; id., 'The Slavic Element in Byzantine Asia Minor in the Thirteenth Century', *B* 18 (1946–8), 69–83; id., 'Observations on the Demography of the Byzantine Empire', *Thirteenth International Congress of Byzantine Studies: Main Papers, XIV*, Oxford, 1966, pp. 18–19; Ahrweiler, 'Smyrne', pp. 19–22.

[78] Miklosich and Müller IV, p. 78, l. 19.

[79] Ibid., p. 25, l. 11.

course large numbers of Latins serving in the Nicaean armies. Some even held estates in the neighbourhood of Smyrna,[80] but in terms of numbers they did not make any very important contribution to the population of the Nicaean Empire. Their political importance was, on the other hand, quite out of proportion to their relatively small numbers.[81]

Just as very few precise data have survived on population, so too the information on the level of prices is very scarce. The main conclusions that can be drawn are that the price paid for arable land was reasonably close to the official value laid down by the surveyors of the time.[82] There were variations from district to district and from year to year. These may reflect the varying quality of the land and possibly, too, supply and demand.[83] They might also be the result of other circumstances, such as the settlement of some lawsuit, when a higher price than usual might be paid.[84] Three sales of olive trees are recorded between August 1231 and March 1232. The price of olive trees remained very steady at just over $\frac{1}{3}$ nomisma[85] each. But the little information that there is for the years on either side points to much higher prices being paid. In 1213 27 olive trees fetched 70 nomismata[86] and in 1234 22 young olive trees were sold for 16 nomismata.[87] It is interesting that when half of these were sold 25 years later they only fetched 4 nomismata.[88] There is a contrast between the

[80] e.g. Syrgares (Miklosich and Müller IV, pp. 7, 36–42, 61, 81–2, 135); Syraliatos (ibid., p. 94); Syr Adam (ibid., pp. 79, 91–2, 103–4).

[81] e.g. the role they played in the usurpation of Michael Palaiologos. See above, pp. 81–2.

[82] Th. I. Uspenskij, 'Vizantijskie zemlemery. Nabljudenija po istorii seljskago khozjajstva', *Trudy VI arkheologičeskago s'ezda v Odesse 1884* g. Odessa, 1888, II, pp. 302–8; G. Ostrogorsky, 'Löhne und Preise in Byzanz', *BZ* 32 (1932), 312–15.

[83] e.g. when one George the Eunuch was building up property in the neighbourhood of Palatia (Miletos) between Oct. 1212 and Mar. 1213 he was consistently paying $\frac{1}{2}$ nomisma per *modios* (1/12 hectare) (Miklosich and Müller VI, pp. 156–65). Between 1225 and 1250 the monastery of Lemviotissa paid about 1 nomisma per modios for the land it bought (ibid., pp. 191, 195, 197, 205). Between 1251 and 1256 the monastery of Xerochoraphiou was paying altogether lower prices for land from a $\frac{1}{4}$ nomisma to 1/17 nomisma per *modios* (Wilson and Darrouzès in *REB* 1968, pp. 36, 38).

[84] e.g. Miklosich and Müller IV, pp. 155–7, esp. p. 156, ll. 5–6.

[85] Ibid., pp. 60–1, 77–8, 134–5.

[86] Ibid., pp. 118–19.

[87] Ibid., pp. 64–5.

[88] Ibid., pp. 132–3.

relative stability of land prices and the far less stable prices paid for olive trees. The information is too slight to attempt a detailed explanation.

More important is the evidence provided by these transactions of the circulation of money among the peasantry. There are just a few examples of payments in kind. In 1250 a peasant sold part of a vineyard for 13 sheep and their young; it is noticeable that the other partners in the sale preferred to receive cash.[89] There are two instances when peasants received donkeys in part payment for the land they were selling.[90] It is possible that the peasantry sometimes sold their property to obtain corn needed to tide them over to the next harvest. In March 1213 a peasant sold a field for 1 nomisma and 2 bushels (*modioi*) of corn.[91] On the other hand, there are not the signs of destitution among the peasantry of western Asia Minor under the emperors of Nicaea that, for instance, one finds in the 1270s among the peasantry of Thessaly. They were forced to sell their property to great landowners in order to survive.[92]

Sometimes peasant property became so subdivided that it became uneconomical to work. In 1246 the monastery of Lemviotissa acquired a water-mill. It had originally belonged to four peasant families. They were forced to sell it to the monastery, not out of poverty, but because there were so many of them that they were not able to carry out the work properly because they were always quarrelling.[93] Partible inheritance prevailed among the peasantry. The subdivision of property that resulted was one of the factors that allowed the great landowners to build up their estates by buying peasants out of unprofitable plots of land.

[89] Miklosich and Müller IV, pp. 200–1.

[90] Ibid. VI, pp. 230–1. A particularly difficult example concerns the monastery of St. Mary Kechiosmene near Palatia. In 1250, as a result of an agreement made four years earlier with the abbot, one Manuel Palaiologos sold a field of 15 *modioi* *εἰς βοΐδιον καματηρὸν ἀρεστὸν ἕν, εἰς ὑπέρπυρα τρία καὶ μοχθηρὸν ἕν*. What it is difficult to decide is whether the price was 3 nomismata and 1 *mochthyron* (billon *trachy*?) but he received its equivalent—1 plough ox—or he received both the plough ox and the money. If the first alternative is correct, it does leave open the possibility that in some cases the price was stated in money but paid in kind (ibid. VI, pp. 191–3).

[91] Ibid. VI, pp. 162–4.

[92] Ibid. IV, pp. 400–8.

[93] Ibid., pp. 196–7.

It was the great landowners who not only gained most from the renewed prosperity of western Asia Minor, but who were also chiefly responsible for the reconstruction of the countryside.[94] The initiative seems to have come from the emperor himself. Large tracts of land were appropriated to the imperial demesne. John Vatatzes took particular care over the management of the imperial estates and through the appointment of skilled stewards was able to increase their profits. Estates were also granted out to the aristocracy who were encouraged to improve the land.[95] One of the reasons why John Vatatzes founded monasteries may have been to bring land back into production.[96] The period of the Nicaean Empire saw a growth of the great estate at the expense of peasant property. This was part and parcel of the return to order in the countryside. On the face of it, the consolidation of small peasant properties in the hands of a single owner must have made for a more profitable concern.

Landowners tended to reside in the towns or cities close to their estates. As a general rule, they probably tried to concentrate their property reasonably close to their chief residence. For example, in 1216 a member of the Gavalas family sold an estate at Phygella because it did not lie sufficiently close to the fortress of Ephesos where he lived and he found it difficult to collect its receipts. Instead he intended to buy property closer to Ephesos.[97] Much of the land of the plain of Memaniomenos outside Smyrna belonged to the Smyrniot nobility, though it is true that they were faced with increasing competition from the aristocratic houses of the Nicaean court.[98]

Landowners invested in urban property not only in the large cities such as Magnesia[99] and Smyrna,[100] but also in smaller centres such as Mantaia[101] and Petra[102] which lay

[94] See Miklosich and Müller IV, p. 3, ll. 10–17, p. 8, ll. 19–20, p. 13, ll. 4–5, p. 17, ll. 4–5, ll. 13–17, p. 21, ll. 2–4, p. 25, ll. 10–11, ll. 23–5, p. 20, ll. 29–30.

[95] Pachymeres I, p. 71, ll. 2–5; Gregoras I, pp. 41–2, p. 43, ll. 10–15.

[96] See Miklosich and Müller IV, p. 18, ll. 27–9.

[97] Ibid. VI, pp. 174–6.

[98] H. Glykatzi-Ahrweiler, 'La Politique agraire des empereurs de Nicée', *B* 28 (1958), 54–5, 63–4.

[99] Miklosich and Müller IV, p. 267, ll. 5–6.

[100] Ibid., p. 25, ll. 4–6, pp. 55–6.

[101] Ibid., p. 31, ll. 9–11, pp. 125–6.

[102] Ibid., pp. 169–70.

close to Smyrna. They clearly had business interests in the cities. There is the example of a member of a family that was fairly prominent under the emperors of Nicaea owning property at Nymphaion.[103] This included four cloth workshops and a tower containing a bakery and a workshop. These brought him in the very large annual rent of 200 nomismata. He also owned a share in a perfume factory and houses. There are examples, too, of monastic houses having some of their dependent peasants settled in the cities and ports of the Empire.[104] The other large employer was the state. Armourers paid by the state worked in several cities of the Nicaean Empire.[105] The silk industry which grew up at Nicaea was very probably controlled by the state. After the recovery of Constantinople it continued to produce silk for the imperial court.[106]

The manufactures carried on in the towns and cities of the Nicaean Empire were mainly for local consumption and designed to meet basic needs. Besides weaving, which would also have been carried on in the countryside in peasant households,[107] the leather trade must have been essential. Apparently, Philadelphia was a centre of this manufacture at the time of the Nicaean Empire.[108] Perhaps a more important function of the towns and cities, leaving aside their military and administrative role, was as centres of consumption and markets for the surrounding countryside. They did not of course furnish the only markets. There were also country fairs.[109] The division of labour between town and countryside was by no means clear-cut. Even a great city, such as Smyrna, had vineyards and fields within its walls, and its inhabitants

[103] Ibid., p. 286, ll. 4–5, ll. 16–17. The man in question was one Goudeles Tyrannos. A man of this name is found in 1252 in joint command of a Nicaean army (Acropolites I, p. 90, ll. 6–7).

[104] Miklosich and Müller IV, pp. 2–3, 20, ll. 22–3, p. 24, ll. 9–10; V, p. 11, ll. 18–20.

[105] Scutariotes, p. 285, ll. 18–23.

[106] Sathas I, p. 152, ll. 21–2. In the late thriteenth century Nicaea was famous for a silk stuff known as cendal (Bratianu, *Commerce génois*, p. 111).

[107] e.g. Nicetas Choniates, p. 858, ll. 15–16. Anyphantor or 'Weaver' was a family name at Smyrna (see Ahrweiler, 'Smyrne', p. 93).

[108] Draeseke in *BZ* 1894, p. 500.

[109] These seem often to have been connected with local monasteries (e.g. Nicetas Choniates, p. 664, ll. 4–5; Zepos, *Ius*, I, p. 661, ll. 24–5; Miklosich and Müller IV, pp. 107, l. 25, 110–11).

also possessed common fields outside.[110] It is likely that Smyrna, like other Mediterranean cities,[111] included in its population a large body of agricultural labourers. Shortly before coming under Nicaean rule, the port of Lampsakos on the Hellespont had a recorded population of 163 adult males. No fewer than 113 of these were engaged in agriculture.[112]

Almost without exception, the cities of western Asia Minor had come in the centuries of the Arab invasions to be concentrated within citadels. It was hardly to be expected that further major changes would take place during the comparatively short period of exile in the sites and general layout of the major cities of western Asia Minor, but their upkeep appears to have been one of the chief cares of the emperors of Nicaea. At Smyrna[113] John Vatatzes carried out extensive reconstructions at the western end of the old Hellenistic citadel on Mount Pagos, creating an inner fortress. This was almost certainly the Neokastron of Smyrna attested by the middle of the thirteenth century, when houses and monasteries had already been built within its walls.[114] It is just possible that this 'New Fortress' may have been the harbour fortress at Smyrna, even though there is no record of its existence until the early fourteenth century.[115]

At Ephesos the classical site was gradually abandoned during the period of the Arab invasions and the centre of the city was moved to the neighbouring hill where the renowned church of St. John the Theologian had been constructed in the reign of Justinian I. In their present form the fortifications of the citadel that grew up around the church appear to date from the period of exile.[116]

There are other instances where classical sites in western Asia Minor were abandoned in the course of the Middle

[110] Miklosich and Müller IV, p. 12, ll. 5, 23, pp. 46–8, 51–4, 67, 125–6.

[111] e.g. Tyre (see J. Prawer, 'Étude de quelques problèmes agraires et sociaux d'une seigneurie croisée au XIIIe siècle', *B* 22 (1952), 55).

[112] Tafel and Thomas II, pp. 208–9.

[113] H. Grégoire. *Recueil des inscriptions grecques chrétiennes d'Asie Mineure*, I. Paris, 1922, Nos. 81–2; W. Müller-Wiener, 'Die Stadtbefestigungen von Izmir, Siğacik, und Çandarli', *Istanbuler Mitteilungen*, 12 (1962), 59–85.

[114] Miklosich and Müller IV, pp. 55–6.

[115] Müller-Wiener, art. cit., p. 84; Lemerle, *Émirat d'Aydin*, pp. 41–4.

[116] H. Vetters, 'Zum byzantinischen Ephesos', *JOBG* 15 (1966), 273–87.

Ages, but in many cases, perhaps the majority, the old sites were retained. At both Pergamon[117] and Palatia (Miletos)[118] the ancient theatre formed the core of the medieval citadel. Theodore Laskaris's description of Pergamon shows that the Byzantine city seemed a miserable affair beside the ruins of the Hellenistic city. To him the modern houses appeared like mouseholes beside the works of the ancients.[119]

The city of Nicaea was something of an exception. It seems to have retained its original Hellenistic street-plan. Great efforts were made by the emperors of Nicaea to refurbish it. Its broad straight streets, which must have contrasted with the narrow winding allies of other cities, were thought worthy of praise.[120]

The other capital of the Nicaean Empire was Nymphaion near Smyrna. It must have grown rapidly[121] after John Vatatzes had made it his residence at the beginning of his reign.[122] There is no evidence that it had ever been of much importance before this. A citadel was built on the summit of a neighbouring hill, but the emperor's palace[123] stood in the plain below, close to the site of the modern village.

The cities of the Nicaean Empire may be divided into two groups. There were the great fortress cities of the north, such as Nicaea, Prousa, Nikomedeia, and Pontic Heraklea; and there were the cities of the west, which were closely linked with the capital of Nymphaion. The two groups were connected by a route via Achyraous (Balikesir). But this town passed into the hands of the Latins, together with the rest of north-western Asia Minor, by the terms of the treaty which Theodore I Laskaris concluded with the Latin Emperor Henry of Hainault, probably in 1212.[124] It was only

[117] Theodore Lascaris, pp. 107–8.

[118] Th. Wiegand (ed.), *Milet. Ergebnisse der Ausgrabungen und Untersuchungen seit dem Jahre 1899*, II. 3, Berlin/Leipzig, 1935, pp. 117, 127.

[119] Theodore Lascaris, pp. 107–8.

[120] See Andreeva, *Očerki*, pp. 20–1; R. Janin, 'Nicée. Étude historique et topographique', *EO* 24 (1925), 482–90; A.-M. Schneider, *Die römischen und byzantinischen Denkmäler von Iznik-Nicaea* (Istanbuler Forschungen, 16), Berlin, 1943, pp. 1–6.

[121] See Miklosich and Müller IV, pp. 285–7.

[122] Blemmydes, pp. 6–7.

[123] See S. Eyice, 'Le Palais byzantin de Nymphaion près d'Izmir', *Akten des XI. Internationalen Byzantinisten-Kongresses*, Munich, 1958, pp. 150–3; Ahrweiler, 'Smyrne', pp. 42–4.

[124] Acropolites I, pp. 27–8.

recovered in 1224. This must have meant that meanwhile the Nicaean Empire was cut into two unequal halves. Communication between them was either by a direct route over Mount Olympos,[125] or, possibly, through the Latin-held territories, since stages were fixed between Adramyttion, which was in Latin hands, and Pergamon in Nicaean territory.[126]

In general, the road system of western Asia Minor was little affected by the loss of Constantinople. The Seljuq conquest of the greater part of Asia Minor meant that the direct routes from Constantinople into Asia Minor became extremely hazardous. Dorylaion (Eskişehir), the key to these routes, was never effectively reoccupied. Byzantine expeditions against the Seljuqs tended to be concentrated along the road that led down the Maiander valley towards Konya.[127] This development makes the choice of Nymphaion as the capital of the Nicaean Empire easier to understand. It lay on the main road to the Seljuq frontier via Sardes, Philadelphia, and Tripolis. It was also linked directly with Ephesos, at the head of the road leading up the Maiander valley.[128] There were of course roads linking it with Smyrna and Magnesia. These three places were the hub of the Nicaean Empire. Nymphaion was equally well placed for the European campaigns of John Vatatzes and Theodore Laskaris. Lampsakos and the Hellespont could be reached either by way of Pergamon and Adramyttion or by way of Kalamos, which was protected by a fortress called Kavallares.[129] It became an important route centre during the period of the Nicaean Empire. It was at the meeting-place of roads from Nymphaion, which lay a day's journey away,[130] from Sardes, and from Achyraous.[131]

[125] Gregoras I, p. 18, ll. 19–20; cf. Anna Comnena, XIV, v. 7: (ed. Leib), p. 168, ll. 18–22; Cinnamus, p. 38, ll. 18–19.

[126] Acropolites II, pp. 15–16.

[127] See Ramsay, *Hist. Geography*, pp. 78–80.

[128] See Ahrweiler, 'Smyrne', p. 17.

[129] Scutariotes, pp. 294–5.

[130] See H. Golubovich, 'Disputatio Latinorum et Graecorum seu Relatio apocrisariorum Gregorii IX de gestis Nicaeae in Bithynia et Nymphaeae in Lydia 1234', *Archivum Franciscanum Historicum*, 12 (1919), 464.

[131] Acropolites I, p. 28, ll. 3–4; Scutariotes, pp. 294–5; A. Chroust, *Quellen zur Geschichte des Kreuzzuges Kaiser Friederichs I* (Monumenta Germaniae Historica. Scriptores Rerum Germanicarum, N.S. V), Berlin, 1928, p. 73, ll. 3–5. For the position of Kalamos close to the ancient Appollonis, see Ramsay, *Hist. Geography*, pp. 129–30; Tomaschek, 'Topographie', p. 96; Ahrweiler, 'Smyrne', p. 73.

Along these roads and along the coasts of Asia Minor some local trade must have been carried on, but there is very little evidence for it. Monasteries at least found it worth their while to obtain exemption from tolls and custom duties charged on internal trade.[132] They may have been shipowners. The monastery of St. John of Patmos was exempted from customs duties and port taxes for two ships.[133] Local trade was presumably mostly in foodstuffs, while it is possible that there was some traffic in salt.

There were salt pans near Smyrna belonging to the state. Their overseer was instructed by the emperor to give 200 measures of salt to the monastery of Lemviotissa each year.[134] This monastery also acquired a salt pan on its own account.[135] Its neighbours were an important member of the metropolitan of Smyrna's administration and a member of a prominent Smyrniot family.[136] Fish, too, was an important article of consumption. The same monastery went to a great deal of trouble and expense to build a fish-pond (*vivarion*) at the mouth of the river Hermos. It seems to have been on a massive scale. Ditches were dug to let in water from the Hermos and, it seems, a windmill (*τὰ ἐξ ἀνέμου*) was built, presumably to regulate the supply of water.[137] One of the witnesses of a document of 1234 concerning this fish-pond was one Constantine Ignatios who is described as a shipowner (*naukleros*).[138] The ports of the western coast of Asia Minor, of which Smyrna was one of the most important, must each have had some shipping engaged in coastal traffic, but this is the only evidence of it.

There is some evidence of foreign trade. Ships sailed to and fro from Anaia, which served as a port for Ephesos, to the

[132] Miklosich and Müller VI, pp. 165–6, 183; Wilson and Darrouzès in *REB* 1968, p. 21; Dölger, *Reg.* 1687, 1783.

[133] Miklosich and Müller VI, pp. 165–6, 183; Dölger, *Reg.* 1687, 1783.

[134] Miklosich and Müller IV, pp. 284–5; Dölger, *Reg.* 1716, 1764, 1878.

[135] Miklosich and Müller IV, pp. 48–51.

[136] i.e. John Kampanes, *sakelliou* and *primikerios* of notaries (see Ahrweiler, 'Smyrne', p. 113) and a member of the Petritzes family (see ibid., pp. 173–4). A certain Pithianos also possessed a share in the salt pans, but nothing further is known about him.

[137] Miklosich and Müller IV, p. 3, ll. 10–17, p. 17, ll. 13–17, p. 21, ll. 2–4, pp. 240–1, 242–4.

[138] Ibid., p. 244, ll. 15–16.

ports of the Syrian coast. They were probably western ships. Among other things they served the pilgrim trade.[139] Luccan and Pisan merchants are occasionally attested at the port of Adramyttion.[140] Goods from India and Egypt were on sale at the market of Magnesia.[141] Foreign luxuries, such as caviare, could be obtained by members of the Nicaean court.[142]

The evidence for direct trade with the West is rather slight. It is true that in 1219 Theodore I Laskaris concluded a treaty with the Venetians of Constantinople granting them the right of free trade within his dominions. His subjects, on the other hand, were to pay customs duties when trading at Constantinople.[143] There are a relatively large number of Venetian commercial documents surviving from the period of the Latin Empire, but they provide absolutely no evidence that the Venetians took advantage of this treaty.[144] One of the reasons for this must have been the attempt made by John Vatatzes in the 1230s to drive them out of Crete.[145]

In 1234 the Venetians made a treaty with Caesar Leo Gavalas, the ruler of Rhodes, who in the previous year had been confronted with a Nicaean invasion of his island. The alliance was directed against John Vatatzes. The Venetians were to be allowed freedom of trade on the island.[146] Again, there is no evidence that the Venetians ever exploited this treaty. Nor are there any signs at this period of the flourishing trade which was to exist in the fourteenth and fifteenth

[139] Blemmydes, pp. 28–9; Gregory of Cyprus, p. 181, ll. 9–10, p. 183, ll. 25–8.

[140] W. Heyd, *Histoire du commerce du Levant*, I, Amsterdam, 1959, pp. 305–6; S. Borsari, 'I rapporti tra Pisa e gli stati di Romania nel duecento', *RSI* 67 (1955), 487–8.

[141] Scutariotes, p. 286, ll. 9–12; Theodore Lascaris, pp. 98, 264–5.

[142] Theodore Lascaris, p. 81, l. 83.

[143] Tafel and Thomas II, p. 206, ll. 5–19.

[144] Cf. Morozzo della Rocca and A. Lombardo, *Documenti del commercio veneziano nei secoli XI–XII*, II, Turin, 1940, No. 594. This document is dated Candia, Mar. 1221. By it Giovanni Longo authorized Domenico Zane to obtain satisfaction for a loan made the previous June by Longo to one Marco Minoto who was travelling to Indromites (Adramyttion). This is the only sign of trade between Crete and the ports of western Asia Minor, but at that date Adramyttion was still in Latin hands.

[145] F. Thiriet, *La Romanie vénitienne au môyen âge. Le dévéloppement et l'exploitation du domaine colonial vénitien (XIIe–XVe siècles)* (Bibliothèque des Écoles françaises d'Athènes et de Rome, 193), Paris, 1959, pp. 97–9.

[146] Tafel and Thomas II, pp. 319–22; Acropolites I, pp. 45–6; Blemmydes, pp. 62–3.

centuries between Crete and the western coasts of Asia Minor,[147] or that Chios was of much commercial importance. Rhodes was certainly coveted by the Genoese, who seized it for a short time in 1249, but they were driven out by a Nicaean force which conquered the island.[148]

The Genoese were to receive, at least on paper, very generous commercial privileges in the Nicaean Empire by the terms of the treaty of Nymphaion which they concluded in May 1261 with Michael VIII Palaiologos.[149] There are no signs that they had previously shown any real interest in establishing trading connections with the Nicaean Empire. This was partly because the Nicaean Empire was allied with their great enemy, Frederick II Hohenstaufen. It was also because during the period of the Latin Empire and the supremacy of Venice in the trade of Constantinople there was little direct commerce between Genoa and Constantinople, with the exception of a single venture of 1251.[150] It may also have been that while the Venetians and the Genoese had goods to export, western Asia Minor, as yet, had few products demanded by the West.

Another factor that has to be borne in mind is that the Nicaean Empire lay between the two major trade routes of the eastern Mediterranean. The first was dominated by the Venetians and led via Crete and Negroponte (Euboea) to Constantinople.[151] The second led from the Crimea to Sinope and thence across Asia Minor to the Seljuq capital of Konya. The route continued to Antalya and Alanya on the southern coast of Asia Minor. These ports were in direct contact with those of Cyprus, Syria, and Egypt.[152]

International trade was concentrated during the period of the Nicaean Empire at Constantinople and Konya. It is likely that the Nicaean Empire received from these centres the foreign goods it required. Even in the early years of the

[147] Thiriet, op. cit., pp. 328–37.

[148] Acropolites I, pp. 86–8.

[149] Zepos, *Ius*, I, pp. 488–95.

[150] M. Ballard, 'Les Génois en Romanie entre 1204 et 1261. Recherches dans les minutiers notariaux génois', *Mélanges d'archéologie et d'histoire*, 78 (1966), 467–501.

[151] e.g. Morozzo della Rocca and Lombardo, op. cit. II, Nos. 518, 530, 537, 582, 592.

[152] C. Cahen, 'Le Commerce anatolien au début du XIIIe siècle', *Mélanges L. Halphen*, Paris, 1951, pp. 91–101; *Pre-Ottoman Turkey*, pp. 163–8.

Nicaean Empire, when pirates made the crossing of the Bosphoros hazardous, merchants still made the journey from Constantinople to Nicaea.[153]

After the Mongol invasion of Asia Minor in 1243 both political and commercial links between the Nicaean Empire and the Seljuqs of Rum became closer. Large amounts of corn and other foodstuffs were exported from the Nicaean Empire to the Seljuq territories which were apparently suffering from famine. These imports were paid for in gold.[154] Caravansarays were built along the roads joining Laodikea (Denizli) to Konya and to Antalya. One was built near Laodikea in 1253/4, presumably to cater for the increased traffic between the Nicaean Empire and the Seljuq state.[155] Some trade to the Nicaean Empire may have come directly via Antalya without making a detour to Konya. This seems to have been an accepted route from Thessalonica.[156]

Some efforts were made by John Vatatzes to discourage foreign imports. His economic policy was one of autarky.[157] The idea of self-sufficiency was deeply engraved on the Byzantine mentality. It was not just that the Empire ought to be self-supporting, but that the emperor and the aristocracy ought to be so as well. John Vatatzes's autarkic policies had two sides to them. On the one hand, the existing wealth of the state was not to be squandered except in its best interests. On one occasion John Vatatzes upbraided his son for going out hunting dressed in silks and cloth of gold: did the prince not realize that these were the 'blood of the Romans'? They were not to be wasted in amusements, but should be used for the benefit of his subjects. They were only to be worn for the reception of foreign ambassadors in order to impress them with the wealth of the Empire.[158] The other side of this policy was his enactment of a sumptuary law which compelled his subjects to wear garments of home-produced cloth.

[153] Heisenberg, 'Neue Quellen', II, p. 39, ll. 17–21, pp. 44–5.

[154] Gregoras I, pp. 42–3.

[155] Erdmann, *Das anatolische Karavansaray*, I. pp. 59–61, 67–72.

[156] Acropolites I, p. 61, ll. 15–19.

[157] See D. Xanalatos, 'Wirtschaftliche Aufbau- und Autarkiemassnahmen im XIII. Jahrhundert (Nikänisches Reich 1204–1261)', *Leipziger Vierteljahrsschrift für Südosteuropa*, 3 (1939), 129–39.

[158] Pachymeres I, pp. 38–9.

This was designed to limit the import of cloth from the Moslem countries and from Italy.[159]

How successful this measure was is of course impossile to say. It was aimed specifically against cloth imports, about which there is no information whatsoever, although it is clear that other foreign goods continued to be imported. On the face of it, the Nicaean Empire must have been reasonably self-sufficient, as the export of foodstuffs to the Seljuqs seems to show.

The gold that this trade procured appears to have been the source of the considerable reserves of treasure that John Vatatzes and his son Theodore II were able to build up.[160] It is therefore rather surprising that John Vatatzes was forced to devalue his gold coinage. According to the historian George Pachymeres it was of only 16 carats, a fineness that was maintained in the coinage of his son.[161] Modern analysis has shown that the fineness of Vatatzes's gold coinage varied from $15\frac{3}{4}$ to $18\frac{1}{4}$ carats. The only example of Theodore II's gold coinage that has been analysed so far bears out Pachymeres's figures.[162] During the twelfth century the Byzantine gold coinage was struck at a theoretical standard of $20\frac{1}{2}$ carats fineness.[163] This may have been maintained in the early gold coinage of John Vatatzes, since it is apparently not impossible that some gold coins of $20\frac{1}{2}$ carats attributed to John II Komnenos should be reattributed to John III Vatatzes.[164] Vatatzes's reign therefore saw a very serious debasement of the gold coinage. How is this to be explained, when, on the one hand, his treasury was full and, on the other, there seems from the 1240s at least to have been a healthy balance of trade?

Bearing in mind John Vatatzes's extremely rudimentary economic lore, one can be sure that debasement was a question

[159] Gregoras I, pp. 43–4; Dölger, *Reg.* 1777.

[160] Pachymeres I, pp. 68–9, p. 71, ll. 8–9; Scutariotes, p. 286, ll. 7–8.

[161] Pachymeres II, pp. 493–4. See D. A. Zakythinos, *Crise monétaire et crise économique à Byzance du XIIIe au XVe siècle*, Athens, 1948, pp. 8–9; Hendy, *Coinage and Money*, pp. 246–54.

[162] T. Bertelè, 'Il titolo degli iperperi della zecca di Nicea', *Thirteenth Congress of Byzantine Studies: Supplementary Papers (Summaries)*, Oxford, 1966, pp. 95–7.

[163] See Hendy, op. cit., pp. 14–16.

[164] Ibid., p. 248.

of necessity. It could be for no other reason than that gold was in short supply. This was for a number of reasons. Asia Minor does not possess any known sources of gold. The emperors of Nicaea would have been dependent upon existing stocks that cannot in any case have been very great and whatever gold came by way of trade. Until the 1240s when gold started to flow in from the Seljuqs, there can have been little influx and most probably a net outflow of gold; this would have gone in part to pay for the cloth imports that John Vatatzes tried to stem. Another factor that has to be borne in mind is the heavy demand of the West for gold, which resulted in a drain of gold from Africa and the Levant to western Europe. This culminated in 1231 in the minting by Frederick II of the gold *augustalis* and in 1252 in the almost simultaneous issue of gold coinages by Genoa and Florence.[165]

It is difficult to believe that the Nicaean Empire would have been shielded from this long-term monetary movement. One of the terms of the treaty of Nymphaion allowed the Genoese to export from the Nicaean Empire gold *hyperpyra* and Seljuq dinars (*turchifari*).[166] The currency difficulties of the Nicaean Empire are illustrated much earlier by one of the articles of the 1219 treaty between Theodore I Laskaris and the Venetians of Constantinople. Both parties undertook not to copy one another's coinage.[167] This was obviously an attempt to bring some sort of order to the monetary situation prevailing in 'Romania' after 1204. The main coinage in circulation was a billon coinage issued by the Latin authorities and imitating earlier Byzantine types.[168] This is as far as one can safely go. One of the likely effects of this billon coinage would have been to drive gold coins out of circulation. It is not without interest in this connection that the Latin authorities of Constantinople derived important revenues from the melting down and refining of gold.[169]

Even assuming that the gold stocks of the Nicaean Empire

[165] See R. S. Lopez, 'Back to Gold, 1252', *Economic History Review,* Ser. ii. 9 (1956–7), 219–40; A. M. Watson, 'Back to Gold—and Silver', ibid., Ser. ii. 20 (1967), 1–34.

[166] Zepos, *Ius*, I, p. 294, ll. 25–6.

[167] Tafel and Thomas II, p. 207, ll. 14–16.

[168] Hendy, *Coinage and Money*, pp. 191–217.

[169] Acropolites I, p. 163, ll. 9–15.

remained reasonably stable, there were other reasons why they would have become insufficient for the needs of the Empire.[170] Investment in land and its improvement and the resulting return to prosperity would have begun to place a strain on inelastic supplies of gold and silver. But this might not have been as serious as the rapid expansion of government expenditure. The unsuccessful expeditions launched between 1230 and 1234 against Rhodes and Crete were followed in 1235 and 1236 by the equally unsuccessful siege of Constantinople by a joint Nicaeo-Bulgarian force. It will be remembered that it was exactly in these years that the price of olive trees suddenly shot up. Expenditure must have increased still further after 1242, when the emperors of Nicaea were involved in continual campaigning in Europe and a large body of Latin mercenaries had to be maintained. It is at this juncture that gold began to flow in from the Seljuq territories and this probably allowed a stabilization of the monetary situation.

Debasement was the obvious solution to a lack of ready cash. There would be the profit made on the debasement as well as the usual profits of the mint. In this connection it is interesting that, although Nicaean coins appear to have circulated in relatively small numbers, the Nicaean emperors issued a very large number of different types.[171]

Debasement of the coinage was not necessarily a disaster. It may even have been one of the conditions of continued agricultural expansion. It would have been a way of meeting the resulting need for an increasing supply of currency. Debasement was not the only solution to a lack of ready cash on the part of the government. Another was to shift as much government expenditure as possible on to the primary producer by means of grants of state rights and revenues to soldiers and members of the aristocracy (*pronoiai*) and by paying a larger proportion of their allowances in kind (*siteresia*).

As might have been expected, the economy of the Nicaean Empire was more primitive than that of the fallen Byzantine

[170] See C. Cipolla, 'Currency Depreciation in Medieval Europe', in S. Thrupp (ed.), *Change in Medieval Society: Europe North of the Alps (1050–1500)*, London, 1965, pp. 227–36, esp. p. 228.

[171] See Hendy, *Coinage and Money*, p. 224.

Empire and on a far smaller scale. It was mainly agricultural and largely untouched by the direct currents of international trade. Its coinage was not only debased, but its volume was much smaller than that of the pre-1204 Byzantine coinage. Unlike the latter, it was not of much importance as an international medium of exchange.

The Byzantine coinage had been one of the instruments by which the emperors of Byzantium were able to impose a degree of economic unity on the lands bordering the Aegean. This in turn was one of the foundations of the strength of the Empire. This economic unity was undermined during the period of exile. The region broke up into a number of units, more or less self-contained, where a local currency circulated. John Vatatzes condoned this situation by continuing to issue a separate Thessalonican coinage after his conquest of the city in 1246.[172]

The break-up of the economic unity of the Byzantine Empire was already being prepared by developments in the twelfth century. On the one hand, Constantinople's central role in the Byzantine economy was slightly undermined by the flowering of provincial centres which appears to have been the result of Latin penetration of the internal trade of the Empire; on the other, the provinces became increasingly alienated from Constantinople as a result of the government's harsh fiscal policies as it sought out new sources of revenue. It was the fall of Constantinople that made these trends irreversible. The recovery of Constantinople did not lead to a renewal of the economic unity of the Aegean region. Instead, it placed new burdens upon the Anatolian provinces which they could not meet.

[172] Hendy, *Coinage and Money*, pp. 290–5.

VII

THE STRUCTURE OF RURAL SOCIETY IN THE NICAEAN EMPIRE

The period of exile saw a decisive stage in what has been called the 'feudalization' of the Byzantine state. Outwardly, it was a process by which the great estate became the basis of the organization of rural society. Its roots can be traced back to the ninth century, when the growth of great estates began to undermine the integrity of the free peasant commune which had dominated the rural society of the Byzantine Empire for the preceding two hundred years. At first, the imperial government was determined to resist a development that appeared to weaken the very foundations of the state, but in the course of the eleventh century it began to come to terms with the growth of the great estate.

This change in the direction of government policy became evident after Alexios I Komnenos (1081–1118) had ascended the throne. Two features of his agrarian policies were of particular importance for the development of Byzantine society. One was negative: he continued a policy of according a degree of immunity (*exkousseia*) to the great landowners from the payment of taxes to the imperial treasury and from the interference of the imperial administration. It did not necessarily entail the grant of a complete immunity. The other feature was more positive and more clearly marks a new departure: public rights and revenues were granted to private individuals. These grants might only be temporary in which case they were called *pronoiai* or *oikonomiai*; or they might be of a more permanent nature and led to the establishment of franchises known as *ktemata* or *zeugelateia*.[1]

These two different kinds of immunities continued to exist

[1] See Každan, *Agrarnye Otnošenija*, pp. 95–9; G. Ostrogorskij, 'Pour l'histoire de l'immunité à Byzance', *B* 28 (1958), 165–254; H. Glykatzi-Ahrweiler, 'La Concession des droits incorporels. Donations conditionnelles', *Actes du XIIe Congrès International d'Études Byzantines, Ohrid, 1961*, II, Belgrade, 1964, pp. 103–14; D. Angelov, 'Die bulgarischen Länder und das bulgarische Volk in den Grenzen des byzantinischen

side by side throughout the later history of the Byzantine Empire. Men continued to build up estates by the traditional means of purchase and marriage alliances; and, in the case of the Church, by the soliciting of gifts as well. There was perhaps a tendency for the different kinds of immunities to be assimilated to one another, since a landowner did not necessarily possess only property enjoying the same kind of privileged status. If he exercised public authority over part of his estates, it was natural that he should try to extend this privilege to the remainder.

It was the alienation of public authority that was decisive for the shaping of late Byzantine society; for it created a new and superior interest in property. A private individual was now interposed between the subject and the state; a new layer was added to the accretion of rights and obligations that provided the framework of Byzantine society. The nature and direction of change within late Byzantine society was to be determined to a large degree by how this new layer modified, and was modified by, the earlier deposits.

It is possible that the alienation of public authority had still not gone very far by the end of the twelfth century. It was not yet particularly common to grant *pronoiai* in return for military service.[2] Franchises were scattered with no great regularity through the provinces of the Empire. Their greatest concentration appears to have been in the Peloponnese and mainland Greece.[3] In western Asia Minor there seem to have been very few outside the Maiander valley, where the Kontostephanos and Kammytzes families among others held franchises.[4] Around Smyrna the Constantinopolitan monastery of the Pantokrator may have succeeded in converting one of its estates into a franchise;[5] and the patriarchate and the monastery of Rouphianon possibly held franchises as well.

Reiches im XI.–XII. Jahrhundert (1018–1185)', *Thirteenth Congress of Byzantine Studies: Main Papers V*, Oxford, 1966, pp. 5–8.

[2] See P. Lemerle, 'Recherches sur le régime agraire à Byzance: la terre militaire à l'époque des Comnènes', *Cahiers de Civilisation Médiévale*, 2 (1959), 265–81; A. Hohlweg, 'Zur Frage der Pronoia in Byzanz', *BZ* 60 (1967), 288–308.

[3] Tafel and Thomas I, p. 258, ll. 7–10, p. 264, ll. 2–7, p. 267, ll. 3–4, pp. 469–72, 486–7.

[4] Ibid., p. 479, ll. 3–4.

[5] Miklosich and Müller IV, pp. 184–5.

Otherwise, the countryside around Smyrna was dominated by the patrimonial estates of local landowners, of whom the Metropolitan of Smyrna was probably the most important, while the communal rights of several villages appear to have survived intact.[6]

It is often assumed that the growth of privileged estates was the root cause of the Empire's weakness in the last years of the twelfth century. Indirectly, this may have been the case. The imperial government was forced to exploit its remaining sources of revenue ever more ruthlessly. This was a cause of the alienation of the provinces from the central government. The growth of franchises may have contributed to this in another way: they were granted in the main to members of the imperial house and of the great court families, as well as to Constantinopolitan monasteries. In other words, it was another way in which the provinces were oppressed by Constantinople. The disorder that reigned in the provinces was to a great extent a reaction against central authority; it must be remembered that two of its most determined opponents at the turn of the twelfth century were Leo Sgouros in the Argolid and Theodore Mangaphas at Philadelphia. Both were representatives of local families and interests; neither belonged to the court aristocracy.[7]

The immediate legacy bequeathed by the House of Angelos to Theodore I Laskaris was a state of anarchy. This was rendered still worse in western Asia Minor by a series of foreign invasions. Peasants and landowners alike took advantage of the situation to appropriate lands to which they had only dubious claims.[8] The wholesale seizure of property brought into existence a tangle of conflicting claims; their solution was to be one of the most pressing administrative tasks that faced the emperors of Nicaea. It was begun under Theodore I Laskaris and was to all intents and purposes completed during the reign of his successor, John Vatatzes. The result was not only a considerable redistribution of property, but

[6] See H. Glykatzi-Ahrweiler, 'La Politique agraire des empereurs de Nicée', *B* 28 (1958), 54–5.

[7] See Nicetas Choniates, pp. 522–4, 799–807; Stadtmüller, *Michael Choniates*, pp. 179–83; A. Bon, *Le Péloponnèse byzantin*, pp. 173–4, 204–5.

[8] See Miklosich and Müller IV, pp. 217–18, 290–5; ibid. VI, pp. 176–9; Wilson and Darrouzès in *REB* 26 (1968), 13–15, 19–20.

also the alienation of public rights on a very large scale. This was part and parcel of the restoration of order in the countryside, but in the process a decisive step was taken in the 'feudalization' of the state.

At first, it did not run counter to imperial interests. Theodore I Laskaris was able to secure possession of extensive estates in western Asia Minor which had formerly been the property of Constantinopolitan monasteries. Both the village of Vari near Smyrna, which had belonged to the monastery of the Pantokrator, and the estate of Pyrgos at the mouth of the river Maiander, previously a possession of the monastery of Panachrantos in Constantinople, were brought under state control.[9] It would seem that much property without a clear owner must have passed into the hands of the state. There are even hints that the emperors of Nicaea proceeded with a policy of forefeiting to the state all the land they needed.[10]

The exact extent of the crown lands of the emperors of Nicaea is impossible to ascertain. Contemporaries lay great emphasis on their considerable size.[11] An enumeration of imperial estates attested in the sources does not lead to any definite conclusion, except that they were widely scattered over western Asia Minor.[12] Near Smyrna it would seem that the Crown ceased to be one of the greatest landowners about the year 1234, when extensive lands from the imperial estates of Palatia were granted to the monastery of Lemviotissa[13] and perhaps to members of the court aristocracy.[14]

The emperors of Nicaea certainly disposed of sufficient property to grant out estates and were also able to create *pronoiai* and franchises. The historian Theodore Skoutariotes attributed the extension of *pronoiai* and franchises that occurred during the period of exile to the work of John Vatatzes.[15] In general terms, he may well be correct, but

[9] Miklosich and Müller IV, pp. 185–7, 217–18; ibid. VI, pp. 176–9, 180–2.

[10] Gregoras I, p. 42, ll. 1–6.

[11] Ibid.; Pachymeres I, p. 69, ll. 5–7; Scutariotes, p. 286, ll. 22–5.

[12] See Miklosich and Müller IV, pp. 142–4, 146–8, 175–6; ibid. VI, pp. 204–5, 227–9, p. 211, ll. 19–23; H. Grégoire, *Recueil des inscriptions grecques chrétiennes d'Asie Mineure*, I. Paris, 1922, p. 119.

[13] Miklosich and Müller IV, p. 9, ll. 18–19, pp. 142–4, 146–8.

[14] Ibid., pp. 232–3, 234–5.

[15] Scutariotes, p. 286, ll. 18–22.

pronoiai had already been created along the coasts of western Asia Minor under Theodore I Laskaris.[16] Around Smyrna only a single *pronoia* is attested during the reign of Theodore I Laskaris.[17] At least in this district the creation of *pronoiai* on a large scale seems to have been left to his successor.[18]

Pronoiai normally consisted of the grant of revenues and services owed by the inhabitants of a particular district, but they could be made up of other rights belonging to the state. Rights over the river Hermos near Smyrna, for instance, went to form *pronoiai* during the period of exile. The source from which a *pronoia*-holder derived his revenue is perhaps not as important as the difference in the size of the revenues granted. Some *pronoiai* were of modest proportions. They were granted to *stratiotai* serving in the imperial army and by the end of the period of exile their value may have been standardized at forty *hyperpyra* per annum.[19] More valuable *pronoiai* probably went to those serving in the lower ranks of the imperial administration, such as *vestiaritai*.[20] Western mercenaries seem to have been generously rewarded by the Nicaean government. The 'imperial liege knight' Syrgares held no fewer than three villages in *pronoia* in the neighbourhood of Smyrna about the year 1230.[21] *Pronoiai* were therefore employed as a means of financing both the administration and the army; the widespread use of the *pronoia* for this end was almost certainly an innovation of the period of exile. *Pronoiai* were also granted to members of the aristocracy and even to members of the imperial family. A village near the mouth of the river Maiander was granted in *pronoia* to George Komnenos

[16] See Miklosich and Müller VI, p. 166, ll. 11–12, p. 178, ll. 33–4.

[17] i.e. the village of Vari, which was granted before 1207 to the imperial *vestiarites* Basil Vlatteros (Miklosich and Müller IV, pp. 185–7, 217–18).

[18] The following holders of *pronoiai* are attested in the Smyrna district (1222–61): Nicholas Adam, knight, *c.* 1260 (Miklosich and Müller IV, pp. 79, 91–2); John Alopos, *prokathemenos* of Smyrna, *c.* 1235 (ibid., pp. 36–9); Michael Angelos, *stratiotes*, *c.* 1259 (ibid., p. 241); Constantine Kalegopoulos, *vestiarites*, *stratiotes*, *c.* 1234 (ibid., p. 242); Kadianos, *vestiarites*, *c.* 1239–46 (ibid., pp. 54, 247); Monomachos, *stratiotes*, *c.* 1239 (ibid., p. 157); Michael Petritzes, *stratiotes*, *c.* 1257 (ibid., pp. 69–72); Syrgares, 'imperial liege knight', *c.* 1230 (ibid., p. 7, l. 11, pp. 36–42, 61, 81–2, 135); Varycheir, *stratiotes*, *c.* 1259 (ibid., pp. 153–5).

[19] See Pachymeres I, p. 18, ll. 14–15.

[20] See above, note 18.

[21] See Glykatzi-Ahrweiler in *B* 28 (1958), 58.

Angelos, who is described as the Emperor Michael VIII Palaiologos's uncle.[22]

The holders of *pronoiai* therefore represented a broad social spectrum. They ranged from the uncle of an emperor to men from the lowest ranks of society.[23] The irascible Nikephoros Blemmydes came into conflict with a *stratiotes* called Skordyllios who held a *pronoia* near Ephesos. He had originally been an innkeeper.[24] Around Smyrna it seems to have been more usual for the holders of *pronoiai* to come from families long established in the region. This became increasingly the case as the thirteenth century wore on. Some of the *pronoia*-holders came from families that possessed quite substantial estates.[25]

Franchises too appeared in increasing numbers in the region of Smyrna during the period of exile. As far as one can tell, none of the great aristocratic families had been established in the district before 1204. In the course of John Vatatzes's reign members of the Tarchaneiotes, Vranas, Philes, Doukas, Gavalas, and Zagaromates families all acquired rights of property around Smyrna.[26] They must have been introduced into the region by John Vatatzes, who made near-by Nymphaion the capital of his Empire.[27]

The structure of their estates only becomes clearer after 1261. But by then purchases of property and the accident of inheritance had often obscured the nature of the original grants of property made by the emperors of Nicaea. They appear to have been of two kinds: the grant of a *zeugelateion* and the concession of a *ktema*. The former was essentially the grant of a block of demesne land. Its exact size was always given.[28] The holder enjoyed a complete immunity; and any peasants settled there would have to pay their taxes to him.[29] Such grants were almost certainly in perpetuity.[30] The *ktema*

[22] Miklosich and Müller VI, pp. 212–14.

[23] Cf. Nicetas Choniates, p. 273, ll. 3–8.

[24] Theodore Lascaris, pp. 298–9.

[25] e.g. the Planites and Petritzes families; see Ahrweiler, 'Smyrne', pp. 173–4.

[26] See Glykatzi-Ahrweiler in *B* 28 (1958), 59–60.

[27] e.g. the *protovestiarites* George Zagaromates was granted a *zeugelateion* near Smyrna by John Vatatzes shortly before 1235 (see Miklosich and Müller IV, p. 11, ll. 18–19, pp. 232–3).

[28] See H. Delehaye, *Deux typika byzantins de l'époque des Paléologues*, Brussels, 1921, p. 131, ll. 13–21; Miklosich and Müller IV, pp. 142–4; 232–3, 235–6.

[29] Miklosich and Müller IV, p. 9, ll. 18–19, p. 20, ll. 13–14, p. 24, ll. 1–2.

[30] Ibid., pp. 235–6; cf. ibid., pp. 233–4.

was a grant of state revenues and rights. Its value is always given in *hyperpyra*; its size is seldom recorded.[31]

Ktemata were franchises in the fullest sense. Their holders were forced to establish their own administrations.[32] In practice, they were often content to take over existing village institutions; in some cases, this led to a blurring of the exact nature of the franchise. The village of Panaretos, to the east of Smyrna, originally formed part of Syrgares's *pronoia*. After his death it passed into the possession of the noblewoman Eirene Vranaina. A dispute involving two of her peasants was brought before her to be settled. She sent the case to the village court for judgement. The guilty party was threatened with a fine, but it was to be payable not to her, but to the state.[33]

A rather clearer picture of the structure of the great estate and the privileges it might enjoy can be obtained from an examination of the grants made by the emperors of Nicaea to the Church. We have already seen that these were on a great scale.[34] This was a reflection of the need the emperors felt for ecclesiastical support, both morally through the act of prayer and perhaps practically as a balance to the aristocracy. Among John Vatatzes's foundations was the monastery of Lemviotissa near Smyrna. Since this monastery is not marked out by contemporaries as a foundation of particular significance, the benefactions it received from the emperors of Nicaea were presumably not very lavish in comparison with those made to more favoured foundations. The basic endowment of the monastery was a single village—that of Vari—which had previously constituted the *pronoia* of Basil Vlatteros.[35] John Vatatzes supplemented this with other gifts of land, particularly from the imperial estates of Palatia;[36] and he bought for it the monastery of St. George Exokastrites outside the walls of the old castle of Smyrna.[37] Smaller benefactions came from peasants and landowners. Often

[31] See Delehaye, op. cit., p. 131, ll. 4–13, p. 132, ll. 3–16, 17–20.
[32] See below, p. 259.
[33] Miklosich and Müller IV, pp. 80–4 esp. p. 83, ll. 14–15.
[34] See above, pp. 47–8.
[35] Miklosich and Müller IV, pp. 1–4.
[36] Ibid., pp. 142–5, 146–50.
[37] Ibid., pp. 43–4.

these were nothing more than a few olive trees or a field. Occasionally they were more substantial. The monastery was also rich enough to round off its possessions by buying up property in the neighbourhood.

The foundation charter of the monastery was provided by a chrysobull of 1228. Its rights of full ownership (*despotikon dikaion*) of its properties were confirmed and it was to enjoy an immunity (*exkousseia*) for them. It was thereby exempted from the payment of taxes and dues and from the performance of various services to the state, with the exception of the payment of the two chief taxes, which were known as *sitarkia* and *agape*.[38] in 1232 the dependency of St. George Exokastrites was freed from the payment of *sitarkia*;[39] and there is no longer any question of the payment of *sitarkia* and *agape* in the chrysobull issued to the monastery in 1235, or in any of its subsequent chrysobulls. It therefore seems safe to conclude that by 1235 the monastery was completely exempted from the payment of taxes to the state. A preliminary step towards this appears to have been taken by the imperial administration in the previous year when it fixed the taxes and services due to the monastery from the peasants of Vari.[40]

It was carefully laid down in the monastery's chrysobulls that it was not simply the monastery that was exempted from the payment of taxes to the state, but also the peasants settled on its estates. In 1227 the abbot was allowed to settle some landless peasants on properties belonging to his monastery. They were to be exempted from the payment of all manner of taxes, including those of *sitarkia* and *agape*.[41] It was also specified in the monastery's chrysobulls that not only sheep belonging to the monastery, but also sheep belonging to its peasantry were exempted from a pasturage tax called *ennomion*.[42]

The monastery was also exempted from the payment of the profits of justice (*aer*) due on the village of Vari.[43] This presumably meant that it possessed full jurisdiction over the

[38] Miklosich and Müller IV, pp. 3–4.
[39] Ibid., pp. 45–6.
[40] Ibid., pp. 182–3.
[41] Ibid., pp. 248–9.
[42] Ibid., p. 17, ll. 27–30.
[43] Ibid., p. 4, l. 6, p. 17, l. 30, p. 21, l. 22.

village. After 1235 the Lemviotissa estates were 'cut off' from the surrounding administrative district and the imperial administration was forbidden access to them.[44] Even so, the monks were obliged to obtain imperial permission to carry out a survey of their estates; this then had to receive imperial confirmation.[45] In this way, the emperor was able to keep a check on the rights which had been granted away.

How typical this pattern of privileges was is of course impossible to tell. But it is interesting to note how the process begins as the grant of a degree of immunity from taxation for a particular estate and ends as a complete franchise from which the imperial administration was to be entirely excluded. Although there may be a legal basis for the distinction of different kinds of immunities, there was no such clear distinction in practice; the government was under strong pressure to allow a tax immunity to be converted into a full franchise.

The period of exile therefore saw not only a large-scale redistribution of property, but with this went the creation of franchises and immunities comprising administrative and fiscal rights. It is a process that can be seen most clearly around the city of Smyrna, but it was also happening in other parts of western Asia Minor: in the Maiander valley,[46] on the island of Cos,[47] and around the city of Nicaea.[48]

Its impact perhaps only began to be felt from about the middle of John Vatatzes's reign; and its full effect only became clear after the recovery of Constantinople. About the year 1235 landholding in the region of Smyrna still retained some of the features it had possessed before 1204. Some villages still maintained their communal rights;[49] and the local landowners appear to have held on to their family estates.[50] They formed a tightly knit group, united by marriage ties. The Gordatos family which owned considerable property at

[44] Ibid. IV, p. 224, ll. 30–1, p. 251, ll. 11–13.

[45] Ibid. IV, p. 221, ll. 3–6.

[46] Ibid. VI, pp. 176–9, 195–6, 201–2.

[47] Ibid., pp. 208–10.

[48] Zepos, *Ius* I, pp. 661–2. Cf. Delehaye, *Typica*, pp. 131–4.

[49] e.g. Mantaia, Rouze, Petra, Prinovari (see Miklosich and Müller IV, pp. 6–16).

[50] e.g. Levounes, Phagomodes, Petritzes, Artavasdes, Alethinos, Lestes, Mantei(anos) (see ibid.).

Mantaia near Smyrna was allied with two other prominent local families, the Thrakeses and the Petritzes.

THE GORDATOS, PETRITZES, AND THRAKESES FAMILIES[51]

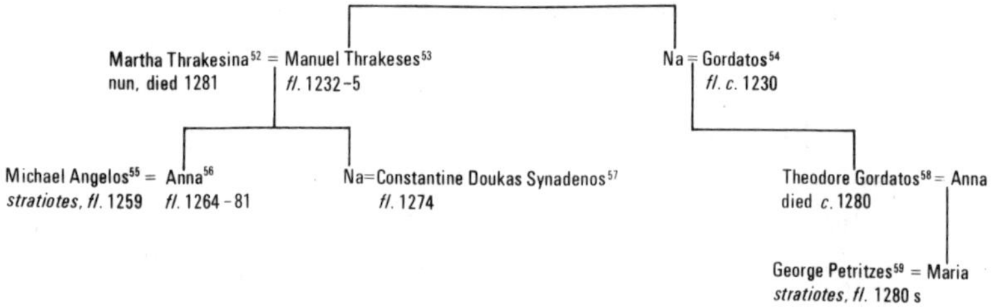

The members of these families played an active part in local affairs. Some held positions in the metropolitan of Smyrna's administration; some entered imperial service; increasingly they became *stratiotai* holding *pronoiai*.[60]

During the period of exile they seem to have been able to resist the encroachments of the new landowners, but the underlying weakness of their position became clear after 1261. Their family estates were broken up and passed into the hands of the new-comers. Sometimes this occurred as the result of a marriage with one of the incoming families,[61] sometimes as the result of brute force,[62] sometimes because the family decided to sell off its estates.[63] In some cases, this

[51] See Ahrweiler, 'Smyrne', pp. 170, 173–4, 177.
[52] Miklosich and Müller IV, pp. 94–5, 106, 112–13.
[53] Ibid., p. 59.
[54] Ibid., p. 8.
[55] Ibid., pp. 241, 244.
[56] Ibid., pp. 94, 106, 112, 169, 244.
[57] Ibid., p. 106.
[58] Ibid., pp. 113, 125–6, 126–8.
[59] Ibid., pp. 99–101, 130–1.
[60] See pp. 125–6 and note 18.
[61] Miklosich and Müller IV, p. 181, ll. 1–2. Cf. ibid., p. 12, ll. 24–5, 31.
[62] Ibid., pp. 102–3.
[63] See ibid., pp. 73–4, 130–1. In the plain of Memaniomenos the monastery of Lemviotissa acquired property from the Kaloeidas, Petritzes, Thrakeses, and Tyrannos families between 1266 and 1287 (ibid., pp. 102–3, 159–60, 161–3, 169–75). It had made no purchases in this region before 1261.

was because they were getting into debt. George Chrysoverges, a member of an old-established family, was forced to borrow $1\frac{1}{3}$ lb. of silver from a member of the Vranas family. When he died about the year 1281 his widow was not able to repay the sum.[64] In the 1260s a *stratiotes* called George Petritzes was forced to borrow from the monks of Lemviotissa in order to equip himself properly.[65] Parallel with the indebtedness of some of the old families went the increasing impoverishment of local monasteries, which were forced to seek the protection of the more powerful imperial foundations.[66]

The peasantry were clearly more vulnerable than the local nobility. Before 1204 some peasant families in the neighbourhood of Smyrna were reasonably well off, at least in terms of land, while some appear to have been related to members of the local nobility.[67] As we have seen, some communal rights had also been preserved. In the first instance, *pronoiai* and franchises were to a large extent created out of these communal rights.[68] Later, the incoming landowners began to compete for the patrimonial property of the various peasant families. Before 1261 their activities tended to be concentrated on property in the plain of Memaniomenos. It was only after 1261 that they began to penetrate the hilly region to the east of Smyrna.[69] The buying out of peasantry does not necessarily mean that they were especially poor or oppressed. The great landowners were simply in a very good position to exploit the peasant land market. The ownership of adjoining property gave them rights of pre-emption and they made full use of these to buy up peasant property.[70]

[64] Ibid., pp. 114–15.

[65] Ibid., p. 161, ll. 21–4.

[66] e.g. the monastery of Eerinon (ibid., pp. 170–1). Cf. A. Visijakova, 'Khozjajstvennaja organizatsija monastyrja Lemviotissy', *VV* 25 (1927), 36.

[67] e.g. the Kolelos family (see Miklosich and Müller IV, pp. 237–8), the Kretikos or Dermatas family (see ibid., pp. 150–3, 155–7, 158–9, 163–5, 174), and the Gounaropoulos family (see ibid., pp. 183–7, 191–6, 200–1). See Ahrweiler, 'Smyrne', pp. 116, 171.

[68] e.g. the communal rights of Prinovari were still in existence in 1235 (see Miklosich and Müller IV, pp. 15–16), but soon afterwards they became part of the franchise of the Vranas family (ibid., pp. 225–6).

[69] e.g. Theodore Komnenos Vranas appears to have been buying up property on a large scale in the region of Mantaia in the 1270s (ibid., pp. 31, 73, 95–6, 113–15, 122, 136).

[70] See ibid., pp. 55–6, 115–17, 155–7.

The peasantry were certainly under such pressure to sell their land that sales were sometimes revoked and a new transaction begun.[71] In some cases, peasants appear to have been paid inflated prices by landowners who were anxious to round off their property.[72]

The period of exile saw the beginning of important changes in the distribution of property in western Asia Minor. Members of the court aristocracy were first granted property rights by the emperors in the region and then began to buy up property from local people, both landowners and peasantry. The introduction of this new class of landowners does not appear to have had very serious consequences for the local nobility until after 1261, when many of them got into debt and began to sell off their estates. Entry into imperial service and the conversion of family estates into *pronoiai* provided a less and less adequate defence against the encroachment of the new-comers. For the peasantry the consequences of these changes were more immediate. The new landowners were not only acquiring peasant property on what seems to have been a large scale; the creation of franchises and *pronoiai* also affected the status of the peasants settled on these lands. They now owed their taxes and labour services to the holders of these grants; they became their *paroikoi* or dependent peasants. In other words, the holders of these grants acquired rights of lordship over the peasantry.

At first, this may have meant little change in their way of life. The dues and labour services which they owed their new lord were fixed by the state and cannot have been very different from those that they had previously owed to the state.[73] The new lord was normally obliged to establish his own administration,[74] but, as far as justice was concerned, it seems to have been usual for him to work through the existing village institutions.[75] The peasants' subjection to a lord brought with it one benefit in particular: they acquired a patron who

[71] Miklosich and Müller IV, pp. 115–17, 155–7, 165–9.

[72] e.g. the monastery of Lemviotissa was buying up arable land at Vari at a price of approximately 1 *hyperpyron* the *modios*, *c.* 1225–50, and in some cases paying an annual rent (*epiteleia*) as well (see ibid., pp. 191–2, 195–8, 200–1, 205).

[73] See Miklosich and Müller IV, pp. 182–3; Dölger, *Reg.* 1740.

[74] See Ahrweiler, 'Smyrne', pp. 162–3.

[75] See below, pp. 259, 263.

would support them in their quarrels with neighbouring villages and landowners. On occasions, he might represent them before the imperial administration.[76] It is also true that, as peasants settled on privileged property, they escaped much of the oppression associated with the imperial administration. There was of course a gloomier side to the picture. The dependants of a great landowner were only too ready to take advantage of his prestige to pursue their own quarrels, by force if need be. About the year 1241 the notary of a village near Smyrna used the power of his lord, the Grand *droungarios* Gavalas, to dispossess a peasant of some property he had bought.[77]

There are signs, on the other hand, that the peasantry found subjection to a lord increasingly irksome. By 1244 *paroikoi* on the Lemviotissa estates were abandoning their holdings and seeking refuge in neighbouring towns and villages.[78] In the years after the recovery of Constantinople they began to withhold rent and labour services from the monastery.[79] One example, in particular, illustrates the disquiet occasioned by the prospect of reduction to the status of a dependent peasant. In March 1242 the monk Maximos Planites, who was the head of an important local family, gave the monastery of Lemviotissa the family estate. His brother and his mother were to have a life interest in half the estate and were to pay the monastery an annual rent (*epitelesmos*) of $1\frac{1}{2}$ *hyperpyra*. They were to come under the monastery's protection, but it was stipulated that they were not to be considered *paroikoi* of the monastery. The monastery was not entitled to demand from them any of the incidents connected with dependent status.[80]

What did dependent status entail for a peasant? How did it differentiate him from other peasants? First of all, there is difficulty of terminology. *Paroikos* is a general term which simply indicated dependent status; and it has been argued that in the course of the twelfth century it came to be used

[76] Miklosich and Müller IV, pp. 41–3.

[77] Ibid., pp. 165–9. For the dating of this incident, see ibid., pp. 254–5; Dölger, *Reg.* 1772.

[78] Miklosich and Müller IV, pp. 261–2; Dölger, *Reg.* 1784.

[79] Miklosich and Müller IV, pp. 255–6; Dölger, *Reg.* 2004A.

[80] Miklosich and Müller IV, pp. 66–9.

for peasants in general. Peasants settled outside privileged property would automatically be *paroikoi* of the state (*demosiakoi paroikoi*).[81] In 1235 some of the inhabitants of Mantaia near Smyrna were so described.[82] The state was quite at liberty to grant away its rights over its *paroikoi* to the holders of franchises and *pronoiai*.[83] In 1209 an inhabitant of Mantaia called John Poleas was paying his taxes directly to the state.[84] By 1228 he had become a *paroikos* of the *pronoia*-holder Syrgares.[85]

It cannot be assumed that the status of state *paroikoi* and that of other *paroikoi* was therefore identical. In the eyes of the state there was a dividing line between peasants who paid their taxes (*telos*) to the state and those who paid a *morte* or tithe to the holders of privileged property or, under certain circumstances, to agents of the state.[86] The former held their property by hereditary right; the latter, in theory, had no hereditary rights in the land they cultivated. This belonged in full ownership (*despotikon dikaion*) to the lord who received their tithe.[87]

This ruling was made by the Emperor Michael VIII Palaiologos in 1262 apropos of a property dispute involving the monastery of St. John of Patmos. He presumably intended it to serve as a guideline for the imperial administration in the settling of disputes over peasant property that had come to form part of a privileged estate. It is unlikely that the distinction drawn in this ruling corresponded to the real condition of peasant property, but was rather a deliberate simplification.

Paroikoi continued to act as though their holdings remained their hereditary property and disposed of it freely. Their

[81] See Ostrogorskij, *Paysannerie*, pp. 20–4.
[82] Miklosich and Müller IV, p. 38, l. 29.
[83] e.g. ibid. VI, pp. 254–5.
[84] Ibid. IV, p. 121, l. 16.
[85] Ibid., p. 81, ll. 11–33.
[86] It might be argued on the basis of this ruling that state *paroikoi* were *paroikoi* paying *morte* to agents of the state, as opposed to other peasants who continued to pay *telos* to the state. Since the evidence is so fragmentary and since the distinctions drawn in the ruling are rather artificial, it would be rash to dismiss the argument out of hand. Against it is an example from the early fourteenth century which shows state *paroikoi* paying *telos* to the state (Miklosich and Müller VI, pp. 254–5).
[87] Ibid., pp. 210–14; Dölger, *Reg.* 1912.

lords appear to have accepted this situation.[88] The payment of *morte* was certainly taken during the period of exile as a sign of dependent status,[89] but there are also examples of *paroikoi* paying their lords *telos*.[90] This was a public charge and represented the basic taxation owed by a peasant household to the state.[91] It was these revenues that often went to create a franchise or a *pronoia*. *Telos* would now be paid by the peasant to his lord, rather than to the state. *Morte*, on the other hand, was a rent of a private character. There are a number of examples of peasants who had illegally sown fields belonging to the monastery of Lemviotissa being ordered to pay the monastery a *morte*.[92] It seems possible that the purpose behind the distinction drawn in the ruling between *telos* and *morte* was to emphasize that what had originally been a public charge had been converted into a private rent. It also emphasized that real rights of ownership lay not with the peasant, but with his lord.

The reality was more complicated. Peasants did not hold property only in a single village nor was it conveniently subject to a single lord. The dividing line between peasants owing taxes to the state and those settled on privileged property would not be a clear one. At first, the creation of a franchise or a *pronoia* would have had little effect on peasant society. They were outwardly fiscal devices whereby the state transferred some of its revenues to a private individual. The implications of these grants for the peasantry remained to be worked out.[93] Tradition and the organization of peasant society indicated that the peasantry would retain a considerable degree of independence. Administrative and judicial convenience demanded that the condition of the peasant and his property should be carefully regulated; and this meant defining more exactly the nature of the subjection of a *paroikos* to his lord. The result of these countervailing tendencies was

[88] See Ostrogorskij, *Paysannerie*, pp. 45–52; Ahrweiler, 'Smyrne', pp. 39–40.

[89] Miklosich and Müller IV, p. 35, l. 18, p. 39, l. 6, p. 40, l. 13.

[90] Ibid., p. 7, ll. 1–13, pp. 182–3; ibid. VI, pp. 208–10, pp. 254–5.

[91] See N. G. Svoronos, *Recherches sur le cadastre byzantin et la fiscalité aux XIe et XIIe siècles*, Paris, 1959, pp. 139–41; Ostrogorskij, *Féodalité*, pp. 310–12.

[92] Miklosich and Müller IV, p. 145, l. 18, p. 218, l. 8, p. 220, l. 1, p. 231, l. 34ff., p. 235, ll. 9–24, p. 254, l. 31.

[93] See Každan, *Agrarnye Otnošenija*, pp. 101–2.

a considerable degree of uncertainty as to the rights that a lord could exercise over his *paroikoi*.

The problem was twofold: what rights did a lord have over the person of one of his *paroikoi* and what rights did he possess over his property? Theoretically, the personal status of a *paroikos* approached serfdom. He was granted to his lord for life;[94] he was not allowed to abandon his holding;[95] and his lord could dispose of him as he liked. In May 1261 the widow of the *panhypersevastos* George Zagaromates gave one of her *paroikoi* to the monastery of Lemviotissa together with all the rights that she possessed over him through her *praktikon*.[96] This illustrates the way in which *paroikoi* came to be considered as objects of property, but it also shows that the powers which a lord possessed over his *paroikoi* were not completely arbitrary. They were laid down in the *praktikon* granted to a landowner by the imperial administration. This was an official record of the property, rights, and revenues that a lord possessed.[97]

The rights of justice that a lord possessed over his *paroikoi* are again not absolutely clear. There are certainly instances of *paroikoi* taking some quarrel before their lord;[98] and with the grant of a franchise often went the profits of justice.[99] But this did not mean that the peasantry were denied access to the imperial law courts. In July 1235 the inhabitants of the village of Potamou near Smyrna, who were *paroikoi* of the 'imperial knight' Syrgares, petitioned the Emperor John Vatatzes directly for a settlement of a dispute that they had with the monastery of Lemviotissa over the hamlet of Sphournou.[100] It is true that two years later Syrgares appeared on their behalf in the imperial court,[101] but this only seems to emphasize the confusion that existed over a peasant's judicial status. It is possible that, as individuals,

[94] Miklosich and Müller VI, p. 195, ll. 20–1.

[95] Ibid. IV, pp. 261–2; Dölger, *Reg.* 1784.

[96] Miklosich and Müller IV, p. 236, ll. 11–26.

[97] See Ostrogorskij, *Féodalité*, pp. 259ff.; Dölger, *Finanzverwaltung*, pp. 100–2; Scoronos, *Le Cadastre de Thèbes*, pp. 59–63.

[98] See Miklosich and Müller IV, pp. 80–4.

[99] See Każdan, *Agrarnye Otnošenija*, pp. 96, 98–9; Ostrogorskij in *B* 28 (1958), 237ff.

[100] Miklosich and Müller IV, p. 37, ll. 13–24.

[101] Ibid., pp. 41–3.

paroikoi were justiciable before their lord, but, as a community, continued to have access to the public courts.

As we have seen, the ruling of 1262 laid down that the holding of a *paroikos* belonged to his lord; and it was certainly the case in the thirteenth century that the holders of franchises and *pronoiai* claimed and won disputed property on the grounds that it belonged to one of their *paroikoi*.[102] Again, the legal position does not do full justice to the complexities of peasant life. As long as a *paroikos* performed his obligations to his lord, he appears to have had security of tenure. In some ways, his rights of ownership were more far-reaching than this suggests. As we have seen, a lord could not prevent his *paroikoi* buying and selling property. All he demanded was that the purchaser of property belonging to one of his *paroikoi* should assume the latter's responsibilities for it. This meant, in practice, not that the new owner became a *paroikos*, but that he paid the lord a rent called an *epiteleia*. This was paid theoretically at a rate equivalent to the property's original fiscal assessment.[103]

This due appears for the first time during the period of exile and provided an excellent instrument for adapting the fiscal rights associated with franchises and *pronoiai* to the existing structure of property.[104] At the same time, it meant that lordship became more complex. It was possible for a *paroikos* to sell off all the property he held on his lord's estates. This would presumably have meant that the lord would have had greater difficulty in exacting his rights, but sometimes it might suit a great landowner to have *paroikoi* settled outside his estates. *Paroikoi* belonging to the monastery of Lemviotissa lived in Smyrna and others belonging to Nea Mone were settled at the port of Chios. They owed their lords rent and labour services.[105] These constituted the real bond between lord and *paroikos*. In theory, it implied that *paroikoi* were entirely subject to their lord's will; in practice, they retained a considerable degree of independence.

This contrast must have been the cause of considerable

[102] Ibid., pp. 69–72, 93–4, 165–9.

[103] See H. Glykatzi, 'L'Épitéleia dans le cartulaire de Lemviotissa', *B* 24 (1954), 72–6, 87–90.

[104] See below, pp. 228–31.

[105] Miklosich and Müller IV, pp. 2–3, p. 20, ll. 22–3; ibid. V, p. 11, ll. 18–20.

friction between the lord and his peasantry. Landowners might seek the help of the administration against their recalcitrant peasantry.[106] As the ruling of 1262 shows, the government defined the legal rights that a lord had over his peasantry and their property in a way that favoured the former. Certainly, in legal terms, the condition of *paroikoi* would appear to have deteriorated in the course of the thirteenth century.

What subjection to a lord meant in real terms for a peasant during the period of exile cannot be known, for there is scarcely any evidence about the total rent that a lord received from a *paroikos*; and hardly anything is known about the nature and the number of *corvées* performed by a *paroikos* in the course of a year. The *praktika* of the fourteenth century show that they varied according to the substance of each *paroikos*. The peasantry were not a homogeneous group; there were great variations in wealth and property.[107]

An impression of these differences can be derived from the division of the peasantry, for fiscal and administrative purposes, into four classes: *zeugaratoi*, *voidatoi*, *aktemones*, and *aporoi*, depending upon the amount of land and the number of beasts that they possessed. The first two classes possessed regular holdings called *zeugaria* and *voidata* respectively. Their exact size varied. In origin, they corresponded to the amount of land that could be worked with the aid of a yoke of oxen or a single ox. The *zeugaratoi* would normally possess a yoke of oxen and the *voidatoi* a single ox. The *aktemones* and the *aporoi* did not possess regular holdings nor was it usual for them to have any plough beasts.[108]

Aktemon and *aporos* were fiscal terms. The peasants belonging to these classes are to be identified with the labourers who are frequently attested during the period of exile. Sometimes they are called labourers (*douleutai*), sometimes hired men (*misthioi*), sometimes even hired labourers (*misthioi douleutai*). They were usually *paroikoi*. During the period of exile

[106] Miklosich and Müller IV, pp. 255–6, 261–2; Dölger, *Reg.* 1784, 2004A.

[107] See Ostrogorskij, *Féodalité*, pp. 312–22; Každan, *Agrarnye Otnošenija*, pp. 170–6.

[108] See Ostrogorskij, *Paysannerie*, pp. 29–30; F. Dölger, *Byzanz und die europäische Staatenwelt*, Ettal, 1953, pp. 226–7; Oikonomidès, in *REB* 22 (1964), p. 160, ll. 17–19, pp. 169–70.

the monasteries of Lemviotissa,[109] St. John of Patmos,[110] and Nea Mone[111] all possessed hired labourers. They must have been employed to work the demesne land. In some cases an estate would be worked entirely by labourers; there would be no *paroikoi* settled there with regular holdings. Labourers may not have possessed any regular holdings on their lords' estates, but they were housed with their families and they possessed some property. They were expected to pay their lords a small money rent and to perform labour services as well.[112]

Labourers sometimes belonged to that class of peasants called 'free and unknown to the administration'.[113] These were not free peasants as opposed to *paroikoi*, but vagabonds and refugees.[114] They possessed no property and they had no settled abode. As a result, they were not inscribed in any tax registers. The prominence of this class during the period of exile must reflect the dislocation of society that followed the fall of Constantinople.[115] In 1227 Abbot Gerasimos was allowed to settle members of this class on the Lemviotissa estates;[116] and in 1260 others who were established on these estates were confirmed in the monastery's possession.[117] It would seem that, as this class of peasants was virtually outside the state's control, the government was willing to grant them to the landowners on whose estates they were settled. In this way they were brought back into the administrative framework of the state.

In the twelfth century the state kept a very careful check on the numbers of peasants settled on the estates of great landowners.[118] The open-handedness with which the

[109] Miklosich and Müller IV, p. 215, l. 1, p. 288, l. 23.

[110] Ibid. VI, pp. 182–3, 208–10; the *praktikon* of Constantine Diogenes, duke of the islands of Leros and Kalymnos, of Sept. 1254. This document is unpublished. Professor Nikos Oikonomides of the University of Montreal very kindly let me consult a transcript which he had made of it.

[111] Miklosich and Müller V, p. 11, ll. 18–26.

[112] See ibid. VI, p. 182, ll. 28–30, pp. 208–10; *praktikon* of Constantine Diogenes.

[113] Miklosich and Müller VI, pp. 179–80, 200, l. 21. See Každan, *Agrarnye Otnošenija*, pp. 134–6.

[114] Miklosich and Müller IV, pp. 222–3; Dölger, *Reg.* 1884. See Ostrogorskij, *Paysannerie*, p. 42; id., *Féodalité*, pp. 330–47.

[115] e.g. Oikonomides in *REB* 25 (1967), 125, ll. 14–15.

[116] Miklosich and Müller IV, pp. 248–9; Dölger, *Reg.* 1715.

[117] Miklosich and Müller IV, pp. 222–3; Dölger, *Reg.* 1884.

[118] e.g. Miklosich and Müller IV, pp. 317–18.

emperors of Nicaea granted away landless peasants has been taken as a sign that the control exercised by the state over the great estates was being relaxed.[119] It is not a view that can easily be accepted. The state had good reason for allowing the settlement of unspecified numbers of landless peasants on the great monastic estates. It was a way of bringing order into the countryside. It did not mean that the imperial administration did not keep a close watch on the rights that the state possessed over peasants and their property.[120] The principle that a landowner was only entitled to the number of *paroikoi* registered in his *praktikon* was not abandoned. In 1263 a list was drawn up of the peasants settled on the Patmos estates on the islands of Cos and Leros. Two reasons were given for doing this: it ensured, on the one hand, that the monastery would make no further additions to its labour force and, on the other, that the state would not deprive the monastery of any of the peasants to which it was entitled.[121]

The emperors of Nicaea kept equally strict control over the rights and revenues granted out in *pronoia*. The principle that a *pronoia* was a possession of the state and not the hereditary property of its holder was strictly maintained under the emperors of Nicaea until almost the very end of the period of exile. Despite the stubborn resistance of the heirs of Basil Vlatteros, the village of Vari which had formed his *pronoia* passed as an imperial donation to the monastery of Lemviotissa.[122] Syrgares's *pronoia* was broken up and granted out to others.[123] It is possible to trace how a *pronoia* constituted of the rights and revenues accruing from a stretch of the river Hermos near Smyrna passed from the *vestiarites* Kalegopoulos to another *vestiarites* Kadianos and finally to the *stratiotes* Michael Angelos.[124] The state's control over *pronoiai* was further strengthened during the period of exile as a result of a decision made in June 1233 by John Vatatzes's chief minister Demetrios Tornikes. This made it illegal for *paroikoi*

[119] See Ostrogorskij, *Paysannerie*, pp. 34–5.
[120] e.g. Miklosich and Müller IV, pp. 85–6.
[121] Ibid. VI, p. 215, ll. 7–10.
[122] See Miklosich and Müller IV, pp. 194–5.
[123] See Glykatzi-Ahrweiler in *B* 28 (1958), 58.
[124] See Miklosich and Müller IV, pp. 239–44, 247.

settled on a *pronoia* to alienate their property to the *pronoia*-holder; for this practice had led to the conversion of property which should have remained under the state's control into the hereditary possession of the *pronoia*-holder.[125]

Michael Palaiologos abandoned the strict control that the emperors of Nicaea had exercised over *pronoiai* and great estates. To ensure the success of his usurpation, he was forced to buy the support of the most influential sections of society. The privileges of the monasteries[126] and of the great aristocracy[127] were confirmed and extended. The principle that a *pronoia* was merely a temporary grant made by the state was replaced by the understanding that it might become the hereditary property of its holder.[128] At a period of great weakness, the government was not able to resist the mounting pressure for the relaxation of state control over landed property. This pressure was itself the consequence of the rising expectations of the army and aristocracy which grew out of the agrarian policies of the emperors of Nicaea.

In the short term, there can be little doubt that these policies were beneficial to the state. Means had to be found to support an army and an administration at a time when the revenues available to the state were limited; and a *modus vivendi* with the aristocracy had to be established. The granting out of state rights and revenues proved to be an excellent way of achieving these ends. It explains why the emperors of Nicaea were able to harness the limited resources of their state so effectively, but this state of affairs would only last as long as the imperial administration was able to maintain a degree of control over the rights and revenues that had been granted away.

The emperors of Nicaea did not initiate the policy of ceding public rights and revenues. They were only following a line of policy laid down by the emperors of the House of Komnenos, but in western Asia Minor they carried it through on a much greater scale than had ever been contemplated

[125] See ibid., pp. 198–200; Dölger, *Reg.* 1734; Ostrogorskij, *Féodalité*, pp. 65–9.

[126] See G. Rouillard, 'La Politique de Michel VIII Paléologue à l'égard des monastères', *EB* 1 (1943), 73–4.

[127] Pachymeres I, p. 97, ll. 15–18.

[128] Ibid., p. 97, ll. 18–22; Ostrogorskij, *Féodalité*, pp. 93–6.

before. Its effects on the structure of society were therefore much more far-reaching. It produced changes in society that were inimical to continuing state control of the rights and revenues that had been temporarily alienated. Landowners turned the right to collect taxes and exact labour services from the peasantry into rights of lordship over their persons and property. The great estate replaced the village as the basis of the organization of rural society. This process of interposing a new layer of authority between the state and the subject has been termed the 'feudalization' of the Byzantine state. If it has to be thought of in terms of western European feudalism, it comes much closer to the 'bastard feudalism' of the later Middle Ages than to the 'classic feudalism' of the High Middle Ages. It was essentially the rights of lordship accruing from a grant of state revenues.

The development of late Byzantine society went counter to the long-standing traditions of autocratic government. The administrative structure of the state began to change in response to the 'feudalization' of society. As more public authority came into private hands, there was less and less need for a highly developed bureaucracy; and the emperor was forced to associate the aristocracy in government. At the same time, in order to protect himself and the imperial prerogative, the emperor had to control the apparatus of government all the more closely through his own servants. This again pointed to the need for a simpler structure of the administration.

The contradiction between autocracy and an aristocratic structure of society was now brought into the heart of government. It was to be one of the chief sources of weakness of the later Byzantine Empire. The agrarian policies of the emperors of Nicaea did not create this contradiction, but their long-term effects were to exacerbate it. Ironically, these policies were to provide, in the short run, a basis for reconciling these opposing tendencies in government and society. The emperors of Nicaea gained the benefits of their policies. It was left to their successors to discover their drawbacks, for the full effect of the large-scale creation of franchises and *pronoiai* was not felt in western Asia Minor until after 1261.

Only then did the great court families come to dominate rural society. During the period of exile society remained much better balanced. The traditions of the village community and the entrenched position of the local nobility held back the advance of the great estate. This was a state of affairs that favoured reasonably effective imperial administration.

PART IV

THE CENTRAL ADMINISTRATION

INTRODUCTION. THE RESTORATION OF CENTRAL GOVERNMENT

The loss of Constantinople in 1204 entailed the loss of the central organs of government together with the administrative archives. This marks a break in Byzantine history, but not a complete break. The Nicaean administration was founded on institutions existing before 1204.

The Byzantine administrative system of the twelfth century owed its structure to the reforms of Alexios I Komnenos (1081–1118). They were characterized by a tendency to greater centralization.[1] Instead of a number of treasuries, the *vestiarion* or wardrobe became the sole central treasury. The whole of the financial administration was subordinated to the Grand Logariast,[2] while the remainder of the civil service came under the newly created office of the logothete of the *sekreta*.[3] The *sekreta* or administrative agencies provided the basic framework of the central administration. Each was responsible for a different aspect of administration, kept its own archives, and produced such imperial documents as related to its field of competence.

Outside the framework of the *sekreta* there lay what might be called the imperial 'cabinet'. Its core was the private imperial chancery at the head of which was the *protasekretis*. Its members also included the *epi tou kanikleiou*, the *mystikos*, and the *epi ton deeseon*. They were formally engaged in the production of imperial chrysobulls, but this meant in practice that they wielded great power in the government.[4]

Even closer to the emperor stood the *mesazon* or 'intermediary'. This title, first attested in the mid-eleventh century, was descriptive of a function and did not give its holder any rank in the court hierarchy. The *mesazon* is perhaps best described in the twelfth century as a kind of imperial private secretary

[1] See, in general, Ahrweiler, *Byzance et la mer*, pp. 200–5.

[2] See Dölger, *Finanzverwaltung*, pp. 15, 17–18, 26–7.

[3] See Ch. Diehl, 'Un Haut Fonctionnaire byzantin, le logothète (τῶν σεκρέτων)', *Mélanges offerts à M. Nicolas Iorga*, Paris, 1933, pp. 217–27.

[4] Dölger, *Byz. Diplomatik*, pp. 61–4.

responsible for the dispatch of the emperor's administrative business. In practice, he often acted as a chief minister.[5]

The loss of the central organs of government in 1204 was not irreparable. In the first place, the area of the Nicaean Empire was considerably smaller than that of the fallen Byzantine Empire; in the second, although the central administrative archives had been destroyed, those of the provincial administration almost certainly survived. Finally, the imperial 'cabinet' formed an adequate basis for the restoration of the central administration. This obvious administrative expedient was to leave its stamp not only on the administration of the Nicaean Empire, but also on that of the restored Byzantine Empire after 1261. The central administration lost its bureaucratic structure and came to depend ever more strictly on the person of the emperor.

It is possible to trace the steps by which Theodore I Laskaris rebuilt the central administration at Nicaea. At first, he relied very heavily upon members of his immediate family and also upon the officers of his household, such as the steward (*epi tes trapezes*)[6] and the keeper of the wardrobe (*protovestiarios*).[7] To these must be added the holders of the offices of *epi tou kanikleiou*[8] and of *mystikos*,[9] which now seem to be firmly attached to the imperial household. They are all found carrying out missions for the emperor in the provinces, laying the foundations for the restoration of central government.

This restoration must have begun soon after Theodore I Laskaris had brought the local rulers to heel. This he achieved in the course of 1205 and 1206. From June 1207 comes the earliest surviving product of the Nicaean chancery. This is an imperial rescript dealing with disputed property in the region of Smyrna.[10] The experiences of the historian

[5] See H.-G. Beck, 'Der byzantinische "Ministerpräsident"', *BZ* 48 (1955), 321–7; J. Verpeaux, 'Contribution à l'étude de l'administration byzantine: ὁ μεσάζων', *BS* 16 (1955), 270–3.

[6] Oikonomides in *REB* 25 (1967), 120, ll. 19–21.

[7] E. Miller, *Recueil des historiens des croisades. Historiens grecs II*, Paris, 1881, pp. 664–5.

[8] Wilson and Darrouzès in *REB* 26 (1968), 14, ll. 5–7. The *epi tou kanikleiou* Basil Chrysomalles is specifically mentioned here as an *oikeios* of the emperor, that is a member of the imperial household.

[9] Oikonomides in *REB* 25 (1967), 125, ll. 4–5, 17–18. The *mystikos* is described as *panoikeiotatos* to the emperor.

[10] Miklosich and Müller IV, pp. 217–18; Dölger, *Reg.* 1676.

and former Grand Logothete Niketas Choniates tend to support the view that by about the year 1207 a Nicaean government began to be firmly established. He arrived at Nicaea in 1206 expecting to find a place waiting for him at the court of Theodore Laskaris. Instead, he met with what he considered a total lack of regard for his learning and administrative experience. He was reduced, he claimed, to near starvation. In desperation, he sought the favour of a former patron, Basil Kamateros,[11] who was now the power behind the throne.[12] At first, Kamateros rebuffed him, but within a year he had become the official rhetor of the Nicaean court. At the same time, he was probably raised to the high judicial office that he held at the time of his death, which occurred about the year 1214.[13] He was also made head of the emperor's chamber.[14] Choniates's career at Nicaea appears to show that by about the year 1207 Theodore Laskaris had need of trained administrators.

Soon some permanent fiscal and judicial institutions came to be added to the rudiments of a household administration. The office of Grand Logothete, before 1204 the head of the civil service, reappears. In 1216 a dispute involving the monastery of St. Paul in Latros and the inhabitants of the town of Sampson was heard before the Grand Logothete John Strategopoulos at a tribunal held in the imperial court. Among those assisting at this tribunal was a secretary of the imperial wardrobe.[15] At about the same time, Demetrios Tornikes became Theodore Laskaris's *mesazon*.[16] The main features of the Nicaean central government now appear to be present. The *mesazon* acted as chief minister and co-ordinated the administration. There was a division between the fiscal administration, which was centred on the wardrobe, and the other aspects of the administration. Apart from the wardrobe there were no institutions distinct from the imperial court. The *sekreta* were never re-established. The civil service, such as it was, comprised the imperial secretaries who were

[11] E. Miller, op. cit, pp. 662–6.
[12] See Michael Choniates II, p. 258, ll. 3–6.
[13] See ibid. I, p. 357, l. 25; II, p. 325, ll. 13–15.
[14] Ibid. I, p. 345, ll. 28–32.
[15] Miklosich and Müller IV, pp. 290–5, esp. p. 290, ll. 10–11.
[16] Ibid. VI, pp. 176–9; Michael Choniates II, pp. 356–7.

attached to the court and possibly some members of the imperial household (*oikeioi*).

Administrative continuity between the reign of Theodore I Laskaris and that of his successor John Vatatzes was ensured by the *mesazon* Demetrios Tornikes and by Andronikos Palaiologos, who had been appointed Grand Domestic—and thus commander-in-chief of the army—by Theodore Laskaris.[17] They continued in their posts under John Vatatzes until the time of their deaths, which by a curious coincidence occurred in the same year, 1247.[18] Their deaths, following so closely upon the Nicaean conquests in Macedonia, made necessary some degree of reorganization in the central administration.[19] Other reforms were contemplated by John Vatatzes's son, Theodore II Laskaris, but essentially the central government of the Nicaean Empire continued in the mould laid down by his grandfather.

[17] Gregoras I, p. 69, ll. 11–12.
[18] Acropolites I, pp. 83–4, p. 93, ll. 10–11.
[19] Ibid., p. 91, ll. 1–5.

VIII

THE EMPEROR AND HOUSEHOLD GOVERNMENT

Care for my troops rouses me from my bed at day-break. I receive ambassadors in audience during the morning and then I inspect the army. I devote the middle of the day to my studies. Afterwards, mounted on horseback, I receive the petitions of those who have not been able to join others within the gates of the palace. In the evening I execute judgements . . . and at night busy myself with the details of the campaign.[1]

This description of how Theodore II Laskaris spent his day gives an insight into the part which the emperor played in day-to-day administration. There is little more that can be added, except that the emperors of Nicaea were—John IV Laskaris must obviously be excluded—very able men who supervised the running of their government very carefully.

They naturally supposed that the policies they formulated and the decisions they took were in the best interests of the Empire. At the same time, they must also have been influenced by various groups and individuals. Virtually nothing is known about the different factions at court, but the pressure brought to bear upon the emperor by individuals is often apparent. The people who had most influence with the emperor do not always seem to have held the highest offices. Nikephoros Blemmydes is one example; Michael Palaiologos's sister Eulogia another. Blemmydes does not appear to have represented any particular interest at court, but Eulogia collected around her a group of men who were instrumental in forwarding Michael Palaiologos's usurpation.[2]

Although the emperor was not impervious to outside pressures, he normally relied for counsel on a small picked body of advisers (*ekkritoi, logades*) drawn from the upper ranks of the court hierarchy. For much of John Vatatzes's reign this powerful inner council seems to have consisted of the *mesazon*

[1] Theodore Lascaris, p. 58, ll. 63–75.

[2] Pachymeres I, pp. 127–9, 166–7.

Demetrios Tornikes and the Grand Domestic and commander-in-chief Andronikos Palaiologos.[3]

In September 1246 John Vatatzes learnt of the death of the Bulgarian tsar. He called together his chief advisers; and it was the Grand Domestic who urged the immediate invasion of the Bulgarian territories in Macedonia.[4]

Theodore II's inner council certainly included the *protovestiarites* Karyanites,[5] his favourites the *protostrator* John Angelos[6] and the Mouzalon brothers, and from time to time George Akropolites.[7]

At times of crisis the emperor appears to have assembled the chief office-holders and generals in full court. This is what happened at the beginning of Theodore II's reign when such a council was summoned to debate what measures should be taken to counter the Bulgarian invasion of Macedonia. George Mouzalon's proposal that the emperor should immediately embark upon an expedition against the Bulgarians was accepted.[8] But at one point in the winter of 1255–6 this campaign seemed to be on the verge of disaster. Theodore called together a council consisting not only of the Byzantine generals present, but also of the commanders of the Latin and Kouman contingents. They advised him to retreat. He agreed to consider this proposal and went away to his chamber to discuss it with his closest advisers. The emperor finally came down on the side of those who wished to continue the advance.[9]

The imperial court was also called together by the emperor to act as a tribunal to hear the cases of high treason.[10] Its composition and procedure varied from occasion to occasion. It was normally constituted by the chief magistrates and commanders who happened to be present with the emperor. On at least one occasion the patriarch and the episcopal bench were also invited to attend.[11] The emperor acted as

[3] Acropolites I, p. 66, ll. 14ff.
[4] Ibid., pp. 73–4.
[5] Ibid., p. 159, ll. 19–21.
[6] Ibid., p. 160, ll. 10–15.
[7] Ibid., p. 128, ll. 19–20, pp. 134–5.
[8] Ibid., pp. 109–11; Scutariotes, p. 291, ll. 16–19.
[9] Acropolites I, pp. 120–1.
[10] Scutariotes, p. 278, ll. 6–10; Acropolites I, pp. 92–100; Blemmydes, pp. 49–50.
[11] Blemmydes, p. 49, ll. 10–16.

president, but he could delegate his authority to a panel of judges.[12] It was usual for the emperor to appoint a prosecutor, but there were occasions when Theodore II Laskaris acted as public prosecutor.[13]

As we have already seen, the imperial court in its consultative and judicial aspects was almost certainly identical with the senate. One can also see that its powers were limited. The final decision always remained with the emperor. He was not obliged to act upon its advice nor were its decisions as a court of law binding upon the emperor.[14] Essentially, it was called by the emperor to sound out opinion. On the other hand, the occasions on which it was called were fairly well defined. Trials for treason seem to have come before it as a matter of course while serious matters of foreign policy appear to have been referred to it. When the Seljuq sultan asked for Nicaean aid against his brother, Theodore II's immediate reaction was to seek the advice of a council (*boule*).[15]

The court met as a council or a tribunal wherever the emperor happened to be. Michael Palaiologos was tried for treason at Philippi in Macedonia, for example.[16] The imperial court, or at least an important part of it, accompanied the emperor on his travels and campaigns. Many of the great festivals of the year were celebrated away from the imperial palace of Nymphaion, although it was usual to return there during the winter months.[17]

The imperial court was the centre of the administration, but this produced certain difficulties after the Nicaean conquest of Macedonia. While John Vatatzes was campaigning in Europe, his son Theodore was left behind as viceroy of the Asiatic provinces.[18] When Theodore became emperor and had to campaign in Europe, he appointed his favourite George Mouzalon viceroy.[19] As viceroy Theodore appears to

[12] Acropolites I, p. 93, ll. 8–9, p. 99, ll. 6–10.

[13] Pachymeres I, p. 33, ll. 2–3. The metropolitan of Philadelphia Phokas appears to have acted as prosecutor in Michael Palaiologos's trial for treason (Acropolites I, pp. 96–7).

[14] Blemmydes, pp. 49–50.

[15] Pachymeres II, pp. 610–11.

[16] Acropolites I, p. 92, l. 26.

[17] Ibid., p. 68, ll. 1–2, p. 85, ll. 1–2, pp. 175–6; Andreeva, *Očerki*, pp. 55–60.

[18] Acropolites I, p. 67, ll. 3–10, p. 71, l. 20.

[19] Scutariotes, p. 292, ll. 3–4; Sathas VII, p. 518.

have travelled extensively through the provinces of Asia Minor.[20] The only fixed institution appears to have been the wardrobe or *vestiarion* which controlled the fiscal administration. It was not attached to the imperial court but was permanently housed in the city of Magnesia.[21]

Until the administrative reforms that Michael Palaiologos carried out when he first became emperor, the *vestiarion* remained the only distinct administrative institution. The imperial court was not divided into definite administrative departments. It is possible to see emerging a rudimentary chancery organization, but much day-to-day administrative and judicial business was simply delegated by the emperor to whomsoever happened to be at hand.[22] Such an unsystematized structure of administration clearly had its disadvantages. As Michael Palaiologos had learnt to his cost, imperial justice could be very arbitrary.[23] He therefore created a tribunal known as the imperial *sekreton* to serve as the chief organ of justice.[24]

The nucleus of the imperial court was provided by the imperial household. This consisted of the great household officers, such as the *protovestiarios*, the steward (*epi tes trapezes*), the butler (*pinkernes*), and the chamberlain (*parakoimomenos*). These offices were originally reserved for eunuchs, but since the twelfth century they had come to be held by members of the upper nobility.[25] Under the emperors of Nicaea the holders of these offices were entrusted with important military commands.[26] Beneath them came the lesser household officers and the ordinary members of the household (*oikeioi*).

Under the emperors of Nicaea the members of the imperial household came to play an essential role in administration. They provided one of the links between the central government and the provinces. They were entrusted with a variety of missions. Sometimes these appear to have involved only

[20] See Andreeva, *Očerki*, p. 101.

[21] Scutariotes, p. 286, ll. 7–8; Pachymeres I, p. 68, ll. 4–8, p. 71, ll. 8–9.

[22] Acropolites I, p. 91, ll. 1–5.

[23] Ibid., pp. 99–100.

[24] Pachymeres I, p. 92, ll. 2–8; V. Laurent, *Les Bulles métriques dans la sigillographie byzantine*, Athens, 1932, No. 723.

[25] R. Guilland, 'Fonctions et dignités des eunuques', *EB* 2 (1944), 202.

[26] See above, p. 62, below, p. 182 and n. 4.

temporary responsibilities;[27] others were of a more permanent nature. Under the Laskarids every recorded duke or governor of the theme of Thrakesion was a member of the imperial household. Even the Butler John Kantakouzenos held this office during the 1240s,[28] while another household officer, the Chamberlain Alexios Krateros, was involved in many aspects of provincial administration over a period that stretches from before 1216 to at least 1227.[29]

THE *MESAZON*

This system of government was co-ordinated and supervised for much of the period of exile by the *mesazon* Demetrios Tornikes. He came from a family of Armenian origin.[30] His father and his grandfather had been men of considerable influence in the administration of the Angeloi.[31] He was related by marriage to the Palaiologoi; and his family became one of the most powerful at Nicaea. It derived great prestige from the singular title of 'Beloved Brother of the Emperor' that John Vatatzes had bestowed upon him.[32] He was one of the central figures of the Nicaean court.

Demetrios Tornikes is described as *oikonomos ton koinon* by the historian George Akropolites.[33] This has given rise to the belief that this was the title of a new office specially created for Tornikes. It has recently been shown that it was simply a description of the function he performed in the government of the Nicaean Empire.[34] It can mean little more than 'the administrator of public affairs', in other words chief minister. It was an unofficial position and seems to have been distinguished from his role as *mesazon*.[35]

[27] See Miklosich and Müller IV, pp. 215–16; VI, pp. 201–2; Dölger, *Reg.* 1802, 1871A.

[28] Ahrweiler, 'Smyrne', pp. 144–5.

[29] Ibid., p. 140.

[30] N. Adontz, 'Les Taronites à Byzance', *B* 11 (1936), 30–44; Darrouzès in *REB* 23 (1965), 149, 152–5, 163, 165–7.

[31] His grandfather held the office of *epi tou kanikleiou* and later the office of logothete of the drome; his father held the latter office at the time of the fall of Constantinople (see Dölger, *Byz. Diplomatik*, p. 55; Darrouzès in *REB* 26 (1968), p. 96, n. 3, p. 108, n. 22).

[32] Pachymeres I, p. 64, ll. 14–17.

[33] Acropolites I, p. 90, l. 24, p. 93, l. 20.

[34] R.-J. Loenertz, 'Le Chancelier impérial à Byzance au XIVe et au XIIIe siècles', *OCP* 26 (1960), 298–9.

[35] Acropolites I, p. 66, ll. 15–16.

A *mesazon* was not necessarily chief minister. In 1259, for instance, this position was held by Andronikos Tornikes,[36] but there is absolutely nothing to suggest that he was also chief minister. On the other hand, the specific functions of the *mesazon* gave him a central role in late Byzantine administration. A key to an understanding of these functions is provided by the *dia*-formulae found on a large number of documents emanating from the imperial chancery from the twelfth century onwards.[37]

On all such documents which have been preserved in the original the formula simply consists of the word 'through' (*dia*), followed by the name of an official. For instance, the Patmos archives have preserved an original imperial order (*horismos*) of April 1244 which bears the simple formula: 'through Demetrios Tornikes'.[38] In contrast, the majority of those *dia*-formulae which bear Tornikes's name and which have been preserved in the cartulary of the monastery of Lemviotissa, run as follows: 'signed below, as is the custom for the *mesazontes*: through Demetrios Tornikes'.[39] On one occasion, an even longer formula is employed: 'notice given through Demetrios Tornikes, as is the custom of those mediating (*mesazontes*) imperial responsibilities and requirements'.[40] It is apparent that the longer *dia*-formulae preserved in the Lemviotissa cartulary are the work of a copyist anxious to make plain the significance of the *dia*-formulae.

They support Professor Dölger's contention[41] that the *dia*-formulae preserve the names of officials responsible for intervening with the emperor on behalf of petitioners. They also show that this was the *mesazon*'s specific function. As the name has always suggested, the *mesazon* acted as an intermediary between the emperor and his subjects. Demetrios Tornikes received a letter about the year 1217 from the exiled Archbishop of Athens, Michael Choniates. He is addressed as *mesazon* and implored to intervene with the Emperor Theo-

[36] Miklosich and Müller IV, p. 222.

[37] F. Dölger and J. Karayannopulos, *Byzantinische Urkundenlehre* (Handbuch der Altertumswissenschaft XII. 3.1), Munich, 1968, pp. 37–8.

[38] Miklosich and Müller VI, p. 183; Dölger, *Reg.* 1783.

[39] Miklosich and Müller IV, pp. 45, 145, 200, 220, 241, 249, 250, 284.

[40] Ibid., p. 139, ll. 6–10.

[41] F. Dölger, *Aus den Schatzkammern des Heiligen Berges*, Munich, 1948, I, p. 23, n. 4.

dore Laskaris, in the hope that the emperor might see fit to provide him with comforts to cheer his exile on the island of Keos.[42]

The *mesazon*'s role as a mediator between emperor and people gave him a central role in the government largely because of a practice that lay at the heart of late Byzantine administration, and one that presumably became more widespread with the disappearance of the administrative departments. It was normal for a person who believed himself to be wronged to petition the emperor directly, and to obtain an imperial order instructing an appropriate official of the provincial administration to examine the complaint.[43] Similarly, the emperor might be petitioned for the grant of some favour or for the confirmation of privileges, even on one occasion for the confirmation of a man's will.[44] Petitioning, as in most medieval administrations, was the usual means by which the wheels of government were set in motion.

Some of the imperial orders which were issued in response to a petition bear a *dia*-formula.[45] In 1216, for example, two monks of the monastery of St. John the Theologian on the island of Patmos brought an imperial order to the Chamberlain Alexios Krateros. It was endorsed: 'through Demetrios Tornikes', and it instructed him to hand over to the monastery an important estate.[46] A similar example concerns the Lemviotissa monastery. By a deed of 1227 the governor of Smyrna handed over to it a dependency in the city. Incorporated at the beginning of this document is an imperial order instructing him to carry this out. It too is endorsed, 'through Demetrios Tornikes'.[47] This order has also been copied separately into the cartulary. It does not bear any *dia*-formula.[48]

[42] Michael Choniates II, pp. 356–7. For the dating see G. Stadtmüller, *Michael Choniates*, p. 266.

[43] e.g. Miklosich and Müller IV, pp. 36–9; Dölger, *Reg.* 1750–1.

[44] Miklosich and Müller IV, p. 58, ll. 27–8.

[45] See Dölger, *Reg.* 1296, 1340, 1423, 1439, 1570, 1636, 1641, 1714–17, 1727, 1733, 1734, 1739, 1755, 1770, 1783, 1866, 1871, 1877, 1913A, 1935, 2121, 2131, 2208, 2512, 2519–20, 2534, 2538, 2577.

[46] Miklosich and Müller IV, pp. 176–9. For the dating of this document, see H. Glykatzi-Ahrweiler, 'Note additionelle sur la politique agraire des empereurs de Nicée', *B* 28 (1958), 135.

[47] Miklosich and Müller IV, p. 45, ll. 2–3.

[48] Ibid., pp. 43–4; Dölger, *Reg.* 1717.

The exact reason for this omission defies explanation. Possibly it was just an oversight on the part of the copyist. What it does show is that, at least in the Lemviotissa cartulary, the original endorsement of an imperial order with a *dia*-formula has not always survived. This slightly weakens the contention that, since only a small proportion of imperial documents are so endorsed, the *dia*-formula can only denote unofficial intervention on behalf of a petitioner by some official.[49]

There could certainly be unofficial intervention with the emperor. On at least two occasions, Nikephoros Blemmydes interceded with Theodore II Laskaris to obtain favours for his friends.[50] But all the evidence points to the conclusion that the position of *mesazon* was at the very least a semi-official function with reasonably well-defined duties. The presence of the *dia*-formula seems to indicate that the *mesazon* had a very important part to play in dealing with petitions presented to the emperor. He was not simply the receiver of petitions. This was the job of the *epi ton deeseon*.[51] The only real possibility is that he assisted the emperor in trying the petitions. The *dia*-formula would then indicate *either* imperial orders dictated by the *mesazon or* this in itself might mean that the petition had been tried by the *mesazon* without reference to the emperor.

The dispatch of petitions must have provided the *mesazon* with the bulk of his work, but the *dia*-formula is not simply limited to documents issued by the imperial chancery in response to petitions. It is also found on imperial legislation[52] and on treaties with foreign powers.[53] This is good evidence that the *mesazon* assisted the emperor in all aspects of his administrative work.

Demetrios Tornikes exercised very broad powers in the administration that at times appear to have gone beyond the functions of a *mesazon*. In April 1234 Tornikes sent a dispatch in his own name to a governor of Smyrna, instructing him

[49] Dölger, *Schatzkammern*, p. 23, n. 4.

[50] Theodore Lascaris, p. 303, ll. 10–13, pp. 305–6.

[51] R. Guilland, 'Etudes sur l'histoire administrative de l'Empire byzantin: le maître des requêtes. '*Ο ἐπὶ τῶν δεήσεων*', *B* 35 (1965), 99–100.

[52] Dölger, *Reg.* 1465–6.

[53] Ibid. 2026, 2104.

to hand over land from some imperial estates to the monastery of Lemviotissa. This task had originally been entrusted by the Emperor John Vatatzes to the Duke of Thrakesion John Doukas Kourtikes. He was unable to carry it out, as he was employed elsewhere on imperial business.[54] In normal circumstances, one would have expected an imperial order to have been sent to the governor of Smyrna, not a dispatch from Tornikes. It shows that at times the *mesazon* could take decisions without reference to the emperor.

The emperor also delegated judicial work to Tornikes. In the 1230s he was responsible for giving judgement in two long-standing disputes over property involving the monastery of Lemviotissa. They had already been the object of numerous petitions to the emperor by all the parties concerned. The provincial authorities were instructed to look into their complaints and, if need be, try the cases. They were not able to produce satisfactory decisions. These disputes were therefore brought before the emperor who then appointed Tornikes to hear them.

Tornikes's career shows how powerful a figure the *mesazon* could become in Byzantine government, but the office of *mesazon* was not an indispensable part of the administration. After Tornikes's death this function is not again recorded until the very end of the period of exile. Possibly John Vatatzes was unwilling to see such wide powers concentrated in the hands of another man. It is equally possible that there was nobody capable of fulfilling the exacting duties that Tornikes had carried out. His administrative responsibilities were entrusted by the emperor to 'whomsoever happened to be at hand', while his chancery duties were divided among a number of secretaries, including the historian George Akropolites.[55]

Towards the end of Vatatzes's reign Phokas, the Metropolitan of Philadelphia, seems to have acted as chief minister. He is described as the emperor's assistant and 'adviser on secular affairs'.[56] Theodore II Laskaris wrote to him at the end of his father's reign asking him to be his adviser, confidant, and minister (*oikonomos*).[57] There is no evidence that he

[54] Miklosich and Müller IV, pp. 146–50; Dölger, *Reg.* 1737.
[55] Acropolites I, p. 91, ll. 1–5. [56] Ibid., p. 97, ll. 4–7.
[57] Theodore Lascaris, p. 163, ll. 24–7.

performed the functions of the *mesazon*. His only recorded acts were to lead an embassy to Michael Angelos, the despot of Epiros, in 1252[58] and to conduct the prosecution at Michael Palaiologos's trial for treason in 1253.[59]

No *mesazon* is attested during the reign of Theodore II Laskaris, although his favourite George Mouzalon has obvious claims to be considered his chief minister.[60] The Emperor Michael Palaiologos had no obvious chief minister in the brief period before the recovery of Constantinople, yet during this time Andronikos Komnenos Tornikes and Michael Senachereim are recorded holding the position of *mesazon* simultaneously.[61] This was a practice that became increasingly common under the Palaiologoi.[62] This underlines the fact that, although the *mesazon* played a vital role in the administration, he was not necessarily chief minister.

Senachereim was appointed *protasekretis* at the beginning of Michael Palaiologos's reign. This office was specially revived for him by the emperor; it placed him at the head of the imperial tribunal.[63] He was responsible for drafting the text of the oaths which Michael Palaiologos exchanged with the young John Laskaris.[64] Such work was well outside the competence of the *protasekretis*. It is much more likely that he undertook it in his capacity of *mesazon*. The *mesazon* would normally have been present at the imperial court and he sometimes followed the emperor on his campaigns in Europe. Demetrios Tornikes accompanied John Vatatzes on his expedition in 1242 against Thessalonica.[65] There were

[58] Acropolites I, p. 82, ll. 3–6.

[59] Ibid., p. 92, l. 4, pp. 96–8.

[60] See Pachymeres I, pp. 42–3; Theodore Lascaris, pp. 267–8.

[61] Miklosich and Müller IV, p. 222; ibid. VI, pp. 201, 214; Dölger, *PARASPORA*, p. 431, n. 3; Dölger, *Reg.* 1866, 1871, 1877, 1913A.

[62] Beck in *BZ* 48 (1955), 312; Verpeaux in *BS* 16 (1955), 285.

[63] Pachymeres I, p. 92, ll. 4–8; Laurent, *Bulles métriques*, No. 723; I. Ševčenko, 'Léon Bardalès et les juges généraux ou la corruption des incorruptibles', *B* 19 (1949), 257. A Senachereim holding the office of *protasekretis* appears in a patriarchal document that has been dated to the year 1247–8 (Laurent, *Regestes*, No. 1308). Since there is no doubt that Senachereim only became *protasekretis* at the beginning of Michael Palaiologos's reign, the only possible explanations are: (1) that the document should be redated; (2) that in this document we are dealing with an officer of the patriarchal administration.

[64] Pachymeres I, p. 96, ll. 3–4.

[65] Acropolites I, p. 66, ll. 15–16.

of course occasions when the *mesazon*'s duties took him away from the imperial court. Senachereim happened to be at Nikomedeia when news reached him of the recovery of Constantinople, while the emperor, for his part, was still at the palace of Nymphaion.[66]

THE NICAEAN CHANCERY

The emperor was also attended on his travels by at least part of the Nicaean chancery. In the autumn of 1246 George Akropolites accompanied John Vatatzes on his Macedonian campaign and drew up the chrysobulls that were granted to the cities and fortresses that submitted to the Nicaean emperor.[67] Another chancery official, John Makrotos, was present with Akropolites at the trial of Michael Palaiologos, which was held at Philippi in Macedonia.[68]

No clear picture of the chancery organization of the Nicaean Empire emerges until after the death of Demetrios Tornikes. The Nicaean chancery seems to have been attached to the imperial household. There are some resemblances to the private imperial chancery that existed before 1204. The offices of *epi tou kanikleiou* and of *mystikos* which belonged to it reappear by the middle of Theodore I Laskaris's reign. But there is no evidence that the holders of these offices had yet recovered their chancery duties. As we have seen, they appear to have been involved in the re-establishment of provincial administration.[69]

This has all the appearances of a temporary expedient. The *mystikos* was to occupy an important position in the Nicaean central government. Under John Vatatzes this office was held by the monk John Mouzalon, whom George Akropolites considered one of the emperor's astutest ministers. He was one of the council appointed by John Vatatzes in 1242 to assist the Crown Prince Theodore Laskaris, who was left behind as viceroy of the Anatolian provinces while the emperor launched an attack on Thessalonica.[70] There is no reason to

[66] Pachymeres I, p. 149, ll. 6–20.

[67] Acropolites I, p. 79, ll. 1–7.

[68] Ibid., p. 99, ll. 6–9.

[69] See above, p. 148.

[70] Acropolites I, p. 67, ll. 6–9. It is possible that John Mouzalon is to be identified with the *diakonos* who combined the offices of *epi tou kanikleiou* and *mystikos* and to

suppose that the duties of the *mystikos* during the period of exile were any different from those he had exercised before 1204 and was to exercise after 1261. In other words, he was in charge of the emperor's secret correspondence; he was also responsible for protecting the interests of imperial monasteries.[71]

The *epi tou kanikleiou* was to recover his old connections with the chancery, but changes which occurred during the period of exile in the form of imperial chrysobulls must have deprived the holder of this office of the central position that he had previously occupied in the imperial chancery.

No imperial chrysobulls issued in the name of the emperors of Nicaea survive in the original before 1259. All that has survived in the original are four imperial orders (*prostagmata, horismoi*) preserved in the Patmos archives.[72] These apparently show no changes as compared with similar documents issued before 1204.[73] This is to be taken as proof of administrative continuity, at least at one level. But at another there were changes. The imperial chrysobulls issued in the first years of Michael Palaiologos's reign show some important differences when compared with those of the emperors of the twelfth century. For one thing, much greater care was taken over their production, but much more important than this was the disappearance of the 'Legimus' and the connected ἀπέλυθε-formula. Before 1204 these had been among the most solemn marks of authentification adorning an imperial chrysobull. They had also been the responsibility of the *epi tou kanikleiou*.[74] Their disappearance therefore points to fundamental changes in the organization of the

---

whom the Patriarch Germanos II addressed two homilies reproaching him for deriding the patriarch's humble origins (Lagopates, *Germanos II*, pp. 273–87). One Spanopoulos—characteristically nicknamed Saponopoulos by Theodore II—held the office of *mystikos* under that emperor (Theodore Lascaris, p. 231, ll. 24–5). In 1259 Michael Palaiologos promoted his nephew of the same name to this office (Pachymeres I, p. 109, ll. 18–20). In the list given by Pachymeres the office of *mystikos* clearly ranked fairly high in the court hierarchy, coming after the rank of *protosevastos*. This may be taken as an indication of its importance during the period of exile.

[71] Dölger, *Byz. Diplomatik*, p. 64.

[72] F. Dölger, 'Die Kaiserurkunden des Johannes-Theologos-Klosters auf Patmos', *BZ* 28 (1928), 345, 350.

[73] Dölger, *Byz. Diplomatik*, pp. 11–12.

[74] Ibid., pp. 12–14, 16–21, 25, 58–9.

chancery during the period of exile. These stemmed, on the one hand, from the rudimentary machinery of government established at the beginning of Theodore I Laskaris's reign and, on the other, from its systematization after the death of Demetrios Tornikes.

His chancery duties were divided among a number of imperial secretaries. The most notable of these were George Akropolites, John Makrotos, Joseph Mesopotamites, and his subordinate Nikephoros Alyates.[75] Akropolites and Makrotos were employed by the emperor in the preparation of the more noteworthy products of the chancery. This suggests a division of labour within the chancery, just as the subordination of Alyates to Mesopotamites points to the re-establishment of a hierarchy within departments. The division within the chancery was most probably between one department responsible for the production of imperial chrysobulls and another engaged in the preparation of day-to-day administrative documents. Perhaps this reconstruction can be pressed still further. While Akropolites and Makrotos are known to have been in close attendance upon the emperor during his campaigns in Europe, there is some reason to believe that Mesopotamites remained behind at the palace of Nymphaion.

He belonged to the circle of the Crown Prince Theodore Laskaris[76] to whom, as we have seen, the government of the Anatolian provinces was entrusted while his father was away in Europe. Like many of the Nicaean bureaucrats, he came from a family that had provided distinguished administrators before 1204.[77] There is no record that he held any specific office. His duties appear to have gone beyond simply chancery work. In August 1253 a lawsuit which had come before the imperial court at Nymphaion was sent to him for judgement.[78] He died soon afterwards.[79]

[75] Acropolites I, p. 91, ll. 2–5.

[76] Theodore Lascaris, pp. 150–8; Andreeva, *Očerki*, p. 119.

[77] e.g. Constantine Mesopotamites held the office of *epi tou kanikleiou* under Isaac II Angelos (Nicetas Choniates, p. 648, ll. 6–7). In 1195–6 he was made metropolitan of Thessalonica and with the exception of a short break at the turn of the century continued to hold this office until 1227–8 (V. Laurent, 'La Succession épiscopale de la métropole de Théssalonique dans la 1ère moitié du XIIIe siècle', *BZ* 56 (1963), 285–92).

[78] Miklosich and Müller IV, pp. 206–7, 208–9; Dölger, *Reg.* 1879.

[79] Miklosich and Müller IV, p. 208.

His subordinate Nikephoros Alyates, a member of another prominent twelfth-century administrative family,[80] was raised to the office of *epi tou kanikleiou* at the beginning of Theodore II Laskaris's reign.[81] This strongly suggests that he had succeeded Mesopotamites as the head of a section of the chancery. He was soon to experience the emperor's disfavour. He was dismissed from office and his tongue was cut out.[82] He was reinstated at the beginning of Michael Palaiologos's reign and sent on a diplomatic mission to the Sicilian court.[83]

Very little is known about George Akropolites's companion John Makrotos. About the year 1239, when Nikephoros Blemmydes wrote to him from Mount Athos, he was simply an imperial secretary.[84] George Akropolites's career in the Nicaean administration is of course much better documented. It began with his appointment as a tutor to Theodore Laskaris.[85] About the time of Tornikes's death he was raised to the office of General Logothete.[86] It was perhaps in this capacity that he drew up the chrysobulls granted in the autumn of 1246 to the cities of Macedonia that submitted to John Vatatzes.[87]

Akropolites's duties after the death of Demetrios Tornikes were not simply limited to chancery work. He was also entrusted with important diplomatic missions.[88] In the autumn of 1255 he was raised to the office of Grand Logothete by Theodore II Laskaris.[89] He was in constant attendance upon the emperor and appears to have been a member of his inner council.[90] He seems to have begun to acquire that competence in foreign affairs which characterized the office of Grand Logothete in the fourteenth century.[91] Theodore II

[80] e.g. Andronikos Alyates held the office of *epi tou kanikleiou* under Alexios III Angelos (Nicetas Choniates, p. 632, ll. 22–3).

[81] Acropolites I, p. 155, ll. 7–9; Sathas VII, p. 537, ll. 2–4.

[82] Acropolites I, p. 155, ll. 7–9.

[83] Ibid., p. 165, ll. 4–6; Dölger, *Reg.* 1862.

[84] L. G. Westerink, 'Some Unpublished Letters of Blemmydes', *BS* 12 (1951), 55.

[85] Andreeva, *Očerki*, p. 100.

[86] Acropolites II, p. vii.

[87] Ibid. I, p. 79, ll. 1–7.

[88] Ibid., p. 92, ll. 3–6; Dölger, *Reg.* 1806.

[89] Acropolites I, p. 124, ll. 17–18; Sathas VII, p. 525, l. 2. Cf. Acropolites I, p. 131, ll. 8–9.

[90] See above, p. 152.

[91] Pseudo-Kodinos, p. 174, ll. 1–7.

Laskaris entrusted him with the task of drawing up the treaty of May 1256 which he had concluded with the Bulgarian Tsar Michael Asen (1246–56).[92] A rumour that Asen refused to ratify the treaty threw the emperor into a rage. He blamed Akropolites, had him beaten and thrown into prison. A little more than a month later he recalled Akropolites, realizing that his suspicions had been unfounded. Akropolites resumed his accustomed place beside the emperor and they at once began to discuss relations with Epiros.[93] Soon afterwards, there came news of Michael Palaiologos's flight to the Seljuqs. Theodore was frightened that Palaiologos would return with a Muslim army at his back. He turned to Akropolites for advice, who tried to convince the emperor that the consequences of Palaiologos's action would not be as serious as he imagined. He thought that the most likely outcome would be that Palaiologos would seek the good offices of the Seljuq sultan in order to negotiate his safe return.[94] The emperor hastened at once to Anatolia, leaving Akropolites behind as viceroy of the Nicaean provinces in Europe.[95] The next year Akropolites was to fall into the hands of the despot of Epiros; he was not to be rescued until the late autumn of 1259. A year later we find him leading a Nicaean embassy to the Bulgarian court.[96] He continued to occupy an important position in government after the recovery of Constantinople.

As the career of George Akropolites demonstrates, the holders of high chancery offices were men of the greatest importance with wide-ranging functions. They were assisted in the dispatch of their duties by imperial secretaries. Several of these are numbered among the correspondents of Theodore II Laskaris.[97] Some of them were clearly on intimate terms with the emperor and were presumably men of influence within the administration. Their duties were not necessarily confined to chancery work. John Konstomares, an imperial secretary belonging to Theodore Laskaris's circle,[98]

[92] Acropolites I, p. 130, ll. 7–9; Dölger, *Reg.* 1833.

[93] Acropolites, pp. 130–4.

[94] Ibid., pp. 134–5.

[95] Ibid., p. 139, ll. 13–14.

[96] Ibid., p. 175, ll. 26ff.

[97] Theodore Lascaris, No. cxv, pp. 159–61, Nos. cxix–cxxii, pp. 166–71, No. cxxxv, pp. 190–1, No. cxxxvii, pp. 193–4.

[98] Ibid., p. 108, ll. 33–4, No. cxxxviii, p. 195.

was responsible for carrying out an administrative survey in the district of Smyrna in 1238 and in the next year was put in charge of the administration of this region.[99] Another imperial secretary surnamed Phrangopoulos handed over, shortly before 1235, an estate near Smyrna to the wife of a high court dignitary.[100]

The history of the Nicaean chancery provides a good example of the direction that administrative changes followed during the period of exile. There was no complete break with the past. The offices of the old imperial chancery provided an adequate basis for the restoration of the chancery. But far-reaching changes in its structure came about after 1247. These were designed to meet the particular needs of the Empire following the conquest of Thessalonica. The chancery was divided into two parts: one attached to the emperor and responsible for the imperial chrysobulls; the other probably established at the palace of Nymphaion with responsibility for the dispatch of day-to-day administration. This division, like all reconstructions based on rather meagre evidence, is slightly arbitrary. It leaves the impression that the chancery organization of the Nicaean Empire was rather rigid, whereas the most striking aspect of the Nicaean chancery was its fluidity. Its members were not just engaged in chancery work, but in all kinds of administrative activity, not least in the judicial work that came before the imperial court.

THE INSTITUTIONS OF JUSTICE

Before 1204 the central courts of law of the Byzantine Empire had naturally been housed in the city of Constantinople. They disappeared with the fall of the city and were never restored in their old form, even after 1261. But there are elements of continuity. The most obvious is to be found in the imperial office. The emperor, as the embodiment of the law, could judge all manner of cases and could also delegate his judicial authority to whomsoever he pleased. A more tenuous link is provided by the office of Grand Logothete. By the end of the twelfth century the Grand Logothete had acquired his

[99] Miklosich and Müller IV, pp. 85–6, 215, 247, 253; Dölger, *Reg.* 1763, 1767–8; Ahrweiler, 'Smyrne', pp. 159–60.

[100] Miklosich and Müller IV, p. 9, ll. 16–24, p. 232.

own law court.[101] This official seems to have preserved his judicial functions, at least during the reign of Theodore I Laskaris. In 1216 a case involving the monastery of St. Paul in Latmos and the people of the town of Sampson was heard in the imperial court before the Grand Logothete John Strategopoulos.[102] This office is not again attested until 1255 when, as we know, it was granted to George Akropolites. There is no evidence that, as Grand Logothete, he had any judicial duties.

During the period of exile the imperial court became the central judicial institution and the final court of appeal. The question arises of how one differentiates the imperial court as a court of law from its other functions. This is difficult to answer because its procedures as a court of law varied with the type of case tried, and as far as high treason is concerned no set procedures appear to have been established.

As we have seen, after the battle of Antioch in 1211 the former Emperor Alexios III Angelos fell into the hands of the Nicaeans. The members of the senate and the military commanders sought from the Emperor Theodore Laskaris the right of trying the former emperor for high treason. Their request was granted.[103] Alexios was found guilty and condemned to be blinded and imprisoned.

A rather different procedure was adopted at the most celebrated trial held under the emperors of Nicaea—Michael Palaiologos's trial for treason which took place at Philippi in the winter of 1253.[104] The emperor appointed a panel of

[101] Ibid., p. 305.

[102] Ibid., pp. 290–5.

[103] Scutariotes, p. 278, ll. 6–10.

[104] Acropolites I, pp. 92–100; Pachymeres I, pp. 21–3. Nikephoros Gregoras's account (I, p. 49, ll. 7–21) is superficial and adds nothing to those of Akropolites and Pachymeres. Akropolites was an eyewitness and his account is very detailed. Pachymeres's account differs from the former on two important points: (1) Whereas Akropolites insists that Palaiologos was suspected of treasonable relations with the Bulgarians, Pachymeres suggests that he had entered into treasonable correspondence with the despot of Epiros. Palaiologos, according to Pachymeres, was at the time governor of 'the western parts' and was willing to surrender the region under his command to the despot and hold it from him. This tallies with Akropolites's information that in the spring of 1253 the emperor appointed Palaiologos as one of the military governors of the district of Vodena in Thessaly. Treasonable connections with Epiros seem much more likely an explanation of John Vatatzes's suspicions than any such connections with the Bulgarians, especially as they apparently related to the period immediately after the conquest of Thessalonica (1246)

judges headed by Phokas, the Metropolitan of Philadelphia, and including Akropolites and Makrotos, to hear the case. The judges informed the accused that in order to prove his innocence he would have to undergo the ordeal by hot iron. They would then give their verdict on the basis of the proof offered by the ordeal. It was confidently expected that Palaiologos would be found guilty, but the trial did not go according to plan. The accused refused to undergo the ordeal. Phokas came and admitted his failure to obtain a conviction to the emperor. The case now passed into the emperor's hands. He failed to coerce the judges into bringing in a verdict condemning Palaiologos. He was himself under strong pressure from the army and his court, who were convinced that Palaiologos was innocent. The emperor reluctantly agreed that no case could be made out against him. Even so, Palaiologos was not released until he had taken a solemn oath administered by the patriarch that he would remain loyal to the emperor and his successors.

A different procedure was adopted in a trial for treason that occurred in the reign of Theodore II Laskaris. An office-holder was charged with treason on the grounds that one of his servants had slandered the emperor by suggesting that his reign would be neither long nor prosperous, and that he was the source of the slander. He denied all knowledge of the matter. The case was heard before the assembled court and army, but reinforced by the presence of the patriarch and other church dignitaries. The emperor consulted them first. They deemed that the man should be condemned to death. The members of the court and army, in their turn, agreed

---

when Palaiologos was governor of Serres. This does not of course rule out the possibility that John Vatatzes saw in the rumours connecting Palaiologos and the Bulgarians suitable evidence on which to convict Palaiologos. (2) Pachymeres does not mention the episode of the ordeal by hot iron. He limits himself to saying that the emperor did not allow Palaiologos to prove his innocence through trial by combat. He emphasizes that Palaiologos was kept in prison after the trial and was only released through the intercession of the patriarch who persuaded the emperor that oaths would be a sufficient guarantee of his loyalty. Akropolites, too, finishes his account of the whole affair by mentioning the oaths that Palaiologos was forced to take.

In its general emphasis Pachymeres's account may come nearer the truth than that of Akropolites, but there is nothing in the former that allows us to impugn the accuracy of the details provided by the latter.

with this verdict. The emperor then turned to Nikephoros Blemmydes who happened to be present and asked his opinion. Blemmydes replied that he did not believe the man to be worthy of death and recommended him to the emperor's mercy. It was probably George Mouzalon who protested that the general verdict should not thus be flaunted, but the emperor stood by Blemmydes's advice.[105]

This account of the procedures followed in trials for treason held during the period of exile is drawn from narrative sources. It is therefore instructive to compare them with the official procedure recommended to Andronikos Palaiologos by his father Michael VIII Palaiologos in the chrysobull of 1272 which defined Andronikos's powers as co-emperor.[106] He was to hold the trials of both soldiers and civilians in the presence of his councillors and to act on their advice. Cases involving higher officials were only to be heard with the consent of the great men attending him, and any judgement was to be submitted to the emperor for a final decision.

The variety of procedures adopted in trials for treason seems to have stemmed out of conflicting principles. Were such trials to go before the nobility and army, or were they to be heard by an imperial tribunal where the judges were appointed by the emperor and ordeal might be employed? A compromise seems to have been reached by Theodore II Laskaris. The opinion of the court, army, and Church was consulted, but the final judgement rested with the emperor. Blemmydes was extremely dissatisfied with this arrangement. It seemed to him to mark a break with Byzantine traditions of justice. There was no prosecutor and no testing of the evidence. The decision was bound to be arbitrary because those consulted simply gave the verdict that the emperor demanded.[107]

With the disappearance of law courts distinct from the imperial court, justice came to depend ever more closely upon the emperor. The giving of justice must have become one of his chief tasks. Theodore II Laskaris was accustomed to go out on horseback to hear the cases of those who had

[105] Blemmydes, pp. 48–50.
[106] Heisenberg, 'Palaiologenzeit', p. 40, ll. 59ff.
[107] Blemmydes, p. 49, ll. 7–10.

been unable to obtain a hearing in the imperial court.[108] This practice anticipates the cavalcade (*kavalikeuma*), which played such an important part in late Byzantine court ceremonial. A horn was sounded to signal the emperor's approach and men could hand their petitions to an official known as the *epi ton deeseon* who would, in his turn, pass them on to the emperor.[109]

Not all the cases brought before the imperial court would be examined by the emperor personally. A special tribunal might be set up,[110] as happened in the case which has already been mentioned involving the monastery of St. Paul in Latmos and the people of Sampson. The case came before the Grand Logothete John Strategopoulos. Associated with him were two judges. They were assisted by five assessors, all of whom were drawn from the ranks of the imperial administration and court nobility.[111] The judges considered the written evidence and oral testimony produced by the two parties and came to their decision on this basis.

In other similar cases a simpler procedure was adopted. The emperor would not set up a special tribunal, but would delegate judgement to a high-ranking member of the administration, such as the *mesazon* Demetrios Tornikes or Joseph Mesopotamites. Possibly such officials had recognized judicial functions, since another prominent administrator under John Vatatzes, the Grand Logariast Demetrios Karykes, is actually described as a judge; and this appears to have formed part of his official title.[112] The procedure followed in these cases was reasonably clear-cut. The official would summon both parties before him and would then come to a decision on the basis of the evidence produced. In some cases, the evi-

[108] Theodore Lascaris, p. 58, ll. 63–75.

[109] Pseudo-Kodinos, p. 173, ll. 1–15, p. 183, ll. 24–7; Heisenberg, 'Palaiologenzeit', pp. 39–40; Guilland in *B* 1965, pp. 99–100.

[110] This is described either as *τὸ ἐν τῇ βασιλικῇ αὐλῇ δικαστήριον* (Miklosich and Müller IV, p. 290) or as *τὸ τῆς βασιλείας μου βῆμα* (Wilson and Darrouzès in *REB* 1968, No. 3, p. 15, ll. 5–6).

[111] Miklosich and Müller IV, pp. 290–5. The judges were: John Strategopoulos, *sevastos* and Grand Logothete, John Angelos, the emperor's servant (*doulos*), Alexios Krateros, the emperor's servant (*doulos*). The assessors were: Michael Hyleas, *protopansevastos*, Alexios Komnenos, *eugenestatos*, Michael Chilarenos, *panhypersevastos sevastos*, Theodore Angelos, a member of the emperor's household (*oikeios*), Nicholas Kaloethos, *grammatikos* in the imperial wardrobe (*vestiarion*).

[112] Blemmydes, p. 13, l. 1, p. 55, l. 15.

dence was treated in a rather high-handed fashion. A dispute over the hamlet of Sphournou near Smyrna came before the *mesazon* Demetrios Tornikes. It was admitted that one of the parties, the 'imperial knight' Syrgares, had no rights in Sphournou, but Tornikes ordered that the property should be divided between him and his opponent, the monastery of Lemviotissa.[113] To ensure that his judgement was respected, a judge could threaten a party disobeying it with a heavy fine.[114] The final stage of the procedure was for an imperial order to be sent to the provincial authorities, instructing them to put the judgement into effect.

This *ad hoc* method of appointing judges seems to have proved more and more inadequate. One of Michael Palaiologos's first acts as emperor was to establish a permanent central tribunal, the imperial *sekreton*, under the presidency of the *protasekretis*.[115]

It is possible to reconstruct the judicial procedures followed at the Nicaean court, but it is more difficult to uncover the legal principles upon which Nicaean judges came to their decisions. A high proportion of the cases of which details survive were straightforward disputes over property. The judges were simply faced with the problem of assigning ownership on the basis of the evidence presented by the parties, but, as the case of Sphournou outlined above shows, judgement might go right against the evidence. The *mesazon* Demetrios Tornikes apparently gave no grounds for his decision in this case, but he did in another case involving the monastery of Lemviotissa, which he heard in June 1233. It concerned a long-standing quarrel which the monastery had had with an imperial *vestiarites* over the possession of some fields. Tornikes dismissed the latter's claims on the grounds that they were based on the sale of those fields by a *paroikos* to the holder of a *pronoia* that had formerly included those fields. The *paroikos* had possessed no right to alienate them in this manner, since

[113] Miklosich and Müller IV, pp. 41–2; Dölger, *Reg.* 1753.

[114] e.g. Mesopotamites threatened the villages of Mantaia with a fine of 1,000 *hyperpyra*, should they continue to molest property belonging to the monastery of Lemviotissa (Miklosich and Müller IV, pp. 206–7, 208–9, 210–11; Dölger, *Reg.* 1813, 1815, 1879).

[115] Pachymeres I, p. 92, ll. 3–8; V. Laurent, *Bulles métriques*, No. 723; Ševčenko in *B* 19 (1949), 257.

such a practice would lead to the conversion of property that should have remained under the control of the state into the hereditary possession of the *pronoia*-holder.[116]

The fall of Constantinople certainly did not prevent the transmission of the corpus of Byzantine law. An abridgement, the Synopsis Minor, may possibly date from the reign of John Vatatzes,[117] but its practical importance is very hard to gauge. There is very little sign that a formal legal education based on the study of Roman law survived.[118] The problem is that, while private law saw very little development after the early eleventh century, public law underwent far-reaching changes, but these were never assimilated to the theory of Byzantine law.[119] Consequently, the gap between the theory and the practice of law grew even wider and the formal study of law less essential. The changes in public law, like practically all legal innovations in Byzantium, were effected by means of imperial novels and chrysobulls. From the period of exile virtually no new imperial legislation has survived. John Vatatzes issued a chrysobull reviving a novel of Manuel I Komnenos, protecting church property from the exactions of imperial officials.[120] Perhaps this lack of legislation indicates that any changes in public law that occurred under the emperors of Nicaea were likely to be the result of interpretations of existing legislation.

In the field of criminal law there was one striking innovation during the period of exile. In both Epiros and the Nicaean Empire the ordeal by hot iron is found in use. It was almost certainly borrowed from the West. The obvious means of transmission were the numerous western mercenaries in Byzantine service both before and after 1204. Michael Palaiologos's trial for treason provides the most famous occasion in Byzantine history when the ordeal was employed.[121] At his trial both trial by combat and ordeal by

[116] Miklosich and Müller IV, pp. 198–200; Dölger, *Reg.* 1734; Ostrogorskij, *Féodalité*, pp. 65–9.

[117] P. Collinet, in *Cambridge Medieval History* IV, p. 722.

[118] The *protasekretis* Michael Senachereim, it is true, is said to have been learned in the laws (Pachymeres I, p. 92, ll. 5–6).

[119] H. J. Scheltema in *Cambridge Medieval History* IV, part 2, p. 72.

[120] Zepos, *Ius* I, pp. 387–9; Dölger, *Reg.* 1301, 1380, 1720.

[121] See G. Czebe, 'Studien zum Hochverratsprozesse des Michael Paläologos im Jahr 1252', *BNJ* 8 (1931), 59–98; Geanakoplos, *Michael Palaeologus*, pp. 21–6.

hot iron were used, though for different purposes. Trial by combat was employed to decide conflicting evidence.[122] This form of the ordeal may have been introduced into Byzantium before 1204, for Palaiologos claimed that by an ancient custom the emperor might allow a man accused of treason to clear himself in this way.[123]

Trial by combat was forbidden to Palaiologos. The only way in which he was to be allowed to prove his innocence was through the ordeal by hot iron. This he resolutely refused to do.[124] As we know, he was released after taking solemn oaths of loyalty to the emperor.

The ordeal by hot iron continued to be employed under Theodore II Laskaris. Men suspected of using magic to make the emperor ill were required to prove their innocence by submitting to this ordeal. They spent the three days before their ordeal in fasting and in prayer. Their hands were bound in order to prevent the application of ointments that might lessen the effect of the ordeal. The ordeal itself consisted in taking hold of a hot iron which had been blessed and in walking three paces with it. The historian George Pachymeres who has left us this description was an eyewitness of these trials and records that some actually came through the ordeal unharmed.[125] The ordeal by hot iron, as described by Pachymeres, is identical with that employed in western Europe, except in one important respect. In western Europe it was customary to bind the hands after the ordeal and not before.

What emerges most clearly from the use of the ordeal during the period of exile was the distaste with which it was viewed by the Byzantines. Even Phokas, who was in charge of Michael Palaiologos's trial, was forced to admit that it was not a Byzantine institution nor one sanctioned by ecclesiastical usage, but was of barbarian origin and unknown to the Byzantines.[126] Similarly, Demetrios Chomatianos, Archbishop of Ohrid from *c.* 1217 to 1234, pronounced that the ordeal by hot iron was fitting only for barbarians and completely

[122] Acropolites I, pp. 94–6.
[123] Pachymeres I, p. 22, ll. 1–5.
[124] Acropolites I, pp. 96–8.
[125] Pachymeres I, pp. 32–3.
[126] Acropolites I, p. 98, ll. 4–9.

outside the traditions of Byzantine law and ecclesiastical canons.[127] Its abolition by Michael Palaiologos was universally acclaimed.[128]

It was in the practice of law that contemporaries seem to have felt that the emperors of Nicaea were drifting furthest from Byzantine traditions. Both Nikephoros Blemmydes and George Pachymeres were extremely critical of the way in which trials for treason were conducted under Theodore II Laskaris.[129] It was not just that the ordeal had been introduced, but that the old judicial procedures were being abandoned. Witnesses were not brought forward; the customary oaths were not given; the accused's previous life was not taken into account, nor finally did the judges' verdict have to be unanimous. Too often, the emperor simply imposed his own verdict. This is the other side of the simplification of the machinery of government.

THE RECRUITMENT AND TRAINING OF OFFICIALS

All titles, whether of office or dignity, were included in the court hierarchy. As a result, it is difficult to discern any well-established pattern in the careers of the dignitaries of the Nicaean court. The trouble is, of course, that the careers of only a handful of these men are known in detail; and most of them were to hold some of the chief positions in the state. Very little is known of the careers of those who did not reach the chief offices of state. Even so, the impression remains that the career structure within the Nicaean administration was extremely rudimentary. The members of the imperial household and the imperial clerks provided the reservoir from which a large proportion of future office-holders were drawn.

The holders of the higher ranks of the court hierarchy do not appear to have followed any well-defined *cursus honorum*. It may be that lower down in the administration and palace services there were recognized paths of promotion. George

[127] J. B. Pitra, *Analecta sacra et classica spicilegio Solesmensi parata*, VII, Paris, 1891, No. 127, cols. 525–8 (I owe this reference to the kindness of Professor Donald Nicol, King's College, London); Zepos, *Ius* VII, pp. 531–2.

[128] Pachymeres I, p. 92, ll. 14–17. The ordeal appears to have survived in Byzantium in a purely private form (see Cantacuzenus II, pp. 171–3).

[129] Blemmydes, p. 49, ll. 7–10; Pachymeres I, p. 33, ll. 3–6.

Akropolites held the offices of Grand Logariast and General Logothete before being promoted by Theodore II Laskaris to the office of Grand Logothete, while Hagiotheodorites, the logothete of the flocks under Theodore II, was made logothete *ton oikeiakon* by Michael Palaiologos.[130] Constantine Margarites, one of Theodore's generals, was successively *tzaousios* of the imperial retinue (*taxis*), and *archon* of the imperial retinue before being made Grand *Archon* by Theodore II.[131]

The chief positions of the court hierarchy went in the main to the members of a handful of noble families. In the administration, too, many officials came from old administrative families. But recruitment, generally, was from a much wider area than an examination of the chief office-holders would suggest. Two considerations must be taken into account. The emperors of Nicaea retained control over court patronage, even if its successful exercise depended in part on their respect for the aspirations of the great noble houses. Moreover, importance within the administration did not depend exclusively upon the office or dignity held.

In the lower and middle reaches of the administration and army a career was open to talents. Foreigners were recruited into Nicaean service. Command of the Nicaean navy was briefly given to an Armenian called Geoffrey.[132] John Vatatzes welcomed a Latin called William into his service and raised him to a position in the court hierarchy.[133] Greeks from Epiros found their way into the ranks of the Nicaean administration and army. There is the example of an Epirot noble called Glavas who deserted to the Nicaeans in 1252. He was honoured with the title of *kouropalates* and towards the end of Theodore II Laskaris's reign he was entrusted with the task of securing possession of the important Black Sea port of Mesemvreia.[134] The conspirators who engineered the fall of Thessalonica in 1246 were rewarded with positions at court and in the administration. Of the leaders of the plot, one

[130] Pachymeres I, pp. 53–4, 109, ll. 21–2.

[131] Acropolites I, p. 123.

[132] Ibid., p. 59, ll. 14–21.

[133] Pachymeres II, p. 546, ll. 13–14.

[134] Acropolites I, p. 90, ll. 18–19; Pachymeres I, p. 350, ll. 8–11; Gregoras I, p. 60, ll. 19–24.

Tzyrithon was made Grand *chartoularios* and granted estates near Smyrna.[135] Another Demetrios Iatropoulos was first made governor of Philadelphia and then promoted in 1260 to the office of logothete *ton oikeiakon*.[136] Others were to hold office in the local administration of Thessalonica.[137]

The emperor's control of patronage did not simply mean that men of humble origins might be advanced in the imperial service. This did of course happen, as in the case of Constantine Margarites. He came from an Anatolian peasant family and began his career in the army of his native theme. He attracted the attention of the Emperor John Vatatzes who took him into his own service.[138] The fortunes of young men of noble birth depended upon the emperor's favour, too. Michael Palaiologos was given high command at a very early age because of the promise that the Emperor John Vatatzes discerned in him.[139] George Akropolites was a member of a noble family resident in Latin-occupied Constantinople. He was sent to the Nicaean court by his dying father and his education was entrusted to the Emperor John Vatatzes who advised him to follow an administrative career. No doubt, the emperor's—and the empress's—interest in a protégé helped Akropolites in the early stages of his career.[140]

The most spectacular example of the way imperial favour could advance a man's career is provided by the ascent of the brothers George and Andronikos Mouzalon to the top of the court hierarchy. They were not of noble birth, but they did have the advantage of having been brought up with the Crown Prince Theodore Laskaris. They entered the imperial palace as *paidopoula* or pages and became companions of the young prince.[141]

The pages played an important part in the ceremonial of

[135] Acropolites I, p. 79, ll. 26–7; Miklosich and Müller IV, pp. 215–16.

[136] Theodore Lascaris, p. 197; Pachymeres I, p. 125, ll. 1–2.

[137] e.g. Kampanos was *prokathemenos* of Thessalonica in 1262 (Dölger, *Schatzkammern*, No. 121/2).

[138] Acropolites I, p. 123, ll. 6–18.

[139] H. Grégoire, 'Imperatoris Michael Palaeologi de Vita Sua', *B* 29–30 (1959–60), 451, ll. 11–31; A. Dmitrievskij, *Opisanie liturgičeskikh rukopisej*, I, Kiev, 1895, p. 790, ll. 21–3.

[140] Acropolites I, pp. 46–7, 49–50, 62–4.

[141] Pachymeres I, pp. 23–4, 41–2.

the Byzantine court.[142] It is by no means certain that they came, as a rule, from noble families. None of those serving at the Nicaean court whose names are known was of noble birth.[143] A page might be charged with quite important missions. One of the pages of the Nicaean court was entrusted with the task of delivering a letter written by the Emperor John Vatatzes to the German Emperor Frederick II.[144] It is reasonable to suppose that service as a page at the imperial court formed an essential part of the training for an administrative career.

There were other young men at court called *archontopouloi*. They too took part in some of the court ceremonies, but they came from noble families and were often related to the emperor.[145] They were surprisingly numerous. There were at least 52 of them at the Nicaean court just before the recovery of Constantinople. They were all granted *pronoiai* at the standard rate for *archontopouloi*.[146] The *archontopouloi* were originally a regiment recruited by Alexios I Komnenos from the sons of soldiers slain in battle.[147]

At the age of about seventeen the young men who had been brought up at court had to decide whether they would take up an administrative or a military career.[148] The *archontopouloi* may well have been those preparing for a military career. It was not unknown for a young man to change careers, but, as a rule, this would only happen at the emperor's express wish.[149]

The young men whom the emperor had accepted into his household would receive their schooling at court. Those chosen at about the age of seventeen for an administrative career would be expected to go on to complete a higher

[142] Nicetas Choniates, p. 639, ll. 26–7, p. 736, ll. 28–30; Pseudo-Kodinos, p. 172, ll. 4–6, 174, ll. 16–18, 176, ll. 7–8, 191, ll. 16–19, 25–6, 192, ll. 2–4, 211, ll. 4–7, 215, ll. 1–2, 16–18, pp. 215–16, 226, ll. 8–9, 230, ll. 13–14, 232, ll. 5–9.

[143] Besides the Mouzalon brothers, two other pages are known at the Nicaean court: Valaneidiotes (Pachymeres I, p. 33, ll. 21–3) and Padyates (see note 144 below).

[144] Miklosich and Müller III, p. 72, l. 7. Cf. Theodore Lascaris, p. 230, ll. 25–6.

[145] Pseudo-Kodinos, p. 202, ll. 19–21, 212, ll. 4–14.

[146] Miklosich and Müller VI, pp. 207–8; Dölger, *Reg.* 1891.

[147] Anna Comnena VII. vii. 1–2; (ed. Leib) II, p. 108, ll. 15–28.

[148] Dmitrievskij, op. cit., p. 790, ll. 20–1; Acropolites I, p. 49, ll. 10–21.

[149] See Pachymeres I, p. 496, ll. 1–4.

education but they had to go outside the imperial court to receive it.

During the period of exile, schooling (*enkyklios paideusis* or *grammatike*) was to be had in the cities of western Anatolia and was almost certainly available to a relatively large proportion of the population. Higher education was more restricted and probably of rather low quality. Nikephoros Blemmydes was forced to go to a teacher settled in the Latin-occupied Troad to complete his higher studies.[150] Gregory of Cyprus complained about the quality of the education available at Nicaea. Its masters could teach grammar and poetry, but not the more advanced rhetoric and philosophy.[151] This charge is supported by what we know of the curriculum of the school founded by Theodore II at Nicaea. It embraced grammar, poetry, rhetoric, and philosophy (*organike*) but only one of the six pupils had progressed beyond the first part of the course.[152]

Despite the generally low standard of higher education during the period of exile, it was a period that produced a number of distinguished scholars, notably Nikephoros Blemmydes and his two pupils George Akropolites and Theodore II Laskaris. They were able to pursue advanced studies in philosophy, mathematics, and astronomy and thus helped to preserve the corpus of Byzantine learning. It was their work that provided the foundation of the revival of learning that took place after the recovery of Constantinople.[153]

The emperors of Nicaea did much to ensure the continuing vitality of Byzantine scholarship. John Vatatzes, and obviously Theodore II Laskaris, took a deep interest in education and learning. They founded libraries, patronized scholars, and had manuscripts collected and copied.[154] This to some extent compensated for the destruction of the chief institutions of higher education at Byzantium which resulted from the fall

[150] Blemmydes, pp. 4–6, p. 65, ll. 6–11.

[151] Gregory of Cyprus, pp. 181–3.

[152] Theodore Lascaris, pp. 274–5.

[153] See Andreeva, *Očerki*, pp. 128–42; P. Tannery, *Quadrivium de Georges Pachymère* (Studi e Testi, 94), The Vatican, 1940, pp. xvii–xxxiii; Hunger in *JOBG* 8 (1959), 123–37.

[154] Scutariotes, p. 291, ll. 6–11, p. 297, ll. 18–22; Blemmydes, pp. 33–4, 36–7. See Hunger in *JOBG* 8 (1959), 124–5.

of Constantinople. The emperors of Nicaea tried to preserve something of these institutions. The office of 'consul of the philosophers' survived the fall of the City. It was held before 1214 by the future patriarch Theodore Eirenikos.[155] Before 1204 the holder of this office had been the head of the faculty of philosophy in the University of Constantinople.[156] During the period of exile he seems to have supervised higher education. When Blemmydes had completed his higher studies, the Emperor John Vatatzes ordered the 'consul of the philosophers' Demetrios Karykes to examine him. Examination was viva voce. Blemmydes was asked to debate the proposition: 'Blessed is he who walks not in the counsel of the ungodly.' Needless to say, Blemmydes was perfectly satisfied that he had emerged victorious.[157]

Until Theodore II Laskaris established a school at Nicaea attached to his foundation, the Church of St. Tryphon,[158] there was no special court school. The Emperor John Vatatzes was content to send promising young men to private teachers for their higher education. George Akropolites was sent with four other young men to be taught by one Theodore Hexapterygos. After Hexapterygos's death, they went to the monastery of St. Gregory the Wonderworker near Ephesos, where they were instructed in philosophy by Nikephoros Blemmydes. The emperor provided him with special funds and supplies for the support of his pupils.[159] This system of private eduction was not particularly successful. Two of Blemmydes's pupils so disliked their teacher that they denounced him to the local authorities, accusing him of malversating property belonging to the former metropolitan of Ephesos.[160] Although Blemmydes was cleared of the charges, he refused ever again to accept pupils from the emperor.[161]

The school founded by Theodore II Laskaris at Nicaea met the need for a permanent institution of higher education to

[155] Nicephorus Callistus Xanthopulus, *Enarratio de episcopis Byzantii*, in Migne, *P.G.* 147, col. 465, ll. 11–12.

[156] F. Fuchs, *Die höheren Schulen von Konstantinopel im Mittelalter* (Byzantinisches Archiv, 8), Leipzig-Berlin, 1926, p. 50.

[157] Blemmydes, pp. 55–9. See Andreeva, *Očerki*, pp. 139–40.

[158] Scutariotes, p. 297, ll. 18–22; Theodore Lascaris, pp. 271–6.

[159] Blemmydes, p. 29, ll. 7–11.

[160] Ibid., pp. 29–30.

[161] Ibid., pp. 31–2; Theodore Lascaris, pp. 325–9, esp. p. 328, ll. 92–3.

which young men from the court could be sent for their final studies. It too was endowed with special funds and supplies. Theodore II established two chairs, one of grammar and one of rhetoric. As we have seen, the number of pupils was very small, amounting to no more than six.[162]

Higher education was absolutely essential for a successful administrative career. The small numbers of young men sent from the court at any given time to receive such an education suggests that there was no great need for a large number of trained administrators and points to the simplification of the administration. On the other hand, scholarship was much esteemed and teaching was often the prelude to a successful career. John Vatatzes was so impressed by the learning which Nikephoros Blemmydes displayed at his viva voce that he immediately took him into the administration.[163] 'The consul of the philosophers' Demetrios Karykes, who examined Blemmydes, had earlier been one of his teachers. He was much respected for his learning. He was responsible in 1234 for giving the official reply to some papal emissaries in a disputation on the procession of the Holy Ghost.[164] He also held the office of Grand Logariast. He was clearly an important figure in the Nicaean administration in the 1220s and 1230s.[165] George Akropolites is an obvious example of how important a good education was for a successful career in the Byzantine administration. The Emperor John Vatatzes himself pointed out to him that the study of philosophy would open up the path to the highest offices and honours.[166] A less obvious example is provided by the career of Michael Senachereim who became *protasekretis* and *mesazon* at the beginning of Michael Palaiologos's reign. He began his career as the holder of the chair of grammar at Theodore II Laskaris's school at Nicaea.[167]

Normally speaking, the training for an administrative or military career was concentrated in the imperial court. The emperor would take young men, usually but not always from

[162] Scutariotes, p. 297, ll. 18–22; Theodore Lascaris, pp. 271–6.

[163] Blemmydes, p. 60, ll. 1–11.

[164] Ibid., pp. 63–4.

[165] Ibid., pp. 12–13, 55, ll. 14–18.

[166] Acropolites I, p. 49, ll. 12–21.

[167] Theodore Lascaris, p. 273, ll. 46–7.

noble families, to be brought up in the imperial court. They might serve as pages or, less formally, as *archontopouloi*. Their education and future career were carefully supervised by the emperor. It was a system that helps explain the predominance of members of the great families in the chief offices of state, but it left the emperor with a firm control over the exercise of patronage.

Naturally, the emperor might recruit into his service men who had not been brought up at court. As we have seen, the emperor's servants came from very diverse backgrounds, but there are no examples from the period of exile of the emperor taking into his service men who had begun their careers in the household of some great court dignitary. This sometimes happened after 1261. When the Despot John Palaiologos died, the members of his household were taken by his brother, the Emperor Michael VIII Palaiologos, into imperial service; and some of them received important offices.[168]

Some of the great noble households must have been on a lavish scale and must have contained men of ability. Service in these households cannot have offered such great rewards or such prestige as imperial service, but it did provide a possible alternative to an education and training centred on the imperial court. The great nobles took young men into their households to serve as pages.[169] They may also have helped promising young men with their education, for it was to the grandees of the Nicaean court that Gregory of Cyprus turned in his search for somebody willing to sponsor his higher education.[170]

Connection, patronage, and status, just as in medieval Europe, were the essence of politics and administration in the later Byzantine Empire. The firm control that the emperor exercised over patronage and status must be accounted one of the most important bases of his effective authority. Yet this should not disguise the fact that, to be successful, imperial patronage had to be employed in such a way as to reconcile imperial authority and aristocratic privilege.

[168] Pachymeres I, pp. 216–17.
[169] Cf. Michael Choniates II, p. 180, ll. 11–24.
[170] Gregory of Cyprus, pp. 181–3.

IX

THE MILITARY ORGANIZATION OF THE NICAEAN EMPIRE

The Nicaean armies were a formidable force. They were rarely defeated; and their roll of victories included victory over the Seljuqs at the battle of Antioch (1211), victory over the Latins of Constantinople at the battle of Poimanenon (1224), and victory over the Franks of Achaea at the battle of Pelagonia (1259). They conquered Thrace and Macedonia and held these provinces against attacks from Epiros and Bulgaria. Their final success was of course the recovery of Constantinople in 1261.

The maintenance of these armies placed a very heavy burden in terms of men, money, and supplies upon the Nicaean Empire. This was particularly the case after the conquest of Thessalonica in 1246; and it made necessary quite important changes in the structure of command and the nature of recruitment.

The military organization of the Nicaean Empire owed much, as one would expect, to Theodore I Laskaris.[1] He tried as far as possible to restore the military organization that had existed in the twelfth century. He relied very heavily on foreign troops. At the battle of Antioch Latin mercenaries formed nearly half the Nicaean army. They were wiped out almost to a man in the battle.[2] Three years later, in 1214, Theodore's army was said to consist of Germans, Turks, Armenians, and Latins from Constantinople.[3]

At the beginning of Theodore's reign command was entrusted in the majority of cases to his immediate relatives,[4] but the emperor took over personal command of his armies

[1] Scutariotes, p. 282, ll. 10–12.

[2] Acropolites I, p. 16, ll. 6–8, 16–20; Gregoras I, p. 18, ll. 17–18, p. 19, ll. 24–5.

[3] Heisenberg, 'Neue Quellen' III, p. 9, ll. 2–5, 10, 19. Cf. ibid. II, p. 37, ll. 15–31.

[4] See above, p. 62. The only exception would seem to be one Dermokaites (Acropolites I, p. 29, ll. 4–5; cf. Miklosich and Müller IV, p. 294).

during the most crucial campaigns. He was in command at the Battle of Antioch, and he led the expedition which finally secured Paphlagonia for the Nicaean Empire in the autumn of 1214.[5]

By the end of his reign the office of Grand Domestic had reappeared. Since the reforms of Alexios I Komnenos at the end of the eleventh century the holder of this office had been the commander-in-chief of the Byzantine armies with over-all responsibility for the military organization of the Empire.[6] Theodore I Laskaris appointed to this office Andronikos Palaiologos, the father of the future emperor Michael VIII Palaiologos.[7]

Andronikos Palaiologos continued to hold this office until his death in 1247. He led the first Nicaean expedition against Rhodes in 1233[8] and was in command of both Nicaean expeditions against Thessalonica. At the conclusion of the successful campaign of 1246 he was left at Thessalonica as viceroy of the newly conquered provinces.[9]

Under the command of the Grand Domestic Andronikos Palaiologos came the commanders of the various units that went to make up the Nicaean field army. They came from the aristocracy and held high court offices and dignities. For example, during the campaign of 1242 against Thessalonica they included the *protovestiarios* Alexios Raoul, the Steward (*epi tes trapezes*) Nikephoros Tarchaneiotes, the *protosevastos* Theodore Kontostephanos, and the Grand *chartoularios* John Petraliphas.[10]

Naturally enough, not every expedition was entrusted to the command of the Grand Domestic at this time. The Nicaean forces sent by John Vatatzes in 1225 to secure possession of the city of Adrianople were led by a member of the Kamytzes family and the *protostrator* John Ises.[11] The *protostrator* was theoretically the Grand Domestic's deputy.[12] The

[5] Heisenberg, 'Neue Quellen' III, pp. 25–6.
[6] See R. Guilland, 'Le Grand Domésticat à Byzance', *EO* 37 (1938), 53–64.
[7] Gregoras I, p. 69, ll. 11–12.
[8] Acropolites I, p. 45, ll. 23–4.
[9] Ibid., p. 66, ll. 16–18, pp. 83–4.
[10] Ibid., p. 66, ll. 18–20.
[11] Acropolites I, pp. 38–41.
[12] Pseudo-Kodinos, p. 168, ll. 1–27. Cf. ibid., p. 173, ll. 16–29.

Nicaean army which attempted to conquer Crete in 1234 was commanded by a man called Kalothetos.[13]

After Andronikos Palaiologos's death the emperor did not appoint a new Grand Domestic; command was therefore divided among a number of generals. The reason for this may have been similar to those that persuaded John Vatatzes to leave the position of *mesazon* unfilled after the death of Tornikes. He was perhaps reluctant to allow power within the state to be concentrated in so few hands. Also the defence of the newly conquered provinces in Europe required a more flexible system of command. On the one occasion in the last years of John Vatatzes's reign that the bulk of the Nicaean field army was brought together to face the Epirot forces, over-all command was entrusted to the Steward Nikephoros Tarchaneiotes, who was temporarily invested with the powers of the Grand Domestic.[14] He may have been officially promoted to this office soon afterwards.[15]

A new generation of commanders appears on the scene at this time, men such as Michael Palaiologos, John Makrenos, Alexios Strategopoulos, and Goudeles Tyrannos.[16] They belonged to noble houses, but had not yet been raised to office, with the exception of Michael Palaiologos who had been made Grand Constable before the end of John Vatatzes's reign.[17] Of the previous generation the *protovestiarios* Alexios Raoul continued to hold command.[18]

The generals who were prominent in the last years of John Vatatzes's reign did not long enjoy the favour of his son Theodore II Laskaris. The new emperor took over command of the Nicaean armies during the two-year campaign against the Bulgarians. The office of Grand Domestic was held in

[13] Tafel and Thomas II, p. 325, ll. 17–18. He is possibly to be identified with a certain Domestic of the Schools called Kalothetos who was a correspondent of Theodore II Laskaris (Theodore Lascaris, No. cxxxviii, p. 196). Theodore is not able to disguise how much he dislikes the man.

[14] Acropolites I, p. 89, ll. 15–16.

[15] Ibid., p. 55, ll. 15–17; Pachymeres I, p. 34, l. 1, p. 127, ll. 17–20. He is probably to be identified with the Grand Domestic of the Imperial Table mentioned in an epitaph composed by Manuel Philes (Philes, No. 88, pp. 125–6, ll. 8–9; see Nicol, *Kantakouzenos*, pp. 138–40).

[16] Acropolites I, p. 90, ll. 6–7. Makrenos appears again in 1262 with the title of *parakoimomenos* as one of the Byzantine commanders in the Peloponnese (Pachymeres I, pp. 206–7). On Goudeles Tyrannos, see Ahrweiler, 'Smyrne', p. 170.

[17] Acropolites I, p. 134, ll. 10–12.

[18] Ibid., p. 92, ll. 15–21.

turn by the brothers George and Andronikos Mouzalon, but neither appears to have been given military command.[19]

At the end of Theodore's reign command of the main field army in Asia Minor was entrusted to the *protovestiarites* Karyanites,[20] while the *protostrator* John Angelos was placed in command of the Nicaean forces in Europe.[21] These appointments were made by Theodore II Laskaris on his death-bed and formed part of the measures he took to ensure the peaceful succession of his son. They also met one of the most serious military problems facing the emperors of Nicaea. This was the increasing difficulty they had in co-ordinating the defence of Asia Minor with the occupation of Macedonia.

Theodore II Laskaris was made aware of other weaknesses in the military organization of his Empire right at the very beginning of his reign. There was a lack of trained troops. The force that he led against the Bulgarians in the winter of 1254/5 was got together very hastily and was recruited as he marched towards the enemy.[22] Not all by any means were trained soldiers. During his second campaign against the Bulgarians he drafted his huntsmen into the field army.[23] At the end of his reign he had to send a detachment of levies to reinforce the Nicaean defences in Europe.[24]

To remedy these deficiencies Theodore undertook a far-reaching reorganization of the army. It is extremely doubtful that he lived to see all his plans carried out. Their completion was left to Michael Palaiologos. In Theodore's eyes, the chief weakness of the Nicaean army was its heavy reliance upon foreigners, especially Latin mercenaries. He objected to the vast sums of money that had to be expended upon their wages. He wanted instead to build up an army that was recruited wholly from his own subjects.[25] To this end, he reduced the privileges and the wages of the western mercenaries.[26] But there was much more to his military reforms than simply this, as can be seen from his creation of two new

[19] Scutariotes, p. 291, ll. 16–19; Acropolites I, p. 124, ll. 4–8.
[20] Acropolites I, pp. 159–60. [21] Ibid., p. 160, ll. 3–15.
[22] Ibid., p. 111, ll. 3–7.
[23] Ibid., pp. 124–5.
[24] Ibid., pp. 146–7.
[25] Theodore Lascaris, pp. 58–9.
[26] Pachymeres I, p. 54, ll. 18–20.

military offices, those of the Grand Stratopedarch and of the Grand Archon. The former was specially created for his favourite George Mouzalon in the autumn of 1255.[27] The holder of this office was responsible for the commissariat.[28] With the great increase in the scale of Nicaean military operations since 1242 it must have become essential for the organization of supplies to be overhauled and put under the control of a single official. There are grounds for supposing that Mouzalon was entrusted with responsibility for overseeing Theodore Laskaris's military reforms. It was he who assisted the emperor in the measures taken against the Latin mercenaries.[29]

The creation of the other new office, that of Grand Archon, appears to be connected with a reorganization of the command of the imperial retinue. This body formed the nucleus of the field army. At the beginning of his reign Theodore Laskaris appointed Constantine Margarites to the new post of *archon* of the imperial retinue (*allagion* or *taxis*). Soon afterwards, he was promoted by the emperor to the new office of Grand Archon.[30] It is not likely that this gave him new duties; it was simply a means of advancing him in the court hierarchy.

Margarites was among the most prominent commanders during Theodore Laskaris's first campaign against the Bulgarians. As *archon* of the imperial retinue and later Grand Archon, he would have been the effective military commander of the imperial retinue. Some of the subordinate commands of the imperial retinue, for instance, the posts of *allagator* and Grand *tzaousios*,[31] are attested during the period

[27] Acropolites I, p. 124, ll. 4–7; Andreeva, *Očerki*, p. 36.

[28] Pseudo-Kodinos, p. 174, ll. 10–13. See R. Guilland, 'Études sur l'histoire administrative de l'Empire byzantin: le stratopédarque et le grand stratopédarque', *BZ* 46 (1953), 63–90.

[29] Pachymeres I, pp. 54–5.

[30] Acropolites I, p. 122, ll. 3–4, p. 123, ll. 6–18. *Allagion* was used at least by the beginning of Michael Palaiologos's reign to mean a regiment of the field army, the equivalent of the earlier *tagma* (Pachymeres I, p. 310, l. 4; Heisenberg, 'Palaiologenzeit', pp. 40–1; Miklosich and Müller IV, p. 179, ll. 1–3; Pseudo-Kodinos, p. 187, ll. 6–8). *Taxis* has very many different usages: it could mean, for instance, the hierarchy of the imperial court, but here it is clearly the equivalent of the term *syntaxis* which is used by the Pseudo-Kodinos to mean the imperial retinue (Pseudo-Kodinos, p. 175, ll. 7–11, p. 182, ll. 18–21, p. 185, ll. 1–14, p. 196, ll. 17–28). That *allagion* and *taxis* could be used interchangeably is proof that the imperial retinue had a military as well as a ceremonial function.

[31] See Guilland in *REB* 18 (1960), 85–6.

of exile. In fact, Margarites held the latter post at the beginning of his career in the imperial service.[32]

The regiments of the Vardariots and the Varangians, which were so prominent in the Byzantine armies of the eleventh and twelfth centuries, were attached to the retinue of the emperors of Nicaea. The Vardariots, who were under the command of a *primmikerios*, maintained order in the imperial camp.[33] The Varangians had special responsibility for guarding the imperial treasury at Magnesia,[34] but at least some of them accompanied the emperor on his travels.[35]

In the mid-fourteenth century the imperial retinue was commanded, at least in theory, by the Grand *primmikerios.*[36] This office was held during the period of exile by Constantine Tornikes, the son of the *mesazon.* He was appointed to this office by John Vatatzes and was given military command, but in the spring of 1255 he was dismissed both from his command and from office by Theodore II Laskaris for incompetence and cowardice.[37] He was replaced in office by John Angelos, who was also entrusted with a military command,[38] but the commands they held, as Grand *primmikerios*, were of forces garrisoning strategic points in Macedonia, not of those belonging to the imperial retinue. On the other hand, as we shall see, their troops were almost certainly detachments of the field army.

A very important section of the Nicaean field army consisted of foreigners. The most prominent of these were the Latin mercenaries. They are always found in close attendance upon the emperor, and were presumably loosely attached to the imperial retinue. They possessed considerable political power: their indignation was one of the factors which led to Michael Palaiologos's acquittal on a charge of high treason, and they were consulted in the autumn of 1258 over the choice of a new regent. They came under the command of the Grand Constable, an office which seems to have been created by

[32] Acropolites I, p. 123, ll. 6–18.
[33] Ibid., p. 131, ll. 26–8.
[34] Pachymeres I, p. 71, ll. 9–12.
[35] Ibid., p. 103, ll. 5–8.
[36] Pseudo-Kodinos, p. 175, ll. 7–11.
[37] Acropolites I, pp. 113–14; Theodore Lascaris, p. 252.
[38] Acropolites I, p. 115, ll. 5–7, p. 124, ll. 9–10.

John Vatatzes for Michael Palaiologos.[39] The effect would have been to integrate the Latin mercenaries more closely within the military organization of the Empire. They were paid wages, but some of them, who are described as imperial liege knights (*kavallarioi*), held *pronoiai*.[40] There can be no doubt that the Latin mercenaries served as heavy cavalry. They were recruited in the main from Constantinople,[41] but they also came from the Venetian territories in the Levant[42] and possibly also from the Crusader states.[43]

Another foreign element in the Nicaean field army was the corps of Kouman troops, known as the *skythikon*. They too were consulted over the choice of a new regent in the autumn of 1258.[44] They were recruited from the ten thousand Koumans settled by John Vatatzes in Thrace and Asia Minor in 1241.[45] This settlement provided the Empire with much-needed man-power at a crucial juncture in its history. Kouman troops featured prominently in the Nicaean campaigns in Europe and played a distinguished part in the surprise attack that restored Constantinople to the Empire.[46] How they were organized is difficult to discover. They retained their tribal customs and social structure.[47] Some of their chiefs were taken into imperial service and prospered. At least one noble Byzantine family of the Palaiologan era was descended from a Kouman chieftain.[48] One of Theodore II Laskaris's trusted servants was a Kouman named Kleopas. He was placed in joint command of a Nicaean army.[49] On the other hand, the Koumans' loyalty was sometimes doubtful. In 1256 those

[39] Acropolites I, p. 134, ll. 10–12; Pachymeres I, p. 21, ll. 1–5, p. 54, ll. 15–16; Pseudo-Kodinos, p. 175, ll. 12–14. See R. Guilland, 'Le Grand Connétable', *B* 19 (1949), 99–111.

[40] Pachymeres I, p. 54, ll. 18–20; Ahrweiler, 'Smyrne', pp. 23–4.

[41] Heisenberg, 'Neue Quellen' II, p. 37, ll. 15–31; ibid. III, p. 9, ll. 2–5, 10, 19.

[42] Tafel and Thomas II, p. 207, ll. 20–1.

[43] See *Registres de Grégoire IX*, ed. L. Auray, Paris, 1896–1955, II, No. 4156.

[44] Acropolites I, p. 158, ll. 18–20.

[45] Ibid., p. 65, ll. 16–20; Gregoras I, p. 37, ll. 4–9.

[46] Pachymeres I, p. 86, l. 2, pp. 137–8, 140–1, p. 143, ll. 9–12; Acropolites I, p. 66, l. 12.

[47] See Jean, Sire de Joinville, *L'Histoire de St. Louis*, ed. Natalis de Wailly, Paris, 1867, pp. 330–2.

[48] See above, p. 105.

[49] Scutariotes, p. 293, ll. 10–17; Theodore Lascaris, p. 259.

settled in Macedonia, numbering some four thousand, deserted to the Bulgarians and inflicted a crushing defeat on a Nicaean army near Didymoteichos.[50] In this battle their use of the bow enabled them to mow down the Nicaean troops from a distance. It was their skill as archers that made them particularly valuable for the Nicaean army. The Koumans do not seem to have had a special commander; small detachments of Koumans, numbering perhaps 300 men, were sometimes distributed among various commanders.[51]

The Turks only begin to form an important element in the Nicaean armies after Michael Palaiologos's return from exile among the Seljuqs.[52] There was an important contingent of them at the battle of Pelagonia where they were almost certainly commanded by Nikephoros Rimpsas, a Turk who had been converted to Christianity.[53]

In the course of Michael Palaiologos's reign the organization of the Byzantine field army assumed a much clearer shape. Its nucleus was provided by the imperial retinue together with the *latinikon* and the *skythikon*. But other regiments (*allagia*) were recruited from both the European and the Anatolian provinces of the Empire. At the same time, troops from the field army were stationed in the cities of the European provinces of the Empire. They were known as *megaloallagitai*.[54] In the early fourteenth century the *megalon allagion* of Thessalonica is recorded as well as that of Hierrisos in the Chalkidike.[55]

Two developments are involved here, both of which can be traced back to the period of the Nicaean Empire. On the one hand, provincial troops were drafted into the field army; on the other, units of the field army were used to garrison the strategic centres of Thrace and Macedonia. This can be traced back to the earliest stage of the Nicaean conquest. As early as 1237 the fortress of Tzouroulon, one of the keys to the control of Thrace, was put under the command of the

[50] Acropolites I, pp. 125–6.
[51] e.g. ibid., p. 139, ll. 6–7.
[52] Ibid., p. 148, ll. 4–19.
[53] Ibid., pp. 168–9, 170–1. Cf. Pachymeres I, p. 329, ll. 1–2.
[54] Pachymeres I, p. 310, ll. 2–11; Pseudo-Kodinos, p. 187, ll. 4–8, p. 196, ll. 17–28.
[55] Dölger, *Schatzkammern*, No. 50, l. 4, Nos. 66–7, ll. 452–3.

Steward Nikephoros Tarchaneiotes.[56] He was succeeded as governor by another prominent Nicaean commander, John Petraliphas.[57] This process becomes much clearer after the conquest of Thessalonica in 1246. For example, in 1252 Michael Palaiologos and the *protovestiarios* Alexios Raoul were left in command of units of the field army (*stratopeda*) garrisoning the fortress of Vodena in Macedonia.[58] At the beginning of Theodore II Laskaris's reign Alexios Strategopoulos and the Grand *primmikerios* Constantine Tornikes were commanding a detachment of the field army quartered at Serres. They were ordered in the spring of 1255 to unite their force with the main field army.[59] At the end of this campaign Constantine Margarites and the emperor's uncle Manuel Laskaris were left behind by the emperor with a body of troops from the field army to garrison Didymoteichos and to protect Thrace, while the emperor returned to Asia Minor.[60] In the autumn of 1256, when the emperor again returned to Asia Minor, he made careful dispositions for the defence of the frontier of his European provinces against the Greeks of Epiros. Detachments of the field army, including Paphlagonians and Koumans, were stationed at Thessalonica under the command of the emperor's uncle Michael Laskaris.[61] It is not absolutely certain that the other commanders appointed at this time by Theodore Laskaris were also given detachments of the field army. The *skouterios* Xyleas, for instance, was made governor of the fortress of Prilep and commander of the forces stationed around there.[62] These might have come from the field army or they might have been purely local forces.

On the other hand, the distinction between local forces and the field army was becoming blurred. It is in Theodore Laskaris's reign that one first sees provincial troops being drafted into the field army. Paphlagonians played an important part in the defence of the European provinces against the Epirots

[56] Acropolites I, pp. 55–6.
[57] Ibid., pp. 58–9.
[58] Ibid., p. 92, ll. 14–19. The term '*stratopedon*' was used consistently by George Akropolites to mean a unit of the field army.
[59] Ibid., p. 114, ll. 2–6.
[60] Ibid., p. 123, ll. 4–19.
[61] Ibid., p. 139, ll. 2–14.
[62] Ibid.

in the closing years of Theodore Laskaris's reign. They were held in high regard for their valour and discipline.[63] Archers from the Anatolian frontier fought at the battle of Pelagonia[64] and took part in the siege of Galata in 1260.[65] In the period after the recovery of Constantinople archers drawn from the Anatolian march of Magedon played a prominent part in the Byzantine campaigns in the Peloponnese.[66] Not all the provincial troops were of the same high quality as the Paphlagonians. There was always a danger that the local forces in the European provinces would desert either to the Bulgarians or to the Epirots.[67] When in 1257 Michael Palaiologos was sent to reinforce the Nicaean commanders in Europe, he was given a body of troops recruited in Macedonia. They were described as very poorly trained.[68] The policy of drafting provincial troops into the Nicaean field army was obviously an expedient forced upon Theodore Laskaris by the critical situation existing in the European provinces. It may also have been part of his declared policy of building an army recruited entirely from his own subjects.

It is of course difficult to estimate the size of the Nicaean field army. Towards the end of the period of exile the individual units seem to have varied in strength from about 300 to 500 men.[69] The only reliable figure for the total size of the Nicaean field army is that of 2,000 given as the number of Nicaean troops at the battle of Antioch in 1211. No fewer than 800 of these were Latin mercenaries.[70] The very modesty of these figures provides strong grounds for believing them to be accurate. By the end of the period of exile the Nicaean forces must have been considerably larger than this.[71] After 1261 Michael Palaiologos was putting very large forces into the

[63] Ibid., p. 139, l. 6, p. 147, ll. 22–3, p. 148, l. 11, p. 161, ll. 6–7.

[64] Ibid., p. 169, ll. 3–5.

[65] Pachymeres I, p. 122, ll. 11–12.

[66] Ibid., p. 205, ll. 15–16, p. 220, ll. 6–10, p. 310, l. 10.

[67] e.g. Acropolites I, p. 114, ll. 22–3.

[68] Ibid., p. 145, l. 4.

[69] Ibid., p. 139, ll. 5–7, p. 144, ll. 5–10, pp. 147–8.

[70] Ibid., p. 116, ll. 6–8, 16–20; Gregoras I, p. 18, ll. 17–18, pp. 19–20.

[71] There are no reliable figures for the total size of the Nicaean forces at the battle of Pelagonia. There is, however, a tradition preserved in the Chronicle of the Morea (ed. Kalonaros, ll. 3696–3711) that they comprised 27 *allagia*. Reckoning on 400 to 500 men to the *allagion* this gives a total of 10,800 to 13,500 men.

field. The army which he sent to the Peloponnese in 1263 was no less than 6,000 strong;[72] and, at least on paper, the imperial retinue alone consisted of 6,000 men, divided into twelve units of 500, each with its own banner.[73]

Under Michael Palaiologos the normal means of providing for the soldiers of the field army was by grants of *pronoiai*.[74] There were *pronoia*-holders in the Nicaean army from the beginning of Theodore I Laskaris's reign. The *vestiarites* Basil Vlatteros, who was serving under the emperor's brother Alexios, held a valuable *pronoia* in the neighbourhood of Smyrna as early as 1207.[75] At this time a *vestiarites* was a high-ranking officer;[76] and it is no surprise that Vlatteros should have been granted a *pronoia*. There was a very great extension of the *pronoia* system under John Vatatzes.[77] The grants were not of uniform value. Many seem to have provided rather modest revenues.[78] It was these variations in the value of the *pronoia* that made it such an effective means of financing the army.

It has been suggested that holders of *pronoiai* were obliged to furnish a certain number of followers for the field army,[79] but this view seems to have little support in the sources and assumes that all *pronoiai* produced large revenues. This is not to say that the great men of the Empire did not have their own households and retinue. Some retainers must have followed their lords on campaign, but there is no reason to suppose that, like the *bucellarii* of the early Empire, they formed a significant proportion of the army. The soldiers of the Nicaean field army were certainly accompanied on campaign by servants who were paid wages. They were popularly known as *tzouloukonai*. They were camp followers who hoped to make their fortunes out of the pickings of war. Only in exceptional circumstances were they called upon to fight. In the autumn of 1246 John Vatatzes encouraged them to storm

[72] Ostrogorsky, *Byzantine State*, p. 483.

[73] Pseudo-Kodinos, p. 196, ll. 17–21.

[74] Pachymeres I, p. 55, l. 18, p. 92, ll. 9–10, p. 97, ll. 18–22; Heisenberg, 'Palaiologenzeit', pp. 40–1.

[75] Miklosich and Müller IV, pp. 217–18; Dölger, *Reg.*, No. 1676.

[76] Anna Comnena IV, iv, 3; (ed. Leib) I, p. 152, ll. 1–2.

[77] Scutariotes, p. 286, ll. 19–22.

[78] See above, pp. 125–6.

[79] See I. Ševčenko, 'On the Preface to a Praktikon by Alyates', *JOBG* 17 (1968), 65–72.

the unfortified lower city of Serres. They were very poorly armed.[80] Thus *pronoiai*-holders were accompanied on campaign by servants, but these could hardly be described as soldiers; and there is no reason to suppose that these were furnished as a condition of holding a *pronoia*.

The revenues that a soldier of the field army received from his *pronoia* were supplemented by wages. These were paid in kind (*siteresia*).[81] Possibly he would have received money payments (*rogai*) as well. Shortly before 1261 we hear of an inspection being carried out of the provisions (*siteresion*) stored for the imperial army at a place called Hagios Kosmas, which was probably on the island of Cos.[82] The official responsible for this had very wide powers: he was able to order a junior official to carry out a fiscal survey of the whole of the island of Cos.

The reforms of Theodore II Laskaris and the Nicaean conquest of Thrace and Macedonia tended to blur the distinctions between the field army and the provincial armies. The armies of the themes were restored by the emperors of the house of Komnenos. Manuel Komnenos created the theme of Neokastra to defend western Asia Minor against Turkish raids.[83] The army of this theme was still in existence under the emperors of Nicaea. Constantine Margarites began his career by serving in its ranks. No other army of an Anatolian theme is attested during the period of exile, but there is a strong presumption that, if the army of the theme of Neokastra continued to exist, the same would be true of the armies of the other Anatolian themes.

There is a dearth of evidence about the organization of the armies of the themes under the emperors of Nicaea. They would have come under the command of the duke or governor of the theme and the stratopedarch of the theme would have had a special responsibility for their organization.[84]

In Asia Minor the main task of these armies seems to have been garrisoning the cities and fortresses. The captains of the fortresses of the theme of the Optimates came under the

[80] Acropolites I, p. 75, ll. 1–10.
[81] Ibid., p. 53, ll. 13–16; Pachymeres I, p. 97, l. 22.
[82] Miklosich and Müller VI, pp. 208–10.
[83] Nicetas Choniates, pp. 194–5; Ahrweiler, 'Smyrne', pp. 123–30.
[84] See below, pp. 252, 255.

command of Michael Palaiologos who was governor of this theme in the opening years of Theodore II Laskaris's reign.[85] The captains of fortresses were known as *kastrophylakes*. They were not only appointed to local fortresses in Anatolia, Thrace, and Macedonia, but also to the great fortress cities of the Empire, such as Smyrna. They had an important role to play in local administration.[86]

The soldiers of the garrison were commanded by a *tzaousios* who was appointed by the emperor, but who presumably came under the orders of the *kastrophylax*.[87] During his service in the army of the theme of Neokastra Margarites attained the rank of *tzaousios*.[88]

The defence of the Anatolian frontier was one of John Vatatzes's main concerns. He established villages close to the fortresses in order that they should be properly supplied with foodstuffs and money.[89] When he heard of the Mongol invasion of the Seljuq territories in 1243 he ordered supplies of corn to be stored in each fortress for years in advance, while large quantities of arms were got together and carefully registered.[90]

The fortresses were garrisoned by soldiers recruited from those known as 'foreigners and free', that is people not registered as tax-payers. It was stipulated that these soldiers should not be *paroikoi*. They were each given full possession of abandoned plots of land in the neighbourhood of the fortresses.[91] The system of peasant soldiers had clearly not completely disappeared. Constantine Margarites came from a peasant family.[92]

[85] Acropolites I, pp. 134–5; Pachymeres I, p. 24, ll. 15–16.

[86] See below, pp. 266–8.

[87] Sathas VI, p. 647, ll. 16–26.

[88] Acropolites I, p. 123, ll. 9–11.

[89] Pachymeres I, p. 69, ll. 5–11.

[90] Ibid., p. 134, ll. 2–9.

[91] G. Ferrari, 'Formulari notarili inediti dell'età bizantina', *Bulletino dell'Istituto Storico Italiano*, 33 (1913), No. 18, pp. 55–6. There is every reason to believe that this formula reflects the conditions existing in the Nicaean Empire. It receives strong support from the information given by George Pachymeres about John Vatatzes's measures for the defence of the Anatolian frontiers. In addition, it is known from a marginal note that the collection of formulae from which it comes was copied in 1259. (See N. Oikonomides, 'Contribution à l'étude de la pronoia au XIIIe siècle', *REB* 22 (1964), 158–9.)

[92] Acropolites I, p. 123, ll. 6–9.

Other vestiges of the system of recruiting the armies of the themes from the local peasantry appear to have survived. The essence of this system in the tenth century was that the holders of what were known as military lands were obliged either to serve in person in the army of their local theme or to furnish a substitute. This obligation was known as *strateia*. In the course of the eleventh century it became the normal practice to commute this service.[93] As a result, *strateia* came to be considered a form of taxation burdening a certain class of holdings. By the thirteenth century a *stratia* [*sic*] had come to mean—on the island of Cos—a kind of holding, but it is not known whether its holder owed any military service.[94] That *strateia* retained something of its original significance is suggested by a document of 1274. Sometime previously there had been a demand for *strateia*. As a result the peasants of Vari near Smyrna were forced to borrow fifty-five hyperpyra from their lord, the abbey of Lemviotissa.[95] The most likely explanation of this incident is that the peasants had commuted any military services that they might have owed.

On occasion, local levies of troops might be raised in the provinces. They served as archers and infantry and supported the soldiers of the field army. At times of particular crisis a corps of levies might be sent to strengthen the Nicaean forces.[96] On what basis these levies were raised it is not possible to say, nor is it known whether they formed part of the organization of the armies of the themes.

Indeed, such is the nature of the evidence that it is not possible to come to anything but the most tentative conclusions about the military organization of the Nicaean Empire. As we have seen, there is very little information available about military organization at the provincial level. What does seem to be clear is that local units were drafted on an increasingly large scale into the field army. This process was to all

[93] See *Actes de Dionysiou*, I, No. 1, pp. 40–2; P. Lemerle, 'Recherches sur le régime agraire à Byzance: la terre militaire à l'époque des Comnènes', *Cahiers de Civilisation Médiévale*, 2 (1959), 265–7.

[94] Miklosich and Müller VI, pp. 217–18. Nothing in this document supports Professor Ahrweiler in her contention (*B* 1958, p. 135) that a *stratia* was the equivalent of a *pronoia*.

[95] Miklosich and Müller IV, p. 256, ll. 5ff.

[96] Acropolites I, p. 111, ll. 3–7, p. 120, ll. 3–10, pp. 146–7.

intents and purposes completed by Michael Palaiologos very soon after the recovery of Constantinople. The borderers had previously lain outside the administrative structure of the Empire. Their chiefs had enjoyed very generous treatment at the hands of the emperors of Nicaea. They were now forcibly enrolled in the imperial army and each man was granted a *pronoia* worth forty *hyperpyra*. This was much less than the revenues they had previously obtained from their own property. It probably represents the standard rate of *pronoia* granted to the ordinary soldiers of the field army.[97]

THE NICAEAN NAVY

The Nicaean Empire possessed a navy from its earliest days. At the very beginning of his reign Theodore I Laskaris assembled a fleet on the Sea of Marmora in an attempt to challenge the position of the Latins. This fleet was very small, numbering scarcely more than a dozen vessels, and met with very little success. Naval activity on the Sea of Marmora seems to have ended temporarily as a result of the treaty which Theodore Laskaris concluded with the Latins in 1214; and by the terms of the treaty made with the Venetians in 1219 no Nicaean warship was to be sent against Constantinople.[98]

Theodore I Laskaris also seems to have possessed an Aegean fleet. This consisted of seventeen galleys and was under the command of John Steiriones, who had been commander of a Byzantine fleet during the reign of Isaac II Angelos.[99] In the spring of 1207 it sailed into the Sea of Marmora in an unsuccessful attempt to blockade the city of Kyzikos, which was in Latin hands.[100] Soon afterwards Steiriones was sent by Laskaris to fetch the exiled Archbishop of Athens, Michael Choniates, from the island of Keos.[101]

There is a tradition that Theodore Laskaris captured Marco Sanudo, the Duke of Naxos, in a sea battle,[102] but

[97] Pachymeres I, p. 18, ll. 2–17.

[98] See Tafel and Thomas II, p. 207, ll. 17–23; Ahrweiler, *Byzance et la mer*, pp. 304–5, 311–13.

[99] Nicetas Choniates, pp. 636–7.

[100] Villehardouin II, pp. 290–2, 294–5.

[101] Michael Choniates II, p. 159, ll. 26–9.

[102] J. K. Fotheringham, *Marco Sanudo, Conqueror of the Archipelago*, Oxford, 1915, pp. 65–6.

it was not until the beginning of the reign of his successor, John Vatatzes, that the Nicaean navy brought the important islands of Lesbos, Chios, Samos, Ikaria, and Cos under Nicaean rule.[103] The island of Rhodes, which was ruled by members of the Gavalas family, was not incorporated in the Nicaean Empire until 1249.[104] An expedition of 1233 failed to secure the island for John Vatatzes.[105] Three years earlier, a Nicaean fleet of thirty-three galleys under the command of the Grand Duke Auxentios had been sent to bring reinforcements to the Cretans who had risen against the Venetians. They captured the fortresses of Rethymnon and Milopotamos, but in 1233 thirty Nicaean galleys were wrecked off the coast of Kythera; and the Venetians were gradually able to restore their position in Crete.[106]

The Venetians were able to strengthen their hold on Crete by a treaty concluded in 1234 with the ruler of Rhodes, who promised not to give any aid to John Vatatzes.[107] A new danger threatened both the Venetians and the Nicaeans when in 1248 the island of Rhodes was seized by the Genoese. They were driven out in the following year by a Nicaean expedition led by the Butler (*pinkernes*) John Kantakouzenos, but only after he had received reinforcements brought from Smyrna by a Nicaean fleet.[108]

The Emperor John Vatatzes maintained another naval force on the Sea of Marmora, and along the Hellespont. As soon as Lampsakos on the Hellespont had fallen into his hands (1224), he built a small fleet at the shipyards of Olkos which lay close by.[109] Shortly afterwards, he was forced to burn it to prevent it falling into the hands of the Latins.[110] This experience did not deter him from having other fleets constructed for service on the Sea of Marmora. They helped the Nicaean forces gain a foothold in southern Thrace and they kept open the Nicaean lines of communication across the Hellespont from Lampsakos to Gallipoli.[111]

[103] Gregoras I, pp. 28–9.
[104] Acropolites I, p. 88, ll. 12–14. [105] Ibid., pp. 45–6.
[106] Thiriet, *La Romanie vénitienne*, pp. 97–9.
[107] Tafel and Thomas II, pp. 319–22.
[108] Acropolites I, pp. 86–8.
[109] Ibid., p. 36, ll. 9–12. [110] Ibid., p. 37, ll. 4–6.
[111] See Ahrweiler, *Byzance et la mer*, pp. 318–19, 324.

The other main task of the Marmora fleet was to blockade the city of Constantinople, but this it failed to do. As one of its commanders, Manuel Kontophre, complained, Greek seamanship was far inferior to that of the Latins.[112] In 1235 the Nicaean fleet blockading Constantinople was driven off by the Latin defenders with the loss of twenty-four galleys. In the following year the Nicaean fleet was unable to prevent Geoffrey Villehardouin, the Frankish prince of Achaea, from bringing relief to the city.[113] In 1241 a Nicaean fleet of thirty galleys was utterly defeated in a battle on the Sea of Marmora by a much smaller Latin fleet.[114] It was this background of defeat that compelled Michael Palaiologos to secure the services of a Genoese fleet as part of his plans for the conquest of Constantinople.

As a result of Alexios I Komnenos's reforms, the Grand Duke became the commander-in-chief of the Byzantine navy.[115] Of the holders of this office recorded for the period of the Nicaean Empire only Auxentios seems to have had command of a Nicaean fleet. The fact that Michael Palaiologos was honoured with this title when he became regent suggests that it had become purely honorific.

Theoretically, the Grand *droungarios* of the fleet was the Grand Duke's lieutenant.[116] This office is attested in the reign of John Vatatzes, when it was held by a member of the Gavalas family.[117] There is no evidence that this man was given any naval command. It is true that another member of this family, the ruler of Rhodes, appears to have been in command of a Nicaean fleet which attacked the Venetian port of Abydos at the mouth of the Hellespont in 1235.[118] This may mean that on this occasion John Vatatzes was forced to engage the services of the Rhodian fleet.

The command of the Nicaean fleets does not seem to have been entrusted to the holder of any particular office. Manuel

[112] Acropolites I, p. 59, ll. 14–22.

[113] J. Longnon, *L'Empire latin de Constantinople*, Paris, 1949, p. 173.

[114] Acropolites I, pp. 59–60.

[115] Ahrweiler, *Byzance et la mer*, p. 209; R. Guilland, 'Les Chefs de la marine byzantine', *BZ* 44 (1951), 222–34.

[116] Ahrweiler, *Byzance et la mer*, pp. 210–11; Guilland, art. cit., pp. 219–21.

[117] Miklosich and Müller IV, pp. 254–5.

[118] Thiriet, *La Romanie vénitienne*, p. 98, n. 2.

Kontophre, who only held the dignity of *sevastos,* was made commander of the Nicaean fleet on the Sea of Marmora in 1241, but he was almost immediately replaced by the Armenian Geoffrey. He was reinstated in the following year and was put in command of the Nicaean galleys which accompanied Vatatzes on his expedition against Thessalonica.[119] The fleet that brought reinforcements in 1249 to the Nicaean forces on the island of Rhodes was commanded by the *protosevastos* Theodore Kontostephanos.[120] In 1242 he was one of the military commanders of the Nicaean forces on the expedition against Thessalonica.[121]

The fleet commanded by Kontostephanos, including horse-carrying galleys, was fitted out at Smyrna. This city was the main Nicaean naval base on the Aegean and must have possessed shipyards.[122] Lampsakos, as we have seen, was the chief naval base on the Hellespont.[123] Nicaean fleets never seem to have been much larger than thirty galleys[124] and were often much smaller.

The Nicaean navy suffered heavy losses in the attempt to take the island of Crete and to blockade the city of Constantinople. Yet the emperors of Nicaea seem to have had relatively little difficulty in equipping new fleets. The burden of equipping and manning these fleets must have fallen, as in the past, on the coastal areas of the Empire.[125] There seems to have been a close connection between the city of Smyrna and the Nicaean navy. Not only was a fleet fitted out here, but the naval tax known as *ploimoi,* which helped finance the fleet, was collected annually from Smyrna and the surrounding district under the emperors of Nicaea.[126] Smyrna was one of the chief cities of the theme of Thrakesion. Perhaps it is no coincidence that Manuel Kontophre, one of the

[119] Acropolites I, p. 59, ll. 14–21, p. 66, ll. 13–14; Ahrweiler, 'Smyrne', pp. 143–4.

[120] Acropolites I, p. 87, ll. 17–19.

[121] Ibid., p. 66, ll. 18–20.

[122] Ibid., p. 87, ll. 14–17; Ahrweiler, *Byzance et la mer*, p. 437.

[123] Acropolites I, p. 36, ll. 9–12, p. 45, ll. 17–19; Ahrweiler, op. cit., p. 437. Kyzikos and Kios may also have been naval bases at this time (see Ahrweiler, op. cit., pp. 319, 436–7).

[124] See above, pp. 196–8.

[125] See Ahrweiler, op. cit., pp. 205–11, 271–9.

[126] Miklosich and Müller IV, pp. 249–53. See below, p. 225.

commanders of the Nicaean fleet, should have been governor of this theme in 1240,[127] just before he took over command of the Nicaean navy. Again, it may be no coincidence that during his term as governor of this theme the collection of *ploimoi* was one of his main concerns.[128] The sailors of the Marmora fleet appear to have been recruited from soldiers stationed in Bithynia, Kyzikos, and along the shores of the Hellespont.[129] It is just possible that at least in the early years of the Nicaean Empire the Grand Duke retained some responsibility for the organization of the navy and for supervising it at the provincial level. In 1209 the Grand Duke Theodotos Phokas, an uncle of Theodore I Laskaris, was responsible for carrying out some mission for the emperor in the theme of Thrakesion.[130] He may even have been acting as duke of the theme.[131] In the twelfth century the office of Grand Duke was sometimes combined with the governorship of the important maritime theme of Hellas.[132]

The military organization of the Nicaean Empire was founded upon the reforms of the emperors of the house of Komnenos. This can be seen particularly clearly in the special taxes which were levied to support the army and navy, but an examination of these is better left to the next chapter which deals with the fiscal system of the Nicaean Empire.

In the course of the period of exile there were many changes in the military organization of the Empire. The direction these took reflects two trends. On the one hand, the changes came about as a result of the pressure which the

[127] See Ahrweiler, 'Smyrne', pp. 143–4. Another governor of Thrakesion, Theodore Kryvitziotes, who held this post in 1260 (Miklosich and Müller IV, pp. 223–4; Dölger, *Reg.* 1884), is later found in command of a fleet of one galley and three galliots (Tafel and Thomas III, pp. 196–7); but Professor Ahrweiler (*Byzance et la mer*, p. 322, n. 3) is quite wrong to connect this with his activities as governor of Thrakesion. It is specifically stated that he was then *capitaneum* of Rhodes. It should be emphasized that Manuel Kontophre did not combine the office of governor of Thrakesion with command of the Nicaean navy, but that there is a strong possibility that as governor of Thrakesion he was responsible for the equipping of a fleet.

[128] Miklosich and Müller IV, pp. 249–53.

[129] Heisenberg in *BZ* 1905, p. 219, ll. 30–8.

[130] Miklosich and Müller VI, pp. 153–6.

[131] A document of 1221 or 1236 (ibid., pp. 182–3) refers to the late *protopansevastohypertatos* who had acted as duke of Thrakesion. It seems not impossible that it is referring to Phokas, who held the honorific title of *panhypersevastos*.

[132] Ahrweiler, *Byzance et la mer*, pp. 271–9. e.g. Eumathios Philokales (see A. Bon, *Le Peloponnèse byzantin*, pp. 197–9).

Nicaean conquests in Europe placed upon the resources of the Empire; on the other, they reflect the way Nicaean central administration came to be concentrated in the imperial household. The imperial retinue became the core of the field army. The chief commands were given very often to the holders of the most important household offices. At the same time, military and naval commanders had a very large part to play in all aspects of the administration. They were frequently governors of provinces. This is perhaps not unexpected. More surprising is their involvement in the fiscal administration of the Empire. Both the Grand Domestic Andronikos Palaiologos[133] and the *protostrator* John Ises[134] were responsible for carrying out fiscal surveys.

This particular example reinforces the impression one has of an administration where there was little division of labour, where distinctions between departments were of the slightest, and where it had become normal to entrust a very wide range of administrative and military duties to the officers and members of the imperial household.

[133] Pachymeres I, p. 222, ll. 3–5.
[134] Miklosich and Müller VI, p. 181, ll. 11–12, p. 190, ll. 7–8.

X

THE FISCAL ORGANIZATION OF THE NICAEAN EMPIRE

The Byzantine fiscal system was developed from that of the late Roman Empire. It was one of the real strengths of the Byzantine Empire and is central to any study of the Byzantine administrative system. Any examination of it has to be carried out along a very broad front. It is not enough simply to investigate the nature of the taxes raised and the type of organization necessary to assess and collect them. It is also essential to consider all aspects of the supervision of landed property. The handing over of property and the settlement of disputes over property bulk very large in the documentary sources and appear to have been one of the main preoccupations of the Byzantine administration. For the recipient of property or for the litigants the main consideration was of course the desire for an unimpeachable title-deed, but the administration had a different end in view: its agents tried to ensure that taxes would not be lost to the central administration, or, if the holder of some property was exempted from taxation, that the exact nature of this exemption was recorded. The careful supervision of property by the government was absolutely essential if the fiscal system was to continue to function efficiently.

It goes almost without saying that the fiscal system and the agrarian structure of the Empire were intimately related; and that changes in the one would lead to changes in the other. We have already seen how the agrarian structure was changing. Its evolution was along two main lines: on the one hand, peasant holdings were increasingly absorbed by the great estates, a process which can of course be traced back to the tenth century, if not before; on the other, the owners of great estates were frequently exempted from the payment of taxes to the state or, more positively, state revenues were granted out to soldiers, administrators, members of the nobility, and even monks. This had the effect of creating what amounted to a new form of property imposed on the already existing agrarian system. As we have seen, this new form of property, or as it should more properly be called, the *pronoia* system, was greatly extended during the period of exile.

What effect did these changes have upon the fiscal system? To answer this question two points must be borne in mind. In the first place, every attempt was made to keep in being the fiscal system enshrined in the so-called 'Fiscal Treatise'[1] and to adapt it to the changing agrarian system. This was self-defeating. The core of the fiscal system was the village community which served as the basic tax-unit. Its members were jointly responsible for any arrears that had not been pardoned by the government. But the owners of large estates were able to escape the constraints imposed by this fiscal solidarity, sometimes at the express orders of the central administration, but very often illegally. The result was that the village community came to be less and less effective as a basis of the fiscal system of the Empire. In the second place, it is not until the period of exile that one can detect the emergence of a new fiscal system better adapted to the changes that had taken place in the system of landed property. A due called *epiteleia*, unattested before 1204, makes its appearance; it had a vital role to play in adapting the fiscal machinery to the *pronoia* system. There is also a change in the basic taxes paid to the state. Two new taxes known as *sitarkia* and *agape* appear.

These are only the outward signs of changes that were certainly taking shape in the course of the twelfth century. The fall of Constantinople did not alter the direction of these changes; it simply accelerated the rate at which they were taking place.

It is possible to perceive the general shape of the changes that were taking place in the fiscal system during the period of exile, but their precise nature is much more elusive. The reason for this is that there is no source comparable to the 'Fiscal Treatise' which would allow one to make a theoretical reconstruction of the fiscal system. The evidence is extremely fragmentary. The main impression one has is of considerable

[1] Edition in Dölger, *Finanzverwaltung*, pp. 113–23.

confusion. There is no clear dividing line between the fiscal duties entrusted to the provincial authorities and those carried out by agents sent out by the central government; at times, there does not even seem to be a clear division between officials responsible for collecting taxes and those responsible for their assessment. There are also great gaps in the evidence. For example, one cannot say for sure which official was at the head of the financial administration of the Nicaean Empire.

More evidence would almost certainly help to clear up much of the confusion that surrounds the Nicaean fiscal system, but, as in other aspects of the Nicaean administration, this confusion does seem to be associated with the emergence of a new phase in the history of the Byzantine administration. Again, it was left to Michael Palaiologos to forge a clear-cut fiscal system out of the confusion existing under the emperors of Nicaea. On the other hand, the principles upon which Michael Palaiologos based his reforms follow the directions of change observable during the period of exile. The *vestiarion* or wardrobe became the hub of the fiscal organization, while the collection of taxes was removed from the provincial authorities and entrusted to agents of the central government.

1. THE VESTIARION

The *vestiarion* became the sole central treasury of the Byzantine Empire as a result of Alexios I Komnenos's reforms. At its head was the Grand Logariast, who was responsible for supervising all aspects of the fiscal administration of the Empire. After the fall of Constantinople the *vestiarion* continued to be the sole central treasury, but now, with the disappearance of the *sekreta,* its competence was enlarged to include all aspects of the fiscal administration. Taxes continued to be paid into it, and it remained responsible for the administration of the state's income in kind.[2] Its new areas of responsibility included keeping the fiscal registers[3] and disbursing revenue.[4] This effectively meant that the whole fiscal machinery was concentrated in the *vestiarion.*

[2] Miklosich and Müller IV, p. 285; Dölger, *Reg.* 1878.

[3] Miklosich and Müller IV, pp. 45–6; Dölger, *Reg.* 1729. See Dölger, *Finanzverwaltung*, pp. 30, 97, 104.

[4] Miklosich and Müller IV, p. 9, ll. 1–5. The late Professor Dölger contended (*Finanzverwaltung*, p. 30) that after 1204 the *vestiarion* also took over responsibility

This appears to have been the one fixed institution of the Nicaean administration. After the removal of the imperial residence to the palace of Nymphaion at the beginning of John Vatatzes's reign, it was housed in the near-by city of Magnesia.[5] A subsidiary treasury was established by Theodore II Laskaris in the fortress of Astytzion in the Troad.[6] This was probably done to facilitate the financing of his European campaigns.

Virtually nothing is known about the officials who staffed the *vestiarion* or about the ministers who had charge of the financial administration of the Nicaean Empire. On the other hand, the historians George Pachymeres and Theodore Skoutariotes were at pains to stress the care which the Emperor John Vatatzes lavished upon the finances of his state and to point out the great treasure which he accumulated in the *vestiarion* at Magnesia.[7] Two instances illustrate the emperor's close supervision of the financial administration. On one occasion, he learnt that the two officials who were responsible for receiving taxes paid into the treasury were neglecting their duties. He had one of them beaten so severely that he died; the other was prudent enough to flee to Trebizond.[8] On another occasion, an official was found to have made a wrong tax-assessment. To teach him not to make such mistakes again, the emperor ordered that the amount wrongly assessed should in future be paid by the official.[9] George Pachymeres hints that Theodore II Laskaris abandoned his father's careful financial policies: expenditure became more lavish and taxation was increased, apparently falling heavily on the clergy.[10]

It is possible that Demetrios Tornikes's duties as chief minister included responsibility for the fiscal administration of the Empire, but there is no certain proof of this. During

for the handing over of *paroikoi*. He may be correct, but the instance which he cites as proof of this refers not to the imperial *vestiarion* but to that of the Empress Theodora (Miklosich and Müller VI, p. 216, ll. 10–12).

[5] Scutariotes, p. 286, ll. 7–8; Pachymeres I, p. 68, ll. 4–8, p. 71, ll. 8–9.

[6] Pachymeres I, p. 68, ll. 8–12.

[7] Scutariotes, p. 286, ll. 7–8; Pachymeres I, p. 68, ll. 6–10, p. 71, ll. 8–9.

[8] Pachymeres II, p. 296, ll. 5–13.

[9] Miklosich and Müller IV, pp. 251–2; Dölger, *Reg.* 1748.

[10] Pachymeres I, pp. 69–70; Theodore Lascaris, pp. 57–8.

George Mouzalon's brief regency the administration of the *vestiarion* was entrusted to his brother-in-law Hagiotheodorites, who held the post of logothete of the flocks.[11] It is just possible that he was already head of the *vestiarion* under Theodore II Laskaris.[12]

The office of Grand Logariast is attested during the period of exile. It was held about the year 1240 by George Akropolites at the beginning of his administrative career.[13] It had previously been held by Demetrios Karykes, who also held the post of 'Consul of the Philosophers'. He was responsible for carrying out a fiscal survey in the neighbourhood of Ephesos.[14] Otherwise, there is absolutely no evidence connecting Karykes with the treasury administration.

The office of logariast of the court is also recorded during the period of exile.[15] The holder of this office had an important, if minor, role in the financial administration of the fourteenth century. It was his duty to see that those at court receiving wages had actually received them and, in addition, that they had carried out the duties for which they were paid.[16]

It might be thought that the administration of the *vestiarion* would have been subordinated to the *protovestiarios*. Under the emperors of Nicaea this office was one of the greatest in the state, but its functions appear to have been limited to the ceremonial of the imperial court. As we have seen, the holders of this office might be entrusted with important military commands. There is absolutely no evidence connecting this office with the financial administration of the Empire. It would appear that the functions of this office did not keep pace with the development of the *vestiarion* from imperial wardrobe to central treasury and finally to chief organ of the financial administration. Nor does the *protovestiarites* appear to have had any connection with the treasury administration.

[11] Pachymeres I, p. 53, ll. 13–17.

[12] Theodore Lascaris, p. 223, ll. 8ff. Here Hagiotheodorites is described as ἐξηγητής. It may be a complete coincidence that, according to Pachymeres (I, p. 53, l. 15), he was in charge of (ἐξηγεῖτο) the officials of the imperial treasury.

[13] Acropolites II, p. vii, n. 6, p. 3.

[14] Blemmydes, pp. 12–13, 55, ll. 15–17.

[15] Pachymeres II, p. 296, ll. 11–12.

[16] Pseudo-Kodinos, pp. 186–7.

In the Book of Offices of the Pseudo-Kodinos the head of the treasury administration was known as the president (*prokathemenos*) of the *vestiarion*.[17] This office is first attested in the reign of Michael VIII Palaiologos.[18] It is not at all unlikely that it was specially created by this emperor in order to put an end to the confused situation that appears to have existed during the period of exile in the organization of the *vestiarion*.

2. FISCAL RECORDS

During the period of exile the *vestiarion* was responsible for keeping a variety of fiscal records. Records were kept of the receipts due from various state properties. For instance, the administrators of the state salt pans near Smyrna were instructed to give the monastery of Lemviotissa a certain amount of salt each year. They obtained a receipt from the monks for the salt. This receipt was then presented to the *vestiarion* and the amount of salt given to the monastery was credited to the administrators' account with the *vestiarion*.[19] This procedure is very similar to one used in the Byzantine fiscal administration before 1204.[20]

The *vestiarion* also kept records of the taxes to be raised and of any exemptions that might be accorded. It was directed that an imperial writ of 1232 exempting one of the Lemviotissa estates from the payment of annual taxes amounting to 1 *hyperpyron* should be registered in the *chartia* of the *vestiarion*.[21] But this tells us very little about the precise nature of the fiscal documents preserved in the *vestiarion*, since *chartia* is a general term that simply means documents.[22]

Before 1204 there were two main types of fiscal register kept by the central government. The more important was the cadastral register. It was arranged according to the various fiscal divisions of the Empire. The basic entry was called the *stichos*. It recorded the name of the tax-payer, the property he owned within the village community which, as we have

[17] Ibid., p. 186, ll. 13–17.

[18] Pachymeres I, p. 384, l. 16.

[19] Miklosich and Müller IV, pp. 284–5.

[20] See N. G. Svoronos, 'Notes à propos d'un procédé de techniques fiscales: la ΔΟΧΗ', *REB* 24 (1966), 97–106.

[21] Miklosich and Müller IV, pp. 45–6; Dölger, *Reg.* 1729.

[22] Svoronos, *Le Cadastre de Thèbes*, p. 20, n. 4.

seen, formed the basic fiscal unit, and the taxes he owed to the government together with any tax remissions that he might enjoy.

Less important before 1204 were the *praktika*. These were a detailed record of a man's whole estate, regardless of fiscal divisions. There would be included not only a description of the property he held, but also a list of the peasants settled there and the dues and services they owed him. The taxes he owed to the government would be recorded, as well as any exemptions he might have been granted. *Praktika* were not only registered in the state archives. They were also issued to the holders of estates and served as title-deeds. From the point of view of the administration, the essential difference between the two types of registers was that the one was arranged according to fiscal units, while the other was arranged according to the owners of property.[23]

After 1204 there is no further record of the cadastral register, whereas from the late twelfth century there are frequent references to *praktika* registered in the government archives; and from 1261 onwards a great many *praktika* issued to private individuals or monasteries have been preserved.[24] In the fourteenth century another type of fiscal register came into prominence. It was known as the *megale thesis*. It was made up of the records produced by a periodic fiscal survey known as the *apographe*. These seem to have been filed in this register under the names of the individuals responsible for carrying out the survey. Each provincial authority kept its own *megale thesis;* a master copy of these, which went under the name of 'the imperial book', was held by the central government. Changes in the ownership of property were entered both in the *megale thesis* and in the appropriate *praktika*.[25] There are good reasons for supposing that this register took over from the cadaster as the main fiscal register. It seems to have been very largely composed of the *praktika* drawn up in the course of an *apographe*.[26] A register based

[23] Dölger, *Finanzverwaltung*, pp. 97–102; Svoronos, *Le Cadastre de Thèbes*, pp. 19–26, 57–63.

[24] Dölger, *Finanzverwaltung*, pp. 101–2; Ostrogorskij, *Féodalité*, pp. 262–3.

[25] *Actes de Zographou*, No. xliv, ll. 40–5; *Actes de Dionysiou*, No. xxv, esp. pp. 141–3.

[26] See Dölger, *Finanzverwaltung*, pp. 111–12, esp. p. 111, n. 8. Cf. Svoronos, *Le Cadastre de Thèbes*, p. 63, n. 1.

upon *praktika* corresponded much better to the needs of the administration at a time when more and more property either formed part of great estates enjoying various immunities or was granted out in *pronoia*, and when the village community became less and less important as a fiscal unit.

There is, as we have already seen, no conclusive evidence as to the exact nature of the fiscal records kept in the Nicaean *vestiarion*. But either the central government or the provincial authorities kept a register of military *praktika*[27] and corresponding to this was a register of civil *praktika*.[28] The one would contain details of lands and revenues granted out in *pronoia* to soldiers; the other surveys of private estates together with the details of *pronoiai* granted to civilians.

At the same time, some vestiges of a cadastral register survived after 1204. In the region of Smyrna there are references to the payment of dues to the *stichos* of such and such a person[29] and to the transference of property from the *stichoi* of others to the monastery of Lemviotissa.[30] The *stichos,* it will be remembered, was the essential element of the cadaster. It might be argued that the examples cited above simply show that *stichos* had lost its technical meaning and had come to mean a holding. But it is not as simple as this. In a lawsuit of 1262 the term *biologion* is carefully defined. The question at issue was whether the land of a village near the mouth of the river Maiander was subject to the conventions governing property granted out in *pronoia*, or whether it was property directly under the control of the state. In the latter case, the property would be registered in the *biologia* of the peasants living in the village and they would pay taxes to the state for it.[31] It can be seen that *biologion*, which may be roughly translated as 'account of livelihood', is an exact equivalent of *stichos*. This does not necessarily mean that the *vestiarion* possessed a cadastral register, but it does allow us to conclude that during the period of exile two basic types of fiscal record were kept: one for privileged property and

[27] Miklosich and Müller IV, p. 70, ll. 19–29.
[28] Ibid., p. 318, l. 10.
[29] Ibid., p. 121, l. 16.
[30] Ibid., p. 8, ll. 27–8, p. 25, ll. 1–3, 18–19.
[31] Miklosich and Müller VI, No. lxxxvi, pp. 212–14; Dölger, *Reg.* 1912.

pronoiai; the other for property that still came under the direct control of the state.

3. FISCAL SURVEYS

These records were very largely obtained and kept up to date by means of the two traditional fiscal surveys carried out by the Byzantine administration. The more far-reaching of these was known as the *exisosis*; the more frequent as the *apographe*.

The *exisosis* was carried out by officials known as *exisotai* and the *apographe* by those known as *apographeis*. Both held temporary commissions from the emperor. Under the emperors of Nicaea the execution of both surveys was entrusted to some of the greatest men of the state. The *exisosis* of the province of Skamander was carried out by the Grand Domestic Andronikos Palaiologos and by one Romanos who held the very elevated court title of Caesar,[32] while that of the region of Ephesos was entrusted to the Grand Logariast and 'Consul of the Philosophers' Demetrios Karykes.[33]

Both before 1204 and after 1261 it was a common practice to entrust the *apographe*, or *anagraphe* as it was called before 1204, to the duke or governor of a theme. This was an obvious expedient since the duties of *apographeus* and duke tended to overlap. But this rarely happened during the period of exile. The *apographe* was normally carried out by prominent members of the central administration. That of the theme of Thrakesion was accomplished by, among others, the Chamberlain Alexios Krateros,[34] the *protostrator* John Ises,[35] and the *protovestiarites* Zagaromates.[36] There were of course exceptions. John Kantakouzenos appears to have combined the functions of *apographeus* and duke of Thrakesion,[37] but his position was unusual. In contrast to other holders of this governorship, he held an important household office, that of Butler, and, instead of holding the governorship for the usual term of a single year, he remained in office for at

[32] Pachymeres I, p. 222, ll. 1–6.

[33] Blemmydes, pp. 12–13.

[34] Miklosich and Müller IV, pp. 240–1; ibid. VI, pp. 176–9, p. 181, ll. 9–11, p. 190, ll. 6–7. See Ahrweiler, 'Smyrne', pp. 140, 171.

[35] Miklosich and Müller VI, p. 181, ll. 11–12, p. 190, ll. 7–8.

[36] Ibid. VI, pp. 189–91, 199–201.

[37] Ibid. IV, p. 70, ll. 19–29. See Blemmydes, pp. 34–5.

least six years from *c.* 1242 to *c.* 1249.[38] This was a critical period in the history of the Nicaean Empire: these years saw both the materialization of the Mongol threat in the east and the Nicaean conquest of Macedonia in the west, to say nothing of the annexation of Rhodes and the surrounding islands carried out by Kantakouzenos himself.[39] Among these islands were Leros and Kalymnos. In 1254 their duke, one Constantine Diogenes, was ordered by the emperor to carry out an *apographe* and *exisosis* of these islands.[40] This must have formed an essential part of a reorganization following their incorporation in the Nicaean Empire.

This shows that it was possible for an *exisosis* to be made for individual provinces or regions of the Empire. It seems likely that it was more usual for the *exisosis* to be carried out for the whole Empire and for an *apographe* to be made at the same time. At least, the chronicler Theodore Skoutariotes singled out the general *apographe* and *exisosis* carried out under John Vatatzes as an extraordinary event. It took place soon after the Latins had been driven out of Asia Minor.[41]

Otherwise, the *apographe* does not appear to have been carried out on a general basis, but to have been ordered for individual themes as the need arose. The normal practice was to appoint an *apographeus* to supervise the *apographe* of each theme. He had a number of subordinates to whom specific tasks were entrusted.[42] But, on occasions, the emperor might appoint a separate *apographeus* for a district within a theme[43] or even sanction a special *apographe* for a private estate.[44]

These considerations help to account for the irregular intervals at which the *apographe* appears to have been carried out. On the other hand, it would be true to say that during the period of exile it took place relatively frequently. Between 1216 and 1249 there were no fewer than six *apographai* of the town of Palatia at the mouth of the river Maiander.[45]

[38] Wilson and Darrouzès in *REB* 26 (1968), No. 6, pp. 20–1; Ahrweiler, 'Smyrne', pp. 144–5.

[39] Acropolites I, pp. 86–8.

[40] The *praktikon* of Constantine Diogenes; for details, see above, p. 139, n. 110.

[41] Scutariotes, p. 286, ll. 14ff.

[42] Miklosich and Müller VI, pp. 176–9, 182–3.

[43] Ibid. IV, pp. 85–6, 253; Dölger, *Reg.* 1763.

[44] Miklosich and Müller IV, pp. 182–3; Dölger, *Reg.* 1740.

[45] Miklosich and Müller VI, p. 190, ll. 6–10.

The duties of an *exisotes* and of an *apographeus* often overlapped. Both might be required to hand over property, make out *praktika,* register the number of peasants living on a particular estate, record the size of their families and the nature of their property, and finally fix the amount of taxes and services owed by each household.[46] The essential difference between the *exisosis* and the *apographe* appears to have been that the former entailed a thorough revision of the tax-assessment, whereas the purpose of the latter was to register changes in the holding of land and consequent changes in the payment of taxes.[47]

One of the main aims of the *exisosis* was to make sure that a landowner was not holding too much or too little property in relation to the taxes which he was paying. In the fourteenth century this applied in particular to land granted out in *pronoia.* It was part of the responsibility of the *exisotai* to increase or reduce the value of the *pronoiai* as the case might be.[48] In theory, this ought to have been reasonably easy to do, since the value of the *pronoia* was set out in the holder's *praktikon.* This must have helped to render superfluous that complicated system of rating the value of property known as the *epibole.* Before 1204 it had been the essential basis upon which these reallocations of property were calculated.[49] It should be said that during the period of exile there is no evidence that either of these procedures was carried out. But there is one small feature which underlines how important the *exisosis* was for the agrarian and fiscal organization of the Nicaean Empire. It seems to have been part of the *exisotes*'s duties during the period of exile to dispose of all land and property which was found to be without an owner.[50]

The purpose of the *exisosis* and of the *apographe* may seem simple enough, but these surveys imposed a vast number of different tasks upon those entrusted with their execution. They amounted to nothing less than a periodic surveillance

[46] See ibid., pp. 208–10, 214–16, 217–19; *Praktikon* of Constantine Diogenes.

[47] See Dölger, *Finanzverwaltung*, pp. 79–81; Svoronos, *Le Cadastre de Thèbes*, p. 124.

[48] Cantacuzenus II, p. 62, ll. 7–15.

[49] See Svoronos, *Le Cadastre de Thèbes*, pp. 119–29; id., 'L'Épibolé à l'époque des Comnènes', *Travaux et Mémoires*, 3 (1968), 375–95.

[50] Miklosich and Müller VI, pp. 208–10. Cf. ibid., pp. 207–8.

of all aspects of the holding of land. A very important aspect of this was the settling of disputes over property. This provided the *apographeis* with a large part of their work.

Perhaps a single example will suffice to illustrate the procedures involved. In 1264 David Vroullas, who was responsible for carrying out the *apographe* in the neighbourhood of Smyrna, was called upon to give judgement in a dispute between the monastery of Lemviotissa and the heirs of a soldier called Michael Angelos. The parties were quarrelling over their respective rights in a fish-pond on the river Hermos. Vroullas's judgement favoured the monastery. His decision was based not only upon the documents which both parties produced to support their claims, but also upon the testimony of local people. He made out a document known as an *apokatastasis* in which possession of the disputed property was confirmed to the monastery. It was directed that this property should be entered in the monastery's *praktikon* and should be struck out from that produced by the opposing party.[51]

Other aspects of the work of an *apographeus* are illustrated by another example. In 1238 the imperial secretary John Konstomares[52] was *apographeus* of the *katepanikion*—that is the chief fiscal division of a theme—of Smyrna. A complaint was brought before him by the monks of Lemviotissa. They alleged that a former duke of the theme of Thrakesion, John Angelos,[53] had imposed upon a holding which they had bought from a peasant called Kakavas a tax known as *epiteleia*. This the monks claimed had been done without proper examination. Konstomares upheld the monks' complaint: the state had no right to demand the payment of an *epiteleia* from this property, since he himself had handed over Kakavas elsewhere and had fixed the taxes and dues which the latter owed.[54]

This document raises a great many problems which will have to be considered in detail later, not least the question of the nature of the *epiteleia*. For the moment, it is sufficient

[51] Ibid. IV, pp. 244–7.
[52] See Ahrweiler, 'Smyrne', pp. 159–60.
[53] Duke from 1235 to 1236. See Ahrweiler, 'Smyrne', p. 142.
[54] Miklosich and Müller IV, pp. 85–6.

to underline three general points that it illustrates. In the first place, it shows the way that an *apograheus* was able to check irregularities in the holding of land and in the payment of taxes; he was in a position to scrutinize the work of previous provincial governors. In the second place, it was part of his normal duties to hand over peasants and, as other examples show,[55] property as well. Finally, it was his responsibility to assess the taxes a man owed and the services he was called upon to perform.

The handing over of property and the assessment of taxes were vital aspects of the administration which came under the periodic supervision of the *apographeis*. But in the intervals between their surveys, these tasks might be entrusted by the emperor to a variety of officials. Consequently, the following examination will not be concerned with these aspects of the administration as the special responsibility of the *apographeus,* but will concentrate upon the procedures involved.

4. THE HANDING OVER OF PROPERTY

(a) The handing over of imperial grants of property.

For obvious reasons this is an aspect of government that bulks large in monastic archives and cartularies. It was entrusted to very many different imperial functionaries in addition to the *apographeis*. During the period of exile there are examples of this task being carried out by the governors of themes, by the governors of cities, and by the administrators of imperial estates.[56] The procedure was relatively straightforward. The recipient of an imperial grant would obtain an imperial order specifying the property to be handed over. He would then take this to the official

[55] e.g. Theodore Lascaris, pp. 309–10; Miklosich and Müller VI, pp. 176–9.

[56] The following account is based on the handing over of the following possessions to the monastery of Lemviotissa: (1) the chapel of St. George Exokastrites by the governor (*prokathemenos*) of Smyrna, George Monomachos, in Nov. 1227 (Miklosich and Müller IV, pp. 43–5; Dölger, *Reg.* 1717); (2) two *zeugaria* of land from the imperial estates of Koukoulos by Stephen Kalopyros, their administrator (*epikraton*), in July 1231 (Miklosich and Müller IV, pp. 142–4; Dölger, *Reg.* 1725); (3) six *zeugaria* of land from the same imperial estates by the governor of Smyrna, John Alopos, in Apr. 1234 (Miklosich and Müller IV, pp. 142–4; Dölger, *Reg.* 1737). It is also based on the handing over in Feb. 1216 of the *metochion* of Pyrgos to the monastery of St. John of Patmos by Andronikos Mauropodos, acting on behalf of the *parakoimomenos* Alexios Krateros (Miklosich and Müller VI, pp. 176–9. For the dating of this document, see Glykatzi-Ahrweiler in *B* 28 (1958), 135).

appointed by the emperor to hand over the property in question. The official would either carry this out in person or would delegate the task to one of his subordinates. Whoever finally took on the job collected together the chief men of the city or the village in which the property was situated. A notary was normally included in their number. Then together they made a perambulation of the bounds of the property. The limits thus established were set down in a deed known as a *paradosis* or *paradotikon gramma,* which thereafter served as a title deed. In the case of the chapel of St. George Exokastrites in Smyrna, which was handed over to the monastery of Lemviotissa in 1227, an inventory was also made of the chapel's movable property. This consisted in the main of liturgical books.

The imperial grant of an estate or of a village which enjoyed varying degrees of immunity from taxation and from the imperial administration involved a much longer and much more complicated procedure. The surrender of the village of Vari near Smyrna to the monastery of Lemviotissa must serve as a single example. It was granted to the monastery by John Vatatzes by a chrysobull dated August 1228.[57] The process of handing it over was not completed until March 1235.[58] This village had belonged before 1204 to the Constantinopolitan monastery of Pantokrator and had then been granted by Theodore I Laskaris to Basil Vlatteros as a *pronoia.*[59] After his death his family continued to claim possession of property in the village and disputed Lemviotissa's rights there. Their claims were dismissed by imperial *prostagmata* of August 1232[60] and July 1233,[61] which upheld the monastery's possession of the village. The monastery also had to prosecute a number of other lawsuits, in particular one against the inhabitants of the village of Mantaia.[62] These concerned properties which had originally belonged to the village, but which had already been lost before 1204.[63]

[57] Miklosich and Müller IV, pp. 1–4; Dölger, *Reg.* 1718.
[58] Miklosich and Müller IV, pp. 4–18; Dölger, *Reg.* 1742.
[59] See Glykatzi-Ahrweiler in *B* 28 (1958), 57.
[60] Miklosich and Müller IV, pp. 194–5; Dölger, *Reg.* 1728.
[61] Miklosich and Müller IV, pp. 198–200; Dölger, *Reg.* 1734.
[62] Miklosich and Müller IV, pp. 210–11; Dölger, *Reg.* 1815.
[63] Miklosich and Müller IV, pp. 184–5, 187–9.

In 1234,[64] after the claims of the Vlatteros family had finally been set aside, the Duke of Thrakesion, Constantine Laskaris, was ordered to register the *paroikoi* settled at Vari and to fix the appropriate taxes and dues which they owed to the monastery of Lemviotissa. In December 1234 the stratopedarch of Thrakesion and Philadelphia, Michael Phokas, was instructed by the emperor to carry out a survey (*periorismos*) of all the monastery's possessions.[65] He completed the

[64] Ibid., pp. 182–3; Dölger, *Reg.* 1740. Mme Ahrweiler's attempt ('Smyrne', p. 145, n. 97) to redate the document in question to the year 1249 seems to rest on very questionable grounds, not least that in 1249 John Kantakouzenos continued to hold the office of duke of Thrakesion (see Ahrweiler, 'Smyrne', p. 144). It is therefore unlikely, though not impossible, that Constantine Laskaris, to whom the document is addressed in his capacity as Duke of Thrakesion, could have held that office in 1249.

The document in question is dated August, Indiction 7 (= 1219, 1234, 1249, 1264). Mme Ahrweiler and Dölger agree that the year 1232 can be accepted as the *terminus post quem*. In that year the abbacy of Gerasimos Opsikianos, mentioned in the document as the former abbot, came to an end. But Ahrweiler cannot accept Dölger's *terminus ante quem* of 1240. In that year a Michael Gounaropoulos is mentioned as dead (Miklosich and Müller, p. 195). Dölger identified this man as the Michael Gounaropoulos mentioned in the document in question. But, as Mme Ahrweiler points out, he was probably dead before 1225 and he was certainly dead before 1232 (ibid., p. 190). She prefers an identification with another Michael Gounaropoulos, a nephew of the above, who was still a minor in 1235 (ibid., p. 13). Consequently, the document under discussion, which shows him holding land, must be dated to a period when he had reached his majority, and therefore, according to Mme Ahrweiler, 1249 is the most likely date. In fact, a close examination of the document in question shows that Mme Ahrweiler's identification and dating are quite irrelevant. It is clear that the Michael Gounaropoulos who is referred to in this document is none other than the dead man. This may have been a mistake on the part of the administration or simply a convenient way of referring to his heirs.

This man formerly held 3 *voidatika* of land in the village of Vari. He gave one of these to Vlatteros. This piece of property had since passed into the possession of Lemviotissa. Nevertheless, he was still trying to give it to one of his relatives. Duke Laskaris was instructed to see that this did not happen. There can be no doubt that Vlatteros was the man who had originally held the village in *pronoia*. It is not known when he died, but it must have been before 1228. It seems quite unlikely that a minor in 1235 could have held land and alienated some of it so many years previously. The date of the alienation of the property in question may have been as early as Nov. 1207 (see ibid., pp. 185–7).

One has to put this document into its proper context, namely the dispute between Vlatteros's heirs and Lemviotissa over property alienated to Vlatteros by various members of the Gounaropoulos family. This was a dispute that raged, as we have seen, in the early 1230s. By the late 1240s it had long been settled. Consequently, since there can be no doubt about the *terminus post quem*, the year 1234 must stand as the date of the document in question.

[65] Miklosich and Müller IV, pp. 4–5; Dölger, *Reg.* 1742.

task in the following March.[66] This was the final stage in the handing over of the village to the monastery. To judge from subsequent lawsuits, Phokas's survey served the monastery as a title-deed to the village of Vari as well as to many of its other properties, but it is not a *praktikon* in the true sense. It only preserves records of the *paroikoi* settled on the monastery's estates for the village of Vari.[67] These details were no doubt taken from the *apographe* made in the previous year by Constantine Laskaris.

The handing over of estates seems therefore to have involved four separate stages. First, an imperial chrysobull had to be obtained. In it would be set out the property to be handed over and the rights and immunities that the recipient would enjoy. Then conflicting claims had to be examined. This might take several years. When these had been finally settled, an *apographe* would be made of the estate, that is to say the *paroikoi* settled there would be registered and their taxes, dues, and services would be fixed. The final stage was the establishment of the bounds of the estate and the drawing up of an inventory of all that was contained therein.

The handing over of the village of Vari gives some idea of the efficiency of the Nicaean administration. The *apographe* was ordered in August 1234, the establishment of its bounds in December of that year; and the whole operation was completed by the following March. These tasks were carried out by the duke of a theme and by the stratopedarch of a theme. It is probable that it was normal to entrust tasks of this nature to the provincial authorities. They might, in certain circumstances, have been carried out by an *apographeus*; and certainly, such an operation would later be checked by the *apographeis,* should any irregularities be brought to their attention.

(b) The handing over of pronoiai

The procedure employed for handing over *pronoiai* resembled that described above for large estates, but there was one very important difference. All that was involved in the transfer of Vari into the possession of the monastery of Lemviotissa was

[66] Miklosich and Müller IV, pp. 5–18.

[67] Ibid., pp. 14–16.

the handing over of a specific village and the peasants settled there. It was, at all events, a grant in full ownership, but at this time the grant of a *pronoia* only brought with it certain temporary rights of ownership. It was above all a grant of revenues belonging to the state and, as such, it was only natural that its monetary value (*nomismatike posotes*) should be the first detail to be established.[68] The problem was to find property on which this revenue could be drawn. This led to a somewhat complicated process, some of the details of which have been preserved in a formula dating from the period of the Nicaean Empire.[69]

This formula shows that the holder of a *pronoia* obtained an imperial writ setting out the property on which he was to draw his revenues. He brought it to an official of the provincial administration empowered by the duke to hand over imperial grants of property. This official then handed over to the holder of the *pronoia* the required amount of land and listed the peasants settled there, with details of their families and their substance. If the *pronoia*-holder did not receive the full amount of land to which he was entitled, the remainder was to be handed over as soon as it became available.

N. Oikonomides, who has recently examined this formula, considers that it only describes a temporary stage in the handing over of a *pronoia*. For, though the form employed in the formula resembles that of a *praktikon,* it does not state the taxes, dues, and other services which the peasants would have owed the holder of the *pronoia*. Nor is there any mention of any demesne land that the holder might have possessed; nor, finally, is the value of the *pronoia* given. Oikonomides believes that a full *praktikon* containing all these details would have been made out at a later stage, possibly by the duke of the theme.[70]

In all this he may very well be right, but he also suggests that the monetary value of a *pronoia* was only fixed at this

[68] See *Actes de Zographou*, No. xxix; *Actes de Xéropotamou*, Nos. 9–10.

[69] G. Ferrari, 'Formulari notarili inediti dell'età bizantina', *Bulletino dell'Istituto Storico Italiano*, 33 (1913), 50; N. Oikonomides, 'Contribution à l'étude de la pronoia au XIIIe siècle: Une formule d'attribution de parèques à un pronoiaire', *REB* 22 (1964), 158–75.

[70] Oikonomides in *REB* 22 (1964), 170–4.

later stage. There are grounds for believing this to be mistaken. In May 1261 an imperial official was ordered by the emperor to go to the estate of Palatia and to divide up all the waste property to be found there, together with other appurtenances, into plots of a fixed monetary value (*nomismatike posotes*). He was then to hand them over to Constantine Pepagomenos and fifty-two *archontopouloi* as *pronoiai* according to the value of the *pronoiai* granted to each of these men.[71]

It is immediately apparent that there are differences between the procedure for handing over a *pronoia* described here and that described in the formula; and this, for the simple reason that the document of 1261 and the formula describe different stages in the handing over of a *pronoia*. The former is concerned with property that had never previously been granted out in *pronoia*. We are therefore face to face with the very first stages in the formation of a *pronoia*: land which was to be granted out in *pronoia* was first surveyed by an imperial official and divided up into plots, each having a fixed value. In other words, the monetary value of a *pronoia* was fixed at the outset. The advantage of this is obvious. When these holdings were next granted out in *pronoia*, their value was already known and there was no need for any detailed survey by the provincial administration. The formula makes it quite clear that the official responsible for handing over property to the holder of a *pronoia* simply transferred to him property previously granted out in *pronoia*, but now vacant.[72]

In the course of time, irregularities were almost bound to occur. Property originally granted out in *pronoia*, the village of Vari for example, might later come to form part of a great estate. The holder of a *pronoia* might find ways to increase the value of his *pronoia*. We have seen how Basil Vlatteros bought up property forming part of his *pronoia*. In this, and in many other ways, the original value of a *pronoia* might be falsified. It was the purpose of the *exisosis* either to rectify these changes or to proceed to a new division of the lands set aside for *pronoia*.

It is not known whether the *apographeis* were called upon to keep a check upon the value of *pronoiai*, but it is known

[71] Miklosich and Müller VI, pp. 207–8; Dölger, *Reg.* 1891.
[72] Oikonomides in *REB* 22 (1964), 160, ll. 10–12.

that under Michael Palaiologos it was the practice for the government to increase the value of *pronoiai* out of the surpluses of the *apographeis* (*perisseiai apographeon*).[73] What were these surpluses? A document of July 1231 throws some light on the problem. In that year a member of the imperial household called John Syropoulos was instructed to return fifteen *hyperpyra* 'of the surplus of *hyperpyra* found as a result of your *apographe* on the estates of the monastery of Lemviotissa'. He was to arrange that the remainder of this 'surplus' was paid into the *vestiarion* by the monastery.[74] The first point that has to be emphasized is that this surplus was in money, for the surpluses mentioned in the 'Fiscal Treatise' and in documents of the late eleventh century were in land. These represented property for which the owner was found to be paying no tax, or insufficient tax. The state possessed the right to confiscate such property.[75] Surpluses in land are still met with after 1261. The *apographeus* could transfer them to whomsoever the emperor directed.[76]

By analogy, surpluses in money must represent revenues illegally enjoyed by a landowner; and, in particular, anything over and above the state revenues that he was allowed. Sometimes, even this might be granted to a landowner by the emperor, as the following example shows. In 1196 the Emperor Alexios III granted the monks of Patmos a property on the island of Crete together with the taxes that it owed to the state—which amounted to 48 *nomismata*. In addition, the monastery was to keep any 'surplus income' (*τὴν τῆς εἰσόδου περίσσειαν*).[77]

There can be little doubt that the 'surpluses of the *apographeis*' represented revenues enjoyed by a landowner in excess of the state revenues that he had been granted and other payments that had been officially approved. This underlines the value of the *apographe*. It provided a means both of ensuring that revenue was not lost to the state and of keeping a check on the incomes of the holders of privileged property.

[73] Heisenberg, 'Palaiologenzeit', pp. 37–41, 78; Dölger, *Reg.* 1994.

[74] Miklosich and Müller IV, p. 254; Dölger, *Reg.* 1726.

[75] Svoronos, *Le Cadastre de Thèbes*, pp. 38–9, 45–6, 127–9.

[76] See *Actes de Xéropotamou*, No. 19, pp. 167–8. Cf. Dölger, *Schatzkammern*, No. 17, No. 43/4, ll. 142, 161.

[77] Miklosich and Müller VI, pp. 131–2.

5. THE ASSESSMENT OF TAXES

Inseparable from the handing over of a *pronoia* or other privileged property was the establishment of the taxes and services owed by the peasants settled there. In the case of a *pronoia* or an immunity these would be due to the holder; in other cases they would normally go to the state. The assessment of the taxes and services to be paid by the peasantry might be the responsibility of the *exisotai*[78] or of the *apographeis*.[79] It was also a task often entrusted to the provincial authorities.

These taxes and services naturally varied with the size of the holding and with the number of livestock that a peasant possessed. For fiscal purposes peasant holdings were standardized and the peasantry divided into classes. As we have seen, a peasant might be a *zeugaratos*, a *voidatos*, an *aktemon*, or an *aporos*.[80] *Zeugaratoi* and *voidatoi* held units of land which were called *zeugaria* and *voidata* respectively. In origin, they probably corresponded to the amount of land which could be cultivated on the one hand by a pair of oxen, and on the other by a single ox. Their exact size varied with the quality of the land.[81] They were also fiscal units. The *aktemones* and *aporoi* would not have possessed regular holdings, but they probably held odd plots of land, possibly leased others, and may have possessed some olive trees. The *aktemones* often owned asses, sheep, and goats. Many would have worked as labourers, some as village craftsmen.

In 1234 Constantine Laskaris, then Duke of Thrakesion, was instructed, as we have seen, to make an *apographe* of the village of Vari. His most important task was to inspect the peasantry settled there, to establish them on either *zeugaria* or *voidatika* according to the wealth and substance of each, and to fix the appropriate taxes and services which they were to owe to the monastery of Lemviotissa.[82]

[78] Ibid., pp. 208–10; *Praktikon* of Constantine Diogenes.

[79] Miklosich and Müller IV, pp. 85–6; ibid. VI, pp. 182–3. Cf. ibid. VI, pp. 188–9.

[80] Tafel and Thomas II, pp. 208–9; Oikonomides in *REB* 22 (1964), 160, ll. 17–19, pp. 169–70.

[81] See N. G. Svoronos, 'Sur quelques formes de la vie rurale à Byzance: petite et grande exploitation', *Annales, Economies, Sociétés, Civilisations*, 11 (1956), 331–2.

[82] Miklosich and Müller IV, pp. 182–3; Dölger, *Reg.* 1740.

A document of 1232 known as the *apokope ton psomion*[83] sheds a little light on the procedures involved. It contains a series of tables. These give, on the one hand, the real value of lands of various qualities and the rate at which they were to be taxed, and, on the other, a notional size of the holdings of the different classes of peasant, e.g. a *zeugaratos* would hold 40 *modioi* of land valued at 60 *hyperpyra*; a *monovoidrios* 30 *modioi* valued at 40 *hyperpyra*; and a *pezos* 20 *modioi* valued at 20 *hyperpyra*.[84]

The official concerned would register all the peasant holdings together with any other land on the estate remaining over. Most of this would be valued separately from the peasant holdings, but some of it would be added to the peasant holdings, since the size given for them in the tables was purely notional. Their real size would depend upon the quality of the land available. The notional figure given in the tables provided a starting-point from which it was possible to establish the real size of these holdings, no matter what sorts of land were contained within the bounds of a particular estate or village.

The purpose of the *apokope ton psomion* was to allow the administration to establish the value of an estate (*proasteion*) for purposes of taxation.[85] Nothing is said about the dues and services owed by the peasants to their lord for their holdings. A rough idea of the dues paid by the different classes of the peasantry can be obtained from the so-called *Tributa Lampsacenorum* of 1219. This is an account of the revenues derived from Lampsakos on the Hellespont by its Venetian lords. The *zeugaratoi* each paid roughly 10 *hyperpyra* per annum; the *voidatoi* 5 *hyperpyra*; the *aktemones* between $2\frac{1}{2}$ and 3 *hyperpyra*; and the *aporoi* a single *hyperpyron*. The *aporoi* excepted, they were also called upon to perform corvées; these were commuted

[83] F. I. Uspenskij, 'Vizantijskie zemlemery. Nabljudenija po seljskago khozjajstva' ('Byzantine surveyors. Observations on Agrarian Economy'), *Trudy VI arkheologicheskago s'ezda v Odesse*, II, Odessa, 1888, pp. 302–8. Since the method of dating employed in this document follows a Cypriot convention (see Svoronos, *Cadastre de Thèbes*, p. 125, n. 2), it seems likely that it reflects the administrative practices followed in Cyprus, but these presumably go back to twelfth-century Byzantine administrative practice.

[84] The classes are slightly different from those attested in western Asia Minor; these are given as follows: *zeugaratos, voidatos, aktemon,* and *aporos*.

[85] See Uspenskij, art. cit., pp. 307–8.

to a total payment of 310 *hyperpyra*, at the rate of 4 *hyperpyra* for each *zeugaratos* and *voidatos* and probably a single *hyperpyron* for each *aktemon*.[86]

The basic tax which each tax-payer owed to the state was known as the *telos*.[87] It was of course perfectly possible for the state to alienate its rights to the *telos* of a particular region or village. In this case the tax-payer, as we have seen, would pay his taxes to the beneficiary of the grant and become his *paroikos*, but the rate of payment would have remained exactly the same. The *telos* was assessed on a tax-payer's substance. We have already noted that the peasantry, who formed the vast majority of tax-payers at Byzantium, were divided into fiscal classes on the basis of their substance and were expected to pay the appropriate *telos*.[88]

Besides the *telos* a peasant household had to bear other charges. As we know, in 1238 the *apographeus* Konstomares assessed the taxes and dues that the peasant Kakavas was to pay. He distinguished three categories of taxes for which he was liable. There were first the military dues (*stratiotika zetemata*), secondly, the 'state chapters' (*demosiaka kephalaia*), which consisted of two taxes known as *agape* and *sitarkia*, and finally there were other dues he was called upon to pay, just like other *paroikoi*.[89] It was the second category which would have constituted the *telos* or *demosion*, as it was often called.

Let us begin by examining the two basic taxes raised during the period of exile, the *agape* and the *sitarkia*. It was only with some reluctance that the government exempted the holders of privileged property from the payment of these taxes. It was even laid down that in normal circumstances

[86] Tafel and Thomas II, pp. 208–9. It is not at all certain how the value of the corvées was worked out. Each *zeugaratos* and *voidatos* was certainly expected to commute his corvées at the rate of 4 *hyperpyra*. The total number of peasants of these two classes was 73. Altogether their corvées would have been worth 292 *hyperpyra*. The total value of the corvées, it will be remembered, was 310 *hyperpyra*. The difference is 18 *hyperpyra*; and there happened to be 18 *aktemones* at Lampsakos. This allows one to conclude that the *aktemones* each commuted their corvées at the rate of 1 *hyperpyron*.

[87] See Svoronos, *Le Cadastre de Thèbes*, pp. 139–41; Ostrogorskij, *Féodalité*, pp. 311–12.

[88] e.g. before 1246 a peasant woman of Palatia was paying a *voidiatikion telos* of 1 *hyperpyron* to her local tax authority (Miklosich and Müller VI, pp. 188–9).

[89] Miklosich and Müller IV, pp. 85–6.

these, together with a tax called *ploimoi*, would be paid on all property except that granted out in *pronoia*.[90]

Neither the *agape* nor *sitarkia* are recorded before 1204, but the latter seems to be identical with a tax called *zeugaritikion* which is attested before 1204. It then seems to have been an additional tax payable on plough teams (*zeugaria*).[91] From what has been said about the nature of the *zeugarion*, it is easy to see that plough teams were a fairly accurate reflection of a man's worth and of the land that he cultivated. Consequently, they provided an excellent basis for the assessment of taxation. The change in nomenclature merely reflects the way in which what was originally only an additional tax became a basic one, but it remains something of a mystery why the name *sitarkia* should have been chosen. It literally means 'supplies' and was the Greek term used as an equivalent for the late Roman *annona*. As is well known, a large part of the *annona* was paid in kind, but *sitarkia* was paid in money.[92] Possibly, there is something to be said for Professor Ahrweiler's intuition that the proceeds of the *sitarkia* went towards the costs of provisioning the cities and fortresses of the Empire. In similar vein, she hazards the guess that the revenues derived from the *agape* went towards the payment of subsidies to foreign powers under the terms of treaties (*agapai*) concluded with them.[93] In other words, the proceeds of these basic taxes were set aside to meet some of the essential needs of the state. Ingenious as this hypothesis is, it is not supported by any solid evidence; and it offers no explanation of the basis upon which the *agape* was raised. Given that *sitarkia* was paid on plough beasts and ploughlands,[94] *agape* was presumably the basic tax paid by those without any. On the face of it, it seems likely that *agape* would

[90] Zepos, *Ius* I, p. 663, ll. 3–5.

[91] Svoronos, *Le Cadastre de Thèbes*, p. 139, n. 7; Každan, *Agrarnye Otnošenija*, pp. 141–3; F. Dölger, 'Zum Gebührenwesen der Byzantiner', in *Byzanz und die europäische Staatenwelt*, p. 257, n. 88; Dölger, *Finanzverwaltung*, pp. 53, 59; Ostrogorskij, *Féodalité*, pp. 305, 357–8.

[92] Miklosich and Müller IV, pp. 45–6; ibid. V, p. 13, ll. 10–13; Dölger, *Reg.* 1729.

[93] H. Glykatzi-Ahrweiler, 'La Concession des droits incorporels. Donations conditionnelles', *Actes du XIIe Congrès International d'Études Byzantines*, II, p. 109, n. 35.

[94] *Sitarkia* would not only have been paid on plough teams (*zeugaria*), but also on single oxen, e.g. the *voidiatikon telos* mentioned above, p. 223, n. 88.

have corresponded to the earlier hearth tax known as the *kapnikon*. The latter tax is not recorded during the period of exile, though it does reappear after 1261,[95] when the *agape* is rarely found.

Typical military dues were those such as *ploimoi* and *kontaratoi*. *Ploimoi*, which literally means 'sailors', may have some connection with the naval service owed in the old maritime themes. This underwent a transformation similar to that already noted in connection with military service.[96] It was commuted in the course of the eleventh century for a money payment. Until the reign of John II Komnenos (1118–43) the revenues derived from this source were earmarked for the upkeep of the fleet, but it was then decided, on the advice of the chief financial minister of the day, John Poutzes, that this income should go directly into the imperial treasury; and it became the treasury's responsibility to find the sums needed for the upkeep of the navy.[97]

This measure must have gone a long way towards transforming *ploimoi* from a due for which only certain properties were liable into a regular tax. We have seen that it was one of the chief taxes raised during the period of exile.[98] It was assessed in units of *ploimoi*, which betrays the origins of this tax. Thus, in 1235 the village of Vari, near Smyrna, was assessed at one and a half *ploimoi* out of a total of 150 *ploimoi*. This total presumably represents the number of sailors that the *katepanikion* of Smyrna theoretically owed for naval service.[99] The fiscal value of a *ploimos* is not known. *Kontaratoi*, which literally means 'spearmen', presumably had a history similar to that of *ploimoi*.[100]

The dues that Kakavas was called upon to pay, like any other *paroikos*, were probably the various *angareiai* and

[95] Dölger, *Finanzverwaltung*, pp. 51–3; Každan, *Agrarnye Otnošenija*, pp. 149ff.

[96] See above, p. 195.

[97] Nicetas Choniates, pp. 74–5. See Ahrweiler, *Byzance et la mer*, pp. 211–12, 230–3; Lemerle in *Cahiers de Civilisation Médiévale*, 2 (1959), 274–5; Stadtmüller, *Michael Choniates*, pp. 174, 291; H. Antoniadis-Bibicou, *Études d'histoire maritime de Byzance. A propos du 'Thème des Caravisiens'*, Paris, 1966, pp. 42–5.

[98] See Zepos, *Ius* I, p. 663, ll. 3–5.

[99] Miklosich and Müller IV, pp. 250–2; Dölger, *Reg.* 1748, 1756.

[100] Miklosich and Müller IV, p. 217, l. 3, p. 224, l. 19, p. 251, ll. 1–22. Other military dues may have been: *stypaxoungoi, pissoygrosissa, zeugoamaxia*.

corvées, which were normally commuted for a money payment,[101] and possibly the *morte* or tithe, which *paroikoi* were expected to give their lord.[102] They may also have included the various perquisites that officials of the imperial administration could claim. The governor of a theme, for instance, could demand a due known as 'ducal needs' (*chreiai doukikai*) and there was a similar due called 'needs of the *katepanikion*' (*chreiai katepanikiai*) which presumably went to the officials of the *katepanikion*.[103] Visiting imperial officials were entitled to a payment in kind known as *kaniskia*.[104] They could also expect dues in return for specific tasks that they carried out. The handing over of imperial grants of property brought with it a payment known as *paradotikion,* unless the emperor exempted the recipient of the grant from its payment.[105] When Duke Laskaris carried out his *apographe* of Vari, he was instructed to see that the peasants of the village gave *oikomodoparasporon,* as they had done under previous lords.[106] This has been interpreted as a payment made by peasants to the official responsible for assessing their taxes and services.[107] It is now clear that the *oikomodion,* at any rate, was not such a payment, but a surcharge paid in corn on the basic taxes.[108] *Oikomodoparasporon* must be related to this.

The bane of the Byzantine tax system before 1204 had been the payment of surcharges on the basic taxes and the payment of additional dues to the officials of the imperial administration. These abuses clearly continued to exist under the emperors of Nicaea; indeed, they formed an integral part of the fiscal system. Possibly, the worst excesses were kept in check, since contemporaries praise the justice of John Vatatzes's fiscal administration.

[101] Miklosich and Müller IV, p. 217, ll. 4ff., p. 249, l. 8, p. 255, l. 28; Tafel and Thomas II, pp. 208–9; Dölger, *Finanzverwaltung*, p. 62.

[102] See above, pp. 134–5.

[103] Miklosich and Müller IV, p. 4, ll. 5–6, p. 18, l. 1, p. 21, ll. 19–20, p. 214, l. 14.

[104] Ibid., p. 214, l. 14.

[105] Ibid., p. 146, l. 29.

[106] Ibid., p. 182, l. 18.

[107] See F. Dölger, 'Zum Gebührenwesen der Byzantiner', in *Byzanz und die europäische Staatenwelt*, pp. 251, 256, n. 86.

[108] *Actes de Dionysiou*, No. 26, ll. 14–17, pp. 153–4; J. Bompaire, 'Sur trois termes de fiscalité byzantine', *BCH* 80 (1956), 625–31; Každan, *Agrarnye Otnošenija*, p. 119.

The Nicaean *vestiarion* possessed other sources of revenue which do not fit very easily into the categories of taxes set out by the *apographeus* Konstomares. The pasturage tax, known as *ennomion*, seems to have been of considerable importance during the period of exile. It was payable both on beasts, particularly sheep, and on bees.[109] One of the tasks that Konstomares had to carry out as *apographeus* was to count the number of sheep and assess the *ennomion* that was to be paid.[110] In the eleventh century a global figure would be fixed for the amount of *ennomion* to be paid by each village community; and this would then be divided among the peasants in proportion to the amount of land tax that each paid.[111]

Another important source of revenue was the *aerika*.[112] These were the profits of justice, but they too seem to have been standardized at a global figure for each village.[113]

Finally, there were the custom duties, or, as they were called, *kommerkia*,[114] and other harbour dues. Before 1204 *kommerkia* had provided the Byzantine Empire with one of its most lucrative sources of revenue, even though from the late eleventh century onwards Venice, Genoa, Pisa, and then even monastic houses, were able to obtain varying degrees of exemption from their payment. *Kommerkia* were not only levied on foreign trade, but also on internal trade. As we have seen, foreign trade with the Nicaean Empire was of relatively minor importance, but local trade was brisk; and *kommerkia* continued to be collected. Some monastic houses still found it worth their while to obtain exemption from their payment.[115] The supervision of the customs service appears to have lain with the duke of the theme. This was

[109] Miklosich and Müller IV, p. 4, l. 6, p. 17, ll. 28–9, p. 21, l. 22, p. 250, l. 2, p. 253, ll. 23–8; ibid. VI, p. 223, ll. 32–5. The *praktikon* of Constantine Diogenes (1254) noted that for every 15 head of lambs 9 or 11 aspra were to be taken.

[110] Miklosich and Müller IV, p. 253; Dölger, *Reg.* 1763.

[111] See Každan, *Agrarnye Otnošenija*, pp. 123–4.

[112] See F. Dölger, 'Das aerikon', *BZ* 30 (1929–30), 450–7.

[113] See Tafel and Thomas II, pp. 208–9.

[114] See H. Antoniadis-Bibicou, *Recherches sur les douanes à Byzance* (Cahiers des Annales, 20), Paris, 1963, pp. 109–10, 124–5, 146–55.

[115] Miklosich and Müller VI, pp. 165–6, 183; Dölger, *Reg.* 1687, 1783; Wilson and Darrouzès in *REB* 26 (1968), No. 6, p. 21.

certainly the case while John Kantakouzenos was Duke of Thrakesion.[116]

6. *EPITELEIA*

It will be remembered that the *apographeus* Konstomares had to decide whether or not a property bought by the monastery of Lemviotissa was liable to pay an *epiteleia*. The *epiteleia* was a distinctive feature of the Nicaean fiscal system. Its nature and importance have been the object of a long study by Professor Ahrweiler.[117] Though her main conclusions must certainly stand, a reappraisal of the importance of the *epiteleia* within the context of the Nicaean fiscal system may not be without some value.

The *epiteleia* is not clearly attested before 1204, but it is frequently recorded from the early years of the period of exile onwards. This presumably indicates that it was of spontaneous growth, designed to meet particular needs at a time of considerable dislocation of the administration. This impression is reinforced by the explanations that contemporaries gave of the purpose behind the payment of *epiteleia*.

In 1209 one John Poleas made a gift of some olive trees to a cousin of his. He stipulated that an *epiteleia* of one and a half *nomismata* should be paid to him each year by his cousin on account of these trees. This was for two reasons. In the first place, this was the sum that the state continued to demand from him each year as tax upon these trees; and, secondly, such a payment would in some way give greater validity to the transaction.[118]

The second point is taken up in other documents of the time. In 1216 a member of the Gavalas family sold his share in some family property near Ephesos to the monastery of St. John of Patmos. The monastery was to pay him an *epiteleia* of four *nomismata* annually. Such a payment would ensure that nobody would be able to dispute the monastery's rights of ownership.[119] Much the same reason was given by the Metro-

[116] Miklosich and Müller VI, p. 183; Dölger, *Reg.* 1783; Wilson and Darrouzès in *REB* 26 (1968), No. 6, p. 21.

[117] H. Glykatzi, 'L'Épitéleia dans le cartulaire de Lemviotissa', *B* 24 (1954), 71–93; id., 'A propos de l'épitéleia', *B* 25/7 (1955–7), 369–72.

[118] Miklosich and Müller IV, p. 121, ll. 17–19.

[119] Ibid. VI, pp. 174–6.

politan of Smyrna in 1237 when he sold a field to the monastery of Lemviotissa and demanded the annual payment of one litre of wax as *epiteleia*: not only would this payment make it impossible for anybody to challenge the monastery's ownership of the field; it would also provide a means of informing future metropolitans of the field's fate.[120]

Accordingly, when property changed hands, a payment called an *epiteleia* was frequently made by the new owner to the original one. This was done for two, apparently unrelated, reasons: on the one hand, it was designed to cover the taxes owing on the property which the original owner would still be called upon to pay by the state; on the other, it provided a guarantee of the new owner's rights to the property. The connection was almost certainly that at Byzantium the payment of taxes on a property provided one of the clearest proofs of ownership.[121] As far as the administration was concerned, the person listed to pay taxes on a particular property was its owner. Consequently, the payment of an *epiteleia* was a means of proving that property had changed hands. Its value in the confused situation that existed under Theodore I Laskaris is quite clear. It ensured that the state kept track of changes in the ownership of property and was not deprived of its revenues. It also provided conclusive proof of ownership at a time when many titles to property were uncertain or defective.

It was a temporary expedient, but, as so often, it came to have a permanent role to play. It not only retained its original purpose, but, at the same time, it was developed to meet new needs. As the payment of an *epiteleia* in wax shows, it did not invariably go to cover the taxes that the original owner of a property owed to the state, but had become a formal payment, designed solely as a guarantee of undisturbed ownership. But it was on the fiscal, rather than the legal, side of the *epiteleia* that the most important developments took place. It came to have a vital role to play in integrating privileged property into the fiscal system as a whole.

For example, there are several instances of the monastery

[120] Ibid. IV, pp. 52–3.

[121] See Svoronos in *Travaux et Mémoires*, 1 (1965), 334–7.

of Lemviotissa buying property from peasants who stipulated that the monastery was to pay an *epiteleia* to their lord, Syrgares,[122] who held a valuable *pronoia* in the neighbourhood of Smyrna. There was another case where the same monastery was called upon to pay an *epiteleia* on some property to another holder of a *pronoia*. This *epiteleia* was inscribed in the latter's *praktikon*.[123] These are excellent examples of the flexibility that the *epiteleia* gave to the *pronoia* system. The land market was such that property granted out in *pronoia* could not be expected to remain invariably under the direct control of a *pronoia*-holder, but, as long as an *epiteleia* was paid, the value of the *pronoia* would be maintained intact. It would be registered in the holder's *praktikon* in the same way as were other revenues that went to make up the *pronoia*.

Much the same is true in the case of property that formed part of an immunity. The holder of an immunity did not just possess rights of ownership in his property, but he also enjoyed fiscal rights in it which had originally belonged to the state. When some estates on the island of Cos were granted to the monastery of St. John of Patmos, the taxes paid on them were transferred to the profit of the monastery.[124] Accordingly, the holder of privileged property could alienate some of his property, but would continue to enjoy the fiscal rights that he possessed in it. The new owner would be expected to pay him an *epiteleia* which became under these circumstances a rent. This illustrates how what were originally public rights were converted into private ones, but in many cases, especially when such property was alienated for pious reasons, the original owner renounced his fiscal rights.[125]

One might say that the *epiteleia* was the lubricant of the Nicaean fiscal system. It made it easier for the government to trace where liability lay for the taxes owed on property that had changed hands. At a different level, it also met some of the problems presented by the development of privileged property. In effect, the alienation by the state of fiscal rights created a new sort of property. The *epiteleia* ensured that real

[122] Miklosich and Müller IV, pp. 60–2, 134–5.
[123] Ibid., p. 89, ll. 7–9.
[124] Ibid. VI, pp. 217–18.
[125] See Glykatzi in *B* 25 (1954), 76–87.

property could be alienated, but the fiscal rights inherent in it could be retained. The *epiteleia* appears sometimes as a payment of a public nature, sometimes as a payment of a private nature. It fitted a situation where public rights were being alienated either temporarily or permanently to private individuals.

The very nature of the *epiteleia* was bound to produce uncertainties which the imperial administration was called upon to resolve. The problem facing Konstomares was to determine the circumstances in which the state could demand the payment of an *epiteleia*.[126] His decision indicated two circumstances in which it could *not* demand payment: first, when the property on which the *epiteleia* was due was waste and unproductive; and, secondly, when the original holder of the property had been established on another holding for which he was liable to pay taxes to the state. Konstomares's judgement stresses that an *epiteleia* ought not to be paid on waste property. This might have opened the way to the payment of an *epiteleia* unconnected with the possession of the relevant property. The principle was soon to be established that a man had no obligation to pay an *epiteleia* on property of which for one reason or another he no longer enjoyed possession.[127]

Theoretically, an *epiteleia* ought to give one a fair idea of the rate at which taxation was levied in the thirteenth century. But the rate at which *epiteleia* was paid on land was so ludicrously high that it cannot reflect the rate of taxation. *Epiteleia* on land seems often to have been paid at the rate of 1 *hyperpyron* per *modios*.[128] There are some isolated figures that suggest the more modest rate of 1 *hyperpyron* for every 12 *modioi*,[129] but even this is high compared with the figures given by the *apokope ton psomion*: there arable land of the first quality was listed to pay taxes at the rate of 1 *hyperpyron* for every 48 *modioi*.[130] One can only suggest that the peasants involved in these transactions alienated part of their property

[126] Miklosich and Müller IV, pp. 85–6.

[127] Ibid., pp. 73–4, 89, ll. 4–26.

[128] A table of the rate at which *epiteleia* was paid is given by Každan, *Agrarnye Otnošenija*, p. 159.

[129] Miklosich and Müller IV, pp. 84–5, 131–2.

[130] Uspenskij in *Trudy VI arkheol. s'ezda v Odesse 1884 g.* II, p. 306.

to the monastery of Lemviotissa and then demanded an *epiteleia* equivalent to the taxes due on the whole of it.[131]

On the whole, the *epiteleia* demanded on olive trees[132] was altogether more reasonable and probably nearer to the real rates of taxation. Very frequently, one finds parcels of from 20 to 40 trees paying a sum fluctuating from one to one and a half *hyperpyra*. This compares with the rate of taxation laid down in the *apokope ton psomion* of 1 *hyperpyron* for every 30 olive trees.[133] But it must not be denied that there were also some considerable variations from this figure in the rate at which *epiteleia* was paid on olive trees.

It is therefore impossible to assume that the rates paid in *epiteleia* either on land or on olive trees necessarily reflect the rates of taxation prevailing. On the other hand, the very great variations in the rate at which *epiteleia* was paid show that, while the *epiteleia* may have acted as a lubricant to the fiscal system, it introduced another element of instability.

7. THE COLLECTION OF TAXES

At first sight, there seems to have been some confusion in the machinery for collecting taxes during the period of exile. There are even instances of *apographeis* demanding the payment of taxes.[134] It was one of the basic principles of the Byzantine fiscal system that tax assessment and tax collection should be kept apart;[135] and a natural reaction to a case of an *apographeus* collecting taxes is that this principle was breached during the period of exile. It is quite possible, however, that the *apographeis* in question were exacting payment of taxes owed to the state, but withheld on some pretext or other. This would be well within the general competence of the *apographeus* who was responsible for checking irregularities in the holding of land and the payment of taxes.

Before 1204 the collection of the basic taxes owed by a *katepanikion*—the chief fiscal unit of a theme—was entrusted to

[131] The cases in which an *epiteleia* of 1 *hyp.* per *modios* was demanded all concern the notorious Gounaropoulos family (Miklosich and Müller IV, pp. 191–2, 195–6, 200–1).

[132] See the table prepared by Glykatzi in *B* 24 (1954), 91–2.

[133] Uspenskij, art. cit., p. 306.

[134] Miklosich and Müller IV, p. 253, ll. 19–33; ibid. VI, pp. 188–9; Dölger, *Reg.* 1763.

[135] See Dölger, *Finanzverwaltung*, p. 79.

an official known as the *praktor*, who was appointed by the duke of the theme.[136] During the period of exile the *praktor* and the ducal administration as a whole continued to collect certain taxes. The dukes of Thrakesion and their administration were frequently upbraided for exacting taxes from property that was exempted from payment, but there is never a hint that the collection of the basic taxes of *sitarkia* and *agape* came within their competence. This was entrusted to men known as *apaitetai* or exactors,[137] who were without any doubt tax-farmers.[138]

The *praktores* and other members of the ducal administration continued to collect military dues, such as *ploimoi* and *kontaratoi*, as well as the profits of justice and the payments made in lieu of corvées.[139]

A single document sheds some light on the accounting procedures employed by the ducal administration. Manuel Kontophre, the Duke of Thrakesion, was informed by imperial writ that the monastery of Lemviotissa was exempted from the payment of one and a half *ploimoi*. The monastery would provide him with a document attested by the Metropolitan of Smyrna proving that it was exempted from this payment. This would then serve as a receipt for the missing one and a half *ploimoi* when the duke presented his account at the treasury.[140] This procedure is exactly the same as that which we have seen used by the administrators of the imperial salt pans near Smyrna.[141] It follows a procedure employed before 1204.[142]

It is possible to detect a tendency during the period of exile for the collection of the military dues to be removed from the competence of the ducal administration. It was a task given with increasing frequency to officials known as *vestiaritai*

[136] Sathas VI, p. 627, ll. 14–18; Dölger, *Finanzverwaltung*, pp. 71–4.

[137] Miklosich and Müller IV, pp. 45–6; Dölger, *Reg.* 1729. Cf. Miklosich and Müller IV, p. 261, ll. 3–7.

[138] See Sathas VI, No. 6, p. 645, No. 8, p. 647; Svoronos, *Le Cadastre de Thèbes*, pp. 89–90.

[139] Miklosich and Müller IV, pp. 216–17, 224–5, 249–50, 250, 252; Sathas VI, pp. 641–2; Ferrari in *Bulletino dell'Istituto Storico Italiano*, 33 (1913), 54, ll. 20–31; Dölger, *Reg.* 1756, 1769, 1770.

[140] Miklosich and Müller IV, p. 250, ll. 27–9; Dölger, *Reg.* 1756.

[141] See above, p. 207.

[142] See Svoronos in *REB* 24 (1966), 97–106.

who held their commissions directly from the emperor.[143] The *vestiaritai* are first attested in the late eleventh century, when they formed the Emperor Alexios I Komnenos's bodyguard.[144] They may have acquired some connection with the fiscal administration at the turn of the twelfth century.[145]

The policy of entrusting the collection of the military dues to the *vestiaritai* seems to have been the prelude to a far-reaching reform carried out in all probability by Michael Palaiologos. The purpose of this reform was to bring the entire tax-raising machinery in the provinces under the direct control of the central government. That of the eastern provinces was placed under the authority of the Domestic of the Anatolian Themes; that of the European provinces under the authority of his counterpart, the Domestic of the Western Themes.[146] The *vestiaritai* were placed under their orders.[147] The creation of these offices helped to disentangle the rather confusing situation that existed under the emperors of Nicaea where responsibility for the raising of certain taxes seems to have been divided indiscriminately between the provincial authorities and agents of the central government.

It would be foolish to pretend that the fiscal machinery of the Nicaean Empire functioned perfectly. There were certainly abuses and cases of oppression and inefficiency. No doubt the burden of taxation continued to be very unevenly distributed. But it is perhaps more important that the emperors of Nicaea were able to obtain the financial resources that they needed and that contemporaries were impressed by the justice of the Nicaean financial administration.

The emperors of Nicaea were able to avoid that brutal fiscal administration which so marred the history of the late twelfth century and was a sign of the government's increasing powerlessness. The relative justice of the Nicaean fiscal administration reflected both its greater efficiency and the much

[143] Miklosich and Müller IV, pp. 251–3; Dölger, *Reg.* 1748, 1759.

[144] Anna Comnena IV. iv, 3; (ed. Leib) I, p. 152, ll. 1–2.

[145] Dölger, *Finanzverwaltung*, p. 31, and n. 10.

[146] Pseudo-Kodinos, p. 188, ll. 5–8; Dölger, *Finanzverwaltung*, pp. 20–1; R. Guilland, 'Contribution à l'histoire administrative et à la prosopographie de l'Empire byzantin: les domestiques des thèmes d'Orient et des thèmes d'Occident', *Akten des XI. internationalen Byzantinisten-Kongresses*, Munich, 1958, pp. 206–11.

[147] Miklosich and Müller IV, pp. 229–30, 231–2, 278–9, ll. 4–5.

more effective control that the government exercised over the great landowners. The taxation system seems to have been simplified. The complicated system of surcharges which was an essential feature of the fiscal administration of the twelfth century[148] was very largely abandoned. It is true that during the period of exile monasteries were at pains to obtain exemption from a large number of different taxes, but the number of taxes that were actually raised appears to have been relatively limited.

One of the results of the simplification of the tax machinery seems to have been more effective central control. This is not just a question of the employment of *vestiaritai* to collect certain taxes. The administrative and fiscal surveys allowed the emperors of Nicaea to keep a close check on developments within the provinces. The *apographe,* in particular, served in many ways as a 'commission of the peace' sent out periodically by the central government to check irregularities in the holding of land, the payment of taxes, and the administration in general.

The strengths of the Nicaean government were emphasized by the historian George Pachymeres, when he contrasted its efficiency and honesty with the failings of the Byzantine government of his own day. He complained that under Michael Palaiologos fiscal surveys were no longer entrusted to the great officers of the court, as had been the case during the period of exile, but were carried out instead by men of no account.[149] He also denounced the growing corruption in the higher reaches of the administration. The *mesazontes* now demanded payment for their services. As a result, men well suited for office were passed over, since they were either unwilling or unable to pay the sums demanded.[150] This should perhaps be linked with growing criticism of abuses arising from the sale of offices. Pachymeres's critical attitude towards the governments of Michael Palaiologos and of his son Andronikos II Palaiologos must have contained an element of nostalgia for the happier days of his youth at Nicaea, but it underlines the deterioration which had occurred in the

[148] See Svoronos, *Le Cadastre de Thèbes*, pp. 81ff.
[149] Pachymeres I, p. 222, ll. 1–6.
[150] Ibid. II, p. 208, ll. 6–11.

practice of government since 1261. It was not simply a question of the sale of offices. This was an abiding feature of Byzantine administration, even if there is no evidence that it was practised under the emperors of Nicaea. It was not in itself inimicable to good government, but it was clearly open to abuse, particularly at times when the Byzantine government found itself in financial difficulties, as was the case from the late thirteenth century onwards. Perhaps more serious was the way in which access to the emperor was becoming more and more restricted. This in turn undermined that close co-operation between the emperor and the aristocracy in all aspects of the administration which had characterized Nicaean government.

PART V

THE PROVINCIAL ADMINISTRATION OF THE NICAEAN EMPIRE

INTRODUCTION. THE RESTORATION OF PROVINCIAL ADMINISTRATION

The system of provincial administration developed at Byzantium in the course of the confrontation with the Arabs (7th–10th centuries) goes under the name of the theme system and is characterized by a series of military governorships. In the course of the eleventh century the themes lost most of their military functions and became little more than administrative divisions. They were reorganized by the emperors of the House of Komnenos, who restored their military character. At their head were dukes who possessed both civil and military authority. This reform was completed in the Anatolian provinces during the reign of Manuel I Komnenos.[1]

After his death in 1180 the new provincial organization was under constant pressure from Turkish raids; and there were frequent rebellions. But it was not completely destroyed. The framework survived until the final fall of Constantinople in April 1204.[2]

The Latin conquest of Constantinople intensified the disorder and confusion in the Anatolian provinces. The Latins began the conquest of the north-western parts; the Seljuqs threatened from the east; and local magnates were able to make themselves independent. Theodore I Laskaris was only able to survive this critical period because of the strength of his base at Prousa.[3] The turning-point came, as we know, in March 1205 when the Latins were completely defeated by the Bulgarians at Adrianople. The Latin forces were evacuated from Asia Minor; and Theodore Laskaris very quickly brought western Asia Minor under his authority. The restoration of its provincial administration must have begun almost immediately; for by 1207 the district of Smyrna was being

[1] H. Glykatzi-Ahrweiler, 'Recherches sur l'administration de l'Empire byzantin aux IXe–XIe siècles', *BCH* 84 (1960), 62–5; Ahrweiler, 'Smyrne', pp. 123–30; id., *Byzance et la mer*, pp. 222–5, 271–9.

[2] Miklosich and Müller IV, pp. 320–9; Dölger, *Reg.* 1571, 1633, 1668.

[3] Nicetas Choniates, pp. 797–8.

administered by an imperial official.[4] About this time, too, sales of land begin again, which suggests that conditions were returning to normal.[5]

The restoration of provincial government was temporarily halted by the great Latin offensive of 1211 and 1212 which penetrated as far as Nymphaion[6] and rendered necessary the evacuation of the theme of Thrakesion.[7] As soon as the Latins had withdrawn, this task was resumed. It is at this time that dukes of the Anatolian themes are attested once again.[8] In 1213 a duke of the theme of Thrakesion is recorded. He was the *epi tou kanikleiou* Basil Chrysomalles.[9] It is strange to find a member of the imperial chancery entrusted with the governorship of a theme; and this suggests that in 1213 the task of restoring the theme system was still in its early stages.

Theodore Laskaris continued to rely heavily upon the co-operation of the aristocracy for the maintenance of law and order; and large areas were administered directly by members of the aristocracy and relatives of the emperor.[10] To defend the frontiers of his state and, at the same time, to assert his authority, Theodore Laskaris was forced to leave his capital of Nicaea and undertake expeditions into the provinces.[11]

The evidence for the restoration of provincial government relates almost entirely to the southern half of the Nicaean Empire. Nothing is known, for instance, about the measures which Theodore I Laskaris took to restore administration in the region surrounding Nicaea and Prousa, which had formed the nucleus of his dominions; nor is it known whether a regular provincial government was even set up in Paphlagonia, which Theodore Laskaris annexed in 1214.

[4] Miklosich and Müller IV, pp. 217–18; Dölger, *Reg.* 1676.

[5] e.g. Miklosich and Müller IV, pp. 119–21 (Oct. 1209); pp. 183–4 (Mar. 1208); pp. 185–7 (Nov. 1207); ibid. VI, pp. 151–3 (July 1207).

[6] Acropolites I, p. 27, ll. 16–18.

[7] Miklosich and Müller IV, p. 35, ll. 22–6, p. 38, ll. 29–33.

[8] e.g. of the theme of Mylasa and Melanoudion (ibid. p. 291, ll. 3–5; Dölger, *Reg.* 1693).

[9] Wilson and Darrouzès in *REB* 1968, pp. 13–14; Dölger, *Reg.* 1685.

[10] See above, pp. 61–2.

[11] See Nicephorus Callistus Xanthopulus, *Enarratio de episcopis Byzantii*, in Migne, *P.G.* 147, col. 465, ll. 11–12, 16–19; Heisenberg, 'Neue Quellen', III, p. 8, l. 31.

We are better informed about the region of Skamander which comprised the north-western corner of Asia Minor. It was held by the Latins from 1212 until they were driven out by John Vatatzes in 1224. During this period its defence was entrusted to a Greek called Theophilopoulos who had some Greek regiments under his command.[12] It is unlikely that the Latins made any drastic alterations in the existing administrative arrangements.[13] An *exisosis* of this region was conducted by the Grand Domestic Andronikos Palaiologos and Caesar Romanos[14] soon after it had been recovered from the Latins.[15] This must have been an important preliminary step in the restoration of Nicaean administration in these region.

The establishment of Nicaean administration in the European provinces of the Empire was complicated by the frequent changes of ruler which these provinces had experienced in the period from the fall of Constantinople to the Nicaean conquest. This meant that it had been very difficult for any ruler whether Latin, Greek, or Bulgarian to assert effective central control over these regions. The power of the local aristocracy and of the commanders of the fortresses was strengthened.[16] The establishment of Nicaean authority in its European provinces was rendered still more difficult by their size and situation. Their conquest very nearly doubled the area of the Nicaean Empire; and they were far removed from the palace of Nymphaion, the administrative capital of the Nicaean Empire. John Vatatzes's speedy conquest of Macedonia was only achieved at the price of confirming the privileges of the towns and cities that submitted to him.[17] In other words, he was forced to accept the power of the local aristocracy in provincial administration.

The restoration of provincial administration was among the chief cares of the emperors of Nicaea; and the administrative system which they established in their Anatolian

[12] Acropolites I, p. 29, ll. 7–11.

[13] Cf. Tafel and Thomas II, pp. 208–9.

[14] Pachymeres I, p. 222, ll. 3–5.

[15] See Scutariotes, p. 286, ll. 14ff.

[16] See E. Francès, 'La Féodalité et les villes byzantines', *BS* 16 (1955), 82–8; E. Kirsten, 'Die byzantinische Stadt', *Berichte zum XI. internationalen Byzantinisten-Kongress*, V. 3, pp. 35–46.

[17] Acropolites I, pp. 77–8.

provinces was one of the strengths of their state. They introduced relatively few innovations. Perhaps the most notable was the separation of the offices of duke and of *apographeus*. Their achievement in Anatolia was to carry through the Komnenian reforms which had broken down in the later twelfth century.

It is convenient to treat the administration of the Asiatic and European provinces of the Nicaean Empire separately. This approach is dictated partly by the different circumstances which affected the histories of these provinces and partly by the nature of the sources. We are much better informed about the Asiatic provinces, but it must be stressed at the outset that most of the information which we possess about their administration relates to a small district around the city of Smyrna, and that this does not necessarily give an entirely accurate picture of the administration of other parts of Nicaean Asia Minor.

XI

THE ADMINISTRATIVE DIVISIONS OF THE ASIATIC PROVINCES OF THE NICAEAN EMPIRE

During the period of exile the theme continued to be the chief unit of provincial administration. It has already been noted that the reorganization of the theme system was the work of the emperors of the House of Komnenos. In Asia Minor it was closely connected with the reconquest and defence of the coastlands against the Turks. At first, it was a matter of holding a number of key points from which it was possible to dominate the surrounding countryside. These were gradually grouped together to form themes that very roughly corresponded to the geographical divisions of western Asia Minor, but there was always a tendency, particularly at times of crisis, for the themes to break up and for the original divisions to reassert themselves.[1]

The chief administrative and fiscal division of a theme was known as the *katepanikion*. Its appearance in the course of the twelfth century is connected with the reorganization of the provincial administration carried out by the emperors of the House of Komnenos. It replaced an older division called the diocese (*dioikesis*).[2]

It must be admitted that the administrative divisions of the Nicaean Empire are not always very clear, largely because there was a tendency to disguise all divisions of the theme and sometimes even the theme itself under the term '*chora*' or 'district'. The *katepanikion* was usually divided into *chorai*. These may have coincided with ecclesiastical divisions known as *enoriai*, for these too are often described as *chorai*.[3] In the

[1] See Ahrweiler, *Byzance et la mer*, pp. 185–9, 222–5.

[2] See D. A. Zakythinos, *Le Despotat grec de Morée*, II, Paris, 1953, pp. 58–9; Ahrweiler, 'Smyrne', pp. 126–7.

[3] See Ahrweiler, 'Smyrne', pp. 55–6; Svornos, *Le Cadastre de Thèbes*, p. 56, n. 2.

neighbourhood of Smyrna they usually comprised several villages.[4]

Administrative divisions from earlier phases of Byzantine administration also survived. The *episkepsis* is a case in point. It was originally a fiscal division of a theme, but by the late twelfth century it was a term more commonly employed for estates belonging to members of the aristocracy and the imperial family. This seems to have been its meaning in the thirteenth century.[5]

The administrative divisions of the Byzantine Empire at the end of the twelfth century are set out in great detail in the lists of provinces contained in Alexios III Angelos's chrysobull of 1198 for the Venetians and in the *Partitio Romaniae* of 1204.[6] In these lists each province is set out with its subordinate divisions. Although they are not completely consistent and although discrepancies exist between them, these lists provide a useful starting-point for an examination of the administrative divisions of the Nicaean Empire.

In the north, stretching along the Black Sea coast from the mouth of the river Sangarios to the town of Amastris was the province of Paphlagonia. To its west lay the region of Bithynia, which was divided in the tenth century between the themes of Optimaton and Opsikion. The former comprised the parts opposite Constantinople; the latter, the region about the city of Nicaea which served as its capital.[7] At the end of the twelfth century Bithynia was divided into a number of smaller provinces,[8] but these seem to have been regrouped during the period of exile to form a single province with its capital at Nicaea.[9] The region of Optimaton was not finally recovered from the Latins until 1240 and it may have formed

[4] See Ahrweiler, 'Smyrne', pp. 55–74.

[5] e.g. the *episkepsis* of Sampson held by Savvas Asidenos (Miklosich and Müller IV, p. 292, ll. 5–7, p. 293, ll. 31–2); the *episkepsis* of Petra held by the Empress Theodora, wife of Michael VIII Palaiologos (ibid., pp. 31, 175, 262, 278).

[6] Tafel and Thomas I, pp. 246–80, 464–88.

[7] A. Pertusi (ed.), *Costantino Porfirogenito de Thematibus* (Studi e Testi, 160), The Vatican, 1952, pp. 68–70, 127–33.

[8] Tafel and Thomas I, pp. 269–70, 475–8. See D. A. Zakythinos, '*Μελέται περὶ τῆς διοικητικῆς διαιρέσεως καὶ τῆς ἐπαρχιακῆς διοικήσεως ἐν τῷ βυζαντινῷ κράτει*', *EEBS* 19 (1949), 19; 25 (1955), 130–40.

[9] Acropolites I, p. 101, ll. 20–1, p. 106, l. 3, p. 159, ll. 16–17; Theodore Lascaris, p. 241, ll. 21–2; Blemmydes, p. 16, ll. 24–6; Gregoras I, p. 57, ll. 21–2.

a separate theme for a time,[10] but it had been reunited with the rest of Bithynia by the beginning of Theodore II Laskaris's reign, when Michael Palaiologos was made governor of Bithynia.[11] Tarsia, a frontier district situated on the eastern banks of the river Sangarios not far from the city of Nikomedeia,[12] also came under his authority.[13]

To the south-east of the city of Nicaea lay the frontier town of Malagina, which stood on the banks of the river Sangarios. It was the centre of a province at the end of the twelfth century.[14] A seal has been preserved from this period; it bears the name of Manuel Lykaites who held the combined office of duke and stratopedarch of Malagina.[15] Whether Malagina continued to form a separate province during the period of exile or whether it came under the authority of the governor of Nicaea is not known, but its position was most probably analogous to that of another border city, Philadelphia, which will be examined below.[16]

At the turn of the twelfth century the north-western corner of Asia Minor formed the theme of Opsikion and Aigaion.[17] This region is referred to in the sources of the thirteenth century as Skamander or the Troad. It appears to have formed a province of the Nicaean Empire after its recovery from the Latins,[18] but its official name is not known. It seems to have stretched as far south as the city of Achyraous, and its southern frontier was apparently formed by the mountain of Kiminas, which divided it from the theme of Neokastra.[19]

[10] Zepos, *Ius* I, p. 661, ll. 18–19; Acropolites I, pp. 58–9. Cf. Ch. Ktenas, '*Χρυσόβουλλοι λόγοι τῆς ἐν Ἄθῳ ἱερᾶς βασιλικῆς, πατριαρχικῆς καὶ σταυροπηγιακῆς μονῆς τοῦ Δοχειαρείου*', *EEBS* 4 (1927), 310–11.

[11] Acropolites I, p. 135, ll. 22–4, p. 163, l. 8. George Pachymeres (I, p. 24, ll. 15–16) describes Michael Palaiologos as governor of Mesothynia and commander 'of these Optimates'. Mesothynia appears to have been the learned equivalent for the region of Optimaton.

[12] Ramsay, *Hist. Geography*, p. 191.

[13] Acropolites I, p. 163, l. 8.

[14] Tafel and Thomas I, p. 478. On the position of Malagina, see V. Laurent (ed.), *La Vita Retractata et les miracles posthumes de St Pierre d'Atroa* (Société des Bollandistes: Subsidia Hagiographica, 31), Brussels, 1958, pp. 66–74.

[15] V. Laurent, *Bulles métriques*, No. 407.

[16] See below, pp. 247–8.

[17] Tafel and Thomas I, p. 270, l. 2; Acropolites I, p. 11, l. 24.

[18] Pachymeres I, p. 222, ll. 2–5.

[19] Acropolites I, pp. 27–8.

This theme was created out of the northern parts of the theme of Thrakesion between the years of 1162 and 1173, as part of Manuel Komnenos's measures for the defence of the Asiatic frontiers of his empire. It originally comprised the cities of Chliara, Pergamon, Adramytion, and the surrounding districts.[20] The northernmost point of this theme in the thirteenth century was the village of Kalamos.[21] It lay in the Upper Kaikos valley near the site of the ancient Stratoniceia.[22] Pergamon[23] and Chliara[24] which are also situated in the Kaikos[25] valley, continued to form part of the theme of Neokastra under the emperors of Nicaea, but the port of Adramytion to the north had become the centre of a separate province by the turn of the twelfth century.[26] Its occupation by the Latins from 1212 to 1224 must have confirmed this arrangement.[27]

In the course of the thirteenth century the theme of Neokastra was considerably extended southwards. It came to include the cities of Magnesia[28] and Sardes[29] in the Hermos valley. In geographical terms it therefore came to be formed by two closely related regions, the valleys of the Kaikos and the Hermos. No officials of this theme are recorded during the period of the Nicaean Empire, but, as we have seen, Constantine Margarites began his career in the army of this theme.[30]

The theme of Thrakesion, which lay to the south, was

[20] Nicetas Choniates, pp. 194–5. On the theme of Neokastra, see Ahrweiler, 'Smyrne', pp. 133–7, 163–5.

[21] Acropolites I, p. 28, ll. 3–4.

[22] Ramsay, *Hist. Geography*, pp. 129–30; Tomaschek, 'Topographie', p. 96.

[23] A theme of Pergamon is recorded in the late thirteenth century, when the theme system in Asia Minor was disintegrating (Dölger, *Reg.* 2079). On Pergamon, see H. Gelzer, 'Pergamon unter Byzantinern und Osmanen', *Abhandlungen der königlich en preussischen Akademie der Wissenschaften*, philos. und hist. Kl., Abh. 2, Berlin, 1903, pp. 82–91.

[24] For the position of Chliara, see Ramsay, *Hist. Geography*, pp. 117–18; Tomaschek, 'Topographie', p. 96.

[25] Acropolites I, p. 28, ll. 6–8.

[26] Tafel and Thomas, I, p. 271, l. 1.

[27] Acropolites II, pp. 15–16.

[28] In 1284 the duke and *apographeus* of Neokastra, Manuel Kalampakes, is found handing over property in Magnesia to the monastery of Lemviotissa (Miklosich and Müller IV, pp. 267–9).

[29] Pachymeres II, pp. 220–1.

[30] Acropolites I, p. 123, ll. 6–19.

reconstituted shortly after 1133 as part of the reorganization of the theme system carried out by John II Komnenos, but its size was much reduced by the creation of the theme of Neokastra.[31] The theme of Thrakesion is not recorded in the lists of provinces contained in the chrysobull of 1198 and in the *Partitio Romaniae,* even though a duke of Thrakesion is attested as late as 1189.[32] It had been reconstituted by the year 1213.[33] Its core was then formed by a region known as Kelvianon which comprised the Kaystros valley.[34] The administrative divisions of the theme of Thrakesion during the period of exile give a clearer picture of its extent. They included the *katepanikia* of Smyrna[35] and Anaia,[36] which lay along the Aegean coast, and the *chora* of Pyrgion and Kaloe,[37] which comprised the upper Kaystros valley.[38]

Basil Chrysomalles, whom we have seen holding office in 1213, is the first duke of Thrakesion recorded after 1204;[39] and from 1233 until 1260 the list of those who held this office is almost complete.[40]

The capital of this theme may have remained, as in the tenth century,[41] the city of Ephesos.[42] There are some grounds for believing that Philadelphia was the capital in the middle of the twelfth century,[43] but by the turn of the century it had become the centre of a separate province.[44] Under the

[31] Ahrweiler, 'Smyrne', pp. 123–30.

[32] Nicetas Choniates, pp. 522–3. See Ahrweiler, 'Smyrne', pp. 130–1.

[33] Wilson and Darrouzès in *REB* 1968, pp. 13–14; Dölger, *Reg.* 1685.

[34] Cinnamus, p. 39, ll. 9–14; Acropolites I, p. 12, l. 20, p. 28, ll. 6–8. Both these authors appear to use Kelvianon as an equivalent for Thrakesion. See also Ramsay, *Hist. Geography*, p. 130; Tomaschek, 'Topographie', p. 91.

[35] See Ahrweiler, 'Smyrne', *passim.*

[36] Wilson and Darrouzès in *REB* 1968, p. 21, ll. 2–3, p. 35, l. 1.

[37] Miklosich and Müller IV, p. 154.

[38] See Tomaschek, 'Topographie', pp. 91–2; P. Lemerle, *L'Émirat d'Aydin, Byzance et l'Occident: recherches sur la "Geste d'Umur Pacha"* (Bibliothèque Byzantine, Études 2), Paris, 1957, p. 21, n. 2.

[39] Wilson and Darrouzès in *REB* 1968, pp. 13–14; Dölger, *Reg.* 1685.

[40] See F. Dölger, 'Chronologisches und Prosopographisches zur byzantinischen Geschichte des 13. Jahrhunderts', *BZ* 27 (1927), 307–10; Ahrweiler, 'Smyrne', pp. 138–49.

[41] See Pertusi (ed.), *De Thematibus,* pp. 68–9.

[42] Blemmydes, p. 91, ll. 8–10.

[43] See R. Browning, 'The Speeches and Letters of Georgios Tornikes, Metropolitan of Ephesos (XIIth Century)', *Actes du XIIe Congrès International d'Études Byzantines. Ochride 1961*, II, pp. 424–5.

[44] Tafel and Thomas I, p. 271, l. 3.

emperors of Nicaea, on the other hand, it appears to have been reunited with the theme of Thrakesion, for in 1235 a stratopedarch of the theme of Philadelphia and Thrakesion is recorded.[45] Also subordinated to the theme of Thrakesion during the period of exile was the theme of Maiander. It comprised, as its name suggests, the Maiander valley. Its chief centre in the thirteenth century was the city of Antioch.[46] It had formed a separate province before 1204, but in 1213, when it is recorded again, it was subject to the authority of the duke of Thrakesion;[47] and by the reign of John Vatatzes it had been incorporated into the theme of Thrakesion.[48] A stratopedarch and *paradotes* of Maiander is attested about the year 1247.[49]

It therefore seems to have been the policy of the emperors of Nicaea to reconstitute the themes of Asia Minor, which had been broken up into a number of smaller provinces in the course of the later twelfth century. But border districts, such as Philadelphia and Maiander, were placed under the authority of a stratopedarch and in this way retained some of the autonomy that they had possessed at the turn of the twelfth century.

Some modifications to provincial boundaries naturally took place during the period of exile. In the early thirteenth century the *episkepsis* of Sampson at the mouth of the river Maiander formed part of the theme of Maiander,[50] but by the end of the period of exile it appears to have been transferred to the theme of Mylasa and Melanoudion.[51] This theme comprised those parts of south-western Asia Minor lying south of the Maiander valley. It seems to have been created about the year 1143 out of part of the old maritime theme of Kivyrraiotai and the southern part of the theme of Thrakesion.[52] The *katepanikion* of Larymos which comprised the

[45] Miklosich and Müller IV, p. 18, ll. 14–18.
[46] Acropolites I, p. 15, ll. 21–3.
[47] Wilson and Darrouzès in *REB* 1968, pp. 13–14; Dölger, *Reg.* 1685.
[48] Wilson and Darrouzès in *REB* 1968, pp. 20–1.
[49] Miklosich and Müller VI, p. 190.
[50] Tafel and Thomas I, p. 479; Wilson and Darrouzès in *REB* 1968, pp. 14–15. Cf. Miklosich and Müller IV, pp. 293–4.
[51] Miklosich and Müller VI, p. 210; Dölger, *Reg.* 1910.
[52] Ahrweiler, 'Smyrne', pp. 128–30.

coastal region opposite the island of Rhodes formed its southernmost administrative division.[53] The names of several dukes who governed this theme in the late twelfth century have been preserved.[54] One John Tzykes who held office shortly before 1216 is the first recorded after the fall of Constantinople.[55]

The Nicaean possessions in the Aegean Sea formed a distinct part of the Nicaean Empire. Almost every island seems to have had its own governor. John Palaiologos, brother of Michael Palaiologos, was appointed governor of Rhodes, probably in 1256.[56] Alexios Varangopoulos was *kephale* or governor of the island of Cos in 1258,[57] and a duke of the island of Chios is recorded in the late thirteenth century.[58] We have already seen how in 1254 Constantine Diogenes held the combined office of duke, *apographeus,* and *exisotes* of the islands of Leros and Kalymnos.[59] But it may have been more usual to group together a larger number of islands for the purposes of the *apographe*. In 1263 Leo Eskamatismenos was *apographeus* of the island of Rhodes and the other Cyclades. His activities extended to the islands of Leros and Cos.[60]

[53] Ibid., p. 291, ll. 3–5; Dölger, *Reg.* 1693.
[54] See Miklosich and Müller IV, p. 320, ll. 22–3, p. 325, l. 3.
[55] Ibid., pp. 320–7.
[56] Miklosich and Müller VI, p. 198.
[57] Ibid. VI, p. 187.
[58] Ibid. IV, p. 230, ll. 9–10; Dölger, *Reg.* 2152.
[59] See above, p. 59.
[60] Miklosich and Müller VI, pp. 214–19.

XII

THE ADMINISTRATION OF THE ASIATIC PROVINCES OF THE NICAEAN EMPIRE

1. DUCAL ADMINISTRATION

The theme system rebuilt by the emperors of the House of Komnenos was in the process of disintegration at the turn of the twelfth century. The emperors of Nicaea arrested this process: the themes of western Asia Minor were reconstituted much as they had existed in the reign of Manuel I Komnenos and provided the framework of Nicaean provincial administration. Each theme had at its head a governor who bore the title of 'duke'. This title was given in the tenth century to the governors of important frontier provinces; it was only in the twelfth century that it came to be applied to the governors of themes generally.[1]

The duke was appointed by the emperor and vested with both civil and military powers; he was the emperor's permanent representative in the province to which he was appointed. His term of office during the period of the Nicaean Empire was normally limited to a single year.[2] Of the dukes of Thrakesion who are recorded during this period only the Butler John Komnenos Kantakouzenos held office for a longer term. He first appears as duke of Thrakesion in 1242[3] and he was still in possession of this office in 1249.[4] As we have already remarked,[5] his long tenure of office was almost certainly due to the exceptional circumstances of those years. Equally unusual was Manuel Kontophre's tenure of this office. He was apparently governor of Thrakesion on two

[1] Glykatzi-Ahrweiler in *BCH* 84 (1960), 53–5, 61–4; Ahrweiler, *Byzance et la mer*, pp. 118–30, 222–5; Ahrweiler, 'Smyrne', pp. 125–7; D. Angelov, 'K voprosu o praviteljakh fem v epirskom despotate i nikejskoj imperii', *BS* 12 (1951), 58–64.

[2] See Dölger in *BZ* 27 (1927), 307–10; Ahrweiler, 'Smyrne', pp. 138–48.

[3] Wilson and Darrouzès in *REB* 26 (1968), 20–1.

[4] Acropolites I, pp. 86–7; Dölger, *Reg.* 1798.

[5] See above, pp. 210–11.

separate occasions, first in 1237 and then again in 1240.[6] Another anomaly occurred shortly before the recovery of Constantinople. In 1259 Theodotos Kalothetos appears to have combined the offices of duke of Thrakesion and duke of Melanoudion.[7] Again the circumstances were exceptional. In that year the usurper Michael Palaiologos had need of men whom he could trust in key positions in the provinces just as much as in the central government. Kalothetos was his uncle.[8]

During the period of exile the dukes of Thrakesion were drawn from the court aristocracy. Some were relatives of the emperors of Nicaea[9] and there were also members of the great Byzantine families, such as the Angeloi, the Laskarids, and the Kantakouzenoi, among their numbers.[10] But, with the exception of John Kantakouzenos, none held any important court title. Most of them bore the very common honorary title of *pansevastos sevastos*.[11] A much more important common factor uniting all those who held the office of duke of Thrakesion during the period of exile has so far gone unnoticed. They were all members of the imperial household.

Some of the dukes of Thrakesion went on to occupy other posts in the Nicaean administration.[12] Manuel Kontophre became commander of the Nicaean fleet,[13] while Theodore

[6] Miklosich and Müller IV, pp. 249–50, 252; Dölger, *Reg.* 1756, 1769, 1770. It may well be, as Professor Ahrweiler ('Smyrne', pp. 143–4 and n. 96) suggests, that the dating of the single document (Miklosich and Müller, No. clvii, p. 250), which apparently shows Kontophre holding office in 1237, ought to be emended. It is dated Indiction 10 (= 1237), but this may be a copyist's error, and should be altered to Indiction 13 (= 1240).

[7] Miklosich and Müller IV, pp. 153–4, 208–10; ibid. VI, pp. 201–2.

[8] Cf. F. Dölger, *PARASPORA*, pp. 181–2.

[9] John Doukas Kourtikes, duke 1233–4, was a *syngambros* of the emperor; John Angelos, duke 1235–6, was an uncle of the emperor.

[10] John Angelos, duke 1235–6; Constantine Laskaris, duke 1234–5; John Kantakouzenos, duke 1242–*c.* 1249.

[11] Manuel Kontophre, duke 1237 (?), 1240; Theodore Hikanatos, duke 1239; Theodotos Kalothetos, duke 1259; Theodore Kryvitziotes, duke 1260.

[12] It has been suggested (e.g. by Ahrweiler, 'Smyrne', p. 142) that John Angelos, Duke of Thrakesion 1235–6, is to be identified with the *Protostrator* John Angelos, who held office under Theodore II Laskaris and belonged to his inner circle (see above, pp. 84, 152). But the latter was a comparatively young man (see Acropolites I, p. 124, ll. 9–13), while the former is described as an uncle of the Emperor John Vatatzes. He is probably to be identified with the father-in-law of John Vatatzes's nephew, John Doukas (Acropolites, p. 101, ll. 4–14).

[13] Acropolites I, p. 59, ll. 14–17, p. 66, ll. 13–14.

Kryvitziotes, who was duke of Thrakesion in 1260, was in the following year a member of a Nicaean embassy to Genoa.[14] Normally speaking, the governorship of a province would only have come fairly late in a man's career. Two dukes of Thrakesion, Theodore Hikanatos[15] and Theodotos Kalothetos,[16] died while holding office, and a third, John Kantakouzenos,[17] shortly after his term of office had ended. On the other hand, a governorship might be conferred upon a man, such as Michael Palaiologos, who was still at the beginning of his career, but had already distinguished himself and was marked out for greater things.

Under the duke of a theme came a variety of officials. They can be divided into two groups. There were, on the one hand, the duke's personal staff and, on the other, senior officials of the provincial administration who were appointed directly by the emperor. These included the governors of cities and fortresses and the stratopedarch, who appears to have been the most important official of the theme beneath the duke. He may well have acted as the duke's deputy. Later evidence suggests that the stratopedarch's special duties were connected with the military organization of the theme,[18] but during the period of exile the holders of this office are only found carrying out routine administrative tasks, such as an *apographe* or the handing over of property.[19] They could also authorize the handing over of *paroikoi* to the holder of a *pronoia*.[20] It was an office that seems to have been frequently combined with other posts in the provincial administration; at Malagina with the office of duke[21] and in Maiander with that of *paradotes*.[22] It must be assumed from the title that the *paradotes* of a theme had a special responsibility for the handing over of property and peasants.[23] But this was not by any means a task that was carried out exclusively by the holders

[14] Dölger, *Reg.* 1884, 1892.
[15] Blemmydes, p. 31, ll. 4–11.
[16] Ibid., pp. 91–2.
[17] Miklosich and Müller IV, p. 70, ll. 20–1. See Nicol, *Kantakouzenos*, 14–16.
[18] Pseudo-Kodinos, p. 187, ll. 4–22.
[19] Miklosich and Müller IV, pp. 4–8; ibid. VI, p. 190.
[20] Oikonomides in *REB* 22 (1964), 160, ll. 8–9.
[21] Laurent, *Bulles métriques*, No. 407.
[22] Miklosich and Müller VI, p. 190.
[23] Cf. Oikonomides in *REB* 22 (1964), 160, ll. 8–9.

of this office. As might be expected, the duke was assisted by officials who in theory were responsible for specialized aspects of provincial administration, but in practice were called upon to perform a variety of tasks. It was for this reason that the chief offices of the theme were often combined.

The members of the duke's personal staff were chosen by him, and not appointed by the emperor. The duke possessed a *grammatikos* or secretary.[24] He also possessed a *logariastes,* who had an essential role to play in the fiscal administration of the theme. He was not only responsible for aiding the duke in the collection of certain taxes,[25] but he was also called upon, at least in the late twelfth century, to supervise property. If the legality of a sale of property was in doubt, it might be brought to him for authorization.[26] He might also be sent by the duke to discover whether a landowner was entitled to all the *paroikoi* settled on his estates.[27]

All aspects of provincial administration came within the duke's purview. His chief responsibility was possibly the maintenance of law and order and the general administration of justice within his province. Often it was simply a question of carrying out an imperial order to protect the rights and property of, for instance, a monastery, when these were threatened by outsiders. In the case of the monastery of Lemviotissa, these ranged from members of the great families of the Empire[28] down to the kitchen servants of the palace of Nymphaion.[29] The dukes of Thrakesion were also called upon to protect this monastery from their own administration.[30]

[24] Miklosich and Müller IV, p. 55, ll. 11–12.

[25] Ibid., pp. 214–15; Dölger, *Reg.* 1731.

[26] Miklosich and Müller VI, p. 125, ll. 25–30.

[27] Ibid. IV, pp. 317–18. There remains the problem of the *protovestiarios.* At the end of the twelfth century holders of this office were involved in the financial administration of the theme (Stadtmüller, *Michael Choniates*, p. 295). They are to be distinguished from the court dignitary of the same name. In the early thirteenth century one George was the *protovestiarios* of the Grand Duke Theodotos Phokas (Miklosich and Müller VI, pp. 153–6). He had been responsible for investigating a property dispute along with other local officials, including a *logariastes.* There are thus two possibilities. The *protovestiarios* was *either* an officer of a great noble household *or*, as there is a strong possibility that Phokas was duke of Thrakesion (see above, p. 200, n. 131), an official of the theme administration.

[28] Miklosich and Müller IV, pp. 254–5; Dölger, *Reg.* 1772.

[29] Miklosich and Müller IV, p. 215; Dölger, *Reg.* 1768.

[30] Miklosich and Müller IV, pp. 216–17, 224–5.

Of course, a duke would not always wait for an imperial order before he acted. Disputes and grievances might be brought directly to him; and he would be expected to investigate them.[31] But, whether he was acting on imperial orders or on his own initiative, many of the cases with which he had to deal would have to come before him for judgement. He possessed his own law court. He was the judge, but assessors were present.[32] In all probability, this law court was established on a semi-permanent basis in the capital of the theme; and it was here that complaints against the ducal administration and lawsuits were brought.[33] In the course of his duties a duke travelled throughout his province. He presumably set up court on the way to hear pressing cases, or he might be ordered by the emperor to go away to a particular place to try a lawsuit on the spot. This happened in September 1235 when the Duke of Thrakesion, John Angelos, was ordered to try a dispute involving the monastery of Lemviotissa. His assessors on this particular occasion were the son of the Metropolitan of Smyrna, a member of the metropolitan's administration, and the governor of the fortress of Smyrna.[34] The decision made by John Angelos and his assessors favoured the monastery. It was based on the documents which each party produced and on the oral testimony of local people who had been summoned.[35]

There was another procedure that a duke could adopt in cases brought before him for judgement. In 1268 the monks of Lemviotissa and a member of the Planites family took their quarrel over some olive trees to John Tornikes, who was then duke of Thrakesion. He sent a citizen of Smyrna called Makrenos, who was not apparently connected with the provincial administration in any official capacity, to the village where the trees stood. He was to investigate the matter and to obtain sworn evidence from local inhabitants.[36] It was upon this evidence that Tornikes came to his verdict.[37]

[31] Blemmydes, pp. 29–30; Theodore Lascaris, pp. 298–9; Miklosich and Müller IV, pp. 73–4.
[32] Blemmydes, p. 17, ll. 11–17.
[33] Ibid., pp. 16–17, p. 29, ll. 26–9, p. 91, ll. 5–13.
[34] Miklosich and Müller IV, p. 38, ll. 19–23.
[35] Ibid. IV, pp. 36–9; ibid. VI, pp. 210–12.
[36] Ibid. IV, p. 141, ll. 6–16. Cf. ibid., pp. 73–4.
[37] Ibid., pp. 73–4.

The impression left by the sources is that most of the duke's judicial work concerned property disputes, but this cannot have been the case. How he dealt with serious crimes, such as murder, robbery, and rape, is nowhere recorded, although something is known of the punishments he could impose. Fining was probably the most common penalty. Sometimes fines were exceptionally heavy. In May 1256 the Duke of Thrakesion, George Makrenos, threatened the inhabitants of the village of Manteia with a fine of 1,000 *hyperpyra* if they continued to trouble the monastery of Lemviotissa.[38] In other cases, imprisonment or beating might be considered more appropriate penalties. In 1233 another duke of Thrakesion, John Doukas Kourtikes, inflicted both these punishments upon the *paroikoi* of Vari for refusing to pay the taxes that he had demanded of them.[39]

Apart from his judicial work and the maintenance of law and order, the duke had other responsibilities which have already been touched upon. The military organization of the theme came under the control of the duke. The commanders of the fortresses of his theme were under his orders[40] and he may have continued to command the troops of his theme on campaign. As late as 1248 the Butler John Kantakouzenos, who was then duke of Thrakesion, was sent by the emperor to seize a number of fortresses on the island of Rhodes. He was to prevent them falling into the hands of the Genoese, who had seized the city of Rhodes. This he did, with the help of a small force which he had at his disposal. This was presumably the army of his theme, since the emperor was forced to send him reinforcements from the field army, as soon as a campaign against the Latins of Constantinople had been completed.[41] By the time of the recovery of Constantinople the duke's military duties must have become progressively less important as a result of the enrolment of the provincial armies in the field army.[42] They would have been reduced to little more than the supervision of the *pronoia* system within his province.

[38] Ibid., pp. 211–12.
[39] Ibid., pp. 214–15; Dölger, *Reg.* 1731.
[40] Acropolites I, pp. 135–6.
[41] Ibid., p. 86, ll. 1–14.
[42] See above, pp. 189–91. Cf. Angelov in *BS* 12 (1951), 62, 65.

The duke and his administration were responsible for the handing over of *pronoiai*.[43] The duke was also to be found during the period of exile carrying out *apographai,* handing over peasants and establishing the dues and labour services they owed their lord, and handing over imperial grants of property.[44] These were all tasks regularly carried out by the *apographeis*. In the intervals of the *apographe* the supervision of property seems to have been one of the duke's main responsibilities.

The duke and his administration also had fiscal responsibilities. As we have seen, these did not include the collection of the basic land tax, but were limited to the raising of various supplementary taxes, the military dues among others. The collection even of these was progressively taken out of the hands of the ducal administration and entrusted to *vestiaritai* who held their commissions directly from the emperor.[45]

The profits of justice *(aerika)* accruing to the state remained under the duke's control and were forwarded to him monthly by his agents, who also seem to have been responsible for exacting corvées which were due to the state.[46] The duke and his administration continued to collect the various perquisites to which they were entitled.[47]

Under the Komnenoi the tax-raising machinery in the provinces was largely under the control of the ducal administration; and the financial needs of a theme were the first charge on the sum of the taxes (*achrostichon*) raised from it.[48] This was in contrast to the situation existing during the period of exile, when the duke was losing control over the collection of taxes within his theme. The consequences for provincial administration must have been far-reaching. To finance his administration the duke would have come to rely very heavily on the revenues that remained to him, in other words the profits of justice and the various perquisites which

[43] See above, pp. 217–19.

[44] See above, pp. 210, 216, 221.

[45] See above, pp. 232–4.

[46] Sathas VI, pp. 641–2; Ferrari in *Bulletino dell'Istituto Storico Italiano*, 33 (1913), 54, ll. 20–31; Miklosich and Müller IV, p. 217, ll. 4–6, p. 224, l. 19.

[47] See above, p. 226.

[48] See Dölger, *Finanzverwaltung*, pp. 76–8, 78, n. 4.

his agents could claim. Such exactions had been one of the worst features of the breakdown of provincial administration at the end of the twelfth century.[49] This does not mean that provincial administration under the Laskarids was necessarily as oppressive as it had been under the Angeloi; only that potential abuses remained. Of more immediate consequence was that the relatively large financial autonomy enjoyed by the governors of themes under the Komnenoi must have been severely circumscribed.

The sources leave two distinct impressions about the nature of Nicaean provincial administration. On the one hand, there was an overlap between the areas of responsibility of the ducal administration and those of agents of the central government; on the other, there was a tendency to diminish the duke's real authority. He was losing control over the raising of taxes within his theme; his military responsibilities were also being reduced. He was becoming essentially a civil governor, responsible for carrying out imperial orders that very often precisely defined the courses open to him and left him with little freedom of action.

There can be little doubt that, at least in the Anatolian provinces, the period of exile saw a movement towards greater central control and the more extensive use of agents of the central government in the provinces. The much smaller size of the Nicaean Empire must have made this a more practical policy than had been the case hitherto. This impression of greater central control is reinforced by the fact that much of our information relates to the district of Smyrna which lay only a few miles from the palace of Nymphaion.

The general direction of imperial policy is one thing; how it worked out in practice is another. Dukes were not always able to carry out imperial orders, nor was it always possible to enforce imperial decisions. This state of affairs suggests that the dukes enjoyed more autonomy than might be supposed. It also reflects the very complicated balance of forces that existed at the local level. The duke's actions were not determined solely by imperial orders, but also by local interests. Bishops, landowners, and even village councils

[49] See Stadtmüller, *Michael Choniates*, pp. 169–72; A. Bon, *Le Péloponnèse byzantin*, pp. 167–9.

all had a part to play in local administration; and the duke needed their co-operation.

2. LOCAL GOVERNMENT

There were not only many interests involved in local government; there were also various levels. The chief administrative division of the theme was the *katepanikion*. Its administration was quite distinct from that of the great cities of the Empire, such as Ephesos, Philadelphia, Smyrna, and Nicaea, which came under a governor appointed by the emperor; but towns, such as Palatia and Sampson, did not possess an administration separate from that of the surrounding countryside and formed the centres of the subordinate divisions (*chorai*) of the *katepanikion*.

At the head of each *katepanikion* was an agent appointed by the duke of the theme. He was known as a *praktor* or, more commonly after 1204, as an *energon*.[50] He might be a person of some standing. John Konstomares, an imperial secretary and a member of Theodore II Laskaris's circle, was *energon* of the *katepanikion* of Smyrna in 1239.[51] *Praktores* were also appointed, presumably by the duke, for the towns and districts within each *katepanikion*.[52]

Before 1204 the duties of the *praktor* were primarily fiscal,[53] but during the period of exile they underwent a change and became in the main administrative and judicial. He heard local disputes in his own law court.[54] He collected the proceeds of justice and, as we have seen, forwarded them monthly to the duke of the theme.[55] Though responsible to the duke, the *praktor* might receive orders directly from the emperor. These normally concerned the maintenance of law and order. In November 1253 the *praktor* of the *katepanikion* of Smyrna was instructed by the emperor to fine the inhabi-

[50] These terms were used interchangeably. It does not seem to me possible to establish a precise distinction between them.

[51] Miklosich and Müller IV, p. 247; Dölger, *Reg.* 1767. See Ahrweiler, 'Smyrne', pp. 159–60.

[52] Ferrari in *Bulletino dell'Istituto Storico Italiano*, 33 (1913), 54, ll. 20–31.

[53] See Dölger, *Finanzverwaltung*, pp. 73–7.

[54] Sathas VI, pp. 633–4.

[55] Ibid., pp. 641–2; Ferrari in *Bulletino dell'Istituto Storico Italiano*, 33 (1913), 54, ll. 20–31.

tants of Mantaia 1,000 *hyperpyra* if they continued to trouble the monastery of Lemviotissa.[56]

One incident reveals something of what was involved in the work of a *praktor*. In 1209 the *praktor* of the town of Palatia was called upon to investigate a dispute over the property of a dying monk. He went to see the monk, hoping to discover how he had disposed of his property. When the case came for judgement before the Metropolitan of Miletos, the *praktor* produced as evidence the statement that he had extracted from the monk.[57]

Not all *praktores* were government agents; some were in the service of members of the aristocracy.[58] As we have seen, the grant of an immunity might involve the exercise of public authority; and the beneficiary would be obliged to establish his own administration. It is difficult to evaluate the role played by these *praktores* in local government during the period of exile, since virtually all the evidence of their activities in the region of Smyrna relates to the period after the recovery of Constantinople. There was now a growing distance between the government in Constantinople and the Anatolian provinces. The monastery of Lemviotissa no longer had the same confidence in imperial intervention and was forced to come to terms with local magnates and sometimes even to seek their protection. Their *praktores'* influence in local affairs consequently grew, but their range of duties cannot have changed greatly. They were essentially estate administrators, responsible for upholding their lord's interests and carrying out his orders. This might involve witnessing the sale of property belonging to one of their lord's *paroikoi*[59] or handing over a grant of property that he had made.[60] At other times, the duties of the *praktor* were more those of a village headman. In 1228 the *praktor* of the village of Prinovari went with the priests and other leading inhabitants to settle a dispute that

[56] Miklosich and Müller IV, pp. 210–11; Dölger, *Reg.* 1815.

[57] Miklosich and Müller VI, pp. 153–6.

[58] See Ahrweiler, 'Smyrne', pp. 162–3. To this list should be added Theodore Lapardas, *energon* in Mourmounta in the service of the *panhypersevastina* Zagaromatina (Miklosich and Müller IV, pp. 234–5) and Leo Kaloeidas, *antidoux* of the Empress Theodora's estates of Petra (ibid., p. 279). *Antidoux* was another equivalent for *praktor* (see Ferrari in *Bulletino del'Istituto Storico Italiano*, 33 (1913), No. 32, p. 60, ll. 24–8).

[59] Miklosich and Müller IV, pp. 158–9.

[60] Ibid., pp. 175–6, 234–5.

their village had with the monastery of Lemviotissa over a field. After evidence had been heard on both sides, the representatives of Prinovari agreed before their *praktor* to concede the field to the monastery.[61]

This incident underlines the part that village representatives had to play in local affairs. They were known as *oikodespotai* or 'the better sorts' (*kreittones*). In the tenth century their farms were carefully distinguished from the general run of peasant holdings.[62] There is no evidence that this continued to be the case in the thirteenth century; their legal status was no different from that of the other *paroikoi* in a village.[63] But their very title implies that they continued to form a peasant aristocracy.

Together with the priests of the village, the *oikodespotai* formed a village council which was responsible for the ordering of many aspects of village life. It served as a law court before which local disputes could be brought.[64] Its members were frequent witnesses of sales and gifts of property and were also often called upon to help the imperial administration or the local bishop in their administrative and judicial work. Village officers may have been chosen from their ranks. One of the *oikodespotai* of the village of Prinovari held the post of *oikologos*.[65] The duties attached to this post are not known; they were possibly connected with the apportioning of dues or holdings among the villagers.[66] That peasants were accustomed to arrange such aspects of village life for themselves is suggested by an imperial order of 1234. It instructed the Duke of Thrakesion, Constantine Laskaris, to settle the *paroikoi* of Vari on appropriate holdings and to fix the taxes and services that they were to owe to their lord, the monastery of Lemviotissa. He was strictly enjoined not to allow them to do as they pleased.[67]

There were other and larger local assemblies which brought together representatives from a whole district (*chora*).

[61] Miklosich and Müller IV, pp. 187–8.
[62] Dölger, *Finanzverwaltung*, p. 115, ll. 13–20.
[63] Miklosich and Müller IV, pp. 128, ll. 14ff., 278, ll. 21ff.
[64] Ibid., pp. 80–4.
[65] Ibid., p. 187.
[66] Cf. the due called *oikomodoparasporon*, on which see above, p. 226.
[67] Miklosich and Müller IV, pp. 182–3; Dölger, *Reg.* 1740.

Occasionally, they were constituted by the *oikodespotai* of the villages within the district,[68] but it seems to have been more common for representatives from the local clergy, together with soldiers holding *pronoiai* within the district, to be present as well.[69]

Much of the work of these assemblies must have been routine. They were called upon to witness a variety of documents, such as wills, sales, and marriage settlements.[70] Local disputes might come before them without the intervention of outside authorities,[71] but more often these assemblies were called together at the orders of a member of the imperial administration, of the local bishop, or of the lord of a village within the district. This does not mean that they were therefore completely subservient to whoever had been responsible for calling them together. No doubt pressure could be brought to bear upon them, but these local assemblies sometimes acted in a remarkably independent fashion. Towards the end of the thirteenth century a powerful landowner of the Phokas family called together an assembly of the district of Mantaia near Smyrna to hear his quarrel over some land with the monastery of Lemviotissa. The monks protested that they had no quarrel with Phokas, but the assembly ordered them to go and fetch their deeds. Otherwise, the case would go by default to Phokas, at whose hands the monks had suffered many injustices. After the monks had returned with the necessary documents, the assembly found in favour of the monastery.[72] About the same time the members of another local assembly ordered their lords to return some olive trees to the same monastery.[73]

The formal organization of these local assemblies rested largely with the local clergy; and this may help to explain the independent stand that these assemblies sometimes took. Not only were the local priests included among the members of both village and district assemblies, but the *protopappas* of a district or a parish (*enoria*)—the two seem often to have been

[68] Miklosich and Müller IV, pp. 165–7.
[69] Ibid. IV, pp. 94–5, 128–9; VI, pp. 153–6, 184–7, 228, ll. 8–9.
[70] Ibid. IV, p. 129, l. 1, p. 140, ll. 17–18.
[71] e.g. ibid., pp. 165–7.
[72] Ibid., pp. 128–9.
[73] Ibid., p. 92, ll. 10–21.

coterminous—not infrequently acted as the president of the district assembly.[74] Sometimes his place would be taken by the local notary,[75] but, in any case, the posts of notary and *protopappas* were frequently combined.[76] Each district had its own notary. He was invariably a priest, and he was appointed by the local bishop. His general responsibilities included the drawing up of deeds of sale, wills, and marriage settlements.[77] He also drew up the decisions reached by the local assemblies, of which he seems to have been a permanent member.[78]

The part played by the *oikodespotai* and the other members of these local assemblies in the general administration of the Empire has already been touched upon. They might be called upon to help an *apographeus* to decide rights of property.[79] They played an essential part in the handing over of imperial grants of property and the establishment of boundaries.[80]

The imperial administration and, for that matter, episcopal administrations, had need of the co-operation of these local assemblies, since one of the commonest methods employed by these administrations to settle disputes and to establish rights was the holding of an 'inquest'. This meant that local representatives were called together to bear witness over some dispute before imperial officials or members of the local bishop's administration. This was the procedure employed in 1235 by the Duke of Thrakesion, John Angelos, when he was ordered by the emperor to try the dispute over the hamlet of Sphournou between the monastery of Lemviotissa and the villagers of Potamou.[81] His judgement, based on local testimony, did not put an end to the dispute. It was finally decided by dividing the hamlet between the opposing parties, but the division had to be carried out in the presence of representatives from the surrounding villages.[82]

[74] Miklosich and Müller IV, pp. 165–7; VI, pp. 153–6.

[75] Ibid. IV, pp. 80–4, 93–4, 128–9.

[76] See Ahrweiler, 'Smyrne', pp. 117–18.

[77] Ferrari in *Bulletino dell'Istituto Storico Italiano*, 33 (1913), No. 14, p. 54, ll. 1–18; A. Dain, 'Formules de "commission" pour un "nomikos" et un "exarchos"', *REB* 16 (1958), 166–7.

[78] Miklosich and Müller IV, pp. 80–4, 128–9, 142–4, 165–6.

[79] Ibid. IV, pp. 244–7, esp. p. 245, ll. 29–33.

[80] e.g. ibid. IV, pp. 142–4.

[81] Ibid. IV, pp. 38–9. Cf. ibid. VI, pp. 210–14; Dölger, *Reg.* 1912.

[82] Miklosich and Müller IV, pp. 41–3.

One case, in particular, illustrates the powers of the *oikodespotai* and the functions of local assemblies. It concerns a long-standing dispute over some olive trees given by one John Poleas to his cousin Leo Mouzethras in 1209.[83] Poleas later claimed that his cousin had taken more than he had been given, and in 1228 he brought his case before his lord (*authentes*), the 'imperial liege knight' Syrgares, who sent the case to be heard before the *oikodespotai* of his *pronoia*. The *oikodespotai* of the village of Aurelion,[84] which formed part of Syrgares's *pronoia*, duly assembled together with the notary of the village. After examining some documents they decided that Poleas had no claim to the olive trees. Mouzethras, nevertheless, ceded ten trees to his cousin in the presence of the *oikodespotai* in the hope of thus bringing the case to a close. It was not to be. In 1251, soon after his death, his cousin's son, Thomas Poleas, reopened the quarrel by submitting it to Eirene Komnena Vranaina who had succeeded Syrgares in possession of the neighbouring village of Panaretos. Mouzethras's heir also came and put his case. Eirene Vranaina decided that the quarrel was to go before the *oikodespotai* of Panaretos for judgement. Before the case could be heard, Thomas Poleas picked the crop of olives and damaged the trees. Vranaina now had no alternative but to have Poleas tried by the *oikodespotai*. They upheld the decision of the *oikodespotai* of Aurelion and ordered Poleas to return possession of the trees to Mouzethras's heir. They warned him that he was liable to be excommunicated by the Metropolitan of Smyrna for bearing false witness and forbade him to reopen the case in either a private (*archontikon*) or ecclesiastical court on pain of a fine of twenty-four *hyperpyra* to the state.[85]

This case illustrates much of what must have been typical Nicaean local administration. It shows the way that the holders of privileged property were taking over some of the functions of the imperial administration. We have seen how they had their own agents, and now we see how the peasants settled on their estates brought their quarrels to them; but it is just as important that they should have sent such cases

[83] Ibid., pp. 119–21.
[84] Ibid., p. 82, l. 31.
[85] Ibid., pp. 80–3.

for judgement before a local court composed of *oikodespotai*. The holders of privileged estates simply took over and worked through the existing village organization. The extension of such estates may therefore not have produced such profound changes in the life of the peasantry as is sometimes supposed.

Nor were these local courts necessarily subservient to the wishes of local landowners. Judgement seems to have rested with the members of the court alone; and the sanctions it possessed—the threat of excommunication by the local bishop and a fine payable to the state—were quite independent of the authority of the local lord. It would seem that the *oikodespotai* had sufficient authority to settle disputes among their fellow peasants and to check misdemeanours. Village life thus retained a degree of autonomy, but should the verdict of a local court go against a man of influence, it was not likely to be respected and the case was almost certain to be reopened in a higher court.[86]

3. MUNICIPAL GOVERNMENT

At the head of the municipal government of the major cities of the Nicaean Empire was a governor known as the *prokathemenos*, who was appointed by the emperor.[87] During the period of exile *prokathemenoi* are attested for the cities of Smyrna,[88] Philadelphia,[89] and Ephesos,[90] and in 1267 for the city of Nicaea too.[91] The *prokathemenos* seems to have been the successor of the *katepano,* the governor of a city in the first half of the twelfth century. A seal of a *prokathemenos* has been preserved from the twelfth century. It is therefore likely that the creation of this office is to be connected with a reform of local government carried out under Manuel Komnenos.[92]

Three *prokathemenoi* of Smyrna are recorded during the thirteenth century. George Monomachos had been appointed

[86] See Miklosich and Müller IV, pp. 32–43, 165–9.
[87] Sathas VI, p. 644, ll. 8–17.
[88] See Ahrweiler, 'Smyrne', pp. 155–8.
[89] Theodore Lascaris, p. 197.
[90] Miklosich and Müller VI, p. 176. I am very grateful to Nikos Oikonomides for allowing me to consult the new edition that he is making of this document.
[91] Pachymeres I, p. 246, ll. 18–19.
[92] See Ahrweiler, 'Smyrne', p. 155.

to this office by 1227,[93] but by 1234 he had been succeeded by John Alopos or Alopekos.[94] The next recorded holder of this position was George Kaloeidas, who remained in office from the 1250s to the 1280s.[95] Both Kaloeidas and Monomachos came from Smyrniot families. Members of the Kaloeidas family figure among the Metropolitan of Smyrna's administration. George Kaloeidas possessed land in the plain of Memaniomenos outside Smyrna and a *metochion* of St. George which he gave to the monastery of Lemviotissa.[96] The Monomachos family also had property in the plain of Memaniomenos, as well as in Smyrna itself and in the village of Mantaia.[97] Alopos does not seem to have come from a local family. No other members of this family figure in the Acts of Lemviotissa. Alopos did hold a *pronoia* in the neighbourhood of Smyrna.[98] This too marks him off from the other *prokathemenoi* of Smyrna.

Demetrios Iatropoulos, the *prokathemenos* of Philadelphia, was likewise not a native of the city he was sent to govern. He had been one of the conspirators who had betrayed Thessalonica to John Vatatzes in 1246[99] and under Michael VIII Palaiologos he was to become logothete *ton oikeiakon*.[100] He was a correspondent of Theodore II Laskaris.[101]

The *prokathemenos* had both civil and military powers. In 1267 panic broke out in the city of Nicaea as a rumour spread that the Mongols were approaching the city. The citizens looked to the *prokathemenos* Nicholas Manouelites for leadership; and he set about organizing the city's defence.[102] But in the reasonably peaceful conditions that reigned in Nicaean Asia Minor the *prokathemenos*'s main duties seem to have been judicial. Various local disputes were brought before him to be settled. In September 1230 Abbot Gerasimos of

[93] Miklosich and Müller IV, pp. 44–5.

[94] Ibid., pp. 146–50.

[95] Ibid., pp. 72, 102–3. For dating see Dölger in *BZ* 27 (1927), 306.

[96] Miklosich and Müller IV, pp. 102–3. See Ahrweiler, 'Smyrne', pp. 157–8.

[97] See Ahrweiler, 'Smyrne', p. 156.

[98] Miklosich and Müller IV, p. 38. Alopos's *pronoia* probably comprised the village of Pauchome: cf. ibid., p. 35, ll. 2–9.

[99] Acropolites I, p. 79, ll. 24–5.

[100] Pachymeres I, pp. 124–5, p. 377, l. 10, p. 522, ll. 10–11.

[101] Theodore Lascaris, p. 197.

[102] Pachymeres I, pp. 246–7.

Lemviotissa produced the will of a monk named Valkes before the *prokathemenos* of Smyrna, George Monomachos. He believed that it would prove that some salt pans disputed by the monk's family belonged to the monastery. Monomachos and other *archontes* of Smyrna were able to persuade the family to make out a deed recognizing the monastery's rights to the salt pans. It was signed by Monomachos.[103] Other deeds which brought lawsuits to an end are signed and witnessed by *prokathemenoi* of Smyrna.[104] Bearing the Valkes case in mind, there is good reason to suppose that they had a part to play in the settlement of these disputes as well. In 1258 the *prokathemenos* of Smyrna, George Kaloeidas, was present (with other *archontes* of the city) as a witness in a case involving the monasteries of Lemviotissa and Kalyphas, which was heard before the Metropolitan of Smyrna.[105]

The *prokathemenos* might carry out more general administrative tasks. Both Monomachos and Alopos were responsible for handing over imperial grants of property to the monastery of Lemviotissa. Alopos actually deputized for the Duke of Thrakesion, John Kourtikes, who was involved on imperial business elsewhere.[106]

At Smyrna the *prokathemenos* was assisted in his duties by the *kastrophylax*. A *kastrophylax* was appointed by the emperor to the command of a fortress and its garrison.[107] The origins of this office have been traced back to the middle of the eleventh century.[108] *Kastrophylakes* were not only appointed to the great fortress-cities of the Empire, but also to the numerous fortresses scattered throughout the provinces.[109] One imagines that in these smaller places their powers were not just limited to the command of a fortress, but that they also pos-

[103] Miklosich and Müller IV, pp. 48–51.

[104] Ibid., pp. 69–72, 192–4.

[105] Ibid., pp. 55–6.

[106] Ibid., pp. 43–5, 146–9.

[107] Sathas VI, pp. 644–5.

[108] N. Oikonomides, 'The Donations of Castles in the last quarter of the eleventh century (Dölger, *Reg.* No. 1012)', *Polychronion. Festschrift Franz Dölger zum 75. Geburtstag*, Heidelberg, 1966, p. 417 and n. 12.

[109] e.g. *kastrophylakes* are recorded for the fortresses of Pelion and Pardovounon on the island of Cos during the thirteenth century (Miklosich and Müller VI, pp. 184, 228).

sessed considerable influence in local administration. Even in the city of Smyrna the duties of the *kastrophylax* were not entirely military. The *sevastos* Theophylaktos Vrachionites is the only *kastrophylax* of Smyrna attested during the period of exile. He held office in the 1230s. In 1230 he helped the *prokathemenos* of Smyrna, George Monomachos, to settle the dispute between the monastery of Lemviotissa and the Valkes family.[110] In 1235 he was associated with the Duke of Thrakesion, John Angelos, in his judgement of the dispute between the same monastery and the inhabitants of Potamou over the hamlet of Sphournou.[111]

Vrachionites was one of the *archontes* of Smyrna before whom the monk Nikandros Gounaropoulos confessed in 1232, at the request of the *vestiarites* John Ravdokanakes, that he had sold a field to Basil Vlatteros.[112] This confession should be put into the context of the dispute between the monastery of Lemviotissa and the heirs of Basil Vlatteros over property in the village of Vari, which had earlier been ceded by the Gounaropouloi family to Vlatteros.[113] In October 1230 the *vestiarites* Ravdokanakes obtained imperial confirmation of his rights to the disputed property, which had come to him through his marriage to Vlatteros's daughter.[114] In the same month that Gounaropoulos made his confession to the *archontes* of Smyrna, the monastery of Lemviotissa obtained an imperial order which recognized the monastery's claims to the whole of the village of Vari and dismissed those of Vlatteros's heirs.[115] It is therefore reasonable to suppose that the *archontes* of Smyrna were collecting sworn evidence, as part of an investigation of the conflicting claims to the village of Vari. We have already seen how a similar procedure was followed in another dispute involving the monastery of Lemviotissa.[116] We cannot know whether the *archontes* of Smyrna were acting on their own initiative or on orders from the government. What we do know is that the *archontes* formed

[110] Miklosich and Müller IV, p. 50, ll. 32–4.
[111] Ibid., p. 38, ll. 20–1.
[112] Ibid., pp. 189–90.
[113] Ibid., pp. 183–4, 185–7.
[114] Ibid., p. 218; Dölger, *Reg.* 1724.
[115] Miklosich and Müller IV, pp. 194–5; Dölger, *Reg.* 1728.
[116] See above, p. 254.

a distinct group within the city and that they were responsible for aiding the governor and the metropolitan in the execution of their administrative and judicial duties.

Individually, the *archontes* of Smyrna had a part to play in local administration. Of the *archontes* of Smyrna who assembled in 1232 to hear Gounaropoulos's evidence, one Theophylaktos Vrachionites was, as we know, *kastrophylax* of Smyrna. Another Constantine Phagomodes was responsible, *c.* 1235, for assessing *ploimoi* in the *katepanikion* of Smyrna;[117] yet another, the *vestiarites* Isaac Levounes, was head of the commission which collected *ploimoi* from that district in 1235.[118] Other *vestiaritai* were also numbered among the *archontes* of Smyrna.[119] It seems probable that the *prokathemenos* of Smyrna ought to be numbered among the *archontes* of the city as well.[120]

In some instances the title of '*archon*' seems to point to a specific office. The *archon*, holding a commission from the duke of a theme, had authority to hand over *paroikoi* to the holder of a *pronoia*.[121] At Athens at the end of the twelfth century an *archon* had charge of the police force, and another *archon* may have commanded the garrison of the city.[122] But it seems more likely that these examples only show how dependent the imperial administration was on the co-operation of local notables.

The *archontes* of a city were drawn in the main from established local families. They might also hold *pronoiai* in the neighbourhood and serve in the imperial administration. The emperors of Nicaea seem to have realized how important it was to bind this group to the imperial government. During the period of exile the *archontes* of Smyrna were described as the *pansevastoi oikeiotatoi* of the emperor,[123] an epithet that is not easily rendered into English, but indicates their intimacy with the emperor. On another occasion, they were called 'most useful imperial men'.[124] Smyrna was only a few miles

[117] Miklosich and Müller IV, pp. 251–2.
[118] Ibid.
[119] e.g. Michael Kadianos (ibid., pp. 54, 189); Alexios Kapnos (ibid., p. 189).
[120] Ibid., pp. 48–51, 55–6, 69–72, 192–4.
[121] See Oikonomides in *REB* 22 (1964), 160.
[122] Stadtmüller, *Michael Choniates*, p. 147.
[123] Miklosich and Müller IV, pp. 189–90.
[124] Ibid., p. 55, ll. 7–8.

from the imperial residence of Nymphaion. The *archontes* of other towns and cities may not have been bound so closely to the emperor. In 1209 the *archontes* of Palatia seem to have been in the service of the Grand Duke Theodotos Phokas.[125] The exact authority that Phokas exercised over Palatia is not known. In any case, the region was still recovering from the chaos that had accompanied the Latin conquest of Constantinople. As the example of the neighbouring town of Sampson shows,[126] at this time towns tended to pass under the control of the most powerful figure in the neighbourhood. As the emperors of Nicaea built up their administration, so they were able to assert their control.

At the same time—and this is much clearer in the European provinces than it is in the Anatolian ones—the towns and cities maintained a degree of autonomy. This was based upon the considerable local influence possessed by the *archontes* and upon the prestige of the bishop or metropolitan of the city. *Archontes* and bishop did not always work hand in hand. At the turn of the twelfth century Michael Choniates, the Archbishop of Athens, denounced the engrossment of peasant property by the local *archontes.*[127] A bishop was responsible for the welfare of his whole flock. Yet there existed a community of interest between *archontes* and bishop. It was partly based on the bishop's need for the co-operation of the *archontes* in order to carry out his administrative work; and it was reinforced by family connections. It was usual for the members of the bishop's administration to be drawn from exactly those families that supplied a city with its *archontes.* Prominent in the administration of the Metropolitan of Smyrna in the thirteenth century were members of the Alethinos, Chrysoverges, Kaloeidas, and Kastamonites families. These families all possessed estates in the neighbourhood of Smyrna and had other members with positions in the imperial administration.[128]

The *archontes,* for their part, recognized the bishop's role as spokesman for his city and his flock. No single local family

[125] Ibid. VI, p. 153.
[126] See ibid. IV, 293–5; Wilson and Darrouzès in *REB* 26 (1968), 13–15.
[127] e.g. Michael Choniates, I, p. 311, ll. 6–11.
[128] See Ahrweiler, 'Smyrne', pp. 103, 108–14, 170–1.

had the prestige or estates to compare with those of the bishop. In times of crisis a bishop might be called upon to organize the defence of his city, as happened to the Archbishop of Athens, Michael Choniates, in the opening years of the thirteenth century.[129] In the more settled conditions that reigned in Nicaean Asia Minor the bishop still had a vital part to play in local administration.

His influence derived from his office. His administrative work stemmed from his ecclesiastical duties. It is hard to separate the one from the other, but it would be going beyond the scope of an examination of local government to treat those aspects of a bishop's work which relate directly to the internal organization and discipline of the Church.

Most of what will be said about the position of the bishop in local government will relate to the metropolis of Smyrna, since our main documentary source, the Lemviotissa cartulary, contains a great deal of information about the activities of the Metropolitan of Smyrna and his administration. The monastery of Lemviotissa was situated in the *enoria* of Mantaia, which was closely attached to the church of Smyrna and seems to have been the metropolitan's special responsibility. The ecclesiastical officials of Mantaia were almost without exception members of the metropolitan's own administration.[130] Obviously, the metropolitan's authority would have been much less strong in the more distant parts of his province; and to this extent the Lemviotissa cartulary may give a slightly false impression of the metropolitan's influence in local government. Against this, it has be to be remembered that Lemviotissa was an imperial monastery and therefore not under the direct authority of the metropolitan of Smyrna. In most of its disputes the monastery first sought the help of the emperor, but it remains true that many of its disputes had in the end to be brought before the metropolitan.

The Metropolitan of Smyrna's relations with the imperial

[129] Bon, *Le Péloponnèse byzantin*, pp. 173–4.

[130] e.g. Theodore Kallistos, *anagnostes* and *nomikos* of the metropolis of Smyrna and the *enoria* of Mantaia (Miklosich and Müller IV, pp. 33, 56–7, 59–60, 61, 77, 79, 83, 119–20, 191–2, 204); John Laodikenos, *nomikos* of the metropolis of Smyrna and the *enoria* Mantaia (ibid., p. 133); John Phokas, *anagnostes* and *nomikos* of the metropolis of Smyrna and the *enoria* of Mantaia (ibid., p. 134). See Ahrweiler, 'Smyrne', p. 115.

administration oscillated between co-operation and conflict. We have already seen how John Vatatzes was forced to issue a chrysobull protecting the personal property of deceased bishops from the authorities of the theme.[131] The fault did not lie solely with the imperial administration. On some occasions it might be necessary to turn to it for protection against the activities of a bishop. In 1207 Basil Vlatteros sought the aid of the imperial administration on behalf of his relatives, the Gounaropoulos family, who, he claimed, were suffering at the hands of the Metropolitan of Smyrna.[132] Later, in 1245, the then Duke of Thrakesion, the Butler John Kantakouzenos, was to receive orders from the emperor to protect the monastery of Lemviotissa from another Metropolitan of Smyrna.[133]

Co-operation was perhaps more usual. In 1209 the Grand Duke, Theodotos Phokas, was unable to examine a dispute which had been brought before him because he was occupied elsewhere on imperial business; he therefore delegated the matter to the Metropolitan of Miletos.[134] Sometimes, a bishop would work alongside the imperial administration. In 1262 Michael Palaiologos instructed the Bishop of Amazon to assist the Duke of Melanoudion in the examination of a dispute involving the inhabitants of Sampson.[135] In much the same way, Niketas Kalosinaras, a member of the administration of the church of Smyrna, and Constantine Kaloktenes, the Metropolitan's son, were associated in the judgement given by the Duke of Thrakesion, John Angelos, in the Sphournou case.[136]

The sequel throws further light on the part played by bishops in local administration. The decision was not respected and the case was taken to the imperial court, where it was decided that the hamlet of Sphournou should be divided between the contending parties. The task of dividing

[131] Zepos, *Ius* I, pp. 486–7; Dölger, *Reg.* 1720.

[132] Miklosich and Müller IV, pp. 217–18; Dölger, *Reg.* 1676. Cf. Miklosich and Müller IV, pp. 185–7.

[133] Miklosich and Müller IV, pp. 139–40; Dölger, *Reg.* 1785.

[134] Miklosich and Müller VI, pp. 153–6.

[135] Ibid., pp. 212–14; Dölger, *Reg.* 1912.

[136] Miklosich and Müller IV, p. 38, ll. 21–2.

the hamlet was entrusted to the Metropolitan of Smyrna, who in his turn assigned the task to Niketas Kalosinaras,[137]

In this case the Metropolitan's administration was responsible for enforcing a decision of the imperial court. But there is at least one case which was brought before the Metropolitan of Smyrna, precisely because the parties despaired of a settlement by the imperial administration. It concerned a property dispute between the monastery of Lemviotissa and a *stratiotes* named Varycheir. Two imperial rescripts of the year 1259 failed to settle the matter, and four years later the parties reopened the case before the Metropolitan of Smyrna, who succeeded in producing a satisfactory settlement.[138] The imperial administration also had the greatest difficulty in settling another quarrel that the same monastery had, this time with the inhabitants of Mantaia. The monastery found it necessary to seek the metropolitan's confirmation of the imperial acts issued in connection with this affair.[139]

There are other instances of imperial rescripts or various acts of members of the imperial administration being brought to a bishop or a metropolitan for confirmation. This is eloquent testimony of their local prestige. An imperial rescript of 1221 for the monastery of St. John of Patmos only survives in a copy authenticated by the Metropolitan of Crete, Nicholas, who then held the throne of Smyrna *(epidoseos logo)*.[140] Or again, the *periorismos* of the land which was handed over to the monastery of Lemviotissa in 1231 from the imperial estates of Koukoulos was afterwards brought to the Metropolitan of Smyrna for confirmation.[141]

Private deeds too might be brought to the local bishop for confirmation and in some instances for registration as well. In 1212 George Eunouchos bought a field near Palatia and brought the deed of sale to the Bishop of Miletos to be confirmed and registered.[142] Bishops did not systematically

[137] Miklosich and Müller IV, pp. 41–3.

[138] Ibid., pp. 153–7; Dölger, *Reg.* 1868, 1874.

[139] Miklosich and Müller IV, pp. 212–13.

[140] Ibid. VI, pp. 180–2. Cf. Blemmydes, p. 12, ll. 7–9. For dating, see Ahrweiler, 'Smyrne', p. 104.

[141] Miklosich and Müller IV, p. 144, ll. 18–32. Cf. ibid., p. 291, where an act made out shortly before 1216 by an imperial official in support of the monastery of St. Paul in Latmos was confirmed by the Bishop of Miletos.

[142] Ibid. VI, p. 158, ll. 15–18: Cf. ibid. IV, p. 108, ll. 13–18, p. 109, ll. 22–32.

register all documents relating to their diocese, but they did possess their own archives; and it was certainly not just copies of their own acts that were kept there. These archives sometimes proved extremely valuable for local administration. Inquiries were begun in 1216 by the imperial administration into the rights that the Constantinopolitan monastery of Panachrantos[143] had formerly possessed in the *metochion* of Pyrgos, which was situated at the mouth of the river Maiander. The Bishop of Miletos was able to produce documents belonging to the monastery and thus smoothed the way for the transfer of the *metochion* to the monastery of St. John of Patmos.[144]

It should not be forgotten that the notarial organization came under the control of the local bishop or metropolitan. We have already seen how he was responsible for appointing notaries for each district within his diocese from members of the priesthood.[145] The situation within a city was slightly different. At Smyrna in the thirteenth century both the greater and the lesser officials of the Metropolitan's administration often combined their offices with that of *tavoullarios*.[146] This was another term for notary, but in this period it seems only to have been applied to members either of a metropolitan administration or of the Patriarchal Church.[147] Although the *tavoullarioi* of the city of Smyrna were members of the Metropolitan's administration, they do not appear to have formed his regular chancery. His official acts were never drawn up by members of his administration in their capacity as *tavoullarioi*.[148] The documents which they drew up in that capacity all seem to have been private deeds.[149] At their head was an

[143] R. Janin, *La Géographie ecclésiastique de l'Empire byzantin*, part 1: *Le Siège de Constantinople et le patriarcat oecuménique*, vol. 3: *Les Églises et les monastères*, Paris, 1953, pp. 223–4.

[144] Miklosich and Müller VI, pp. 176–9.

[145] See above, p. 262.

[146] Ahrweiler, 'Smyrne', pp. 118–20.

[147] e.g. the priest and *tavoullarios* of the metropolis of Philadelphia, John Sellares (Miklosich and Müller IV, p. 48); the imperial deacon, *ostiarios* of the Patriarchal Church and *tavoullarios*, Leo Helladas (ibid., p. 80). For the *tavoullarioi* of the metropolis of Smyrna, see Ahrweiler, 'Smyrne', pp. 118–20.

[148] See Miklosich and Müller IV, pp. 41–3, 52–4, 84–5, 110–12, 144, 155–7, 189, 258–60.

[149] See ibid., pp. 48–51, 66–9, 69–72, 86–8, 106–9, 152–3, 157–8, 163–4, 169–70, 183–4, 185–7.

officer known as the *primmikerios* of the *tavoullarioi*.[150] This is reminiscent of the organization of the guild of *tavoullarioi* at Constantinople in the tenth century. It was carefully supervised by the imperial administration.[151] In the later Byzantine period the imperial government still claimed the right to appoint the head of the *tavoullarioi* of a particular city,[152] but in practice, as the example of Smyrna shows, the notarial organization in the cities had been annexed to the Metropolitan's administration.

The possession of an archive and the control of the notarial organization did not simply mean that the metropolitan or bishop had a responsibility for the legal transactions that occurred within his diocese. They also meant that he possessed a solid documentary base for his judicial activities. He was more in touch with local conditions; he had the necessary information upon which to arrive at a verdict; and this verdict was all the more likely to be respected for being registered in the archives of his church. The desire that people showed to have imperial acts authenticated by a bishop or metropolitan is perhaps indirect proof of this. In addition, he possessed the sanction of excommunication. This was not only used as a punishment, but also as a way of testing evidence.[153]

In practice, as we have seen, it is difficult to draw a clear-cut dividing line between ecclesiastical and imperial jurisdiction.[154] It was not just that the imperial administration relied upon the support of the local bishop when it came to the settlement of lawsuits. It was also the case that lawsuits begun in imperial courts might later be transferred to an episcopal one. Parties appear to have been able to take their disputes to whichever court they pleased; and there were strong inducements, which have been outlined above, for seeking the arbitration of the local bishop or metropolitan.

Their influence was increased by the over-all supervision that they appear to have exercised over the work of local

[150] See Ahrweiler, 'Smyrne', pp. 112, 113, 115, 118–20.

[151] See I. Dujčev (ed.), *Τὸ ἐπαρχικὸν βιβλίον. The Book of the Eparch. Le Livre du Préfet*, London, 1970, pp. 13–22.

[152] Sathas VI, pp. 645–6.

[153] Miklosich and Müller IV, pp. 82–3; ibid. VI, pp. 154–5.

[154] See above, pp. 51–3.

courts composed of *oikodespotai* and other local representatives. In the Poleas case[155] judgement was finally given on 15 October 1251 by the *oikodespotai* of Panaretos. Two days later it was authenticated by the *chartophylax* of the church of Smyrna, who claimed that the judgement had been carried out by commission of the Metropolitan.[156]

Judicial work was often delegated to members of an episcopal administration. In 1228 the Metropolitan of Smyrna entrusted judgement in the dispute between the monastery of Lemviotissa and the Prinovaritai to his *megas sakellarios* Constantine Varypates. His decision was then brought to the Metropolitan for confirmation.[157] The chief officers of a bishop's administration normally acted as assessors of his court; at Smyrna the *archontes* of the city might sometimes assist as well.[158]

The chief officers of an episcopal administration were known as the *archontes* of the Church; and their role was not dissimilar to that of the *archontes* of the city. They came from the same background. At Smyrna they appear as a body witnessing sales and gifts of property. They were present, for instance, when the *prokathemenos* of Smyrna, George Monomachos, handed over the *metochion* of St. George Exokastrites to the monastery of Lemviotissa.[159]

The episcopal *archontes* were arranged in a hierarchy modelled on that of the Patriarchal Church.[160] At the head came the *oikonomos,* followed at Smyrna by the *chartophylax,* the *sakellarios,* the *skeuophylax,* the *protekdikos,* and the *sakelliou.* The first four titles were often qualified by the epithet '*megas*'. Beneath these offices came other minor ones.[161] Each of these officials had special duties, sometimes administrative and

[155] See above, p. 263.

[156] Miklosich and Müller IV, p. 84, ll. 1–7.

[157] Ibid., pp. 187–9.

[158] Ibid., pp. 55–6, 155–7. The assessors of the metropolitan of Smyrna's court, who tried the lawsuit between the monastery of Lemviotissa and the party of the *stratiotes* Varycheir in Mar. 1263, were all members of the clergy of Smyrna, with the exception of Leo Makrenos who came from an important local family (ibid., p. 157; Ahrweiler, 'Smyrne', p. 146).

[159] Miklosich and Müller IV, pp. 44–5.

[160] See Bréhier, *Institutions*, pp. 500–1; Beck, *Kirche und theologische Literatur,* pp. 98–120.

[161] See Ahrweiler, 'Smyrne', p. 103, n. 173, p. 111, n. 177, pp. 108–14.

judicial, sometimes purely liturgical. The *oikonomos* was responsible for the financial administration of his Church.[162] The *chartophylax* presided over the episcopal court in the absence of the bishop, looked after the archives, and was also responsible for internal discipline within the Church.[163]

As in any state, there were layers of government at Byzantium. The imperial administration was superimposed on local institutions and had to take local interests into account if it was to function effectively. This perhaps helps to explain why it was that the bishop had such influence in local government. He was the acknowledged spokesman of local interests. He possessed a well-organized administration which could be turned to most aspects of local government. There was an understanding with the local nobility. There were of course instances of conflict between a bishop and the imperial administration. The bishop was an important landowner and had to protect and extend his rights of property. This might lead to lawsuits in which the imperial administration might have to intervene.

There was no clash of jurisdiction as such. It seems to have been accepted that a litigant had the right to choose the court in which his lawsuit was to be prosecuted. This sometimes produced uncertainties. Some cases might be heard simultaneously in an imperial and an ecclesiastical court.[164] Uncertainties led on occasion to oppression on the part of the imperial administration. Inquiries, particularly into fiscal matters, were carried out with considerable brutality.[165] Governors abused their powers to seize property unjustly and threatened with violence those, such as Nikephoros Blemmydes, who protested at their conduct.[166] Nor does the imperial administration seem to have been entirely successful during the period of exile in dealing with local violence. Its decisions were often simply ignored; and lawsuits over property dragged on over a long period of time, with accompanying violence which other landowners often found expedient to foster. Peasants and townspeople were supported in their lawsuits by

[162] Pseudo-Codinus (ed. Bonn), pp. 3–4; Beck, op. cit., pp. 106–7.
[163] Beck, op. cit., pp. 109–12.
[164] Blemmydes, pp. 31–2.
[165] Ibid., pp. 29–31, 34–5, 91–2.
[166] Ibid., pp. 16–18.

landowners and persons at court, and there were cases of maintenance.[167]

Two phases can be detected in this pattern of violence and oppression. The first was simply the aftermath of the anarchy that had accompanied the fall of Constantinople; the second can be seen as the result of the introduction of new landowners into western Asia Minor and the great extension of new rights of property. This represented one aspect of the Laskarids' attempt to bring order to the countryside, but it also brought with it numerous disputes as the new landowners tried to extend their rights over peasants and old-established landowning families alike.

It is possible to detect in this situation many of the weaknesses and abuses of Palaiologan government; and these in turn throw into relief the flaws of the government of the Nicaean Empire. Its strong features are less easy to see. Yet compared with the Empire of the Palaiologoi, and, for that matter, compared with the Empire of the Angeloi, the Nicaean Empire appeared to contemporaries as a sound organism; and the very success of the Nicaean Empire seems to bear out their opinion.

The source of this strength was the conviction that the Nicaean Empire was the Byzantine Empire recreated in exile and destined to restore Constantinople as the seat of Empire. This conviction allowed the mobilization of the resources of the Nicaean Empire for defence and later conquest. It also formed a background to the understanding reached by Theodore I Laskaris with local magnates; and this was the first step towards ending the worst aspects of the prevailing anarchy. It did not mean that oppression and violence were entirely eliminated. That would be to misunderstand the nature of medieval government. It was in the nature of government to tolerate a considerable degree of local violence, for it had to take local interests into account and to work through local institutions. If the example of Smyrna is at all representative, one of the strengths of Nicaean government in Asia Minor was that the *archontes* of the city were brought within the framework of imperial government.

The strength of the imperial government did not rest on

[167] Wilson and Darrouzès in *REB* 26 (1968), 20, ll. 12–14.

direct control of all aspects of provincial life and administration. This was an impossibility. It depended rather upon control of the resources of the state. Direct central control over the tax-raising machinery seems to have been reinforced during the period of exile. This is one feature of Nicaean rule; another is the way the emperors of Nicaea were able to exploit their control over the resources of the state. The great families were mollified by grants of estates; and the *pronoia* system was extended in such a way as to support a standing army.

It was exactly in these areas that the imperial administration appeared at its most efficient. Land and rights were handed over with commendable speed. The taxation system and fiscal rights were carefully supervised by commissions that were sent out by the central government at frequent intervals. While it remains true that the emperors of Nicaea reaped the benefits of their control over the resources of the state, the dangers of their policies only became clear after 1261, when the careful balance that they had achieved between imperial supervision and the alienation of imperial rights was lost. Perhaps it was a balance that could never have been maintained for long. At the local level the imperial administration owed much to the work of the *archontes*. Their position was to be undermined by the extension of the estates of members of the court nobility; and as a result the imperial administration became increasingly less effective. One example, in particular, vividly illustrates what was happening in the years after the recovery of Constantinople. In 1275 the emperor's cousin, the *protosevastos, protovestiarios,* and Grand Domestic, Michael Tarchaneiotes, compelled George Kaloeidas, the *prokathemenos* of Smyrna and a member of one of the most distinguished of Smyrniot familes, to surrender to him one of the family's most valuable estates.[168]

[168] Miklosich and Müller IV, pp. 102–3. For the dating of the document in question, see Ahrweiler, 'Smyrne', p. 120.

XIII

THE EUROPEAN PROVINCES OF THE NICAEAN EMPIRE

Apart from the reconquest of Constantinople, the major political achievement of the emperors of Nicaea was their conquest of Thrace and Macedonia. The initial conquest of both Thrace and Macedonia was achieved with surprising ease. In 1235 John Vatatzes was able to occupy the Gallipoli peninsula and southern Thrace as far west as the river Maritsa, under the terms of the treaty which he had concluded with the Bulgarian Tsar John II Asen.[1] Soon afterwards the strategic fortress of Tzouroulon on the main road from Constantinople to Adrianople[2] fell into Nicaean hands.[3] The important cities of northern Thrace, such as Adrianople, Didymoteichos, and Vizye, probably passed under Nicaean control at about the same time.[4] The Latins of Constantinople were able, probably in the year 1240, to recover Tzouroulon and Vizye.[5] These were not restored to the Nicaean Empire until 1247.[6] Nicaean rule in Thrace was now secure. The Latins only held a few places in the neighbourhood of Constantinople, such as Aphameia and Selymvria.[7]

The unsuccessful Nicaean expedition against Thessalonica in 1242 at least secured the Aegean coastlands as far as the mouth of the river Strymon.[8] Then, in the autumn of 1246, John Vatatzes seized Macedonia from the Bulgarians; and in November of that year a plot engineered by some of the lead-

[1] Acropolites I, p. 51, ll. 13–18; Gregoras I, p. 30, ll. 7–12.

[2] See C. J. Jireček, *Die Heerstrasse von Belgrad nach Constantinopel und die Balkanpässe*, Prague, 1877, p. 51.

[3] Acropolites I, p. 55, ll. 14–16.

[4] Ibid., p. 54, ll. 14–15.

[5] Ibid., p. 58, pp. 18–20.

[6] Ibid., p. 85, ll. 1–24; D. I. Polemis, 'A Manuscript Note of the Year 1247', *Byzantinische Forschungen*, 1 (1966), 269–76.

[7] Pachymeres I, p. 110, ll. 5–10.

[8] Acropolites I, pp. 65–6. Cf. Dölger, *Reg.* 1775.

ing citizens of Thessalonica allowed him to enter that city unopposed.[9]

The frontiers of these new conquests were reasonably well defined. The Nicaeans controlled the Rhodope mountains and the passes across them through their fortresses of Tzepaina and Stenimachos; and the upper course of the river Maritsa was established as the official boundary between the Nicaean Empire and the Bulgarian territories. Though lying on the southern bank of this river, the city of Philippopolis was not surrendered to the Nicaeans by the Bulgarians. Further west the Nicaeans controlled the valley of the river Strymon as far north as the fortress of Velbužd (Velevousdion) and the valley of the river Vardar as far north as Skoplje, where the frontiers of the Nicaean Empire marched with those of the kingdom of Serbia.[10] In the mountains to the west of the Vardar valley lay the Epirot outposts of Kastoria, Pelagonia, Ohrid, Prilep, and probably Veles. Closer to Thessalonica the fortress of Edessa (Vodena) remained in the hands of the former emperor of Thessalonica, Theodore Angelos.[11]

All these places were to fall to the Nicaeans in 1252 when they mounted a campaign against Epiros, ostensibly in order to forestall an Epirot attack on their territories in Europe. At the same time, the chieftain who ruled Alvanon, the core of the Albanian lands, was persuaded to change his allegiance from the ruler of Epiros to the emperor of Nicaea.[12]

These conquests appeared to offer further protection to the Nicaean territories in Europe. Control of the Vardar valley was no longer threatened by the Greeks of Epiros. Yet the Nicaean grip on its European territories was not as firm as it appeared. There were only small Nicaean garrisons in the key fortresses; their fortifications had been neglected; and the garrison troops were discontented because of the excessive length of their service.[13] In eastern Macedonia perhaps the majority of people were Bulgarians. They welcomed the Bul-

[9] Acropolites I, pp. 79–83.

[10] Ibid., p. 78, ll. 14ff.; Theodore Lascaris, p. 281, ll. 68–73.

[11] Acropolites I, p. 84, ll. 16–22.

[12] Ibid., pp. 89–92; Dölger, *Reg.* 1806; A. Ducellier, 'L'Arbanon et les Albanais au XIe siècle', *Travaux et Mémoires*, 3 (1968), 367–8.

[13] Acropolites I, p. 108, ll. 4–15.

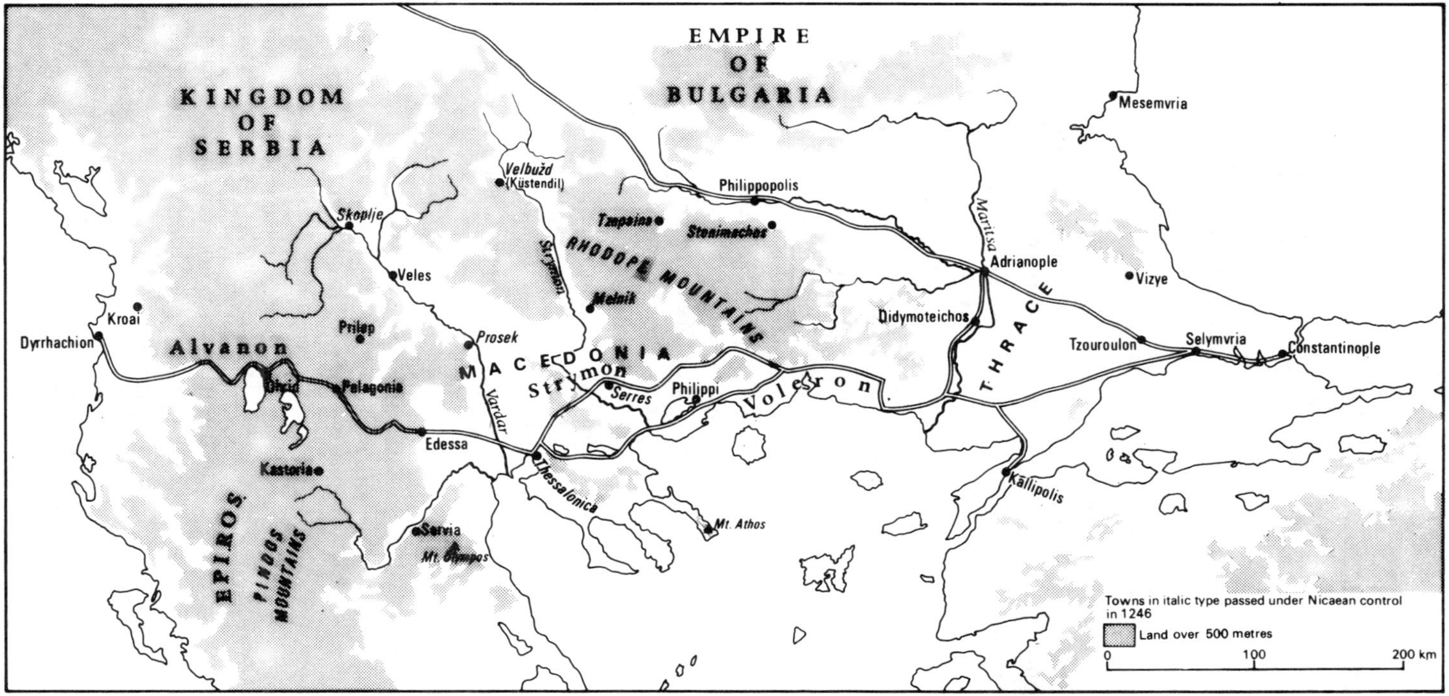

Map 2. The Nicaean Territories in Europe

garian invasion that followed news of John Vatatzes's death late in 1254; very quickly the Bulgarians were able to regain control of the Rhodope region. They even seized a fortress in the neighbourhood of Adrianople.[14] The new emperor Theodore II Laskaris fought two long and hard campaigns against the Bulgarians before a peace treaty was negotiated in the summer of 1256. By it the boundaries which had existed in his father's reign were restored.[15]

He then extorted the surrender of the city of Dyrrhachion and the fortress of Servia from Michael Angelos, the despot of Epiros, as the price of the marriage of the despot's son to his daughter.[16] Before he could take possession of these important places—Dyrrhachion was the chief city of the Albanian coast; Servia, to the north-west of Mount Olympos, blocked any Nicaean advance southwards into Thessaly—news that Michael Palaiologos had fled to the Seljuqs forced him to return to Anatolia.[17] The task was entrusted to the Grand Logothete George Akropolites.[18] He was faced almost immediately with an Epirot invasion; many of the Nicaean commanders went over to Michael Angelos; and he himself was captured.[19] The Nicaean hold on western Macedonia was to remain extremely precarious until the autumn of 1259 when the usurper Michael Palaiologos sent his brother, the *sevastokrator* John Palaiologos, with the bulk of the Nicaean field army to Macedonia. The Epirots and their Frankish allies were completely defeated by the Nicaeans at the battle of Pelagonia. Nicaean armies advanced as far as the Epirot capital of Arta; and the principality of Thessaly recognized Nicaean suzerainty. The Albanian lands, too, returned to the Nicaean allegiance.[20] The Nicaean conquests in Thrace and Macedonia were finally secured. Few additions were to be made to them despite the great efforts mounted after 1261. This is in itself a measure of the Nicaean achievement.

[14] Akropolites, p. 108, ll. 19–20.

[15] Ibid., p. 127, ll. 12–16; Theodore Lascaris, pp. 279–82; Dölger, *Reg.* 1883.

[16] Acropolites I, pp. 132–3.

[17] Ibid., pp. 134–5; Gregoras I, p. 57, ll. 19–21.

[18] Acropolites I, p. 139, ll. 13–14.

[19] Ibid., pp. 140–3, 149–50.

[20] Ibid., pp. 165–72; Pachymeres I, pp. 81–6, 106–7; Gregoras I, pp. 71–5. See Geanakoplos, *Michael Palaeologus*, pp. 47–74.

The European provinces of the Nicaean Empire were of a considerable extent, not much smaller than its Anatolian provinces. They contained a number of the greatest cities of the Byzantine Empire, including Thessalonica, its second city. There was much good farming land. Thrace was a large exporter of corn in the late thirteenth century.[21] The river valleys and coastal plains of Macedonia formed a region that was well adapted to Mediterranean agriculture with its combination of arable and pasture farming with the tending of vineyards and olive groves. The mountains of the northern frontier were rich in gold and silver, but this mineral wealth does not appear to have been exploited on any scale in the thirteenth century.[22]

It is not at all certain that these potentially rich conquests brought any new strength to the Nicaean Empire. Any benefits that might have accrued from them must have been outweighed by the great cost of holding down these territories. They ought to have provided the Empire with a valuable new recruiting ground for its army. The future Grand Logothete George Akropolites witnessed the ceremony by which the inhabitants of Melnik surrendered their city to John Vatatzes in the autumn of 1246. The notables of the city numbered above five hundred. Akropolites was so impressed by them that he exclaimed how valuable an addition they would make to the Nicaean forces.[23] A force was indeed raised from Melnik, but it proved unreliable, deserting in the winter of 1254–5 to the Bulgarians.[24] The town of Veles went over to the Bulgarians at the same time. It was besieged in the summer of 1255 by Theodore II Laskaris. The inhabitants of the town agreed to surrender on condition that they were allowed to leave it with the full honours of war. The emperor accepted their proposals, but soon regretted his decision, when he saw them, about five hundred strong, marching out to join the Bulgarians.[25] John Vatatzes was able to settle a large body of Koumans in Thrace and Macedonia;

[21] Bratianu, *Le Commerce génois*, pp. 119–20.

[22] See D. Kovačević, 'Dans la Serbie et la Bosnie medievales: les mines d'or et d'argent', *Annales. Économies, Sociétés, Civilisations*, 15 (1960), 248–58; Sp. Vryonis, 'The Question of the Byzantine Mines', *Speculum*, 37 (1962), 13–15.

[23] Acropolites I, pp. 77–8.

[24] Ibid., pp. 114–15.

[25] Ibid., p. 118, ll. 7–9.

these certainly played a prominent part in the Nicaean armies, but at times they were unreliable too. At the end of 1255 they deserted to the Bulgarians.[26] Even as late as 1260 Michael Palaiologos had to make a detour to Adrianople where a rebellion was brewing.[27]

The turbulence of the European provinces of the Nicaean Empire can be explained by their past history. The emperors of Nicaea were the heirs of more than half a century of political instability. Macedonia and Thrace had been the scene of the wars between Byzantium and the emerging Bulgarian state at the end of the twelfth century. After the fall of Constantinople to the Latins these regions were disputed between the Bulgarians, the Latins, and the Greeks of Epiros. In the late 1220s they were briefly united under the rule of Theodore Angelos, the Epirot leader, who had made himself emperor at Thessalonica. He was defeated in 1230 by the Bulgarians, who annexed the whole of Macedonia with the exception of Thessalonica and the surrounding region.

This political instability was reinforced and possibly in part caused by population movements within the Balkans. By the mid-eleventh century the Vlachs and the Albanians, after centuries of obscurity, had begun to re-emerge and to press down from the mountains to the plains.[28] Less than a century later, the Koumans were crossing the Danube in very large numbers and began to settle in the Balkans. They caused considerable destruction and transferred their nomadic way of life to the plains of Thrace.[29] The Vlachs too were nomads; and in certain areas the appearance of these pastoralists must have had serious results for agriculture. It is about this time that Thessaly, which is very well suited to arable farming, began to be known as Great Vlachia.[30]

Just as disturbing were the effects of war. The wars of the Bulgarian ruler Kalojan in the early thirteenth century

[26] Acropolites I, pp. 125–6.

[27] Pachymeres I, pp. 125–6.

[28] See P. Charanis, 'Observations on the Demography of the Byzantine Empire', *Thirteenth International Congress of Byzantine Studies: Main Papers XIV*, pp. 15–17; Wolff in *Speculum*, 24 (1949), 180–90, 198–201, 203–6; Ducellier in *Travaux et Mémoires*, 3 (1968), 353–68.

[29] Nicetas Choniates, pp. 561–2, 691–2; Acropolites I, pp. 53–4, esp. p. 54, ll. 1–2.

[30] Nicetas Choniates, p. 841, ll. 14–15; Acropolites I, p. 61, ll. 25–6.

against the Latins of Constantinople for the control of Thrace took on the aspect of slave-raiding expeditions.[31] It must have been about this time that some of the Greeks of Philippopolis emigrated to the greater safety of Melnik.[32]

The instability of society was reflected in the fragmentation of political power. By the late twelfth century various men had established themselves as independent rulers in Macedonia. The Vlach chieftain, Dobromir Chrysos, who set up a principality centred on Prosek in the Vardar valley, is one example.[33] In the 1220s another chieftain, called Sthlavos, ruled the Rhodope region from Melnik; he was able to play off against each other the Bulgarians, Latins, and Greeks of Thessalonica.[34]

Successive conquerors of Thrace and Macedonia attempted to establish some degree of central authority over these regions. Theodore Angelos set about restoring a provincial administration. The themes that had existed before 1204 were resuscitated; governors were appointed and tax collectors were sent out. His authority and that of his successors seems to have been very effective close to the capital of Thessalonica. No fewer than four governors of the theme of neighbouring Verroia are attested in ten years. This suggests that the rulers of Thessalonica were able to limit the term of office of the governor of this theme to a single year.[35] How far Theodore Angelos's administrative reorganization survived the Bulgarian conquest of Thrace and Macedonia in 1230 is difficult to say. The Bulgarian Tsar John Asen was content to rule much of his new territory indirectly and to keep the apparatus of administration to a minimum. He sent out commanders to the fortresses of the region and appointed tax-collectors.[36]

After his death in 1241 the authority of the Bulgarian rulers in Macedonia became weaker; and the fortress commanders must have become virtually independent. This lack

[31] Villehardouin, pp. 204–5, 212–13, 226–7, 228–35, 258–9, 260–3.

[32] Acropolites I, p. 76, ll. 11–20. Cf. Nicetas Choniates, pp. 829–30.

[33] Nicetas Choniates, pp. 643–4, 665–6.

[34] Acropolites I, pp. 38–9.

[35] See D. Angelov, 'K voprosu o praviteljakh fem v epirskom despotate i nikejskoj imperii', *BS* 12 (1951), 60–4, 71–4; D. M. Nicol, *The Despotate of Epiros*, Oxford, 1957, pp. 66–8; D. A. Zakythinos, *Despotat* II, p. 49.

[36] Acropolites I, p. 43, ll. 7–8.

of effective central authority meant that changes in government and society were more pronounced in Macedonia than they were in Anatolia. The Epirot aristocracy possessed great estates and enjoyed immunities at least on the scale of their counterparts in Anatolia,[37] but they appear to have possessed much greater political power at the local level. The desertion of Theodore Petraliphas, the brother-in-law of the Despot of Epiros, Michael Angelos, to the Nicaean side in 1252 has already been mentioned. One result of this was that the city of Kastoria and the whole of the surrounding region passed under Nicaean rule.[38]

In other ways, too, 'feudalizing' tendencies went a great deal further in Macedonia and Epiros than they did in Anatolia. The form these took may appear rather strange when compared with the patterns of society that existed in western Europe; for they are most clearly seen in the towns and fortresses of the region. In the course of the thirteenth century these acquired a considerable degree of autonomy. They were not particularly flourishing centres of commerce. Some suffered in the wars of the period. The town of Serres was reduced to little more than a village as a result of its capture in 1230 by the Bulgarian Tsar John Asen.[39] Thessalonica was cut off from its hinterland for long periods during the first half of the thirteenth century; and it is to be doubted whether on the eve of the Nicaean conquest it was very prosperous.

In the general insecurity of the times the towns served as refuges for the people of the surrounding countryside; they became essentially fortresses. They were dominated not by merchants, but by their *archontes*. George Akropolites divided the representatives of the town of Melnik into three groups. Beneath the *archontes* came those enrolled in the army and then a group whom he describes as the 'better sort'. These would have been the equivalent of the *oikodespotai* that one meets in the villages and towns of Anatolia at this time.[40] The structure of society at Thessalonica must have

[37] See Dölger, *Schatzkammern*, No. 33; *Actes de Xeropotamou*, No. 8; Miklosich and Müller IV, pp. 345–9; Nicol, *Despotate of Epiros*, pp. 215–16.

[38] Acropolites I, pp. 90–1.

[39] Ibid., p. 74, ll. 19–23.

[40] Ibid., p. 77, ll. 16–22. See E. Francès, 'La Féodalité et les villes byzantines au XIIIe et au XIVe siècles', *BS* 16 (1955), 76–96; E. Kirsten, 'Die byzantinischen Stadt', *Berichte zum XI. internationalen Byzantinisten-Kongress*, Munich, 1958, pp. 35–46.

been slightly different. The conspirators who surrendered the city to John Vatatzes in November 1246 were divided into two groups. One seems to have been drawn from the aristocracy of the Angelos court; the other from notables of the city.[41]

When the Latin Emperor Baldwin entered Thessalonica in 1204, he confirmed the privileges of the city;[42] the price that John Vatatzes had to pay in 1246 for its surrender was to issue a chrysobull confirming the customs and rights of the city and guaranteeing its freedom.[43] He had earlier issued similar chrysobulls to other towns and cities in Macedonia that had surrendered to him. The possession of privileges appears to mark off the towns and cities of Macedonia from those in Anatolia, and points to the greater autonomy enjoyed by the nobility in the European provinces. The towns became the preserve of aristocratic privilege.

In content the chrysobulls that John Vatatzes issued to Thessalonica and to other cities in Macedonia must have been similar to that which he granted in 1252 to the town of Kroai in Albania. By it the citizens' property both inside and outside the town was to be free of all taxation.[44]

As the price of a swift conquest, John Vatatzes was forced to come to terms with local autonomy. Not only did he confirm the privileges of the towns and cities that surrendered to him, but those officials and notables that came over to the Nicaean side were handsomely rewarded and often taken into Nicaean service. Dragotas, the Bulgarian governor of Serres, surrendered the town to John Vatatzes. He was rewarded with a large gift of money and a golden cloak and was also made commander of the army of Melnik.[45] The conspirators of Thessalonica, too, were rewarded by John

[41] Acropolites I, pp. 79–80.

[42] Villehardouin, pp. 88–9.

[43] Acropolites I, p. 80, ll. 1–8.

[44] Dölger, *Reg.* 1810. Compare the privileges granted by Michael VIII Palaiologos and his son Andronikos II Palaiologos to the city of Monemvasia in the Peloponnese. The citizens, as a body, were to enjoy complete immunity and freedom from taxation for their hereditary property and were to be free from the payment of customs duties on transactions that took place within the city (Zepos, *Ius* I, pp. 513–15; Miklosich and Müller V, pp. 154–5; Dölger, *Reg.* 1897, 2102).

[45] Acropolites I, pp. 74–5, 114–15.

Vatatzes with money and, as we know, were taken into Nicaean service.[46]

The recognition of local privileges and the integration of local armies, such as that of Melnik, into the Nicaean forces introduced an element of instability into the Nicaean administration of Macedonia. We have already seen how the towns and fortresses of eastern Macedonia almost all went over to the Bulgarians on the death of John Vatatzes and those of western Macedonia to the Epirots at the end of Theodore II Laskaris's reign.

It was difficult to disguise the fact that the Nicaean conquest meant a military occupation. After the campaigning season had ended, it was usual to leave some detachments of the Nicaean field army behind in Europe. These were quartered at strategic points in Thrace and Macedonia, for example at Edessa (Vodena),[47] Serres,[48] and Didymoteichos;[49] and their commanders were probably given administrative powers over the surrounding district.[50] In addition, the chief fortresses were given Nicaean garrisons and commanders. At Melnik the garrison appears to have been quite distinct from the local army.[51] At the same time, the emperors of Nicaea were beginning to restore a regular administration in Macedonia. These aspects of Nicaean rule hardly squared with its apparent toleration of local liberties, which must have become increasingly circumscribed as the re-establishment of an administration progressed. This must have been a cause of considerable resentment.

No very clear picture of administration in the Empire's European territories emerges. Virtually nothing is known about how Thrace was organized. Didymoteichos rather than Adrianople appears to have been the administrative centre.[52] More is known about the administration of Macedonia. It is a confusing picture. This may be because it derives from the narrative of George Akropolites's history; and there are

[46] Acropolites I, p. 79–80. See above, pp. 175–6.
[47] Ibid., p. 92, ll. 19–24.
[48] Ibid., p. 114, ll. 2–6.
[49] Ibid., p. 123, ll. 3–7, 18–19.
[50] Ibid.; Pachymeres I, p. 21, ll. 11–12.
[51] Acropolites I, pp. 114–15.
[52] Ibid., p. 123, ll. 3–4, 24–6. See Zakythinos, *Despotat*, II, p. 54.

virtually no documentary sources which might have made the picture more precise. Perhaps it is much more because the restoration of the administration was still going ahead and was not completed until after 1261, when a series of fiscal surveys were carried out.[53]

In the absence of the emperor, the Nicaean territories in Macedonia were placed under a viceroy who had his seat at Thessalonica. After the conquest of Thessalonica in 1246 John Vatatzes, as we know, left the Grand Domestic Andronikos Palaiologos behind as viceroy. He died soon afterwards and was succeeded by Theodore Philes.[54] The Grand Logothete George Akropolites is the next recorded viceroy; he was appointed to the position in the autumn of 1256. The emperor conferred (*χειροτονήσας*) on him the title of *praitor*,[55] which may have been the official title of the viceroy of Thessalonica.[56]

Before departing for Anatolia Theodore II Laskaris appointed governors for Thessalonica and other key points in western Macedonia. These were then placed under Akropolites's authority. As viceroy, he had very wide powers; he could appoint and dismiss the governors of provinces, military commanders, tax-collectors, and local administrators (*energountes*).[57] He had his own staff and an armed retinue.[58]

His first months as viceroy were spent travelling through western Macedonia and Albania. He dispatched much administrative business on the way, meeting tax-collectors, the governors of towns, and the commanders of the local military contingents.[59] He was travelling in the worst months of the year. He left Verroia in December 1256 and reached Prilep

[53] See G. Rouillard, 'Recensements de terres sous les premiers Paléologues', *B* 12 (1937), 105–6. The *orphanotrophos* Edessenos was responsible for carrying out an *exisosis* in the *chora* and castle of Voleron, the city of Serres together with Melnik and Strymon, and the theme of Thessalonica and Verroia. It has been argued that this survey dates from soon after the Nicaean conquest of Thessalonica (see P. Lemerle, *Philippes et la Macédoine orientale à l'époque chrétienne et byzantine*, Paris, 1945, pp. 222–3). This seems to be mistaken, since the official in question was active in the fourteenth century (see Dölger, *Schatzkammern*, pp. 172, 202).

[54] Acropolites I, pp. 83–4.

[55] Ibid., p. 139, ll. 14–15.

[56] Cf. Theodore Lascaris, p. 254, l. 105.

[57] Acropolites I, p. 142, ll. 12–15.

[58] Ibid., p. 143, ll. 1–2.

[59] Ibid., pp. 139–40.

at the end of February, having secured possession of the fortress of Servia and the city of Dyrrhachion on the way.[60]

The news that the governor of Alvanon intended to go over to the despot of Epiros forced Akropolites to take measures for the defence of western Macedonia. The governor of Thessalonica, Michael Laskaris, a great-uncle of the emperor, was summoned to meet him at Pelagonia where they would take counsel together. The *skouterios* Xyleas, who was governor of Prilep, was also to be present at their meeting. It was decided that Laskaris and Xyleas should concentrate their forces at Pelagonia, while Akropolites went on to Ohrid to settle matters in Alvanon.[61]

Akropolites's measures did not meet with much success. The Albanians were in full revolt; the new governor of Alvanon was besieged in Ohrid. The *skouterios* Xyleas disregarded his orders and rashly attacked the forces of the despot's ally, the ruler of Serbia; he was captured and his army dispersed. Akropolites himself was blockaded in the fortress of Prilep by the forces of the despot. The siege was lifted briefly by the troops of Michael Laskaris and Michael Palaiologos who had been sent to Macedonia in an attempt to restore the situation. They were soon forced to retreat in the face of the Epirot forces. Akropolites held out a little longer; he then surrendered on the understanding that he would be allowed to depart with the full honours of war, but he was nevertheless thrown into an Epirot prison.[62]

Akropolites's activities appear to give a good impression of the powers that a viceroy possessed and the work that he was expected to undertake, but a rather poor one of the structure of the administration over which he presided. The administrative divisions of the Nicaean territories in Europe, for example, are not known with any certainty. It seems probable that the divisions which are found after 1261 were established in the course of the Nicaean period. The existence of the themes of Thessalonica[63] and of Strymon[64] is attested towards the end of the period of exile. Before 1204 they had

[60] Ibid.

[61] Ibid., pp. 140–2.

[62] Ibid., pp. 142–3.

[63] F. Dölger, *PARASPORA*, p. 436, ll. 12–13.

[64] Dölger, *Reg.* 1866.

formed a single province,[65] together with the district of Voleron, a district that stretched along the Aegean coast from the mouth of the Strymon to the mouth of the Maritsa. Their division appears to have gone back to the Nicaean conquest. Voleron was annexed in 1242,[66] before the other Nicaean conquests in Macedonia had been made; and in 1246 the viceroy Andronikos Palaiologos was left as governor of Thessalonica, while his son Michael Palaiologos was made governor of Serres and Melnik, which were the chief places of the theme of Strymon.[67]

On the western and northern frontiers of the Empire the administrative divisions were very small, comprising no more than a town and the surrounding countryside. In the far north the theme of Skoplje is recorded in 1256.[68] It is probable that other towns for which Nicaean governors are attested, such as Ohrid, Prilep, and Veles, continued to form the centres of separate provinces as they had done in the late twelfth century.[69]

The Nicaean governors in Europe almost all held positions at court. Xyleas, the governor of Prilep, held the office of *skouterios* or shield-bearer[70] and was held in high regard by Theodore II Laskaris.[71] Theodore Kalampakes, who was appointed governor of Veles in 1256, was *tatas* of the court.[72] Isaac Nestongos, governor first of Alvanon and then of Ohrid, held the office of steward.[73] He, together with Michael Laskaris and Michael Palaiologos, who also served as governors in Europe, came from among the greatest of the Nicaean families. At a lower level of the administration there were no doubt many officials who came from local families, but this was only exceptionally the case at a higher level. Con-

[65] Tafel and Thomas I, p. 264, ll. 1–2.

[66] Cf. Acropolites I, pp. 65–6.

[67] Ibid., pp. 83–4.

[68] Theodore Lascaris, p. 281.

[69] See Tafel and Thomas I, pp. 259–62, 486–7.

[70] See Pseudo-Kodinos, p. 183, ll. 11–20, p. 196, ll. 14–17. He also bore the emperor's *divellion* or rod of authority.

[71] Acropolites I, pp. 139ff.

[72] Ibid., p. 139, ll. 10–11. The functions of this position are not certainly known. There seems to be some doubt about the accepted opinion that the holder of this office was the crown prince's tutor (see Andreeva, *Očerki*, pp. 41–2).

[73] Acropolites I, pp. 142–3.

stantine Chavaron, who was appointed governor of Alvanon in 1256,[74] belonged, it is true, to a family established in the early twelfth century near Thebes.[75] He himself appears to have come from Alvanon,[76] but he had been brought up at the Nicaean court with Michael Palaiologos.[77] Xyleas was obviously one of Theodore II Laskaris's new men; and George Akropolites hints that he was not of Nicaean origin.[78]

The Nicaean governors in Europe were essentially military governors. As governor of Prilep, Xyleas had a large force under his command.[79] Michael Laskaris, the governor of Thessalonica in the latter part of Theodore II Laskaris's reign, was given a force of Paphlagonians and 300 Koumans.[80] It may have been the usual practice to give a provincial governor in Europe troops from the field army, as these must have been, but when Michael Palaiologos was appointed governor of Dyrrhachion in 1257[81] he raised his troops from Macedonia.[82]

The title given to a Nicaean governor in Europe is not known for certain. George Akropolites normally writes that such and such a person had been placed in charge (*εἰς φυλακήν*) of a particular fortress or district.[83] This might suggest that in many cases these Nicaean governors were simply *kastrophylakes*,[84] but it seems much more likely that these local governors ought to be identified with the *kephalai* who played such a vital role in local administration after 1261.[85] A *kephale* of the island of Cos is recorded in 1258;[86] and in 1266 the

[74] Acropolites I, p. 139, ll. 11–12.

[75] See Svoronos, *Le Cadastre de Thèbes*, p. 72.

[76] Theodore Lascaris, p. 250, ll. 8–11.

[77] Acropolites I, p. 164, ll. 17–19.

[78] Ibid., p. 141, ll. 14–18.

[79] Ibid., pp. 141–2.

[80] Ibid., p. 139, ll. 5–7.

[81] Pachymeres I, p. 26, ll. 14–16.

[82] Acropolites I, p. 145, ll. 2–5.

[83] Ibid., p. 51, ll. 19–21, p. 58, ll. 18–20, p. 84, ll. 1–4, p. 115, ll. 5–8, p. 119, ll. 13–15, p. 123, ll. 4–19, p. 139, ll. 2–14, p. 143, ll. 2–3.

[84] e.g. George Akropolites appointed the Steward Isaac Nestongos *εἰς φυλακὴν τοῦ κάστρου* of Ohrid (Acropolites I, p. 143, ll. 2–3).

[85] See Heisenberg, 'Palaiologenzeit', pp. 68–70; E. Stein, 'Untersuchungen zur spätbyzantinischen Verfassungs- und Wirtschaftsgeschichte', *Mitteilungen zur Osmanischen Geschichte*, 2 (1923–6), 21–2; Zakythinos, *Despotat* II, pp. 64–71.

[86] Miklosich and Müller VI, pp. 186–7.

Sevastokrator Constantine Tornikes appears as *kephale* of the theme of Thessalonica.[87] It seems safe to infer that the post of *kephale* existed in Thrace and Macedonia during the Nicaean period.

The creation of this post fits the conditions of the Nicaean conquest admirably. *Kephale,* as a general term, was often used in the late Byzantine period to denote a military commander.[88] We have already seen how the commanders of contingents of the Nicaean field army might act as military governors of towns and fortresses in Thrace and Macedonia.[89]

The duties that the *kephale* had to perform were not very different from those undertaken by the duke of a theme. For a time, the two offices continued to exist side by side; and there is at least one instance where a provincial governor combined the two offices.[90] Is this simply a question of a changing titulature? Or does the creation of the post of *kephale* mark a new stage in Byzantine provincial administration?

Its origins were similar to those of other provincial governors who are met with in the course of Byzantine history. Like the *strategos* or the duke, the *kephale* was a military commander who acquired administrative duties. A well-integrated provincial administration was to be built around the offices of *strategos* and the duke, but this was not to be the case with the *kephale*; it is in this way that the creation of this post marks a new stage. Provincial government was too fragmented, both in terms of geography and in terms of organization. Instead of a provincial governor with over-all responsibility for the administration of a region, there was a large number of local governors, who were each responsible to the emperor and whose relationship to one another was not at all well defined. In other words, a clear-cut chain of command was lacking.

This was the legacy of the conditions of the Nicaean con-

[87] Dölger, *Schatzkammern*, No. 34.

[88] Acropolites I, p. 126, ll. 12–13; Pseudo-Kodinos, p. 167, ll. 16, 19, p. 175, ll. 8, 13.

[89] See above, pp. 189–90.

[90] i.e. John Tornikes, governor of the theme of Thrakesion in 1268 (see Ahrweiler, 'Smyrne', p. 149).

quest. Normally either the emperor or his viceroy would have been on the spot to co-ordinate the provincial administration. After the recovery of Constantinople this was hardly ever the case. The solution to this problem was to be found in the fourteenth century in the creation of apanages for princes of the imperial house.

The general direction of change in the administrative structure of the Empire also contributed to the weakness of provincial administration after the recovery of Constantinople. It was difficult for a provincial administration to develop around the post of *kephale,* for the simple reason that so much local administration had been entrusted to agents of the central administration. A great deal of routine administration was carried out by commissions of *apographeis*; tax-raising too was taken out of the control of the provincial authorities and was carried out by agents of the central government. The work of the *kephale* was limited to the maintenance of law and order and local defence.[91] His authority was circumscribed still further by the presence of other local officials, such as the *kastrophylakes* and *prokathemenoi.* These were appointed by the emperor and were directly responsible to him; they were not clearly under the authority of the *kephale*.

At first sight, it might seem that these changes would have strengthened the administrative structure of the state and would have enhanced central authority. In reality, they were counter-productive. They emphasized the gap that existed between the provinces and the capital. This must have increased local resentment of the imperial administration. The agents of the central government would not have had any strong local administration to help them in their work. At the same time, the disappearance of an effective local administration would have allowed the growth of local privileges, whether municipal or aristocratic. Exercise of central authority would come to depend more and more upon the recognition of these local privileges; and the holders of these privileges would in turn come to supplant the local administration. The foundations of the administrative system were indeed being eaten away. There was very little to support the

[91] Sathas VI, pp. 642–3.

weight of the central administration, except a sentimental attachment on the part of the provinces to the imperial court and the imperial office.

One of the causes of the weakness of the Empire of the Palaiologoi was that a sound provincial administration was never established in Thrace and Macedonia. The combination of increased centralization and growing local privilege made this impossible. Nicaean administration was much more strongly based in Anatolia. The reforms of the emperors of the House of Komnenos were carried through; and this gave to the Nicaean Empire a sufficiently strong foundation for its mission to restore the Empire to Constantinople. In practical terms, it allowed the emperors of Nicaea to conquer and hold down Thrace and Macedonia, a task that had defeated so many other rulers in the first half of the thirteenth century. At the same time there must have been weaknesses, since the Anatolian provinces were to all intents and purposes lost to the Empire scarcely half a century after the recovery of Constantinople. The cohesion of society and the soundness of the provincial administration were undermined by the growing power of the great families. Their estates were extended at the expense of the local landowning families who had contributed so much to provincial administration during the period of exile. These are developments that only become clear after 1261, when imperial authority became more distant with the return to Constantinople, but their roots go back to an acceptance by the emperors of Nicaea that the aristocracy had a right to dominate society. In the short term, this gave the state much greater cohesion, but it raised a problem that was at the heart of Theodore II Laskaris's struggle with elements among the aristocracy: did domination of society mean that the aristocracy was also to dominate the government?

Certain features of Nicaean government seemed to point in this direction. The development of the judicial and consultative functions of the imperial court seemed to indicate that the part played by the aristocracy in government might be given a constitutional form. Theodore II Laskaris's musings over the nature of friendship at least show that he was aware of this problem and that he felt the need to justify imperial autocracy. But in all sections of society a sentimental reverence for the imperial office went so deep that it was impossible to give constitutional recognition to a development that was circumscribing imperial autocracy. This was the dilemma of the later Byzantine Empire. Imperial autocracy was more or less a fiction, but it was difficult to recognize this fact and for good reasons even more difficult to replace it with a different form of government.

The Byzantine Empire was after all built round the imperial office. The theory of imperial autocracy had hardly changed since the reign of Justinian, even since the time of Constantine the Great. This continuity was one of the strengths of the Empire. It preserved the unity of the Empire through centuries that saw great changes both in its internal structure and its external situation. After the catastrophe of 1204 the imperial office proved a strong enough institution around which to rebuild the Empire in exile at Nicaea. The Emperors of Nicaea were able to win the loyalty of the people of western Asia Minor and to harness its resources. A nucleus was created capable of restoring the integrity of the Byzantine Empire.

The limitations of this restoration only became clear once the seat of empire had returned to Constantinople. The imperial office was less and less able to give effective unity to the Empire. Imperial authority became weaker. This was not because the emperors did not possess an administration, but because power in the provinces came to lie with the great landowners. As a result the imperial administration became increasingly irrelevant and imperial authority increasingly illusory.

At least one Nicaean minister foresaw the dangers which the return of the seat of Empire to Constantinople held in store. The *protasekretis* Senachereim was utterly dismayed by the news of the City's recovery. His words were prophetic: 'Oh, what is this I hear! Has this been saved up for our days! How have we sinned that we should live to see such a disaster! Let no one hope for any further good fortune, now that the Byzantines have set foot in the City once more.'[92]

[92] Pachymeres I, p. 149, ll. 12–15.

BIBLIOGRAPHY

1. CALENDARS AND COLLECTIONS OF SOURCES

E. Barker, *Social and Political Thought in Byzantium from Justinian I to the Last Palaeologus*, Oxford, 1957.

Corpus Inscriptionum Graecarum, IV, ed. A. Boeck, Berlin, 1877.

A. Dmitrievskij, *Opisanie liturgicheskikh rukopisej, khranjashchikhsja v bibliotekakh pravoslavnago vostoka (The Liturgical Manuscripts preserved in the Libraries of the Orthodox East*). Vol. 1: *Typika*, pt. 1, Kiev, 1895; Vol. 2: *Euchologia*, Kiev, 1901; Vol. 3: *Typika*, pt. 2, St. Petersburg, 1917.

F. Dölger, *Regesten der Kaiserurkunden des oströmischen Reiches* (Corpus der griechischen Urkunden des Mittelalters und der neueren Zeit, Reihe A, Abt, 1), Munich/Berlin, 1924–65, 5 vols.

H. Grégoire, *Recueil des inscriptions grecques chrétiennes d'Asie Mineure*, I, Paris, 1922.

V. Laurent, *Les Bulles métriques dans la sigillographie byzantine*, Athens, 1932.

—— *Les Regestes des actes du patriarcat de Constantinople*, I, fasc. 4: *Les Regestes de 1208 à 1309* (Le Patriarcat Byzantin. Recherches de diplomatique, d'histoire et de géographie ecclésiastiques publiées par l'Institut d'Études Byzantines, Paris, Série 1), Paris, 1971.

J. D. Mansi, *Sacrorum conciliorum nova et amplissima collectio*, Florence/Venice, 1759–98, 31 vols.; reprinted J. B. Martin and L. Petit, Paris, 1901– , in progress.

J. P. Migne, *Patrologiae cursus completus. Series graeco-latina*, Paris, 1857–66.

—— *Patrologiae cursus completus. Series latina*, Paris, 1844–55.

F. Miklosich et J. Müller, *Acta et diplomata graeca medii aevi sacra et profana*, Vienna, 1860–90, 6 vols.

E. Miller, *Recueil des historiens des croisades. Historiens grecs* (Académie des Inscriptions et Belles-lettres), Paris, 1875, 1881, 2 vols.

R. Morozzo della Rocca and A. Lombardo, *Documenti del com-*

mercio veneziano nei secoli XI–XIII (Documenti e studi di storia communale e di diritto communale, XIX–XX), Turin, 1940, 2 vols.

J. B. Pitra, *Analecta sacra et classica spicilegio Solesmensi parata*, Paris, 1876–91, 8 vols.

Registres de Grégoire IX. Recueil des bulles de ce Pape, publiées ou analysées d'après les manuscrits originaux du Vatican par L. Auvray (Bibliothèque des Écoles françaises d'Athènes et de Rome, Sér. 2, No. 9), Paris, 1896–1955, 4 vols.

Registres d'Innocent IV. Recueil des bulles de ce Pape, publiées ou analysées d'après les manuscrits originaux du Vatican et de la Bibliothèque Nationale par E. Berger (Bibliothèque des Écoles françaises d'Athènes et de Rome, Sér. 2, No. 3), Paris, 1884–1921, 4 vols.

G. A. Rhalles et M. Potles, *Σύνταγμα τῶν θείων καὶ ἱερῶν κανόνων*, Athens, 1852–9, 6 vols.

K. N. Sathas, *Μεσαιωνικὴ βιβλιοθήκη* (*Bibliotheca graeca medii aevi*), Venice/Paris, 1872–94, 7 vols.

G. L. F. Tafel et G. M. Thomas, *Urkunden zur älteren Handels- und Staatsgeschichte der Republik Venedig* (Fontes Rerum Austriacarum, Abt. 2, XII–XIV), Vienna, 1856–7, 3 vols.

J. et P. Zepos, *Ius graecoromanum*, Athens, 1931, 8 vols.

2. ORIGINAL SOURCES

Acropolitae, Georgii, Opera, ed. A. Heisenberg. I: *Historia, Breviarium historiae, Theodori Scutariotae additamenta*; II: *Scripta minora*, Leipzig, 1903.

Actes de Dionysiou (Archives de l'Athos IV), ed. N. Oikonomidès, Paris, 1968, 2 vols.

Actes de Xéropotamou (Archives de l'Athos III), ed. J. Bompaire, Paris, 1964, 2 vols.

Actes de Zographou, ed. W. Regel, E. Kurtz, and B. Korablev, in *Vizantijskij Vremennik*, 13 (1907), Supplement.

Annae Comnenae porphyrogenitae Alexias, ed. B. Leib, Paris, 1937–45, 3 vols.

Arsenii Autoriani Testamentum in Migne, *P.G.* 140, cols. 947–58.

Blemmydae, Nicephori, Curriculum Vitae et Carmina, ed. A. Heisenberg, Leipzig, 1896.

Blemmydae, Nicephori, Epistolae; Appendix III of *Theodori Ducae Lascaris Epistolae CCXVII*, ed. N. Festa, Florence, 1898.

Cantacuzeni, Ioannis, eximperatoris Historiarum Libri IV, ed. L. Schopen, Bonn, 1828–32.

K. Chatzepsaltes, '*Σχέσεις τῆς Κύπρου πρὸς τὸ ἐν Νικαίᾳ βυζαντινὸν κράτος*', *Κυπριακαὶ Σπουδαί*, 15 (1951), 65–82, texts, 65–6, 75–7.

——"*Η Ἐκκλησία Κύπρου καὶ τὸ ἐν Νικαίᾳ οἰκουμενικὸν πατριαρχεῖον ἀρχομένου τοῦ Ιγ' μ.χ. αἰῶνος συνοδικὴ πρᾶξις τοῦ πατριαρχείου Κωνσταντινουπόλεως σχετικῶς πρὸς τὴν ἐκλογὴν καὶ τὴν ἀναγνώρισιν τοῦ ἀρχιεπισκόπου Κύπρου Ἡσαΐου*', *Κυπριακαὶ Σπουδαί*, 28 (1964), 135–68, text, 141–4.

Χωνιάτου, Μιχαὴλ Ἀκομινάτου, τὰ σωζωμένα, ed. Sp. Lampros, Athens, 1879–80, 2 vols.

Choniatae, Nicetae, Historia, ed. I. Bekker, Bonn, 1835.

Choniatae, Nicetae, Thesaurus Orthodoxae Fidei in Migne, *P.G.* 140.

Choniatae, Nicetae, Orationes et Epistulae, ed. J. A. Van Dieten (Corpus Fontium Historiae Byzantinae, III), Berlin/New York, 1972.

Χρονικὸν τοῦ Μωρέως, ed. P. P. Kalonaros, Athens, 1940.

A. Chroust, *Quellen zur Geschichte des Kreuzzuges Kaiser Friederichs I* (Monumenta Germaniae Historica, Scriptores Rerum Germanicarum, N.S. V), Berlin, 1928.

Cinnami, Ioannis, Epitome rerum ab Ioanne et Alexio Comnenis gestarum, ed. A. Meineke, Bonn, 1836.

Costantino Porfirogenito de Thematibus, ed. A. Pertusi (Studi e Testi, 160), The Vatican, 1952.

A. Dain, 'Formules de "commission" pour un "nomikos" et un "exarchos"', *REB* 16 (1958), 166–8.

J. Darrouzès, 'Le Mémoire de Constantin Stilbès contre les Latins', *REB* 21 (1963), 50–100.

——'Les Discours d'Euthyme Tornikès (1200–1205)', *REB* 26 (1968), 49–121.

H. Delehaye, *Deux typica byzantins de l'époque des Paléologues*, Brussels, 1921.

F. Dölger, *Aus den Schatzkammern des Heiligen Berges. 115 Urkunden und 50 Urkundensiegel aus 10 Jahrhunderten*, Munich, 1948, 2 vols.

Τὸ ἐπαρχικὸν βιβλίον. The Book of the Eparch. Le Livre du Préfet (with an Introduction by I. Dujčev), London, 1970.

Ephraim, *Chronographia*, ed. I. Bekker, Bonn, 1840.

G. Ferrari, 'Formulari notarili inediti dell'età bizantina', *Bulletino dell'Istituto Storico Italiano*, 33 (1913), 41–128.

H. Gelzer, 'Ungedruckte und ungenügend veröffentliche Texte der Notitiae episcopatum, ein Beitrag zur byzantinischen Kirchen- und Verwaltungsgeschichte', *Abhandlungen der königlich bayerischen Akademie der Wissenschaften*, philos.-philol. Classe, 21 (1901), Abh. 3.

H. Golubovich, 'Disputatio Latinorum et Graecorum seu Relatio apocrisariorum Gregorii IX de gestis Nicaeae in Bithynia et Nymphaeae in Lydia 1234', *Archivum Franciscanum Historicum*, 12 (1919), 418–70.

H. Grégoire, 'Imperatoris Michael Palaeologi de Vita Sua', *B* 29–30 (1959–60), 447–76.

Gregorae, Nicephori, Byzantina Historia, ed. L. Schopen, Bonn, 1829–55, 3 vols.

Γρηγορίου τοῦ ἁγιωτάτου καὶ μακαριωτάτου οἰκουμενικοῦ Πατριάρχου περὶ τοῦ καθ' ἑαυτὸν βίου ὡς ἀπ'ἄλλου προσώπου, in W. Lameere, *La Tradition manuscrite de la correspondance de Grégoire de Chypre, patriarche de Constantinople (1283–1289)* (Études de philologie et d'histoire anciennes publiées par l'Institut historique belge de Rome, II), Brussels/Rome, 1937, pp. 176–91.

A. Heisenberg, 'Kaiser Johannes Batatzes der Barmherzige', *BZ* 14 (1905), 160–233.

—— *Nikolaos Mesarites. Die Palastrevolution des Johannes Komnenos*, Würzburg, 1907.

—— 'Aus der Geschichte und Literatur der Palaiologenzeit', *Sitzungsberichte der bayerischen Akademie der Wissenschaften*, philos.-philol. und hist. Klasse, 1920, Abh. 10, Munich, 1920.

—— 'Neue Quellen zur Geschichte des lateinischen Kaisertums und der Kirchenunion. I. Der Epitaphios des Nikolaos Mesarites auf seinen Bruder Johannes; II. Die Unionsverhandlungen vom 30. August 1206; III. Der Bericht des Nikolaos Mesarites über die politischen und kirchlichen Ereignisse des Jahres 1214', *Sitzungsberichte der bayerischen Akademie der Wissenschaften*, philos.-philol. und hist. Klasse, 1922, Abh. 5; 1923, Abh. 2–3, Munich, 1923.

J. M. Hoeck and R.-J. Loenertz, *Nikolaos-Nektarios von Otranto,*

Abt von Casole: Beiträge zur Geschichte der ost-westlichen Beziehungen unter Innozenz III. und Friederich II. (Studia Patristica et Byzantina, 11), Ettal, 1965.

Jean, Sire de Joinville, *L'Histoire de St. Louis*, ed. Natalis de Wailly, Paris, 1867.

Ch. Ktenas, '*Χρυσόβουλλοι λόγοι τῆς ἐν Ἄθῳ ἱερᾶς βασιλικῆς, πατριαρχικῆς καὶ σταυροπηγιακῆς μονῆς τοῦ Δοχειαρείου*', *EEBS* 4 (1927), 285–311.

E. Kurtz, 'Tri sinodalnykh gramoty mitropolita Efesskago Nikolaja Mesarita' ('Three Synodal Letters of the Metropolitan of Ephesus, Nicholas Mesarites'), *VV* 12 (1906), 99–111.

—— 'Christophoros von Ankyra als Exarch des Patriarchen Germanos II', *BZ* 16 (1907), 120–42.

Sp. Lampros, '*Ἀνέκδοτα ἔγγραφα τῆς μονῆς Ξηροχωραφίου ἢ Ἱερᾶς*', *NH* 11 (1914), 401–13.

——'*Κυπριακὰ καὶ ἄλλα ἔγγραφα ἐκ τοῦ παλατίνου κώδικος 367 τῆς βιβλιοθήκης τοῦ Βατικάνου*', *NH* 14 (1917), 14–50; 15 (1921), 141–65.

Lascaris, Theodori Ducae, Epistolae CCXVII, ed. N. Festa, Florence, 1898.

V. Laurent, *La Vita Retracta et les miracles posthumes de St Pierre d'Atroa* (Société des Bollandistes: Subsidia Hagiographica, 31), Brussels, 1958.

R.-J. Loenertz, 'La Chronique brève de 1352', *OCP* 29 (1963), 331–56.

—— 'Lettre de Georges Bardanès, métropolite de Corcyre, au patriarche oecuménique Germain II 1226–1227c.', *EEBS* 33 (1964), 87–118, text, 104–18.

J. Nicole, 'Bref inédit de Germain II, patriarche de Constantinople (Année 1230) avec une recension nouvelle du chrysobulle de l'empereur Jean Ducas Vatacès', *REG* 7 (1894), 68–80, text, 74–80.

M. G. Nystazopoulou, '*Ὁ ἐπὶ τοῦ κανικλείου καὶ ἡ ἐφορεία τῆς ἐν Πάτμῳ μονῆς*', in *Σύμμεικτα*, I (*Βασιλικὸν Ἵδρυμα Ἐρευνῶν-Κέντρον Βυζαντινῶν Ἐρευνῶν*), Athens, 1966, pp. 76–94.

N. Oikonomides, 'Contribution à l'étude de la pronoia au XIIIe siècle. Une formule d'attribution de parèques à un pronoiaire', *REB* 22 (1964), 158–75, text, 159–61.

—— 'Cinq actes inédits du patriarche Michel Autôreianos', *REB* 25 (1967), 113–45, texts, 114–25.

Pachymeris, Georgii, de Michaele et Andronico Palaeologis libri tredecim, ed. I. Bekker, Bonn, 1835, 2 vols.

A. Papadopoulos-Kerameus, '*Θεόδωρος Εἰρηνικός, Πατριάρχης οἰκουμενικός*', *BZ* 10 (1901), 182–92, text, 187–92.

L. Petit, 'Documents inédits sur le concile de 1166 et ses derniers adversaires', *VV* 11 (1904), 465–93.

Philae, Manuelis, Carmina, ed. E. Miller, Paris, 1855–7, 2 vols.

(Pseudo-) *Codini, Georgii, de officialibus palatii Constantinopolitani et de officiis magnae ecclesiae liber*, ed. I. Bekker, Bonn, 1839.

Pseudo-Kodinos, *Traité des Offices*, ed. J. Verpeaux (Le Monde Byzantin, 1), Paris, 1966.

Scutariotae, Theodori, Additamenta ad Georgii Acropolitae Historiam, in *Acropolitae, Georgii, Opera*, I. ed. A. Heisenberg (q.v.), pp. 275–302.

Sphrantzes, Georgios, *Memorii 1401–1477*, ed. V. Grecu (Scriptores Byzantini, V), Bucharest, 1966.

Th. I. Uspenskij, 'Vizantijskie zemlemery. Nabljudenija po istorii seljskago khozjajstva' ('Byzantine surveys. Observations on the History of Agrarian Economy'), *Trudy VI arkheologicheskago s'ezda v Odesse 1884 g.*, II, Odessa, 1888, pp. 272–341.

Villehardouin, *La Conquête de Constantinople*, ed. E. Faral, Paris, 1961, 2 vols.

L. G. Westerinck, 'Some Unpublished Letters of Blemmydes', *BS* 12 (1951), 43–55.

N. Wilson et J. Darrouzès, 'Restes du cartulaire de Hiéra-Xérochoraphion', *REB* 26 (1968), 5–47.

Xanthopuli, Nicephori Callisti, Enarratio de episcopis Byzantii et de patriarchis omnibus constantinopolitanis, in Migne, *P.G. 147*.

3. SECONDARY AUTHORITIES

N. Adontz, 'Les Taronites à Byzance', *B* 11 (1936), 21–42.

P. J. Alexander, 'The Strength of Empire and Capital as seen through Byzantine Eyes', *Speculum*, 37 (1962), 339–57.

H. Ahrweiler, 'L'Histoire et la géographie de la région de Smyrne entre les deux occupations turques (1081–1317), particulièrement au XIIIe siècle', *Travaux et Mémoires*, 1 (1965), 1–204.

—— 'Choma-Aggélokastron', *REB* 24 (1966), 278–83.

—— *Byzance et la mer. La marine de guerre, la politique et les institutions maritimes de Byzance aux VIIe–XVe siècles* (Bibliothèque Byzantine, Études 5), Paris, 1966.

M. A. Andreeva, *Ocherki po kul'ture vizantijskago dvora v XIII veke (Studies in the Culture of the Byzantine Court in the thirteenth century)* (Travaux de la société royale des sciences de Bohême, Classe des Lettres, N.S. VIII, No. 3), Prague, 1927.

D. Angelov, 'K voprosu o praviteljakh fem v epirskom despotate i nikejskoj imperii' ('On the Question of the Governors of Themes in the Despotate of Epiros and in the Nicaean Empire'), *BS* 12 (1951), 56–74.

—— 'Die bulgarischen Länder und das bulgarische Volk in den Grenzen des byzantinischen Reiches im XI.–XII. Jahrhundert (1081–1185) (Sozial-ökonomische Verhaltnisse)', *Thirteenth Congress of Byzantine Studies: Main Papers,* V. Oxford, 1966.

H. Antoniadis-Bibicou, *Recherches sur les douanes à Byzance* (Cahiers des Annales, 20), Paris, 1963.

—— *Études d'histoire maritime de Byzance. A propos du 'Thème des Caravisiens',* Paris, 1966.

M. Ballard, 'Les Génois en Romanie entre 1204 et 1261. Recherches dans les minutiers notariaux génois', *Mélanges d'archéologie et d'histoire*, 78 (1966), 467–501.

N. H. Baynes, *Byzantine Studies and Other Essays*, London, 1955.

H.-G. Beck, 'Der byzantinische "Ministerpräsident" ', *BZ* 48 (1955), 309–38.

—— *Kirche und theologische Literatur im byzantinischen Reich* (Handbuch der Altertumswissenschaft, XII. 2. 1), Munich, 1959.

—— 'Senat und Volk von Konstantinopel. Probleme der byzantinischen Verfassungsgeschichte' *Sitzungsberichte der bayerische Akademie der Wissenschaften,* philos.-hist. Klasse, 1966, heft 6.

T. Bertelé, 'Il titolo degli iperperi della zecca di Nicea', *Thirteenth Congress of Byzantine Studies: Supplementary Papers (Summaries),* Oxford, 1966, pp. 95–7.

J. Bompaire, 'Sur trois termes de fiscalité byzantine', *BCH* 80 (1956), 625–31.

A. Bon, *Le Péloponnèse byzantin jusqu'en 1204* (Bibliothèque Byzantine, Études 1), Paris, 1951.

S. Borsari, 'Federigo II e l'Oriente bizantino', *RSI* 63 (1951), 279–91.

—— 'I rapporti tra Pisa e gli stati di Romania nel duecento', *RSI* 67 (1955), 477–92.

C. M. Brand, *Byzantium Confronts the West 1180–1204,* Cambridge, Mass., 1968.

G. I. Bratianu, *Recherches sur le commerce génois dans la Mer Noire au XIIIe siècle,* Paris, 1929.

L. Bréhier, *Les Institutions de l'Empire byzantin, le Monde Byzantin II* (L'évolution de l'humanité, 32 bis), Paris, 1949.

R. Browning, 'The Speeches and Letters of Georgios Tornikes, Metropolitan of Ephesos (XIIth Century)', *Actes du XIIe Congrès International d'Études Byzantines, Ochride 1961,* II, Belgrade, 1964, pp. 421–7.

—— *Greece—Ancient and Medieval. An Inaugural Lecture Delivered at Birbeck College 15th June 1966,* London, 1966.

J. B. Bury, *The Imperial Administrative System in the ninth century with a revised text of the Kletorologion of Philotheos* (British Academy Supplemental Papers 1), London, 1911.

—— 'The Constitution of the Later Roman Empire', in *Selected Essays of J. B. Bury* (ed. Harold Temperley), Cambridge, 1930.

C. Cahen, 'Le Commerce anatolien au debut du XIIIe siècle', *Mélanges L. Halphen,* Paris, 1951, pp. 91–101.

—— *Pre-Ottoman Turkey. A General Survey of the Material and Spiritual Culture and History c. 1071–1330* (translated by J. Jones-Williams), London, 1968.

P. Charanis, 'Coronation and its Constitutional Significance in the Later Roman Empire', *B* 15 (1940–1), 49–66.

—— 'The Jews in the Byzantine Empire under the First Palaeologi', *Speculum,* 22 (1947), 75–7.

—— 'On the Asiatic Frontiers of Nicaea', *OCP* 13 (1947), 58–62.

—— 'The Slavic Element in Byzantine Asia Minor in the Thirteenth Century', *B* 18 (1946–8), 69–83.

—— 'The Monastic Properties and the State in the Byzantine Empire', *DOP* 4 (1948), 51–119.

—— 'On the Ethnic Composition of Byzantine Asia Minor

in the Thirteenth Century', *Προσφορὰ εἰς Σπ. Κυριακίδην*, Thessalonica, 1953, pp. 140–7.
—— 'The Transfer of Population as a Policy in the Byzantine Empire', *Comparative Studies in Sociology and History*, 3 (1960–1), 140–54.
—— 'Observations on the Demography of the Byzantine Empire', *Thirteenth International Congress of Byzantine Studies; Main Papers, XIV*, Oxford, 1966.
A. A. Christophilopoulou, '*Ἡ σύγκλητος εἰς τὸ βυζαντινὸν κράτος*', *Ἐπετηρὶς τοῦ Ἀρχείου τῆς Ἱστορίας τοῦ Ἑλληνικοῦ Δικαίου*, 7 (1949), fasc. 2.
—— '*Ἐκλογή, Ἀναγόρευσις, καὶ Στέψις τοῦ βυζαντινοῦ Αὐτοκράτορος*', *Πραγματεῖαι τῆς Ἀκαδημίας Ἀθηνῶν*, 22 (1956), fasc. 2.
C. Cipolla, 'Currency Depreciation in Medieval Europe', in *Change in Medieval Society, Europe North of the Alps (1050–1500)* (ed. S. Thrupp), London, 1965, pp. 227–36.
P. Collinet, 'Byzantine Legislation from the Death of Justinian (565) to 1453', *Cambridge Medieval History,* IV, Cambridge, 1923, pp. 706–25.
G. Czebe, 'Studien zum Hochverratsprozesse des Michael Paläologos im Jahr 1252', *BNJ* 8 (1931), 59–98.
R. Devréesse, 'Négotiations ecclésiastiques arméno-byzantines au XIIIe siècle', *Studi bizantini e nedellenici*, 5 (1939), 146–51.
Ch. Diehl, 'Un Haut Fonctionnaire byzantin, le logothète (*τῶν σεκρέτων*)', *Mélanges offerts à M. Nicolas Iorga,* Paris, 1933, pp. 217–27.
F. Dölger, *Beiträge zur Geschichte der byzantinischen Finanzverwaltung, besonders des 10. und 11. Jahrhunderts* (Byzantinisches Archiv, 9), Leipzig/Berlin, 1927.
—— 'Chronologisches und Prosopographisches zur byzantinischen Geschichte des 13. Jahrhunderts', *BZ* 27 (1927), 291–320.
—— 'Die Kaiserurkunden des Johannes-Theologos-Klosters auf Patmos', *BZ* 28 (1928), 332–71.
—— 'Das Aerikon', *BZ* 30 (1929–30), 450–7.
—— *Byzanz und die europäische Staatenwelt. Ausgewählte Vorträge und Aufsätze,* Ettal, 1953.
—— *Byzantinische Diplomatik. 20 Aufsätze zum Urkundenwesen der Byzantiner,* Ettal, 1956.

—— *ΠΑΡΑΣΠΟΡΑ. 30 Aufsätze zur Geschichte, Kultur, und Sprache des byzantinischen Reiches,* Ettal, 1961.

—— and J. Karayannopoulos, *Byzantinische Urkundenlehre* (Handbuch der Altertumswissenschaft XII, 3, 1), Munich, 1968.

J. Draeske, 'Theodoros Laskaris', *BZ* 3 (1894), 498–515.

A. Ducellier, 'L'Arbanon et les Albanais au XIe siècle', *Travaux et Mémoires,* 3 (1968), 353–68.

F. Dvornik, *Early Christian and Byzantine Political Philosphy: Origins and Background* (Dumbarton Oaks Studies IX), Washington D.C., 1966, 2 vols.

E. Erdmann, *Das anatolische Karavansaray des 13. Jahrhunderts,* Berlin, 1961, 2 vols.

S. Eyice, 'Le Palais byzantin de Nymphaion près d'Izmir', *Akten des XI. Internationalen Byzantinisten-Kongresses,* Munich, 1958, pp. 150–3.

A. M. Fontrier, 'Le Monastère de Lembos près de Smyrne et ses possessions au XIIIe siècle', *BCH* 16 (1892), 379–410.

J. K. Fotheringham, *Marco Sanudo, Conqueror of the Archipelago,* Oxford, 1915.

E. Francès, 'La Féodalité et les villes byzantines au XIIIe et au XIVe siècles', *BS* 16 (1955), 76–96.

F. Fuchs, *Die höheren Schulen von Konstantinopel im Mittelalter* (Byzantinisches Archiv, 8), Leipzig/Berlin, 1926.

A. Gardner, *The Lascarids of Nicaea. The Story of an Empire in Exile,* London, 1912.

D. J. Geanakoplos, *Emperor Michael Palaeologus and the West 1258–82. A Study in Byzantine-Latin Relations*, Cambridge, Mass., 1959.

H. Gelzer, 'Pergamon unter Byzantinern und Osmanen', *Abhandlungen der königlichen preussischen Akademie der Wissenschaften,* philos. und hist. Klasse, Abh. 2, Berlin, 1903.

H. Glykatzi, 'L'Épitéleia dans le cartulaire de Lemviotissa', *B* 24 (1954), 71–93.

—— 'A propos de l'épitéleia', *B* 25/7 (1955–7), 369–72.

—— Ahrweiler, 'La Politique agraire des empereurs de Nicée', *B* 28 (1958), 51–66.

—— 'Note additionnelle sure la politique agraire des empereurs de Nicée', *B* 28 (1958), 135–6.

——'Les Forteresses construites en Asie Mineure face à l' invasion seldjoucide', *Akten des XI. Internationalen Byzantinisten-Kongresses,* Munich, 1958, pp. 182–9.

—— 'Recherches sur l'administration de l'Empire byzantin aux IXe–XIe siècles', *BCH* 84 (1960), 1–111.

—— 'La Concession des droits incorporels. Donations conditionnelles', *Actes du XIIe Congrès International d'Études Byzantines. Ohrid, 1961,* Belgrade, 1964, II, pp. 103–14.

B. Granić, 'Kirchenrechtliche Glossen zu den vom Kaiser Basileios II dem autokephalen Erzbistum von Achrida verliehenen Privilegien', *B* 12 (1937), 395–415.

R. Guilland, 'Le Grand Domesticat à Byzance', *EO* 37 (1938), 53–64.

—— 'Fonctions et dignités des eunuques', *EB* 2 (1944), 185–225.

—— 'Études sur l'histoire administrative de l'Empire byzantin. Le Grand Connétable', *B* 19 (1949), 99–111.

——'Études de titulature et de prosopographie byzantines. Le Protostrator', *REB* 8 (1950), 156–79.

—— 'Études de titulature et de prosopographie byzantines. Les chefs de la marine byzantine: Drongaire de la flotte, Grand Drongaire de la flotte, Mégaduc', *BZ* 44 (1951), 212–40.

—— 'Études sur l'histoire administrative de l'Empire byzantin. Le stratopédarque et le grand stratopédarque', *BZ* 46 (1953), 63–90.

—— 'Observations sur la liste des dignitaires du Pseudo-Codinos', *REB* 12 (1954), 58–68.

—— 'Contribution à l'histoire administrative et à la prosopographie de l'Empire byzantin: les domestiques des thèmes d'Orient et des thèmes d'Occident', *Akten des XI. Internationalen Byzantinisten-Kongresses,* Munich, 1958, pp. 206–11.

—— 'Études sur l'histoire administrative de l'Empire byzantin: les commandants de la garde impériale sous les Paléologues. L'*ἐπὶ τοῦ στράτου* et le juge de l'armée', *REB* 18 (1960), 79–96.

—— 'Études sur l'histoire administrative de Byzance. Observations sur le Clétorologe de Philothée', *REB* 20 (1962), 156–70.

—— 'Études sur l'histoire administrative de l'Empire byzantin. Le maître des requêtes. '*Ὁ ἐπὶ τῶν δεήσεων*', *B* 35 (1965), 97–118.

J. Hackett, *A History of the Orthodox Church of Cyprus,* London, 1901.

M. F. Hendy, *Coinage and Money in the Byzantine Empire 1081–1261* (Dumbarton Oaks Studies XII), Washington D.C., 1969.

E. Herman, 'Ricerche sulle istituzione monastiche bizantine: typika ktetorika, caristicarii e monasteri "liberi" ', *OCP* 6 (1940), 293–375.

W. Heyd, *Histoire du commerce du Levant* (translated by F. Raynaud), Amsterdam, 1959, 2 vols.

A. Hohlweg, 'Zur Frage der Pronoia in Byzanz', *BZ* 60 (1967), 288–308.

H. Hunger, 'Von Wissenschaft und Kunst der frühen Palaiologenzeit', *JOBG* 8 (1959), 123–55.

J. Irmscher, 'Nikäa als "Zentrum des griechischen Patriotismus" ', *Revue des Études Sud-Est Européennes,* 8 (1970), 33–47.

R. Janin, 'Nicée. Étude historique et topographique', *EO* 24 (1925), 482–90.

—— *Constantinople byzantine: développement urbain et répertoire topographique* (Archives de l'Orient Chrétien, 4), Paris, 1950.

—— *La Géographie ecclésiastique de l'Empire byzantin*, part 1: *Le Siège de Constantinople et le patriarcat oecuménique*, Vol. 3: *Les Églises et les monastères*, Paris, 1953.

G. de Jerphanion, 'Les Inscriptions cappadociennes et l'histoire de l'Empire grec de Nicée', *OCP* 1 (1935), 239–56.

——'*ΣΑΜΨΩΝ* et '*ΑΜΙΣΟΣ*. Une ville à deplacer de neuf cent kilomètres', *OCP* 1 (1935), 257–67.

C. J. Jireček, *Die Heerstrasse von Belgrad nach Constantinopel und die Balkanpässe*, Prague, 1877.

—— *Geschichte der Serben*, Amsterdam, 1967, 2 vols.

A. P. Kazhdan, *Agrarnye otnoshenija v Vizantii XIII–XIV vv. (Agrarian Relations in Byzantium in the 13th and 14th centuries)*, Moscow, 1952.

E. Kirsten, 'Die byzantinische Stadt', *Berichte zum XI. internationalen Byzantinisten-Kongress*, Munich, 1958.

D. Kovačević, 'Dans la Serbie et la Bosnie médiévales: les

mines d'or et d'argent', *Annales. Économies, Sociétés, Civilisations*, 15 (1960), 248–58.

S. N. Lagopates, *Γερμανὸς ὁ β', Πατριάρχης Κωνσταντινουπόλεως-Νικαίας, 1222–1240. Βίος, συγγράμματα καὶ διδασκαλία αὐτοῦ, ἀνέκδοται ὁμιλίαι καὶ ἐπιστολαὶ τὸ πρῶτον ἐκδιδόμεναι*, Tripolis, 1913.

E. Lappa-Zizicas, 'Un Traité inédit de Théodore II Lascaris', *Actes du VIe Congrès International d'Études Byzantines*, I, Paris, 1948, pp. 119–26.

V. Laurent, 'Un Sceau inédit du protonotaire Basile Kamateros, *B* 6 (1931), 253–72.

—— 'Le Pape Aléxandre IV (1254–1261) et l'Empire de Nicée', *EO* 34 (1935), 26–55.

—— 'La Succession épiscopale de la métropole de Théssalonique dans la première moitié du XIIIe siècle', *BZ* 56 (1963), 284–96.

—— 'La Chronologie des patriarches de Constantinople au XIIIe siècle', *REB* 27 (1969), 129–50.

P. Lemerle, *Philippes et la Macédoine orientale à l'époque chrétienne et byzantine* (Bibliothèque des Écoles françaises d'Athènes et de Rome, 158), Paris, 1945.

—— *L'Émirat d'Aydin, Byzance et l'Occident: Recherches sur la "Geste d'Umur Pacha"* (Bibliothèque Byzantine, Études 2), Paris, 1957.

—— 'Recherches sur le régime agraire à Byzance: la terre militaire à l'époque des Comnènes', *Cahiers de Civilisation Médiévale*, 2 (1959), 265–81.

R.-J. Loenertz, 'Le Chancelier impérial à Byzance au XIVe et au XIIIe siècle', *OCP* 26 (1960), 275–300.

J. Longnon, *L'Empire latin de Constantinople et la principauté de Morée*, Paris, 1949.

R. S. Lopez, 'Back to Gold, 1252', *Economic History Review*, Ser. ii. 9 (1956–7), 219–40.

A. Meliarakes, *'Ιστορία τοῦ Βασιλείου τῆς Νικαίας καὶ τοῦ Δεσποτάτου τῆς Ἠπείρου (1204–1261)*, Athens, 1898.

J. Meyendorff, 'Justinian, the Empire and the Church', *DOP* 22 (1968), 43–60.

W. Miller, 'The Empire of Nicaea and the Recovery of Constantinople', *Cambridge Medieval History*, IV, Cambridge, 1923, pp. 478–516.

D. M. Nicol, 'Ecclesiastical Relations between the Despotate of Epiros and the Kingdom of Nicaea in the years 1215 to 1230', *B* 22 (1952), 207–28.

—— *The Despotate of Epiros*, Oxford, 1957.

—— 'The Fourth Crusade and the Greek and Latin Empires, 1204–1261', *Cambridge Medieval History*, IV, part 1, Cambridge, 1966, pp. 275–330.

—— *The Byzantine Family of Kantakouzenos (Cantacuzenus) ca. 1100–1460. A Genealogical and Prosopographical Study* (Dumbarton Oaks Studies XI), Washington, D.C., 1968.

W. Norden, *Das Papsttum und Byzanz. Die Trennung der beiden Mächte und das Problem ihrer Wiedervereinigung bis zum Untergange des byzantinischen Reiches*, Berlin, 1903.

M. Nystazopoulou, "*Ο "Ἀλανικὸς" τοῦ ἐπισκόπου Ἀλανίας Θεοδώρου καὶ ἡ εἰς τὸν πατριαρχικὸν θρόνον ἀνάρρησις Γερμανοῦ τοῦ β*'", *EEBS* 33 (1964), 270–8.

D. Obolensky, 'Byzantium, Kiev and Moscow: a Study in Ecclesiastical Relations', *DOP* 11 (1957), 21–78.

—— *The Byzantine Commonwealth: Eastern Europe 500–1453*, London, 1971.

N. Oikonomides, 'The Donations of Castles in the last quarter of the eleventh century (Dölger, *Reg.* No. 1012)', *Polychronion. Festschrift Franz Dölger zum 75. Geburtstag*, Heidelberg, 1966, pp. 413–17.

P. Orgels, 'Sabas Asidénos, dynaste de Sampson', *B* 10 (1935), 67–77.

G. Ostrogorskij, 'Löhne und Preise in Byzanz', *BZ* 32 (1932), 293–333.

—— *Pour l'histoire de la féodalité byzantine* (Corpus Bruxellense Historiae Byzantinae, Subsidia I) (translated by H. Grégoire and P. Lemerle), Brussels, 1954.

—— 'Zur Kaisersalbung und Schilderhebung im spätbyzantinischen Krönungszeremoniell', *Historia*, 4 (1955), 246–56.

—— *Quelques problèmes d'histoire de la paysannerie byzantine* (Corpus Bruxellense Historiae Byzantinae, Subsidia II), Brussels, 1956.

—— 'Pour l'histoire de l'immunité à Byzance', *B* 28 (1958), 165–254.

—— *History of the Byzantine State* (translated by J. Hussey), 2nd edn., Oxford, 1968.

D. I. Polemis, 'A Manuscript Note of the year 1247', *Byzantinische Forschungen*, 1 (1966), 269–76.

—— *The Doukai. A Contribution to Byzantine Prosopography*, London, 1968.

J. Prawer, 'Étude de quelques problèmes agraires et sociaux d'une seigneurie croisée au XIIIe siècle', *B* 22 (1952), 5–61; 23 (1953), 143–70.

Sir W. M. Ramsay, *The Historical Geography of Asia Minor* (Royal Geographical Society's Supplemental Papers IV), London, 1890.

—— *The Cities and Bishoprics of Phrygia, being an essay of the local history of Phrygia from the earliest times to the Turkish Conquest*, Oxford, 1895.

L.-P. Raybaud, *Le Gouvernment et l'administration centrale de l'Empire byzantin sous les premiers Paléologues (1258–1354)*, Paris, 1968.

G. Rouillard, 'Recensements de terres sous les premiers Paléologues. Remarques sur la pratique de la chancellerie impériale et des services du fisc', *B* 12 (1937), 105–18.

—— 'La Politique de Michael VIII Paléologue à l'égard des monastères', *EB* 1 (1943), 73–84.

—— *La Vie rurale dans l'Empire byzantin*, Paris, 1953.

A. P. Rudakov, *Ocherki vizantijskoj kul'tury po dannym grecheskoj agiografii (Studies in Byzantine Culture from the Evidence of Greek Hagiography)*, Moscow, 1917.

H. J. Scheltema, 'Byzantine Law', in *Cambridge Medieval History*, IV, part 2, Cambridge, 1967, pp. 55–77.

G. Schmalzbauer, 'Die Tornikioi in der Palaiologenzeit', *JOB* 18 (1969), 115–35.

A.-M. Schneider, *Die römischen und byzantinischen Denkmäler von Iznik-Nicaea* (Istanbuler Forschungen, 16), Berlin, 1943.

I. Ševčenko, 'Léon Bardalès et les juges généraux ou la corruption des incorruptibles', *B* 19 (1949), 247–59.

—— 'On the Preface to a Praktikon by Alyates', *JOB* 17 (1968), 65–72.

G. Stadtmüller, *Michael Choniates, Metropolit von Athen* (Orientalia Christiana Analecta, 33. 2), Rome, 1934.

—— 'Zur Geschichte der Familie Kamateros', *BZ* 34 (1934), 352–8.

E. Stein, 'Untersuchungen zur spätbyzantinischen Verfassungs- und Wirtschaftsgeschichte', *Mitteilungen zur Osmanischen Geschichte*, 2 (1923–6), 1–62.

L. Stiernon, 'Les Origines du despotat d'Épire', *REB* 17 (1959), 90–126.

—— 'Les Origines du despotat d'Épire (suite)', *Actes du XIIe Congrès d'Études Byzantines. Ochride 1961*, II, Belgrade, 1964, pp. 197–202.

N. G. Svoronos, 'Le Serment de fidélité à l'empereur byzantin et sa signification constitutionnelle', *Actes du VIe Congrès International d'Études Byzantines*, I, Paris, 1948, pp. 191–7.

—— 'Le Serment de fidélité à l'empereur byzantin et sa signification constitutionnelle', *REB* 9 (1951), 106–42.

—— 'Sur quelques formes de la vie rurale à Byzance: petite et grande exploitation', *Annales. Économies, Sociétés, Civilisations*, 11 (1956), 325–35.

—— *Recherches sur le cadastre byzantin et la fiscalité aux XIe et XIIe siècles: le cadastre de Thèbes*, Paris, 1959.

—— 'Les Privilèges de l'église à l'époque des Comnènes: un rescrit inédit de Manuel ler Comnène', *Travaux et Mémoires*, 1 (1965), 325–91.

—— 'Notes à propos d'un procédé de techniques fiscales: la *ΔΟΧΗ*', *REB* 24 (1966), 97–106.

—— 'L'Épibolé à l'époque des Comnènes', *Travaux et Mémoires*, 3 (1968), 375–95.

I. Sykoutres, '*Περὶ τὸ σχίσμα τῶν Ἀρσενιατῶν*', *Ἑλληνικά*, 2 (1929), 267–332; 3 (1930), 15–44.

P. Tannery, *Quadrivium de Georges Pachymère* (Studi e Testi, 94), The Vatican, 1940.

F. Thiriet, *La Romanie vénitienne au moyen âge. Le développement et l'exploitation du domaine colonial vénitien (XIIe–XVe siècles)* (Bibliothèque des Écoles françaises d'Athènes et de Rome, 193), Paris, 1959.

W. Tomaschek, 'Zur historischen Topographie von Kleinasien im Mittelalter', *Sitzungsberichte der kaiserlichen Akademie der Wissenschaften in Wien*, philos.-hist. Classe, 124 (1891), Abh. 8.

A. E. Vacalopoulos, *Origins of the Greek Nation: The Byzantine Period, 1204–1461, New Brunswick, N.J., 1970.*

J. Verpeaux, 'Contribution à l'étude de l'administration byzantine: *ὁ μεσάζων*', *BS* 16 (1955), 270–96.

—— 'Les Oikeioi. Notes d'histoire institutionelle et sociale', *REB* 23 (1965), 89–99.

A. Visijakova, 'Khozjajstvennaja organizatsija monastyrja Lemviotissy', ('The Economic Organization of the Monastery of Lemviotissa'), *VV,* 25 (1927), 33–52.

Sp. Vryonis Jr., 'The Question of the Byzantine Mines', *Speculum,* 37 (1962), 1–17.

—— 'The Byzantine Legacy and Ottoman Forms', *DOP* 23/4 (1969–70), 253–308.

A. M. Watson, 'Back to Gold—and Silver', *Economic History Review,* Ser. ii. 20 (1967), 1–34.

T. Wiegand, *Der Latmos,* in *Milet. Ergebnisse der Ausgrabungen und Untersuchungen seit dem Jahre 1899,* III, 1, Berlin, 1913.

P. Wirth, 'Die Begründung der Kaisermacht Michaels VIII. Palaiologos', *JOBG* 10 (1961), 85–91.

—— 'Von der Schlacht von Pelagonia bis zur Wiedereroberung Konstantinopels. Zur äusseren Geschichte der Jahre 1259–1261', *BZ* 55 (1962), 30–7.

P. Wittek, *Das Fürstentum Mentesche: Studie zur Geschichte Westkleinasiens im 13.–15. Jahrhundert* (Istanbuler Mitteilungen, 2), Istanbul, 1934.

R. L. Wolff, 'The "Second Bulgarian Empire". Its Origin and History to 1204', *Speculum,* 24 (1949), 167–206.

D. Xanalatos, 'Wirtschaftliche Aufbau- und Autarkiemassnahmen im XIII. Jahrhundert', *Leipziger Vierteljahrschrift für Südosteuropa,* 3 (1939), 129–39.

D. A. Zakythinos, *Le Despotat grec de Morée,* Paris, 1932–53, 2 vols.

——'*Μελέται περὶ τῆς διοικητικῆς διαιρέσεως καὶ τῆς ἐπαρχιακῆς διοικήσεως ἐν τῷ Βυζαντινῷ κράτει*', *EEBS* 17 (1941) 208–74; 18 (1948), 42–62; 19 (1949), 3–15; 21 (1951), 179–209; 22 (1952), 159–82; 25 (1955), 127–57.

—— *Crise monétaire et crise économique à Byzance du XIIIe au XVe siècle,* Athens, 1948.

I. GENERAL INDEX

Abydos, 198.
Achaea, 26, 198.
Achilles, 31.
Achyraous, 99, 111, 112, 245.
Adam, Nicholas, knight, 125, note 18.
Adramyttion, 112, 114 and note 144, 246.
Adrianople, 183, 279, 282, 284, 288.
Battle of, 12, 239.
Aegean, 1, 11, 104, 120, 247, 249, 279, 291.
Nicaean fleet of, 196, 199.
Africa, 118.
Afyon Karahisar, see Akroinon.
Ahrweiler, Professor Hélène, 3, 200 note 127, 216 note 64, 224, 228, 251 notes 6 and 12.
Akoimetos, Monastery of, 50
Akroinon, 98.
Akropolites, George, 3, 13 note 15, 25 note 82, 30–1, 48, 65, 67, 68, 72, 73, 76, 77, 88, 100, 152, 155, 159, 161, 163, 164–5, 167 and note 104, 168, 175, 176, 178, 179, 180, 283, 286, 292 and note 84.
Grand Logariast, 175, 206.
General Logothete, 164, 175.
Grand Logothete, 73 note 62, 164–5, 175, 282.
Praitor, 282, 289–90.
History of, 3, 288.
Alania:
Theodore, Bishop of, 19.
Alanya, 115.
Albania, Albanians, 25, 280, 282, 284, 287, 289–90.
Alethinos family, 129 note 50, 269.
Alexander, 29, 31.
Alexander IV, Pope, 18.
Alexios I Komnenos, Emperor, 72, 121, 147, 177, 183, 198, 204, 234.
Alexios III Angelos, Emperor, 1, 12, 37, 73, 167, 220, 244.
Alopos, John, *prokathemenos* of Smyrna, 125 note 18, 214 note 56, 265–6 and note 98.
Alvanon, 280, 290, 291, 292.
Governor of, see Chavaron, Constantine, and Nestongos, Isaac.
Ruler of, see Goulamos.
Alyates family, 72.
Alyates, Andronikos, *epi tou kanikleiou*, 164 note 80.
Alyates, Nikephoros, *epi tou kanikleiou*, 72, 163–4.
Amanariotissa, monastery of, 54.
Amastris, 98, 244.
Metropolitan of, 21.
Amazon, Bishop of, 271.
Anaia, 113.
katepanikion of, 247.
Andronikos I Komnenos, Emperor, 61.
Andronikos II Palaiologos, Emperor, 68, 105, 169, 236, 287 note 44.
Angelos, imperial house of, 12, 61, 69, 70, 123, 155, 257, 277.
Angelos, Epirot dynasty, 24, 287.
Angelos family, 69, 251.
Angelos, Demetrios, Despot of Thessalonica, 23, 24 note 80.
Angelos, George Komnenos, uncle of Michael VIII Palaiologos, 125.
Angelos, John, Emperor, then Despot of Thessalonica, 24 note 80.
Angelos, John, uncle of John III Vatatzes, 170 note 111.
Duke of Thrakesion, 213, 251, notes 9, 10, 12, 254, 262, 267, 271.
Angelos, John, 251 note 12.
Grand *primmikerios*, 187.
Protostrator, 84, 152, 185, 251 note 12.
Angelos, Manuel, Emperor, then Despot of Thessalonica, 23, 24 note 80.
Angelos, Michael, Ruler of Epiros, 12.
Angelos, Michael, Despot of Epiros, 24, 25–6 and note 83, 28, 82, 160, 282, 286, 290.
Angelos, Michael, *stratiotes*, 125 note 18, 130, 140, 213.
Anna, his wife, 130.
Angelos, Nikephoros, Despot, 25.

Angelos, Theodore, Emperor of Thessalonica, 20–1, 23, 280, 284, 285.
Angelos, Theodore, *oikeios*, 170 note 111.
Antioch-on-the-Maiander, 248.
Battle of, 14, 29, 31, 73, 98, 167, 182, 183, 191.
Anyphantor, 109.
Aphameia, 279.
'Apokope ton psomion', 221, 232.
Appollonis, 112 note 131.
Aprenos family, 69.
Arabs, 110, 239.
Argolid, 123.
Armenians, 19, 32, 105, 155, 175, 182.
Church, 19.
Bride of Theodore I Laskaris, 41.
Arsenios Autoreianos, Patriarch, 45, 51 and note 30, 54 and note 47, 56, 57, 58, 71 note 47, 73 note 65, 82–93 *passim*.
Arta, 12, 282.
Synod at, 21.
Artavasdes family, 129 note 50.
Asidenos, Savvas, *sevastokrator*, 61, 244 note 6.
Astytzion, 205.
Athens, 11, 268, 269.
Archontes of, 269.
Archbishop of, see Choniates, Michael.
Athos, Mount, 164.
Attaleia (Antalya), 98, 115, 116.
Augustus, 38
Aurelion, 263.
Oikodespotai of, 263.
Auxentios, Grand Duke, 197, 198.

Babylon, 29.
Baldwin I, Latin Emperor, 11, 12, 287.
Balikesir see Achyraous
Balsamon family, 72.
Belissariotes, John and Michael, 11 note 6.
Bishops, 257, 261, 264, 269–70, 271, 272, 273, 274, 276.
Bithynia, 27, 50, 58 note 62, 200, 244–5.
Governor of, see Michael VIII Palaiologos.
Black Sea, 98, 244.
Blemmydes, Nikephoros, 28, 32, 44, 50–1 and note 30, 53, 57, 59, 67, 85, 87–8, 126, 151, 158, 164, 169, 174, 178, 179, 180, 276.
Boniface of Montferrat, 11, 12.
Bosphoros, 116.
Bulgaria, Bulgarians, 12, 13, 21, 22, 23, 26, 27, 32, 77, 152, 165, 167 note 104, 182, 184, 185, 186, 189, 191, 239, 241, 279–81, 283, 284, 285, 287–8.
Alliance with Nicaea, 22, 23, 26, 119.
Archbishop of, 21.
Church in, 2, 21–2.
Macedonian territories, 23
Tsar, 26, 152, 165.

Cadaster, 207–8.
Candia, 114 note 144.
Cappadocia, 101.
Caria, 100.
Caucasus, 19.
Chalkoutzes, 71 note 49.
Chavaron, Constantine, Governor of Alvanon, 291–2.
Chilarenos, Michael, *panhypersevastos*, 170 note 111.
Chios, 104, 115, 137, 197.
Duke of, 249.
Chliara, 99, 246.
Chomatianos, Demetrios, Archbishop of Ohrid, 21, 173.
Chonai, 100.
Choniates, Michael, Archbishop of Athens, 11, 44, 71, 156, 196, 269–70.
Choniates, Nicetas, 29.
Ex-Grand Logothete, 149.
Chrysomalles, Basil, *epi tou kanikleiou*, 148 note 8.
Duke of Thrakesion, 240, 247.
Chrysos, Dobromir, 285.
Chrysoverges family, 131, 269.
Chrysoverges, George, 131.
Constantine the Great, 31, 38, 296.
Constantinople, 1, 2, 4, 9, 10, 11, 12, 13, 14, 15, 16, 17, 26, 27, 28, 29, 32, 33, 37, 47, 52, 55, 61, 63, 71 note 50, 72, 74, 90, 91, 97, 98, 100, 102, 109, 112, 114, 115, 116, 118, 120, 123, 129, 133, 139, 147, 161, 165, 166, 172, 176, 177, 178, 179, 182, 188, 191, 196, 198, 199, 204, 239, 241, 244, 249, 251, 255, 269, 274, 277, 279, 284, 285, 294, 295, 296.

Great Palace, 65.
Monasteries of, 49, 123, 124 and see Panachrantos and Pantakrator, monasteries of.
Nicaeo-Bulgarian siege, 119.
'Sion', 29.
University of, 179.
'*Constitutio Cypria*', 18.
Coronation, 39, 43–5, 89–90, 91, 92.
Corvées see *angareiai.*
Cos, 104, 129, 140, 193, 195, 197, 230, 249, 266 note 109, 292.
Kephale of, 249, 292 and see Varangopoulos, Alexios.
Court hierarchy, 24, 63–4, 65, 77, 174.
Cretans, Crete, 114–15 and note 144, 119, 184, 197, 199, 220.
Metropolitan of, 272.
Crimea, The, 19, 115.
Crusader States, 188.
Currency, 117–20.
Cyclades, 249.
Cyprus, 17–19, 20, 115, 222 note 83.
Archbishop of, see Esaias and Neophytos.

Dalaman Çay see Indos.
Danube, 284.
David, 31, 43, 44.
Denizli see Laodikea.
Dermatas family see Kretikos.
Dermokaites, 182 note 4.
Didymoteichos, 189, 190, 279, 288.
Diogenes, Constantine, duke of Leros and Kalymnos, 211, 249.
Praktikon of, 139 note 110.
Dölger, Professor Franz, 156, 204 note 4.
Dorylaion, 112.
Doukas, imperial house of, 69.
Doukas family, 126.
Doukas, Isaac, *sevastokrator*, brother of John III Vatatzes, 68.
Doukas, John, 251 note 12.
Dragotas, 287.
Duke, governor of a theme, 4, 193, 210, 218, 226, 227, 233, 239, 240, 242, 250–8, 285, 293.
Dyrrhachion, 25, 26, 282, 290.
Governor of, see Michael VIII Palaiologos.

Eerinon, monastery of, 131 note 66.
Edessa see Vodena.
Edessenos, *orphanotrophos*, 289 note 53.
Egypt, 114, 115.
Eirene Laskarina, Empress, 47, 176.
Ephesos, 53, 104, 108, 110, 112, 113, 126, 179, 206, 210, 228, 247, 258.
Church of St John the Baptist at, 110.
Metropolitan of, 58 note 62, 179 and see Mesarites, Nicholas, Klaudiopolites, Constantine, and Nikephoros of Ephesos, Patriarch.
prokathemenos of, 264.
Epiros, Epirots, 12, 20, 21, 23–8, 31–3, 82, 88, 165, 172, 175, 182, 184, 190, 191, 280, 282, 284, 286, 288, 290.
Church in, 15, 20–1, 23–4, 27, 52.
Rulers of, 27, 28, 66, 160, 165, 167 note 104 and see Angelos, Michael, Despot of Epiros.
Esaias, Archbishop of Cyprus, 17.
Eskamatismenos, Leo, *apographeus* of Rhodes and the Cyclades, 249.
Eskişehir see Dorylaion
Euboea, 11, 71 note 49, 115.
Eusebius of Caesarea, 1, 38.

'Fiscal Treatise', 203, 220.
Florence, 118.
'Foreigners and free' see *xenoi.*
Fourth Crusade, 9, 61.
Franchises, 121–3, 127–9.
Franks, 26, 182, 282.
Frederick II, German Emperor, 15–16, 115, 177.
Mints *augustalis*, 118.

Galata, siege of, 191.
Gallipoli, 197, 279.
Gavalas, Rhodian dynasty, 28, 114, 197, 198.
Gavalas family, 108, 126, 228.
Gavalas, Grand *droungarios*, 133, 198.
Gavalas, Leo, Caesar, 114.
Genoa, Genoese, 102, 114–15, 118, 197, 198, 227, 252, 255.
Geoffrey, an Armenian, 175, 199.
George the Eunuch, 106 note 83, 272.
Protovestiarios of Phokas, Theodotos (q.v.), 253 note 27.

Georgians, 19.
Germanos II, Patriarch, 15, 18, 19, 21, 23–4, 29, 47, 50, 52, 58, 161 note 70.
Germans, in Nicaean service, 182.
Glavas, *kouropalates*, 175.
Gordatos family, 129–30.
Gordatos, Anna, 130.
Gordatos, Theodore, 130.
Goulamos, ruler of Alvanon, 25.
Gounaropoulos family, 131 note 67, 216 note 64, 232 note 131, 267, 271.
Gounaropoulos, Michael, 216 note 64.
Gounaropoulos, Nikandros, monk, 267–8.
Greece, 122.
Gregoras, Nikephoros, 25 note 83, 43, 87, 88, 167 note 104.
Gregory IX, Pope, 30.
Gregory of Cyprus, Patriarch, 19, 32, 178, 181.

Hagios Kosmas, 193.
Hagiotheodorites family, 72.
Hagiotheodorites:
  Logothete of the Flocks, 72 note 51, 175, 206 and note 12.
  Logothete *ton oikeiakon*, 175.
  Brother-in-law of Mouzalon, George (q.v.), 84 note 43.
Helladas, Leo, 273 note 147.
Hellas, theme of, 200.
'Hellas', 'Hellenes', 'Hellenikon', 'Hellenis', 29–31.
Hellespont, 58 note 62, 110, 112, 197, 198, 199, 200, 222.
Henry of Hainault, Latin Emperor, 14, 15, 17, 111.
Hermos, 99, 102, 113, 125, 140, 213, 246.
Hexapterygos, Theodore, 179.
Hieras, monastery of, 53, 106, note 83.
Hierissos, *megalon allagion* of, 189.
Hikanatos, Theodore, Duke of Thrakesion, 251 note 11, 252.
Hohenstaufen, 15, 30.
Hyakinthos, Monastery of, 50.
Hyleas, Michael, *protopansevastos,* 170 note 111.

Iatropoulos, Demetrios:
  Prokathemenos of Philadelphia, 176, 265.
  Logothete *ton oikeiakon*, 73 note 62, 176, 265.
Ignatios, Constantine, *naukleros*, 113.
Ikaria, 104, 197.
Ikonion, 112, 115, 116.
'Imperial Book', 208.
'Imperial Cabinet', 4, 147–8.
'Imperial Household', 4, 148–55 passim. Members of, see *oikeios*.
'Imperial liege knight' see *kavallarios.*
'Imperial Monasteries', 51–3.
'Imperial Retinue', 76, 186–7, 192.
'Imperial Secretary' see *grammatikos.*
'Imperial Tribunal' see *sekreton.*
India, 114.
Indos, 100.
Innocent IV, Pope, 16.
'Inquest', 262.
Isaac II Angelos, Emperor, 48, 196.
Ises, John, *protostrator*, 183, 201, 210.
Italy, 117.

Jerusalem, 19.
Jews, 29, 32, 105.
John II Asen, Bulgarian Tsar, 22, 23, 279, 285, 286.
John II Komnenos, Emperor, 99, 225, 247.
John III Doukas Vatatzes, Emperor, 1, 5, 15, 16, 18, 20, 22, 23, 24, 25–6, 27, 29, 30, 32, 40, 41, 47–8, 50, 51, 53, 55, 56, 57, 58, 62, 63, 64, 66, 67, 68, 71, 72 note 53, 73, 75, 76, 88, 93, 100, 101 and note 38, 104, 105, 108, 111, 112, 114, 116, 117, 118, 120, 123, 124, 125, 126 and note 27, 127, 129, 136, 140, 150, 151–3, 155, 159, 160, 161, 164, 167 note 104, 170, 172, 176, 177, 178, 179, 180, 183, 184, 187, 188, 192, 194 and note 91, 197, 198, 199, 205, 211, 215, 226, 241, 248, 251 note 12, 265, 271, 279, 282, 283, 287, 288, 289.
  Protovestiarios or *protovestiarites*, 41.
John IV Laskaris, Emperor, 26, 41, 42, 45, 79, 80–92 passim, 151, 160.
John Kamateros, Patriarch, 13.
Justinian I, Emperor, 2, 38–9, 110, 296.

Kadianos, Michael, *vestiarites*, 125 note 18, 140, 268 note 119.

Epitropos of the monastery of Lemviotissa, 55.
Kaikos (Bakir), 102, 246.
Kakavas, 213, 223, 225.
Kalamos, 112 and note 131, 246.
Kalampakes, Theodore, *tatas* of the court:
Governor of Veles, 291.
Kalegopoulos, Constantine, *stratiotes*, then *vestiarites*, 125 note 18, 140.
Kallistos, Theodore, 270 note 130.
Kaloe, see Pyrgion and Kaloe.
Kaloeidas family, 130 note 63, 265, 269.
Kaloeidas, George, *prokathemenos* of Smyrna, 265–6, 278.
Kaloeidas, Leo, *antidoux* of Petra, 259 note 58.
Kaloethos, Nicholas, secretary to the *vestiarion*, 170 note 111.
Kalojan, Bulgarian Tsar, 12, 21, 284.
Kaloktenes, Constantine, 271.
Kalopyros, Stephen, *epikraton* of Palatia, 214 note 56.
Kalosinaras, Niketas, 271–2.
Kalothetos, Theodotos; uncle of Michael VIII Palaiologos:
Domestic of the Schools, 184 note 13.
Duke of Thrakesion and Melanoudion, 251 note 11, 252.
Kalymnos, 139 note 110, 211, 249.
Duke of, see Diogenes, Constantine.
Kamateros family, 70–1 and note 47.
Kamateros Basil, uncle of Theodore I Laskaris, 44, 62, 70–1, 149.
Kampanes, John, *sakelliou* and *primmikerios* of the notaries of Smyrna, 113 note 136.
Kampanos, *prokathemenos* of Thessalonica, 176 note 137.
Kamytzes family, 69, 122, 183.
Kantakouzenos family, 69, 78, 251.
Kantakouzenos, John, Butler:
Duke of Thrakesion, 155, 197, 210–211, 216 note 64, 228, 250–2, 255, 271.
His wife, see Palaiologina, Eirene (Eulogia).
Kantariotissa, Martyrdom of the 13 Monks of, 19.
Kapnos, Alexios, *vestiarites*, 268 note 119.
Karyanites, *protovestiarites*, 152, 185.
Karykes, Demetrios, Grand Logariast and 'Consul of the Philosophers', 170, 179–80, 206, 210.
Kastamonites family, 269.
Kastoria, 280, 286.
Kato Ptomaion, Monastery of, 54 note 47.
Kavallares, 99, 112.
Kavallarios family, 69, 70.
Kavallarios, Basil, 78.
Kaystros (Küçük Menderes), 102, 247.
Kelvianon, 247 and note 35.
Keos, 11, 157, 196.
Kiminas, Mount, 245.
Kivyrrhaiotai, theme of, 248.
Klaudiopolis, Church of, 48–9.
Klaudiopolites, Constantine, Metropolitan of Ephesos, 53.
Kleopas, 188.
Knidian Peninsula, 100 note 30.
Kolelos family, 131 note 67.
Komnenos, imperial house of, 12, 60, 63, 69, 70, 98, 141, 239, 243, 250, 256, 257, 295.
Komnenos, David, Ruler of Paphlagonia, 13, 61, 98.
Konstomares, John, imperial secretary, 165–6.
Apographeus of Smyrna, 213, 223, 227, 228, 231.
Energon of Smyrna, 258.
Kontophre, Manuel, *sevastos*, 199.
Duke of Thrakesion, 200 note 127, 233, 250–1 and notes 6, 11.
Commander of fleet, 198–200.
Kontostephanos family, 61, 62, 71, 122.
Kontostephanos, Nikephoros, *sevastokrator*, 61.
Kontostephanos, Theodore, *protosevastos*, 71, 183, 199.
Konya see Ikonion.
Kotyaion, 98.
Koukoulos see Palatia (Koukoulos).
Kourtikes, John Doukas, *syngambros* of John III Vatatzes:
Duke of Thrakesion, 159, 251 note 9, 255, 266.
Koumans, 48, 105, 152, 188–90, 283–4, 292.
Kouzenas, imperial monastery of, 52, 53.
Krateros, Alexios, Chamberlain, 155, 157, 170 note 111, 210, 214 note 56.
Kretikos family, 131 note 67.

Kroai, 287.
Kryvitziotes, Theodore, Duke of Thrakesion, 200 note 127, 251–2 and note 11.
Küstendil, see Velbužd.
Kütahya, see Kotyaion.
Kythera, 197.
Kyzikos, 196, 200.
  Metropolitan of, 58 note 62.

Lampsakos, 90, 110, 112, 197, 199, 222, 223 note 86 and see *Tributa Lampsacenorum.*
Laodikea, 98, 100, 116.
Laodikenos, John, 270 note 130.
Lapardas, Theodore, *energon* of Mourmounta, 259, note 58.
Larissa, Metropolitan of, 24.
Larymos, *katepanikion* of, 249.
Laskarids, imperial dynasty of Nicaea, 41, 45, 49, 82, 93, 155, 257, 277.
Laskaris family, 69, 251.
Laskarina, Theodora, daughter of Theodore II Laskaris, 66.
Laskaris, Alexios Komnenos, *eugenestatos* and *sevastokrator*, brother of Theodore I Laskaris, 170 note 111, 192.
Laskaris, Constantine, brother of Theodore I Laskaris, 61.
Laskaris, Constantine, Duke of Thrakesion, 216 and note 64, 217, 221, 226, 251 note 10, 260.
Laskaris, Manuel, *protosevastos*, brother of Theodore I Laskaris, 77, 82, 84, 85, 190.
Laskaris, Michael, brother of Theodore I Laskaris, 77, 82, 85.
  Governor of Thessalonica, 190, 290, 291, 292.
  Grand Duke, 84 note 43.
Latin Empire of Constantinople, 1, 11–12, 15, 16, 22, 43, 114.
  Patriarch, 11.
  Coinage, 118.
Latins, 1, 4, 11, 12, 14, 15, 16, 17, 18, 22, 29, 30, 32, 47, 52, 61, 82, 97, 104, 111, 112, 120, 182, 196, 197, 198, 211, 239–40, 241, 245, 246, 255, 269, 279, 284, 285, 287.
  in Nicaean service, 81–2, 106 and note 94, 119, 152, 175, 182, 185–6, 187–8, 191.
Lemviotissa, imperial monastery of, 47 note 13, 51, 53, 55, 104 and note 61, 106–7 and note 83, 113, 124, 127–9, 130–1 and note 63, 132, note 72, 133, 135, 136, 137, 139, 140, 156, 157, 158, 159, 171, 195, 207, 209, 214 note 56, 215, 216 and note 64, 217, 220, 221, 228, 229–30, 232, 233, 253, 254, 255, 260, 261, 262, 265, 266, 267, 270, 271, 272, 275 and note 158.
  Abbot of, see Opsikianos, Gerasimos.
  Epitropos of, see Kadianos, Michael.
Leros, 139 note 110, 140, 211, 249.
  Duke of, see Diogenes, Constantine.
Lesbos, 54 note 47, 104, 197.
Lestes family, 129 note 50.
Levounes family, 129 note 50.
Levounes, Isaac, *vestiarites,* 268.
Livadarios family, 69.
Local Councils, 257, 260–4.
Longo, Giovanni, 114 note 144.
Lopadion, 99.
Luccans, 114.
Lydda, Archbishop of, 17.
Lydia, 58 note 62.
Lykaites, Manuel, Duke and Stratopedarch of Malagina, 245.

Macedonia, 1, 23, 26, 33, 152, 153, 161, 164, 182, 185, 187, 189, 190, 191, 193, 194, 211, 241, 279–80, 282–4, 285–6, 287–8, 289–90, 291, 292, 293, 295.
Magedon, 99, 191.
Magidia, 99.
Magnates see *megistanes.*
Magnesia, 52, 83, 102, 108, 112, 114, 205, 246.
  Vestiarion at, 154, 187.
Maiander, 61, 71, 97, 100, 102, 105, 112, 122, 125, 129, 211, 248, 273.
  Stratopedarch and *paradotes* of, 248, 252.
  Theme of, 248, 252.
Makestos (Simav), 99, 102.
Makrenos, citizen of Smyrna, 254.
Makrenos, George, Duke of Thrakesion, 255.
Makrenos, John, *parakoimomenos*, 184 and note 16.
Makrenos, Leo, 275 note 158.

Makrinitissa, monastery of, 73 note 65.
Makrotos, John, imperial secretary, 161, 163, 164, 168.
Malagina, 99, 245 and note 15, 252.
Bishops of, 99 note 14.
Duke and Stratopedarch of, see Lykaites, Manuel.
Manfred, ruler of Sicily, 82.
Mangaphas, Theodore, 61, 123.
Manouelites, Nicholas, *prokathemenos* of Nicaea, 265.
Mantaia, 108, 129 note 49, 130, 131 note 69, 134, 215, 255, 259, 261, 265, 272.
Enoria of, 270 and note 130.
Manteianos family, 129 note 50.
Manuel I Komnenos, Emperor, 9, 60, 65, 97, 99 note 14, 172, 193, 239, 246, 250, 264.
Manuel I, Patriarch, 22.
Manuel II, Patriarch, 16, 46, 47, 50.
Marathon, battle of, 29.
Margarites, Constantine, 75–6, 175, 176, 190, 193, 194, 246.
Tzaousios of the army of Neokastra, 194.
Tzaousios of the imperial *taxis*, 175.
Grand *Tzaousios*, 75, 175, 187.
Archon of the imperial *taxis*, 186.
Grand Archon, 76, 175, 186.
Maritsa, 23, 279, 280, 291.
Marmara, Sea of, 11, 196.
Nicaean fleet of, 196–200.
Mauropodos, Andronikos, 214 note 56.
Mavrozomes, Manuel, 13, 61, 100.
Maximos, Patriarch:
Abbot of Akoimetos, 50.
Mela see Vari.
Melanoudion:
Duke of, see Kalothetos, Theodotos.
Melkites, 19.
Melnik, 26, 32, 283, 285, 286, 287, 288, 289 note 53, 291.
Governor of, see Michael VIII Palaiologos.
Memaniomenos, plain of, 103, 108, 130 note 63, 131, 265.
Mesarites, Nicholas, Metropolitan of Ephesos, 51, 53.
Mesemvreia, 175.
Mesopotamites family, 72.
Mesopotamites, Constantine, *epi tou kanikleiou* and Metropolitan of Thessalonica, 163 note 77.
Mesopotamites, Joseph, 72 note 53, 163–4, 170, 171, note 114.
Mesothynia, 245 note 12.
Methodios, Patriarch:
Abbot of Hyakinthos, 50.
Metropolitans, 273–4 and see Bishops.
Michael VIII Palaiologos, Emperor, 26–7, 47, 56, 66, 71 note 50, 73, 78, 79, 80–93 passim, 99, 101, 102, 105, 126, 141, 151, 160, 161 and note 70, 162, 164, 169, 176, 180, 181, 183, 185, 189, 191, 192, 196, 198, 204, 207, 220, 235–6, 244 note 6, 249, 251, 265, 271, 282, 284, 287 note 44, 291, 292.
Grand Constable, 81, 184, 188.
Grand Duke, 83, 84, 198.
Basileopator, 83.
Despot, 83–4, 86, 87, 88.
Governor of Serres and Melnik, 167 note 104, 291.
Governor of Vodena, 190.
Governor of Bithynia and Optimaton, 194, 245 and note 12, 252.
Governor of Dyrrhachion, 290, 291, 292.
Trial for treason, 66, 67, 75, 153 and note 13, 160, 161, 167–8 and note 104, 172–3, 187.
Flight to Seljuqs, 26, 66, 78, 165, 189, 282.
Usurpation, 26, 40, 41, 45, 57, 58, 79, 80–93, 106 note 81.
Government of, 235–6.
Financial Reforms, 234.
Judicial Reforms, 75, 154, 171, 174.
The 'New Constantine', 31.
Michael Asen, Bulgarian Tsar, 165.
Michael Autoreianos, Patriarch, 13, 37, 46, 49, 68.
Miletos see Palatia (Miletos)
Metropolitan of, 259, 271, 272 and note 141, 273.
Milopotamos, 197.
Milvian Bridge, Battle of, 31.
Minoto, Marco, 144 note 144.
Mitylene see Lesbos,
Metropolitan of, 51, 54 note 47.
Monasteries see Akoimetos, Amanariotissa, Eerinon, Hieras or Xerochoraphiou, Hyakinthos, Kato,

Monasteries—*contd.*
Ptomaion, Kouzenas, Lemviotissa, Makrinitissa, Nea Mone, Panachrantos, Pantokrator, Paschasiou, Rouphinianon, St Andreas, St Anthony the Great, St Gregory the Wonderworker, St John of Patmos, St Mary Kechionismene, St Nicholas of Kalyphas, St Panteleemon, St Paul in Latmos, Sosandra, Xerochoraphiou or Hieras.
Monemvasia, 287 note 44.
Mongols, 116, 194, 211, 265.
Monoikos, Bishop of, 54.
Monomachos family, 265.
Monomachos, *stratiotes*, 125 note 18.
Monomachos, Chariton, monk, 54.
Monomachos, Constantine, 54.
Monomachos, George, *prokathemenos* of Smyrna, 214 note 56, 264–7, 275.
Moses, 13, 31.
Moslems, 117.
Mourmounta:
Energon of, see Lapardas, Theodore.
Mouzalon, Andronikos, 78, 152, 176, 177 note 143.
Protovestiarites, 77.
Grand Domestic, 77, 185.
Mouzalon, George, 76–9, 80–2, 85, 87, 152, 153, 160, 169, 176, 177 note 143.
Grand Domestic, 76–7, 185.
Protosevastos, Protovestiarios, and Grand Stratopedarch, 77, 186.
Regent, 42, 69, 79.
Brother-in-law of Hagiotheodorites (q.v.), 84 note 43.
Mouzalon, John, *mystikos*, 75 note 70, 161 and note 70.
Mouzalon, Theodore, *protokynegos* or *protoierakaris*, 77 and note 91, 152.
Mouzethras, Leo, 263.
Mylasa and Melanoudion, theme of, 240 note 8, 248.
Dukes of, see Tzykes, John, and Kalothetos, Theodotos.

Nea Mone, Monastery of, 137, 139.
Negroponte see Euboea.
Neochorion, 103 note 58.
Neokastra, theme of, 193, 194, 245–7.
Army of, 75, 193, 246.
Neophytos, Archbishop of Cyprus, 18–19.
Nestongos family, 69, 82.
Nestongos, George, Butler, 82.
Nestongos, Isaac, Steward:
Governor of Alvanon and of Ohrid, 291, 292 note 84.
Nicaea, 1, 2, 13, 15, 16, 17, 18, 19, 20, 21, 29, 32, 33, 37, 40, 44, 47, 48, 49, 50, 58, 63, 73, 82, 90, 91, 98–9, 101, 111, 116, 129, 148, 149, 155, 178, 240, 244–5, 258, 296.
Borderers, 93.
'A latter-day Athens', 31.
Metropolis of, 48.
prokathemenos of, 264 and see Manouelites, Nicholas.
See St Anthony the Great, monastery of, and St Tryphon, Church of.
Nicholas Laskaris, Emperor, son of Theodore I Laskaris, 42, 68.
Nikephoros of Ephesos, Patriarch, 56, 90–1.
Metropolitan of Ephesos, 50.
Nikomedeia, 111, 161, 245.
Metropolitan of, 58 note 62.
Notary see *nomikos*.
Nymphaion, 48, 63, 83, 89, 90, 109, 111, 112, 126, 153, 161, 163, 166, 205, 240, 241, 253, 269.
Treaty of, 115, 118.

Oath, 65–6, 85, 88, 89, 93.
Ohrid, 280, 290, 291, 292 note 84.
Archbishop of, 20–2 and see Chomatianos, Demetrios.
Governor of, see Nestongos, Isaac.
Oikonomides, Professor Nikolaos, 139 note 110, 218–19, 264 note 90.
Olkos, 197.
Olympos, Mount (Ulus Dag), 99, 112.
Olympos, Mount, 282.
Opsikianos, Gerasimos, Abbot of Lemviotissa, 51, 128, 139, 216 note 64, 265–6.
Opsikion, theme of, 244.
Opsikion and Aigaion, theme of, 245.
Optimates, the, Optimaton, theme of, 193–4, 244, 245 note 12.
Governor of, see Michael VIII Palaiologos.
Ordeal, 75, 167–8 and note 104, 172–4 and note 128.

Oriental Patriarchates, 19–20.
Ottoman Turks, 9, 23.

Pachymeres, George, 30, 65, 67, 69, 73, 76, 85, 87, 117, 161 note 70, 167 note 104, 173, 174, 194 note 91, 205, 235–6.
Padyates, *paidopoulos*, 177 and note 143.
Pagos, Mount, 110.
Palaiologan, Palaiologos, imperial dynasty, 42, 69, 70, 72, 155, 160, 277, 295.
Palaiologina, Eirene (Eulogia), 151.
Palaiologina, Maria (Martha), 78.
Palaiologos, Andronikos, Grand Domestic, 150, 152, 183–4, 201, 210, 241.
  Viceroy of Thessalonica, 183, 289, 291.
Palaiologos, Constantine, Despot, 41, 62.
Palaiologos, Constantine, Caesar and *sevastokrator*, 82, 101.
Palaiologos, John, Grand Domestic, *sevastokrator*, and Despot, 82, 181, 282.
  Governor of Rhodes, 249.
Palaiologos, Manuel, 107 note 90.
Palaiologos, Michael, *mystikos*, 162 note 70.
Palatia (Koukoulos), imperial estates of, 124, 127, 214 note 56, 272.
Palatia (Miletos), 62, 106 note 83, 107 note 90, 111, 211, 219, 223 note 88, 258, 272.
  Praktor of, 259.
  Archontes of, 269.
Panachrantos, Constantinopolitan monastery of, 124, 273.
Panaretos, *prokathemenos* of the *vestiarion*, 73 note 62.
Panaretos, Village of, 127, 263.
  Oikodespotai of, 263, 275.
Pantokrator, Constantinopolitan monastery of, 122, 124, 215.
Papacy, 14, 16, 21–2, 23, 27.
Paphlagonia, Paphlagonians, 13, 50, 61, 91, 98, 101 and note 38, 183, 190–1, 240, 244, 292.
  Monasteries in, 52.
Paphos, Bishop of, 17.
Pardovounon, 266 note 109.
Partitio Romaniae, 244, 247.
Paschasiou, Monastery of, 90.
Patras, Archbishop of, 11.
Patriarch, Patriarchal Administration, Patriarchate, 11, 15, 16, 17, 20, 21, 22, 23, 24, 25, 28, 33, 37, 39–40, 43, 44, 46, 48, 49, 50, 51, 52, 54, 58–9, 152, 168, 273 and note 147, 275.
  Exarchs, 22, 24, 58 and note 62.
Pauchome, 265 note 98.
Pelagonia, 280, 290.
  Battle of, 26, 182, 189, 191 and note 71, 282.
Pelion, 266 note 109.
Peloponnese, 122, 191, 192.
Pepagomenos, Constantine, 219.
Pergamon, 99, 111, 112, 246.
  Theme of, 246 note 24.
Petra, 108, 129 note 49.
  Antidoux of, see Kaloeidas, Leo.
  Episkepsis of, 244 note 6, 259 note 58.
Petraliphas family, 69.
Petraliphas, John, Grand *chartoularios*, 183, 189.
Petraliphas, Theodore, 25, 286.
Petritzes family, 113, 126 note 25, 129 note 50, 130 and note 63.
Petritzes, George, *stratiotes*, 130, 131.
Petritzes, Michael, *stratiotes*, 125 note 18.
Phagomodes family, 129 note 50.
Phagomodes, Constantine, 268.
Philadelphia, 49, 61, 100, 101, 105, 109, 112, 123, 245, 247–8, 258.
  Church of, 48.
  Metropolitan of, see Phokas.
  Prokathemenos of, see Iatropoulos, Demetrios.
  Stratopedarch of, 248 and see Phokas, Michael.
  Tavoullarios of, see Sellares, John.
Philanthropenos family, 69, 70.
Philes family, 69, 70, 126.
Philes, Theodore, 76, 78, 82, 85.
  Viceroy of Thessalonica, 289.
Philippi, 153, 161, 167.
Philippopolis, 280, 285.
Philokales, Eumathios, 200 note 132.
Philomelion, 97.
Phokaia, 102.
Phokas family, 261.
Phokas, Metropolitan of Philadelphia, 52, 153 note 13, 159–60, 167, 173.

Phokas, John, 270 note 130.
Phokas, Michael, *syngambros* of John III Vatatzes:
  Stratopedarch of Philadelphia and Thrakesion, 216–17.
Phokas, Theodotos, *panhypersevastos*, uncle of Theodore I Laskaris, Grand Duke, 62, 200 and note 131, 253 note 27, 269, 271.
  Duke of Thrakesion, 200 note 131, 253 note 27.
Phrangopoulos, imperial secretary, 166.
Phrygia, 105.
Phygella, 108.
Pindos Mountains, 12, 31.
Pisa, Pisans, 114, 227.
Pithianos, 113 note 136.
Planites family, 126 note 25, 133, 254.
Planites, Maximos, monk, 133.
Plousiada, 99.
Poimanenon, Battle of, 29, 182.
Poleas, John, 134, 228, 263, 275.
Poleas, Thomas, 263.
'Politicians', 57.
Pontic Heraklea, 49, 98, 111.
  Church of, 48.
Potamou, 136, 262, 267.
Poutzes, John, 225.
Priene see Sampson.
Prilep, 190, 280, 289, 291–2.
  Governor of, see Xyleas.
Prinovari, 129 note 49, 131 note 68, 259–60, 275.
  Praktor of, 259–60.
  Oikodespotai of, 260.
  Oikologos of, 260.
Prosek, 285.
Prousa, 99, 111, 239, 240.
Pseudo-Kodinos's *Book of Offices*, 76, 207.
Pyrgion and Kaloe, *chora* of, 247.
Pyrgos, *metochion* of, 124, 214 note 56, 273.

Raoul family, 69, 70.
Raoul, Alexios, *protovestiarios*, 77, 78, 183, 184, 190.
Ravdokanakes, John, *vestiarites*, 267.
Rethymnon, 197.
Rhodes, 28, 114, 119, 183, 197, 211, 249, 255.
  Caesar of, see Gavalas, Leo.
  Capitaneum of, see Kryvitziotes, Theodore.
  Governor of, see Palaiologos, John.
Rhodope Mountains, 280, 282, 285.
'Rhomaioi', 'Roman', 'Romania', 29–30, 32, 118.
Rimpsas, Nikephoros, 189.
Romanos, Caesar, 210, 241.
Rome, 16.
Rouphinianon, Monastery of, 48 note 13, 122.
Rouze, 129 note 49.
Ryndakos (Atranos), 102.
Russia, 105.
  Church in, 19, 20.

St. Andreas, Monastery of, 52.
St. Anthony the Great, Monastery of, 47.
St. George-without-the-Castle (Exokastrites), *metochion* of, 127, 128, 214–15 and note 56, 275.
St. Gregory the Wonderworker, Monastery of, 53, 179.
St. John of Patmos, Monastery of, 3, 55–6, 113, 134, 139, 140, 156, 157, 162, 214 note 56, 220, 228, 230, 272, 273.
  Epitropos of, 55–6.
St. John the Baptist, Church of, 110.
St. Mary Kechionismene, Monastery of, 107 note 90.
St. Nicholas of Kalyphas, Imperial monastery of, 53, 266.
St. Panteleemon, Monastery of, 55.
St. Paul in Latmos, Monastery of, 51, 149, 167, 170, 272 note 141.
St. Sophia, Clergy of, 11, 49, 91.
St. Tryphon, Church of, 179–80.
Salamis, Battle of, 29.
Sale of Offices, 236.
Samians, Samos, 104, 197.
Sampson, 61, 149, 167, 170, 258, 269, 271.
  Episkepsis of, 244 note 6, 248.
Sangarios (Sakarya), 99, 102, 244, 245.
Sanudo, Marco, Duke of Naxos, 196.
Sardes, 100, 102, 105, 112, 246.
  Metropolitan of, 48, 58 note 2, 91.
Sava, St., Archbishop of Serbia, 22.
Seljuqs of Rum, 13, 14, 26, 66, 78, 97, 98, 100, 101, 112, 115, 116, 117,

118, 119, 165, 182, 189, 194, 239, 282.
Sultan, 29, 61, 97, 103, 153, 165.
Sellares, John, *tavoullarios* of Philadelphia, 273 note 147.
Selymvria, 11, 279.
Senachereim, Michael, *protasekretis* and *mesazon*, 160–1 and note 63, 172 note 118, 180, 296.
Holds chair of grammar, 180.
Senate, Senators, 37, 67–8, 72–4 and note 65, 85–6, 89, 153, 167.
Serbia, 21, 23, 27, 280, 290.
Archbishop of, see Sava, St.
Church in, 2, 21–2.
Grand Župan of, see Stefan.
Serres, 167 note 104, 190, 193, 286, 287, 288, 289 note 53, 291.
Governor of, see Michael VIII Palaiologos.
Servia, 25, 282, 290.
Sgouros, Leo, 123.
Sicily, 164.
Ruler of, see Manfred.
Sinai, Mount, Monastery of St. Catherine, 20.
Sinope, 115.
Sipylos, Mount, 102.
Skamander see Troad.
Skoplje, 280.
Theme of, 291.
Skordyllios, *stratiotes*, 126.
Skoutariotes, Theodore, 51 note 30, 124, 205, 211.
Dikaiophylax, 73 note 62.
Smyrna, 48, 54, 55, 63, 102–13 passim, 122–37 passim, 140, 148, 166, 192, 194, 195, 197, 199, 209, 213–15 and note 56, 225, 242, 244, 254, 258, 261, 265–9, 272–4, 277.
Archontes of, 108, 113, 266–9, 275.
Energon of, see Konstomares, John.
Kastrophylax of, see Vrachionites, Theophylaktos.
Prokathemenos of, see Monomachos, George, Alopos, John, and Kaloeidas, George.
Katepanikion of, 225, 239, 247, 258, 268.
Metropolitan of, 53, 55, 113, 123, 130, 228–9, 233, 254, 263, 265, 268–75 passim.
State Saltpans at, 113, 207, 233.
Sosandra, Imperial monastery of, 48, 81–2.
Spanopoulos, *mystikos*, 161 note 70.
Sphournou, 136, 262, 267, 271.
Stadia, 100 note 30.
Stefan, Grand Župan of Serbia, 21–2.
Steiriones, John, 196.
Stenimachos, 279.
Sthlavos, 285.
Strategopoulos family, 69, 82.
Strategopoulos, Alexios, Grand Domestic and Caesar, 76, 77, 82, 85, 184, 190.
His father, 101 note 38.
Strategopoulos, Constantine, 77, 82, 85.
Strategopoulos, John, Grand Logothete, 149, 167, 170 and note 111.
Stratoniceia, 246.
Strymon, 279, 280, 291.
Theme of, 289 note 53, 290–1.
Synadenos family, 69.
Synadenos, Constantine Doukas, 130.
Synods, 15, 16, 17, 19–20, 21, 27, 43, 46, 49, 50, 51, 57, 72, 86, 90, 91.
Synopsis Minor, 172.
Syracuse, Church of, 48.
Syrgiannes, 105.
Syrgares, imperial liege knight, 125 and note 18, 127, 134, 136, 140, 171, 230, 263.
Syria, 113, 115.
Syropoulos, John, *apographeus*, 220.

Tarchaneiotes family, 69, 126.
Tarchaneiotes, Michael, *protosevastos, protovestiarios*, and Grand Domestic, 278.
Tarchaneiotes, Nikephoros, Steward, 183, 190.
Grand Domestic, 78, 184 and note 15.
His wife, see Palaiologina, Maria (Martha).
Tarsia, 99, 245.
Thebes, 292.
Themes, 239, 243, 248, 250, 258, 271, 285, 290–1.
Armies of, 176, 193, 195.
Theodora Doukaina, Empress, 66, 204 note 4, 244 note 6, 259 note 58.
Theodore I Laskaris, Emperor, 1, 12, 13, 15, 17, 18, 20, 29, 31, 40, 41–2, 43–4, 47, 49, 50, 51, 53, 61–2, 63, 68, 70–1, 73, 85, 92, 98, 99, 100,

Theodore I Loskaris, Emperor—*contd.* 104, 111, 114, 118, 123, 124, 125, 148–50, 156–7, 163, 167, 182, 184, 192, 196, 200, 215, 229, 239, 240, 277.
Despot, 37.
His Brothers, 40, 61–2, 85.
Marriage to an Armenian princess, 41.
Victory over Seljuqs, 14.
Theodore II Laskaris, Emperor, 16, 26, 28, 30, 31–2, 41–2, 43, 44, 45, 46, 50–1, 52, 57, 59, 72 and note 54, 75, 80, 81, 82, 83, 84, 85, 87, 88, 93, 100, 101, 102, 111, 112, 116, 117, 150, 151–3, 158, 160, 161, 164–5, 168, 169, 173–4, 175, 176, 178, 184 and note 13, 187, 188, 190, 194, 205, 245, 251 note 12, 282, 283, 288, 289, 291, 292.
and aristocracy, 74, 76–9.
and his circle, 76, 81, 84 and note 43, 163, 165, 176, 258, 265, 291, 292.
and education, 179–80.
and military reforms, 185–6, 190–1, 193.
Theodore II Eirenikos, Patriarch, 49 and note 22.
'Consul of the Philosophers', 179.
Theophilopoulos, Governor of the Troad, 241.
Thessalonica, 11, 12, 20, 24, 25, 116, 160, 161, 166, 167 note 104, 175–6, 182, 183, 190, 199, 265, 279–80, 283–4, 285, 286, 287, 291.
Coinage of, 120.
Empire of, 20, 23, 25, 284.
Kephale of, see Laskaris, Michael, and Tornikes, Constantine.
Megalon Allagion of, 189.
Metropolitan of, 91 and see Mesopotamites, Constantine.
Prokathemenos of, see Kampanos.
Theme of, 289–90 and note 53.
Viceroy of, see Palaiologos, Andronikos, Philes, Theodore, and Akropolites, George.
Thessaly, 23, 25, 73 note 65, 107, 167 note 104, 282.
'Great Vlachia', 284.
Thrace, 1, 11, 12, 23, 33, 76, 182, 188, 189, 190, 193, 194, 197, 279, 282–5, 288, 293, 295.
Thrakeses family, 130 and note 63.
Thrakesion, theme of, 199–200 and note 127, 240, 246–8 and note 35.
Dukes of 155, 233, 247, 250–3 and see Angelos, John; Chrysomalles, Basil; Hikanatos, Theodore; Kalothetos, Theodotos; Kantakouzenos, John; Kontophre, Manuel; Kourtikes, John Doukas; Kryvitziotes, Theodore; Laskaris, Constantine; Makrenos, George; Phokas, Theodotos; Tornikes, John.
Stratopedarch of, see Phokas, Michael.
Tithe see *morte.*
Tornikes family, 62 note 9, 69, 70, 155.
Tornikes, Andronikos Komnenos, *mesazon*, 156, 160.
Tornikes, Constantine, 77, 82.
Grand *primmikerios*, 187, 190.
Sevastokrator, 91.
Kephale of Thessalonica, 292–3.
Tornikes, Demetrios, 'Beloved Brother of the Emperor', *mesazon*, 25, 62 note 9, 64, 140, 149–52, 155–61 and note 31, 163, 164, 170–1, 184, 205.
Oikonomos ton koinon, 155.
Tornikes, Euthymios, 11 note 7.
Tornikes, John, Duke of Thrakesion, 254–5, 293 note 90.
Trebizond, 12, 20, 205.
Tributa Lampsacenorum, 222–3.
Trikokkia, 99.
Tripolis, 100, 112.
Trnovo, Church of, 20–22.
Troad, 32, 178, 205, 241, 245.
Governor of, see Theophilopoulos.
Turkomans, Turks, 9, 47, 50, 82, 97, 98, 100, 101, 193, 239, 243.
In Nicaean Service, 182, 189.
Tyrannos family, 130 note 63.
Tyrannos, Goudeles, 109 note 103, 184 and note 16.
Tyre, 110 note 111.
Tzamantouroi see Laskaris family.
Tzepaina, 280.
Tzouroulon, 189–90, 279.
Tzykes, John, Duke of Mylasa and Melanoudion, 249.
Tzyrithon, Grand *chartoularios*, 176.

Udj, 98.
Union of Churches, 14–16, 27, 47, 57.

Valaneidiotes, [Grand Stratopedarch], 78.
paidopoulos, 177 note 143.
Valkes, monk, 266, 267.
Varangians, 187.
Varangopoulos, Alexios, *Kephale* of Cos, 249.
Vardar, 280, 285.
Vardariots, *Primmikerios* of, 187.
Vari, 104 and note 61, 124, 125 note 17, 127–8, 132 note 72, 140, 195, 215, 216 and note 64, 217, 219, 225, 226, 255, 260, 267.
Varychier, *stratiotes*, 125 note 18, 272, 275, note 158.
Varypates, Constantine, *megas sakellarios* of the Church of Smyrna, 275.
Vatatzes family, 69.
Velbuzd (Velevousdion), 280.
Veles, 280, 283, 291.
Governor of, see Kalampakes, Theodore.
Venetians, Venice, 9, 114, 115, 118, 187, 196, 197, 227, 244.
Verroia, 289.
Theme of, 285, 289 note 53.
Verroiotes, *megas diermeneutes*, 73 note 62.
Villehardouin, Geoffrey, Prince of Achaea, 198.
Villehardouin, Theodosios, monk, 56.
Vizye, 279.
Vlachernai, Palace of, 65.
Vlachs, 284, 285.
Identified with 'Hellenes', 30.
Vlatteros family, 216 and note 4.
Vlatteros, Basil, *vestiarites*, 125 note 17, 127, 140, 192, 215, 216 note 64, 219, 267, 271.
Vodena, 167 note 104, 190, 280, 288.
Voleron, *chora* of, 289 note 53, 291.
Vrachionites, Theophylaktos, *kastrophylax* of Smyrna, 267–8.
Vranaina, Eirene Komnena, 127, 263.
Vranas family, 69, 131 and note 68.
Vranas, Theodore Komnenos, 131 note 69.
Vroullas, *apographeus*, 213.

Wardrobe see *vestiarion*.
William, a Latin, 175.

Xerochoraphiou see Hieras, Monastery of.
Xeros, Manuel, 54 note 47.
Xerxes, 29.
Xyleas, *skouterios*, governor of Prilep, 190, 290, 291, 292.

Zaccaria, Benedetto, 102.
Zagaromates, George, 126.
protovestiarites, 126 note 27, 210.
Panhypersevastos, 136.
His wife, 136, 259 note 58.
Zane, Domenico, 114 note 144.
'Zealots', 57.
Zorobabel, 13.

II. INDEX OF TECHNICAL TERMS

achrostikon, 256.
aktemon, 138, 221, 222 and note 84, 223 and note 86.
allagator, 186.
aer, aerika, 128, 227, 256.
agape, 128, 203, 223, 224–5, 233.
allagion, 186 and note 30, 189, 191 note 71.
angareiai, 138, 222–3 and note 86, 225, 233, 256.
annona, 224.
antidoux, 259 note 58.
apaitetai, 233.
apographe, apographeus, 208, 210–14, 217, 219–20, 221, 226, 227, 228, 232–3, 235, 242, 249, 252, 256, 262.
apokatastasis, 213.
aporos, 138, 221–2 and note 84.
archontes, 67–8, 71 and note 50, 85, 266–9, 275, 278, 286.
archontikon, 263.
archontopouloi, 177, 181, 219.

biologion, 209.
bucellarii, 192.

charistike, 53–6.
chartia, 207.
chartophylax, 275–6.
chora, 243–4, 258, 260.
chreiai doukikai, 226.
chreiai katepanikiai, 226.

demosiaka kephalaia, 223.
dioikesis, 243.
douleutai, 138.

enkyklios paideusis see *grammatike*.
ennomion, 103, 128, 227.
energon see *praktor*.
enoria, 244, 261, 270.
ephoros, ephoria, 55–6 and note 51.
epibole, 212.
epiteleia, 132 note 72, 137, 203, 213, 228–3 passim.
epitropos see *ephoros*.
episkepsis, 244 and note 6.
exisosis, exisotes, 210–12, 219, 221, 241, 249, 289 note 53.
exkousseia, 121, 128.

grammatike, 178.
grammatikos, 4, 149, 163, 165, 174, 253.

kaniskia, 226.
kapnikon, 225.
kastrophylax, 194, 252, 255, 266–8 and note 109, 292, 294.
katepanikion, 226, 233, 243, 258.
katepano, 264.
kavalikevma, 170.
kavallarios, 125 and note 18, 188.
kephale, 292–4.
kreittones see *oikodespotai*.
kommerkia, 227, 287 note 44.
kontaratoi, 225, 233.
ktema, ktemata, 121, 126–7.

latinikon, 189.
logariastes, 253 and note 27.

megale thesis, 208.
megaloallagitai, 189.
megistanes, 68–70, 80, 85, 86, 89.
mesazon, 147, 155–61, 235.
misthioi, misthioi douleutai, 138.
monovoidrios, 222.
morte, 134 and note 86, 135, 226.

nomikos, 133, 215, 262, 263, 270 note 130, 273–4.
nomismatike posotes, 218–19.

oikeios, 4, 73, 148 notes 8 and 9, 150, 154–5, 174, 268.
oikodespotai, 260–4, 275, 286.
oikologos, 260.
oikomodion, 226.
oikomodoparasporon, 226, 260 note 66.
oikonomia see *pronoia*.
oikonomos, 56, 155, 275–6.

paidopoula, 76, 176–7, 181.
paradotes, 248, 252.
paradotikion, 226.
paradotikon gramma, 215.
paroikoi, 132–9 and note 86, 171, 194, 204 note 4, 216, 217, 223, 225–6, 252, 253, 255, 259, 260, 268.
periorismos, 216, 272.
perisseia, 220.
pezos, 222.
pissoygrissia, 225 note 100.
ploimoi, 199, 200, 224, 225, 233, 268.
praitor, 289–90, 294.
praktikon, 138, 139, 140, 208–9, 212, 213, 217, 218, 223, 230.
praktor, 233, 258–9 and note 58, 289.
primmikerios of the *tavoullarioi*, 274.
proasteion, 220.
pronoia, 119, 121, 122, 124–6 and note 18, 127, 130, 131, 132, 135, 137, 140–1, 142, 171–2, 177, 188, 192, 193, 196, 203, 209, 210, 212, 215, 217–19, 221, 224, 230, 252, 255–6, 261, 263, 265 and note 98, 268, 278.
prokathemenos, 252, 264–6, 294.
protekdikos, 275.
protopappas, 261–2.
protovestiarios, 253 note 27.

roga, 193.

sakellarios, 275.
sakelliou, 275.
sekreta, 147, 149, 204.
sekreton, 73, 86, 154, 171.
sitarkia, 128, 203, 223–4 and note 94, 233.
siteresion, 119, 193.
skeuophylax, 275.
skythikon, 188, 189.
stichos, 207, 209.
strateia, 195.
stratiotika zetemata, 223, 225.
stratopedarches, 193, 217, 252.
stratopedon, 190 and note 58.
stypaxoungoi, 225 note 100.

tavoullarios, 273–4 and note 147.
taxis, 186 and note 30.
telos, 134 and note 86, 135, 223 and note 88, 224 note 94.
tzouloukonai, 192.

vestiarion, 3, 147, 149, 154, 170 note 111, 187, 204–7, 209, 220, 227.
vestiaritai, 171, 234, 235, 256, 268.
voidata, voidatika, voidatikion telos, 216 note 64, 138, 221, 223 note 88, 224 note 94.
voidatos, 138, 221–2 and note 84, 223 and note 86.

xenoi, 139, 194.

zeugaratos, zeugaria, 138, 221–2 and note 84, 223–4 and notes 86 and 94.
zeugaritikion, 224.
zeugelateion, 121, 126 and note 27.
zeugoamaxia, 225 note 100.

III. INDEX OF OFFICES AND OFFICE HOLDERS OF THE NICAEAN COURT[1]

DESPOT, 24, 41, 64.
See Theodore I Laskaris
Laskaris, Constantine[2]
Palaiologos, Constantine
Angelos, Manuel
Angelos, John
Angelos, Demetrios
Angelos, Michael
Angelos, Nikephoros
Michael VIII Palaiologos
Palaiologos, John

SEVASTOKRATOR, 64, 68.
See Asidenos, Savvas
Kontostephanos, Nikephoros
Laskaris, Alexios
Laskaris, George[3]
Laskaris, Isaac[4]
Doukas, Isaac
Palaiologos, John
Palaiologos, Constantine
Tornikes, Constantine

CAESAR, 64.
See Gavalas, Leo
Romanos
Palaiologos, Constantine
Strategopoulos, Alexios

GRAND DOMESTIC, 64, 183–4.
See Palaiologos, Andronikos
Tarchaneiotes, Nikephoros
Mouzalon, George
Mouzalon, Andronikos
Palaiologos, John
Philes, Alexios[5]

PANHYPERSEVASTOS, 64.
See Phokas, Theodotos
Chilarenos, Michael
Zagaromates, George

PROTOVESTIARIOS, 64, 148, 154, 206.
See John III Doukas Vatatzes
Raoul, Alexios
Mouzalon, George
Raoul, John[6]

GRAND DUKE, 64, 198, 200.
See Phokas, Theodotos
Auxentios
Michael VIII Palaiologos
Laskaris, Michael

PROTOSTRATOR, 64, 183
See Ises, John
Angelos, John
Philanthropenos, Alexios Doukas[7]

GRAND STRATOPEDARCH, 64, 186.
See Mouzalon, George
Valaneidiotes

GRAND PRIMMIKERIOS, 64, 187.
See Tornikes, Constantine
Angelos, John
Angelos[8]

[1] For convenience sake this list of offices follows the order given in the *Book of Offices* of the Pseudo-Kodinos. The offices of *Epi tou Kanikleiou* and of the 'Consul of the Philosophers' are missing from that list and have been inserted here in their appropriate place. I have listed office holders in chronological order and have supplied some details of those who do not appear in the text of the book.

[2] Brother of Theodore I Laskaris: see Bodleian Library, Oxford, Baroc. Ms. 235.

[3] Brother of Theodore I Laskaris: see Miklosich and Müller IV, pp. 35, 38, 40.

[4] Brother of Theodore I Laskaris: see Akropolites I, pp. 34–5; Gregoras I, p. 25, ll. 1–21.

[5] Married to a niece of Michael VIII Palaiologos: see Pachymeres I, pp. 108–9.

[6] Also married to a niece of Michael VIII Palaiologos; the son of Raoul, Alexios: see Pachymeres I, pp. 108–9.

[7] Pachymeres I, p. 109, ll. 15–16.

[8] Uncle of Theodora Doukaina, Empress of Michael VIII Palaiologos; son of Angelos, John (q.v.), the uncle of John III Vatatzes: see Pachymeres I, p. 72, ll. 3–4, p. 109, ll. 16–17; Acropolites I, p. 101, ll. 4–14.

GRAND CONSTABLE, 187–8.
See Michael VIII Palaiologos
GRAND LOGOTHETE, 166–7.
See Strategopoulos, John
Akropolites, George
EPI TOU KANIKLEIOU, 55, 147–8, 155, 161–2.
See Chrysomalles, Basil
Alyates, Nikephoros
PROTOSEVASTOS, 64.
See Hyleas, Michael
Kontostephanos, Theodore
Mouzalon, George
Laskaris, Manuel
Nestongos, Michael[9]
BUTLER, 4, 154.
See Kantakouzenos, John
Nestongos, George
KOUROPALATES
See Glavas
CHAMBERLAIN, 4, 154.
See Krateros, Alexios
Zagaromates, George
Vasiliskos, Basil[10]
GENERAL LOGOTHETE
See Akropolites, George
PROTOVESTIARITES, 206.
See John III Doukas Vatatzes
Zagaromates, George
Mouzalon, Andronikos
Karyanites
STEWARD, 148, 154.
See Tarchaneiotes, Nikephoros
Nestongos, Isaac
GRAND HETAIREIARCH
Phlamoules[11]
Kamytzes, John[12]
Livadarios, Michael[13]
Ramatas, Manuel[14]
Vasiliskos[15]
CONSUL OF THE PHILOSOPHERS, 179.
See Theodore II Eirenikos
Karykes, Demetrios
GRAND CHARTOULARIOS
See Petraliphas, John
Tzyrithon
Palaiologos, Michael[16]
PROTASEKRETIS, 147, 171.
See Senachereim, Michael
MYSTIKOS, 147–8, 161–2.
See Mouzalon, John
Spanopoulos
Palaiologos, Michael[17]
DOMESTIC OF THE SCHOOLS
See Kalothetos, Theodotos
GRAND DROUNGARIOS, 198.
See Gavalas
PRIMMIKERIOS OF THE COURT
Mourtzouphlos, Isaac Doukas[18]
GRAND ARCHON, 186.
See Margarites, Constantine
TATAS OF THE COURT, 291 and note 72.
See Kalampakes, Theodore
GRAND TZAOUSIOS, 186.
See Margarites, Constantine
LOGOTHETE TON OIKEIAKON
See Hagiotheodorites
Iatropoulos, Demetrios
GRAND LOGARIAST, 147, 204.
See Karykes, Demetrios
Akropolites, George
PROTOKYNEGOS
See Mouzalon, Theodore
SKOUTERIOS, 291 and note 70.
See Xyleas
EPI TON DEESEON, 147, 158, 170.

[9] Nephew of Michael VIII Palaiologos: see Pachymeres I, pp. 109, ll. 17–20.
[10] See Pachymeres I, p. 130, ll. 8–9, p. 487, ll. 3–5.
[11] See Acropolites I, pp. 36–7.
[12] See ibid., pp. 38–40.
[13] See ibid., p. 67, l. 10.
[14] See ibid., p. 151, notes.
[15] See Pachymeres I, p. 130, l. 10.
[16] Uncle of Michael VIII Palaiologos: see Pachymeres I, p. 25, ll. 4–5.
[17] Nephew of Michael VIII Palaiologos: see Pachymeres I, p. 109, ll. 18–20.
[18] See Acropolites I, p. 92, ll. 4–6, p. 144, ll. 6–10.

PROTOIERAKARIOS
See Mouzalon, Theodore
Chadenos, Constantine[19]
LOGOTHETE OF THE FLOCKS
See Hagiotheodorites
PRESIDENT OF THE CHAMBER
See Choniates, Niketas[20]
LOGARIAST OR THE COURT, 206.
Angelos[21]
EPI TON KRISEON
See Choniates, Niketas[22]
COUNT OF THE IMPERIAL HORSE
Chadenos[23]

[19] See Miklosich and Müller IV, p. 285.
[20] See Michael Choniates I, p. 345.
[21] See Pachymeres II, p. 296, ll. 12–13.
[22] See Michael Choniates I, p. 345.
[23] See Pachymeres I, p. 27, ll. 5–7, p. 29, ll. 14–15.